1 MONTH FREE READING

at
www.ForgottenBooks.com

English
Français
Deutsche
Italiano
Español
Português

www.forgottenbooks.com

Mythology Photography **Fiction**
Fishing Christianity **Art** Cooking
Essays Buddhism Freemasonry
Medicine **Biology** Music **Ancient
Egypt** Evolution Carpentry Physics
Dance Geology **Mathematics** Fitness
Shakespeare **Folklore** Yoga Marketing
Confidence Immortality Biographies
Poetry **Psychology** Witchcraft
Electronics Chemistry History **Law**
Accounting **Philosophy** Anthropology
Alchemy Drama Quantum Mechanics
Atheism Sexual Health **Ancient History**
Entrepreneurship Languages Sport
Paleontology Needlework Islam
Metaphysics Investment Archaeology
Parenting Statistics Criminology
Motivational

ISBN 978-1-5280-8685-1
PIBN 11001703

THE

UNIVERSITY

REVIEW

Vol. I.

MAY—SEPTEMBER, 1905

SHERRATT & HUGHES
65 Long Acre, London, W.C.
27 St. Ann Street, Manchester
1905

1168-41

1905, Aug. 25 – Sept. 18.
Lowell Fund

INDEX.

INDEX

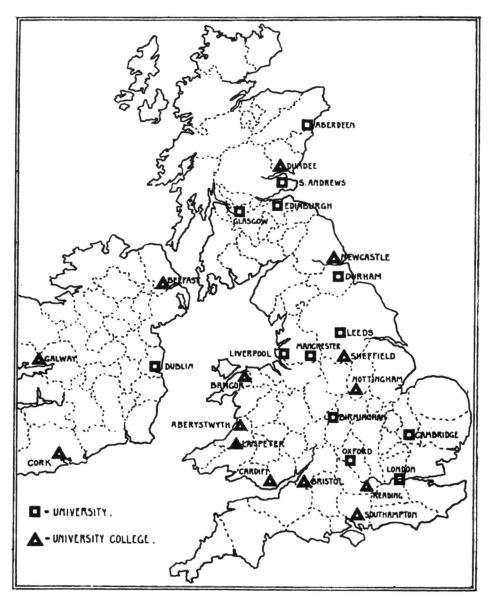

**THE UNIVERSITIES AND UNIVERSITY COLLEGES OF THE
UNITED KINGDOM.**

*(The University Colleges at Aberystwyth, Bangor and Cardiff, constitute the
University of Wales. The Queen's Colleges at Belfast, Cork and Galway,
constitute the Royal University of Ireland.)*

Lowell fund

The University Review

| NO. I. VOL. I. | MAY, 1905. |

The University Movement.

AN INTRODUCTORY NOTE

BY

THE RIGHT HON. JAMES BRYCE, F.R.S., D.C.L. (Oxon.), LL.D. (Edin., Glas., St. Andrews), LITT.D. (Camb., Vict.), M.P.

No change in the organs of its intellectual life which England has seen during the last two or three centuries, is more interesting, or more full of promise for the future, than that which has been effected within our own time by the extension of the old Universities and the creation of new ones. It has been a rapid change, considering the dimensions it has attained, yet it has come so gradually as to have attracted less notice than it deserves.

Fifty years ago, there were in England and Wales only two effective Universities, the two which had come from the twelfth and thirteenth centuries. There was, indeed, an University recently established at Durham, but it was then so small and weak as to count for little; and there was a body called the University of London, but it was then merely an Examining Board, not a teaching institution. The two ancient seats of learning at Oxford and Cambridge had been only slightly affected by modern currents of thought, and gave scant attention to any subjects except the Greek and Latin classics, mathematics, mental philosophy, and history. Even the two latter subjects were at Cambridge little regarded, while Oxford reckoned comparatively few mathematicians and few followers of physical science among teachers or students. These two Universities had, between them. only some two thousand undergraduates, a proportion of about one to nine thousand in the total population of England and Wales.

To-day Oxford has three thousand five hundred and Cambridge two thousand nine hundred students. The teaching staff in both has grown largely, if not in the same proportion. Five new Universities have been founded, one for Wales, with three constituent colleges, others at Manchester, Liverpool, Leeds, and Birmingham. The University of London has become a teaching institution, consisting of a great number of Schools giving high instruction in and around London. The total number of students in these nine Universities of 1905 is (reckoning in all London students) about eighteen thousand. There have also been set up a good many colleges in the large towns; and what is even more remarkable, women's colleges—at least six of which are of unquestioned University rank—have been founded. Each one of these latter gives instruction practically equal to that obtainable at Oxford or Cambridge, whose examinations have been opened to the women students, although the titular honours of a degree are still withheld. This is a striking development, and it has come about so gradually, so smoothly, with so little opposition from any quarter, as to seem to be the result of natural forces, of a strong though quiet stream of opinion. It may indeed be doubted whether the movement does not in one particular point show signs of advancing rather too fast. To extend the name of an University to institutions which do not yet possess the funds required to secure a complete teaching staff of admitted eminence and to provide all the appliances necessary for satisfactory teaching—a step which there seems to be some risk that Governments may under local pressure take—would be no benefit to education, for it would tend to lower the conception of what an University ought to be.

The result of this surprising development has been to create in England a great new body of men interested as teachers and as students in all questions bearing on the progress and working of Universities and Colleges, and to create in particular in those who belong to each several University a wish to know what is passing at the others, what experiments are being tried, what results attained, what are the matters which engage academic thought, and which way the current of that thought flows. There has hitherto been comparatively little communication between the different Universities. Of late years professors and lecturers migrate more frequently than formerly from one to another, as has long been the habit in Germany and in America. But, unlike the Germans, British students have very rarely lived and worked at more than one place; and graduates have felt comparatively little interest in other institutions than their own. The new conditions which we see now make a closer and more constant intercourse between the different seats of learning and science more natural and more necessary than was once the case. Each has begun to feel that it ought to know what the others are doing, and to try to profit by their experience ; and as the Universities, taken altogether, are becoming more potent factors in life as a whole, those who dwell in them are more sensible of a common task, as well as of common principles and ideas leading them forward.

This is not less true because some institutions are devoted more specially to literary or human subjects, and others to the investigation of external nature. It would be a misfortune if the teaching of languages, of history, of philosophy were to be pursued altogether apart from the teaching of physical science, and a like misfortune if the students of science were gathered into institutions from which the human subjects were excluded. The minds of each set of men would suffer through the absence of those whose methods and trend of thought are dissimilar. Still Oxford and Cambridge, themselves in some respects diverse, do both of them differ markedly in traditions and tendencies from Manchester, Leeds, and Birmingham, as these again differ a little from the colleges of Wales and from Liverpool. The two ancient seats will doubtless long retain that primacy which they owe to their brilliant and eventful history, to their venerable aspect, to their external beauty, and to that peculiar type of social life which the existence of colleges, some of which come down from the earlier Middle Ages, has impressed upon them. But they have much to learn from the newer institutions, as these have much to learn from them. The problems of modern life which have become urgent in the great cities where the newer Universities stand, are closely connected with the economic and historical studies pursued in the older Universities, and the relation between those studies and the plans fit to be followed in handling social problems may be compared to the relations between theoretic and applied science. Among the practical questions of educational methods, there are some in which Oxford can give light to Manchester, some in which Manchester can give light to Oxford.

Neither ought the Scottish Universities to be forgotten. They have been, as much as any others in the world, thoroughly popular, accessible to every class in the community, influencing and expressing in the amplest measure the intellectual life of the Scottish people. They have developed along lines unlike those of Oxford and Cambridge, and have set a pattern which in many points the newer English Universities have followed. They too, however, had fifty years ago fallen behind the needs of the time ; and they have still something to gain by being brought into closer touch with those of Southern Britain, to which they often send, and from which they often draw, eminent teachers.

Ireland has, in this respect, as unhappily in many others, been left behind the larger island. Her great historic University, founded by Queen Elizabeth, though illustrated by many distinguished professors and alumni, has been hitherto for the most part identified with one section of the people.   Her other University is an Examining Board—for the Queen's University, which consisted of the three Queen's Colleges, was foolishly extinguished thirty-four years ago.   The problem of the higher education in Ireland has fallen into politics, and into that most troublesome form of politics which is infected by ecclesiastical controversy. Everyone who cares either for Ireland or for education must desire to see this problem solved in a way which shall both meet the sentiment of the people and also secure the breadth and the freedom essential to University teaching of the best type.   Is it too much to hope that the experience, the wisdom, the large and liberal spirit which ought to mark the public opinion of places of teaching and learning everywhere, will be brought to bear upon this question, and that British University thought may help to enlighten and guide statesmen who honestly try to give Ireland what she needs?

That the Universities in the British Colonies ought to be brought into some closer connection with those of the United Kingdom is a feeling which has been growing both here and in the Colonies.   An important conference held in London last summer gave expression to it. Few better ways could be found for drawing the mother and the daughters nearer together, and for making more plain and visible the essential unity of the British people all over the world.

Lastly, we have still much to learn from continental

Europe, particularly from Germany and France, and not less, though in different ways, from the United States. In those countries also there is a constant advance, and many experiments are being tried from a knowledge of which we may profit.   America in particular sets to us a wonderful example in the appreciation which her business men shew of the practical value that belongs to the highest theoretical instruction, and in the energy and liberality with which provision is being made for new branches of study.

Thus there is at this moment, not only a far larger public in Britain directly interested in University matters than ever existed before, but also a greater need for the exchange of ideas and suggestions between those who are at work in different centres, and a greater need also for all the help that can be drawn from a knowledge of what is passing in other countries.   Which ever way we look, we see vistas of work, important and promising work, opening before us.   Hence the necessity for such an organ of intercommunication between teachers and students all over the United Kingdom as this *University Review* is designed to furnish.   Its aim is, as I understand, both to supply information as to what is passing here and abroad, and to express University opinion, focussing, so to speak, the order and the views of those who think upon questions of the higher education.   Both objects are admirable, and ought to win for the enterprise the sympathy of those who realize how much our Universities are now doing. how much more they may do, how various and how splendid may be the contributions they will make to national life.

Universities and Examinations

BY

ARTHUR SCHUSTER,

Sc.D. (Camb.), Ph.D. (Heidelberg), F.R.S.,

Langworthy Professor of Physics in the Victoria University of Manchester.

———

I TAKE it as an axiom that University Reform has been necessary at all times, is necessary at the present moment, and always will be necessary, for though our educational ideals remain the same, the methods by which we strive to approach these ideals are effective only by being in a constant state of flux. In all intellectual pursuits the gain lies in the effort, and it must always be a new effort. This is especially true in educational matters where methods quickly crystallize into mechanical routine.

The question is not, therefore, whether at any particular time University reform is necessary, but rather in what particular direction reform is most needed. I shall take as my guide in this respect the opinion of one who has never been known to speak without good reason, and who, I know, weighed his words well before he uttered them from the Presidential chair of the Royal Society. Sir William Huggins in a recent annual address to that Society, touched upon University education, and I need only quote one passage which contains the essence of his criticism : " Into the dry bones of the present academic system of reading and examination must enter the living breath of the spirit of research." If, after twenty years of serious, though perhaps spasmodic efforts to encourage research, which, at any rate, some of the Universities have made, such criticism is still possible, we may conclude that though the will has not been wanting, the efforts have been fruitless.

Let us for a moment try to disengage our minds from the ties of old traditions, and formulate briefly what the aims of an ideal University should be.

The University must enable the men or women who attend it to carry out effectively the main objects of their lives. There is naturally great variety in the requirements of different students, according to the careers they ultimately intend to pursue; and a complete review of University education would have to consider as to whether it is advisable to include in the same University organisation the pure scholar, the intending politician, the practical engineer, and the newspaper editor. It might simplify matters to have a separate University for each of these vocations, but I shall here assume, what indeed I believe to be well established, that the union of the different branches of learning into a system of personal contact between students of different faculties is one of the essential corner stones of the University building.

We must, therefore, find some ground common to the great variety of interests which the University represents.

Though the early part of our lives is necessarily taken up by the acquisition of knowledge, success in life depends not on what we know, but on the use we make of our knowledge. The application of knowledge no doubt presupposes its existence, but it requires a mental effort of a quite distinct and separate character, and, therefore, also requires a separate training. We are thus led to the two complementary yet often contradictory phases of intellectual activity—the acquisition of knowledge, and the application of knowledge to some useful purpose. The expression useful is here employed in its widest sense, and is not restricted to technical application of a utilitarian character. The writing of a dictionary is in its way as useful as the building of a bridge.

I think it will be found that all the criticisms of University education and most University reforms of recent times have, directly or indirectly, been provoked by the fluctuating opinion of the relative value which is to be attached to the application of knowledge as contrasted with its mere accumulation. In any academical discussion of the subject, there will probably be little difference of opinion; for everyone recognises that, at any rate for the great majority of students, the power of applying existing knowledge is of infinitely greater importance than the mere facility of acquiring and storing it up. The difficulty begins when we face the question of teaching, and try to arrange a course of study in which proper value is given to the power of turning knowledge to a good purpose.   It is much easier to teach if you make the accumulation of knowledge the primary object, and it is so difficult to test by examination anything except the possession of knowledge, that, however good the intentions of the teacher may be, he will unconsciously drop into the old groove, unless forcibly prevented.   This, in my opinion, can only be achieved by a radical change in the present system of awarding University honours.   I do not wish to underrate the educational value of the struggle which aims principally at the acquisition of knowledge, provided it is not made the final object of University education.   The mistake which has been made, is to try to satisfy contradictory requirements by a general system, which really only recognises one part and leaves the other and more important one out of account.

Let us, therefore, in future frankly divide the work of the University into two parts.   The acquisition of knowledge, and the power of applying it ; and let us free the second and higher part of the University from the fictitious test of examination, which, when confined to its proper sphere, will be simplified and rendered more effective.

May I briefly summarise the propositions by means of which I hope to justify my conclusion?

The power of applying knowledge such as is required for success in life can be taught, and, therefore, should be taught in the University.

The power of applying knowledge cannot be tested satisfactorily by examination.

We should recognise that examination serves its

legitimate and very necessary purpose when it tests the existence of knowledge.

If this be accepted, it follows that those portions of University study which are brought under the dominion of examination can only form a part of the University course and should, therefore, only take up a portion of the students' time.

As regards the teaching of applying knowledge, it has long been recognised, at any rate in scientific subjects, that a student does not derive a lasting benefit from his learning until he has had some kind of experience in research. The word "research" has been much abused. The object, as far as it ought to receive a place in University education, is not the accumulation of new facts. The discovery of a new compound in organic chemistry, or the detailed examination of the physical properties of some material may bring out new facts of greater or smaller importance, and at the same time be quite useless as a means of training the reasoning powers.

What I mean by training in research work is the development of that critical power and faculty of independent thought which ought to lead to real success in life, whatever the vocation may be. Mere acquisition of knowledge is not sufficient for the purpose. No problem ever presents itself twice exactly in the same fashion, and whatever his profession may be, a man must ever be ready with some originality and enterprise if he wishes to succeed. The distinction between a good and bad medical man is not that the good doctor remembers better what he has read in books about a particular disease, but that he can cope with new circumstances or complications arising in individual cases, which it is impossible to deal with collectively. Similarly, if an engineer had always to build such bridges or design such bridges as have been built and designed previously, and are described in published works, there would be no need for the engineer to pass through the University. If engineering, on the other hand, is admitted as a University subject, it can only be on the ground that the profession requires men who can deal with fresh and unforeseen circumstances. It is unnecessary to labour this point. The schoolmaster, the commercial man, or the brewer all equally deal with problems which, though they may be old, recur under fresh aspects and require something more than pure knowledge for their solution.

If every problem shows some new difficulties which call for originality, the solution of the problem would probably not be within our powers, did not previous experience, gained by ourselves or others, give us some clue as to how to overcome the difficulties. It is here that the value of the training will show itself.

You have a problem before you, and have to decide how far you can follow the guidance of others, and at what point you must begin to apply your own faculty of independent judgment. The power of utilising the experience gained perhaps by centuries of work, and to fertilize it with that little spark of originality which shall convert a mere repetition of what others have done into proper productive and useful work, constitutes the common basis of research work in all subjects. It is a power which ultimately becomes instinctive, but is capable of being developed by a proper training.

But it is not possible or desirable to apply an examination test which shall distinguish between students who have learned the art of originality, and those who have not.   The essence of research work is in the concentration of the mind on one problem to the exclusion of all others. The essence of examination work is the dispersion of the mind over many problems to the exclusion of the one a person is specially interested in.

Examination serves its own proper function when it tests knowledge.   Incidentally, it gives the advantage to students who possess quickness of thought, readiness of expression, and self-confidence; all these are admirable but not essential qualities.

If I may take it for granted that something is missing in our University courses which should be provided, we are brought face to face with the question: Are we to lengthen the periods of study, or may we in any way save the time of the student in other respects?   The second alternative is the one that deserves our first consideration, for, if a saving of time is possible, we should take advantage of it independently of other considerations.

The degree examinations at present serve a double purpose.   They fix a certain minimum of knowledge which a student must acquire to obtain a degree, and they also separate by a division into classes those students who specially distinguish themselves.   The division into classes is considered necessary in order to give a well-merited start in life to the ablest men and women. But the mistake of this arrangement, to my mind, is this, that the same examination cannot properly at the same time efficiently exclude those who should not obtain a degree and also arrange those who pass in a proper order of merit. An examiner, keeping the second requirement in view, makes his papers too difficult and then has to fix too low a standard as test of a mere pass. The consequence is, that we put too great a strain on our best students and too small a strain on our worse ones.

The evil of the examination system does not lie so much in the cramming to which the weak student has to submit himself, in order to pass, as in the lasting damage it does by wasting the time of the strong student, to whom at present the attainment of a high position in the final tests is often of vital importance.

The greatest defect in our educational system is the spirit of personal competition which it encourages, and this defect is aggravated by the publicity which is given to school and University successes. Our educational problem would be materially simplified if the advertising value which the success of a boy now possesses for the school in which he was trained could be done away with. Something would be gained by abolishing the publicity which is now given to University successes, and we should go further in the same direction by abolishing the division into classes. The public is only concerned with the fact that the student has obtained a degree. Whether he has done well or badly in the examination is a matter between the student, the teacher, and the parent.

Can any sound reason be given for the division into classes besides the purely utilitarian one that it may increase the graduate's prospect in after life, and if we consider the advantage given to the first class man, ought we not also to consider the many disabilities that we inflict on those on whom we have impressed the stamp of inferiority?

It may, no doubt, be reasonably urged that a man or woman is justified in looking for a tangible sign of success. In active life, that success appears in many ways. When a man obtains a lucrative position, he is glad of it, not only on account of its money value, but because it is a sign of success.

I do not wish for a moment to undervalue the motive power of ambition, or to contend that such ambition is not in itself a good thing, but if the arrangement of men into groups at a final examination is to be justified on the ground of its being a sign of the measure of the success which a student has obtained in his University course, surely that kind of success should be aimed at which is in accord with the proper aims of University teaching. If the possession of knowledge is not the highest aim of an University, and if the examination chiefly tests knowledge, it is clearly not the proper basis on which University honours should be awarded. It is a vital point in my argument that a clear distinction should be drawn between the causes which lead to success in real life, and those which lead to success on the lower steps of the educational ladder.

A boy at school should learn what he is told to learn,

and he measures himself against his fellow school boys in a personal competition as to who should do best in a task which is set to a whole form. This is the only competition which is possible, while the acquisition of knowledge is the main object, for then a thorough understanding of what has has been taught can form the only test of success, and such understanding may be satisfactorily tested by examination. The conditions in actual life are altogether different. Success is not for him who can do what others have done before him, just a little better than they have done it, but to him who can strike out a new line of work and do what has not been done before.

Personal competition is not a real factor of success in life, and should be excluded as a factor of success in University education. I do not know whether it will be said that division into classes does not imply personal competition and that Universities have already anticipated my objections by abolishing almost entirely the Order of Merit in their examination lists. This is only partially true. On the contrary, it may be argued that the abolition of the Order of Merit has aggravated the evil. It makes very little difference to a student's career whether his name appears nineteenth or twentieth in the examination list ; for every reasonable man knows that a second examination might reverse the order. If you separate the nineteenth and twentieth by drawing the line between the first and second class just at that point, the small difference that may exist is at once exaggerated into a large one. Still the difference between the top of the second class and the bottom of the first is not a vital one. But now abolish the Order of Merit, and you introduce a gulf across which there is no bridge. You raise the man who just manages to get into the first class to the level of the best man of his year, and you lower the man who just escapes being placed in the first class to the level of the man who is close to obtaining a third. The difference between the nineteenth and twentieth now becomes exaggerated, until it is equal in public estimation to the difference between a genius and a mediocrity.

I am not, however, dealing here with the aspect of the question from the standpoint of justice, but from that of education. The influence on a man's career of his name appearing in the first class is such, that even though he may be absolutely safe in the opinion of his teachers, he will work during his last year under conditions of strain and worry which will shew their evil effects not only on his health, but on the whole benefit he derives from his studies. The true function of a University can only come into play when the student is made to work in a restful spirit which excludes anxiety, and this at present is possible only to those who possess iron nerves.

If you admit that personal competition is undesirable in itself, you have at once a means ready to your hand to find time for the introduction of a higher class of work which at present is almost entirely excluded.

I assume that students enter the University well prepared for their work, and that the University in its legislation should primarily consider those students who, though they may not have any exceptional ability, yet are anxious to learn, and who do not require the constant pressure of an examination immediately in front of them to make them work. Such students, I consider, ought to be able to pass an examination at the end of the second year which should be sufficient to indicate that they possess sufficient knowledge to obtain a degree. I should institute such an examination in each of what we now call our Honours Schools, and I should fix the standard certainly as high as is required at present for the mere attainment of an Honours degree. A student now aspiring to a first class ought to take such an examination in his stride at the end of the second year. There is no doubt, to my mind, that this should be possible, in fact, experience proves it to be the case. There are every year a considerable number of students at Cambridge of sufficient capacity to take the first part of a Tripos at the end of their second year, and this part entitles them to a degree, provided their incapacity is sufficient to oblige them to take three years over it. Among the first ten wranglers in the Mathematical Tripos last year four, including the senior wrangler, only spent two years at Cambridge.

If, then, Cambridge gives high distinctions for examinations which may be taken at the end of the second year, we need not be afraid to establish at that period such an examination as I contemplate. I should not force anyone to take the examination at that period if not ready, and I should allow a student who fails, to take the examination again at the end of the third year. Whether, if passed at the end of the third year, the candidate should be entitled to an Honours or only a pass degree, is a question of secondary importance, which need not be entered into at present. At any rate, no Class should be awarded. The student who passes the qualifying examination at the end of the second year, would then have a complete year which may be entirely given up to research. By research, as I have already indicated, I do not necessarily mean the discovery of new facts, but only the working out of some problem which contains some novelty and requires some originality. That third year should be absolutely free from compulsion as to attendances. The test of the student's work should be found in the account which he is able to give at the end of it. The student who is more sluggish of mind, unless well prepared when he enters the University, would be able to reach the research standard by extending his stay over a fourth year.

My argument if consistently applied leads to the abolition of all classes but there is little hope that such a radical change would be accepted at present, as an intermediate step may abolish the division if it is based on the result of examination only. Many of my objections would fall to the ground if classes were assigned on the result of a piece of work on which the student has concentrated his mind for a whole year. This would practically replace an examination containing unexpected questions ranging over a variety of subjects by an examination containing one question which is known beforehand. The uncertainty which at present gives rise to a harmful strain of mind would be entirely absent. Nor will the judgment of the examiner on a particular piece of work carry with it that sharp distinction of intellectual power which in the popular opinion at present marks the division between a first and second class.   A dissertation may be pronounced to satisfy the examiners to a greater or smaller degree without attaching a permanent label of superiority or inferiority to its author.   A comparative failure in one piece of work may be redeemed by the higher merit of another.

In trying to devise an improved scheme of University courses, I have chiefly kept in view the student of good ability who intends to do his work in life with pleasure to himself and profit to others.   During his University life, such a student lays the foundation of future success, but that success, as I have been trying to show, does only to a small extent depend on an accumulation of knowledge.

Originality of mind is probably most active during that period in which at present we restrain all independent activity by the worry and anxiety of an impending examination.   Those of us who have been so fortunate as to have made, even though only in a very small degree, an addition to human knowledge, realise how much of our work in middle age has had its germ in the thoughts of our youth.   The success and happiness of the nation, I firmly believe, depends on the proper organisation of University teaching.   And that organisation will be beneficial only if it gives suffcient time for quiet thought and sufficient freedom from unnecessary anxiety. As long as the career of a student is made to depend on a chance question, or on the state of his health at a particular moment, the final year of University study must be lost to the healthy and natural development of the mind. I think that in the proposals which I have sketched out, the proper release of the present strain will be found. A minimum of knowledge is required. Let that minimum of knowledge be tested properly and even severely, but let it make no difference whether 80 or 50 per cent. of the examination paper has been answered. The standard of pass might be made much higher than at present without imposing an excessive strain on the average student. When he has shown that he deserves a degree, it is right and proper that an opportunity shall be given him to develop his special powers and to distinguish himself. My proposal secures this by giving a year which is absolutely at the student's disposal to be used under the guidance of his teachers as he thinks fit. If he realises that in this year he will be laying the foundation of his future intellectual activity we may have every confidence that he will employ it to the lasting benefit of himself and to the credit of his University.

Shakspere and Stoicism

BY

E. A. SONNENSCHEIN, M.A., D.LITT. (Oxon.)

Professor of Latin and Greek in the University of Birmingham

IT is, I think, becoming clearer every day that the idea of Shakspere which is entertained by the world at large requires to be modified in the light of wider knowledge of his works and sounder views of the relation of modern to ancient literature generally. The average reader of Shakspere thinks of him as a gifted barbarian who took Nature as his model, and owed as little as possible to "art." I am afraid that the great Milton is partially responsible for popularising this caricature of his brother poet, and not only in the well-known passage of *L'Allegro* :—

> Or sweetest Shakspeare, Fancy's child,
> Warble his native wood notes wild;

but also in his epitaph on Shakspere, where he speaks of his "easy numbers" flowing "to the shame of slow-endeavouring art." This antithesis of nature to art is, if it is not too audacious to say so, a false antithesis—false in all great poetry, and false in regard to Shakspere in particular. But, perhaps, more fatal to a true understanding of our greatest poet is the current antithesis of romantic to classical, as it is commonly interpreted. People fancy that the modern world is separated by a great gulf from the ancient world, and that in studying modern literatures we come into contact with an order of thought and sentiment which is comparable with ancient Greek and Roman thought and sentiment only by way of contrast. And the world will continue to think so, until two things happen: till, firstly, the classics are studied in a more literary and humane fashion in our schools and Universities, and, secondly, the history of our own literature is better understood. When these things happen, it will be seen that what is most characteristically modern in the literatures of modern Europe is indissolubly linked with the great classical tradition, and that our spiritual ancestors in the realms of art and science are to be found not among the Teutons— our corporeal ancestors—but among the Greeks and the Romans, the Romans standing to us in a more intimate relation than the Greeks. Shelley, in the preface to his *Hellas*, said that "we are all Greeks." So we are, but it would be even truer to say that we are all Romans, little as we know it. For what the Greeks originated in art and science the Romans handed on, with characteristic modifications of their own, to the modern world. I am leaving ethics and religion for the moment out of the question; but here, too, an historical study reveals the fact that ancient philosophy, and especially Platonism and Stoicism, was a great factor in the development of, and still forms an element in, all our modern sentiments in these spheres.

These large assertions I cannot attempt to prove in this place. But I will illustrate them by reference to a single passage of Shakspere, the source of which I think I have had the good fortune to discover. I imagine that if anyone wished to point out a characteristically modern passage, he could hardly find a better one for his purpose than that speech of Portia, to which the poet has assigned a central position in the *Merchant of Venice*. It breathes the very spirit of Christian charity; it is a "locus classicus" on the beauty of mercy and forgiveness of injuries, and one of the brightest jewels in the poet's crown:—

> The quality of mercy is not strained;
> It droppeth as the gentle rain from heaven
> Upon the place beneath.

No one, I think, of the countless thousands who have read this speech, has ever doubted for a moment that it was an entirely original creation of the poet's. Yet it is neither more nor less than a beautiful rendering of the leading ideas of the treatise "on Mercy" (*De Clementia*), written by the Roman Stoic philosopher, Seneca, in which he addresses an eloquent appeal to the youthful emperor Nero to exercise his despotic powers in a spirit worthy of his position. Here are the passages in which the key-notes of the whole treatise are struck, but rearranged in the order in which Shakspere has placed them in his rendering :—

<table>
<tr><td align="center">SENECA.</td><td align="center">SHAKSPERE.</td></tr>
<tr><td>Nullum clementia ex omnibus magis quam regem aut principem decet. (I. 3, 3 ; again I. 19, 1.)</td><td>It becomes The throned monarch better than his crown.</td></tr>
<tr><td>Eo scilicet formosius id esse magnificentiusque fatebimur quo in majore praestabitur potestate. (I. 19, 1.)</td><td>'Tis mightiest in the mightiest.</td></tr>
<tr><td>Quod si di placabiles et aequi delicta potentium non statim fulminibus persequuntur, quanto aequius est hominem hominibus praepositum miti animo exercere imperium? (I. 7, 2.)</td><td>But mercy is above this sceptred sway. It is enthroned in the hearts of kings ; It is an attribute to God himself.</td></tr>
<tr><td>Quid autem? Non proximum eis (dis) locum tenet is qui se ex deorum natura gerit, beneficus et largus et in melius potens? (I. 19, 9.)</td><td>And earthly power doth then show likest God's When mercy seasons justice.</td></tr>
<tr><td>Cogitato . . . quanta (Romae) solitudo et vastitas futura sit si nihil relinquetur nisi quod iudex severus absolverit. (I. 6, 1.)</td><td>Consider this, That in the course of justice none of us Should see salvation.</td></tr>
</table>

It is perhaps only an accident that in this last passage even the form of the sentence it similar ; in the English as in the Latin we have an Imperative Mood with a dependent clause. Further, the story of Augustus pardoning Cinna (i. 1—12)[1] may have suggested :—

> It is twice blessed ;
> It blesses him that gives and him that takes.

---

1. This chapter of the *De Clementia* is summed up in the following passage, which I translate literally :

" Cinna, I grant you your life for a second time. From the present day let us be friends ; let us try which of us shows the higher character. I in giving you your life or you in owing your life to me."

Nor are there wanting evidences in other plays of Shakspere that this particular tract of Seneca was known to him.   First of all, the leading idea recurs in *Measure for Measure*, ii. 2 :

> No ceremony that to great ones 'longs
> Not the king's crown . . .
> Become them with one half so good a grace
> As mercy does.

The sentiment of I. 6, 1 recurs in *Hamlet*, II. 2., " Use every man after his desert, and who shall 'scape whipping?" And its continuation may well have suggested a passage in *King Lear*, IV. 6. :

Quotus quisque ex quaesitoribus est qui non ex ipsa ea lege teneatur, qua quaerit? quotus quisque accusator vacat culpa ?	Thou rascal beadle, hold thy bloody hand ! Strip thine own back, etc.

Lit :   " How few officers of the law are not themselves within the reach of the very law under which they prosecute?   How few accusers are themselves innocent?"

In I. 9, 3 we have a reference to the pricking of the names of the proscribed, which Shakspere elaborates in *Julius Cæsar*, IV. 1, though he may have got this from Roman history.   In II. 5, 1 we read " There are old women or girls who are affected by the tears of the greatest criminals, and who if they could would let them out of prison."   This is like *Julius Cæsar*. I. 2 : " Three or four wenches where I stood cried ' Alas, good soul !' and forgave him with all their hearts. . . . . . If Cæsar had stabbed their mothers, they would have done no less."

The following passage of *Titus Andronicus* (if that play is by Shakspere), I. 2 :

> Wilt thou draw near the nature of the Gods ?
> Draw near them then in being merciful.

may obviously be derived from this same source, though it may also come from Cicero, *pro Ligario*, XIII. 32.[1]

No doubt some critics will prefer to regard all such passages as mere 'coincidences.' But I must say a word upon one criticism which has already been passed on my theory. The Poet Laureate, surely in a moment of forgetfulness, has expressed his disagreement with me on the ground that poetry is not made in the fashion which my theory implies. "The white heat, the fine frenzy of the brain, in the moment of such composition, precludes so cold a procedure."[2] If so, of course, my theory would fall to the ground. But together with it would fall another theory which is, I think, universally accepted, namely, that Shakspere was the author of that series of Roman plays which are based on Plutarch—*Julius Cæsar, Antony and Cleopatra, Coriolanus*—to which may be added *Timon of Athens* : for they all contain specimens of that 'cold procedure' which the Poet Laureate declares to be unworthy of a real poet. Either those large sections of all the above plays which are transcripts from Plutarch are not by Shakspere, or there is no *a priori* impossibility of the speech of Portia being a transcript from Seneca.

To me, as one of the unpoetical, this speech of Portia, regarded in the light of my theory, raises in acute form two questions of importance : (1) Did Shakspere know Latin ? (2) How far are certain ethical and religious conceptions in Shakspere specifically modern and Christian ?

---

1. Professor Churton Collins, *Studies in Shakspere*, 1904 (Preface, p. viii.)
2. *Literary Supplement to the Times*, September 23rd, 1904.

(1) The first question which the average man asks when one points to the influence of a classical author on Shakspere, is "What crib did he use?" For did not Ben Jonson tell us long ago that Shakspere had "small Latin, and less Greek?" Well, in this particular case *there was no English translation of the De Clementia in existence at the time when the Merchant of Venice was written* (*i.e.*, somewhere between the years 1594 and 1600). The first English translation was that of the complete works of Seneca by T. Lodge in 1614, *i.e.*, nearly twenty years after the probable date of the *Merchant of Venice*. There was, however, prior to this date a French translation of the *De Clementia*, by A. Cappel, published at Paris in 1578, and this was republished in 1594, and again in 1604; and there was a German translation of this, together with some other of Seneca's works, by Michael Herr, published at Strassburg, part of which bears the date 1536, part 1540. Now, of course, if anyone chooses to think it more likely that Shakspere read his Seneca in a French or German translation than that he read it in the original, I cannot prove the contrary. Yet I think everything points in the other direction. Prof. Churton Collins has shown that Montaigne exercised no influence on Shakspere till after the publication of Florio's English translation, which seems to prove that he had not read him in the original French. As for the German translation, there is not a tittle of evidence in Shakspere's works to show that he knew German, though he may have been in Germany. In a matter like this, we can only proceed by probabilities; and I think most people who know

anything about the relative positions of the study of Latin and modern languages in the schools of the day will agree that it is much more likely that an educated Englishman of the time of Elizabeth was familiar with Latin than that he was familiar with French or German. Besides, it has yet to be proved that Cappel's or Herr's translation ever found its way into England.

Here, then, we have evidence stronger than any that has been hitherto adduced to show that Shakspere was something of a Latin scholar,[1] and, moreover (what has not hitherto been suspected), that he had read one at least of the prose works of Seneca. Where he got his Latin is another question. I hope, by the way, that no "Baconian" will find in this article grist for his mill. Personally, I see no difficulty in accepting the statement of Nicholas Rowe (1709) that he was educated at a "free school"—if not Stratford Grammar School, then some other grammar school.[2] And in any grammar school of the day, it has been shown by careful examination of evidence,[3] the course of reading in Latin for boys of from seven to fourteen years of age was a pretty wide one. There were no "lateinlose Bürgerschulen" in those days.[4]

1. The evidence that the *Comedy of Errors* was based on a reading of the *Menaechmi* in the original is not absolutely conclusive, though it is strong.

2. Local tradition at Stratford still points to Shakspere's desk ; till recently it stood in the Latin room of the school, but has now been removed to the house where the poet was born. The Rev. R. S. de Courcy Laffan, formerly Headmaster of Stratford Grammar School, has kindly allowed me to see a paper in MS. in which he adduces further arguments in favour of Stratford as Shakspere's school.

3. Collected by the late Prof. Spencer Baynes and Prof. Collins.

4. Seneca was much more read in the age of Elizabeth than he is at the present day ; witness the influence which he exercised on the precursors of Shakspere. And in the opinion of Prof. Spencer Baynes (based on school lists of the time) some of the *tragedies* of Seneca probably formed part of Shakspere's school reading. There is, however, no evidence that any of Seneca's prose works were read in schools of the time ; and I think that Shakspere probably got to know the *De Clementia* later in life.

On the other hand little attention was given to antiquities and archæology; so that it is not surprising that there are many slips in Shakspere as to the *mise en scène*, costuming, &c., of his Roman plays.   Perhaps this is the sort of ignorance to which the learned Ben Jonson referred in his well-known saying about "small Latin and less Greek."

(2) But after all, the question of deepest interest raised by the *De Clementia* is not whether Shakspere read it in Latin, or even whether he read it at all.   In any case there remains the fact that the ethical sentiment of the speech of Portia is identical with that of the pagan philosopher.   Nor must it be supposed that the ethical teaching of the *De Clementia* is an isolated phenomenon. On the contrary, mercy and the forgiveness of injuries are characteristic notes in all the writers of the Neo-Stoic school of Rome—Seneca, Epictetus, Marcus Aurelius.

There is probably no school of philosophy which has been so hardly judged as Stoicism.   Its influence upon the world has been incalculable.   The main *differentiae* of modern society as compared with ancient, are, I suppose, broadly speaking, three : the passage from the city-state to the empire-state, the abolition of slavery, and the creation of the Church as distinct from the State.[1]   All these were voiced, or at least anticipated in principle, by Stoicism.   As to the third point, Stoicism, like some other Greek schools of philosophy, linked men together in a unity which was independent of the State, and in which, therefore, there lay the germs of a Church.

1. See the late Professor H. Sidgwick's *Development of European Polity.*

Nor are we fully conscious of the debt which we owe to Stoicism as a religious philosophy. The high seriousness and lofty morality taught by this school the world passes by with a shrug of indifference : its charities —extended to slaves and even to the lower animals, ὅσα ζώει τε καὶ ἕρπει θνήτ᾽ ἐπὶ γαῖαν,[1] 'all things that live and creep upon the earth'—are put down to rhetoric or insincerity ; and men are content merely to 'shiver at its apathy.' But its apathy was, after all, only meant as a protest against emotion in the wrong place. What the Stoics objected to was the basing of mercy (*clementia*) upon mere emotion, mere softness of heart (*misericordia*). May not the reason for this indifference of the world at large towards a noble school of thought be found partly in the fact that Stoicism stands too near to ourselves to be seen clearly? They say that if you show a man his own likeness in a mirror he will sometimes turn from it in disgust. Stoicism is essentially a philosophy not of despair, but of confidence and almost defiant optimism. Many of the fundamental ethical principles which are generally regarded as specifically Christian had been developed independently by the Porch. The idea of the fatherhood of God and its corollaries—the brotherhood of man and the law of love— in a word, the whole idea of basing morality directly upon a religious theory of the Universe is characteristically Stoic.

The striking phrase τοῦ γὰρ καὶ γένος ἐσμέν, "for we are

---

1. *Hymn of Cleanthes*, 3rd Century B.C.

also his offspring," quoted by St. Paul, and the use of the word πατήρ in addressing the Deity are common to the hymn of Cleanthes and the prologue to the Φαινόμενα of Aratus. In view of these facts it is no matter of surprise that Stoicism has contributed to Christianity some of its cardinal terms: πνεῦμα (*spiritus*), συνείδησις (*conscientia*), αὐτάρκεια (*sufficientia*), and even λόγος, in their special religious senses, have come to us through the Stoics. The phrase πολιτεία τοῦ κόσμου, *civitas communis hominum et deorum*, "city of God," is only one of many links that connect the early Greek Stoics with Marcus Aurelius and Marcus Aurelius with St. Augustine. Nor did some of the chief of the early Fathers of the Church, notably St. Augustine, fail to recognise the affinities of Christianity to earlier religious systems. " *Seneca saepe noster* " says Tertullian ; " *Seneca noster* " says Jerome ; and the recognition went so far as to lead some zealot to manufacture a correspondence between Seneca and St. Paul, which was intended to account for their resemblances. Some passages in Seneca are indeed startling enough to awaken a suspicion of some contact between him and Christianity. He several times speaks of God as *parens noster*, and as " within us " *(prope est a te deus, tecum est, intus est)*; he calls Him *sacer spiritus (sacer intra nos spiritus sedet;* cf. i. Corinthians, 3, 16, and 6, 19). Yet these terms are in reality stoical property ; the " God within " of Seneca is the same as the *dominans ille in nobis deus* of Cicero, and the *divinae particula aurae* of Horace. Stoicism was penetrated through and through with the enthusiasm of the conviction that Reason, man's

prerogative, is an emanation from, or part of, the Deity. [1]
And if Seneca has some striking parallels to the ethical
teaching of the Sermon on the Mount, these are only
deductions from that fundamental ethical principle of
Stoicism by which it is linked not less with Aristotle than
with Christianity : *hominem sociale animal, communi bono
genitum.* [2]

If, then, the characteristic features of Shakspere's
religious conceptions are, as Prof. Churton Collins says,
the omnipresence of God, conscience as a divine monitor,
and the efficacy of prayer, we must not assume that on
these points Shakspere speaks from a point of view which
is Christian as opposed to Stoic, though no doubt his
beliefs came to him in the first instance from the religion
of Christ, for which he had a profound reverence.   But
it is in the purely ethical sphere that Stoic influence
shows itself most clearly in Shakspere.   It has coloured
his whole moral ideal.   At least I know of none of his
characters that strikes one as drawn with greater sympathy than Horatio ; and in him the poet has come very
near to a picture of the Stoic " wise man " :

> A man that fortune's buffets and rewards
> Hast ta'en with equal thanks : and bless'd are those
> Whose blood and judgement are so well commingled,
> That they are not a pipe for fortune's finger
> To sound what stop she please. *Give me that man
> That is not passion's slave,* and I will wear him
> In my heart's core, aye, in my heart of heart.

---

[1] For modern expressions of this leading conception of Stoicism see Pope's
Essay on Man :
　　　　" This light and darkness in one chaos joined
　　　　　What shall divide ?   The God within the mind."
and the passages in Emerson's *Divinity School Address* of 1838 where he speaks
of the "Indwelling Supreme Spirit."
[2] Seneca, *De Clem.* i. 3, 2.

The "passion" spoken of is clearly not merely animal passion; it is that tyranny of emotion which leads to infirmity of purpose and judgement. And Horatio, speaking of himself when he tries to drink the poisoned cup, says :

> I'm more an antique Roman than a Dane.

* * *

But if, on the one hand, Shakspere knew Latin, there is some evidence that he did not know Greek well—at any rate, that he was not in the habit of using his knowledge for practical purposes. In dealing with the Greek classics he seems to have relied mainly on translations. In some cases he may have used Latin versions, but in the case of Plutarch he was thrown back upon North's English translation, which was dependent upon a previous French translation by Amyot. Now there is one passage in which this third-hand material on which he worked has exercised a curious and, I think, an unfortunate influence on his treatment. In *Julius Cæsar*, act v., scene 1, Cassius asks Brutus what he intends to do if the battle goes against them; they are just about to meet Octavius and Antony on the field of Philippi :—

> If we do lose this battle, then is this
> The very last time we shall speak together :
> What are you then determined to do?

And Brutus replies :—

> Even by the rule of that philosophy
> By which I did blame Cato for the death
> Which he did give himself; I know not how
> But I do find it cowardly and vile,
> For fear of what might fall, so to prevent
> The time of life : arming myself with patience
> To stay the providence of some high powers
> That govern us below.

The grammatical construction is not very clear: but the general sense is plain.   Brutus thinks suicide wrong. Then Cassius asks:

> Then, if we lose this battle,
> You are contented to be led in triumph
> Thorough the streets of Rome ?

And Brutus replies :—

> No, Cassius, no : think not, thou noble Roman,
> That ever Brutus will go bound to Rome ;
> He bears too great a mind.

And this resolve is in harmony with his subsequent act.   The battle went against him, and he threw himself upon his sword, held by his servant Strato.   In the passage just quoted, Brutus changes his mind ; first he thinks suicide wrong, then, stung apparently by the taunt of Cassius about being led in triumph through the streets of Rome, he says he will kill himself rather than fall alive into the hands of the enemy.   This is hardly worthy of Brutus, and hardly consistent with the passage in Act iii, Sc. 2, where he is represented as already prepared for suicide.   But the poet was in a difficulty ; he could not reproduce what North's Life of Brutus gives, for the simple reason that it is self-contradictory.   We read there, after the question of Cassius :

> Brutus answered him, being yet but a young man and not over-experienced in the world : " I trust (I know not how) a certain rule of philosophy, by the which I did greatly blame Cato for killing himself, as being no lawful or godly act, &c. *But now being in the midst of danger I am of a contrary mind.* For if it be not the will of God that this battle fall out fortunate for us, I will . . . . . . rid me of this miserable world," &c.

But the present tense " I trust " (if it is a present tense)

is inconsistent with the next sentence.   Now let us turn
to Plutarch himself.   The Greek may be thus translated :—

> Brutus answered: "When I was a young man[1] and inexperienced
> in life I was led, I know not how, into a presumptuous utterance in
> the way of philosophy.   I blamed Cato for having taken his own
> life, regarding it as an unholy and unmanly act to evade one's
> destiny and not to accept fearlessly whatever befalls, but to run
> away from it.   But now, in my present circumstances, I am of a
> different opinion ; and if heaven should not decide the present
> issue according to our wishes, I have no desire hereafter to put
> other hopes and enterprises to the proof, but will throw up my
> hand and be content."

He is comparing his opinions at different periods of
his life.   When he was a younger man he held that
suicide was cowardly ; but now he thinks it justifiable, or
even a duty to oneself, under certain circumstances.
The words " I trust (present tense) a certain rule of
philosophy " of North's translation are a ludicrous mis-
translation of Amyot's "je feis (= fis) un discours de
philosophie"; and moreover North has got his inverted
commas in the wrong place.   The result is that the great
dramatist, in despair at the muddle, cuts the knot by
turning one speech into two, and representing Brutus
as changing his mind in the course of the conversation.
I think it is pretty clear that Skakspere had not the
Greek of Plutarch before him when he wrote this.

But this passage, like the speech of Portia, raises
further questions as to the poet's ethical and religious
conceptions, and their relation to Christianity on the one
hand and Stoicism on the other.   It is noteworthy that
his attitude towards suicide is different in this play from

---

1. *i.e.*, comparatively young.   Brutus was born in 85 B.C., and was therefore
39 years old at the date of Cato's suicide.

what we find in *Hamlet*, in *Cymbeline*, and in *King Lear*.
In *Hamlet* (I. 2) "the Everlasting" has "fixed his canon
against self-slaughter;" Imogen might have committed
suicide but that

> Against self-slaughter
> There is a prohibition so divine
> That cravens my weak hand.

Gloucester prays

> Let not my worser spirit tempt me again
> To die before you please.

But in *Julius Cæsar* we hear no word of disapproval of
the act of Brutus and of Cassius and of Portia, except
what Brutus himself says in the speech quoted above.
Antony voices the general feeling of the play (and may
not we add of the audience—whatever we may think
about the poet himself) when he says

> This was the noblest Roman of them all.

The explanation of this difference of attitude clearly is
that the poet has entered so thoroughly into the feelings
of the Romans of the time of Brutus, that he has given
dramatic expression in this play to a sentiment which was
opposed to his own, and opposed to Christianity; though
it would be difficult to point to any passage in the
Scriptures in which a "divine prohibition" against self-
slaughter, as distinct from murder in general, is to be found.

But is, then, the passage above quoted, in which
Brutus for a moment condemns suicide, inconsistent with
the antique feeling on this subject? Not at all. Shakspere
does not explicitly tell us what system of philosophy he
had in mind when he spoke of a "rule" against suicide.
But no doubt he had noticed, and perhaps marked in his

copy of Plutarch, the statement that Brutus was acquainted with *all* the sects of the Greek philosophers and understood their doctrines ; "*but above all the rest he loved Plato's sect best*" (North's Plutarch, ch. 2).   Cicero, too, tells us that Brutus was a Platonist.[1]   Now, if we turn to Plato, we find that suicide is condemned, and condemned on the identical ground on which the Christian sentiment against it rests.   This comes out in a well known passage of the *Phædo*, and also in the following passage of the *Laws* (ix. 873) :

> And what shall he suffer who slays him, who of all men is his own best friend?   I mean the suicide, who from sloth or want of manliness imposes on himself an unjust penalty. . . . Such men shall be buried alone and ingloriously on the borders of the twelve provinces of the land, and no column or name shall mark the place of their interment.

a curiously interesting passage when we reflect on the customs which prevailed till quite recently in respect to the burial of suicides.   Be it remembered that there were Latin translations of Plato in existence in Shakspere's day.   But even if in the field of ethics Brutus (like his teacher Antiochus) was a Stoic, as is indeed likely, and as seems to be implied by Shakspere in the passage (iv. 3), where Cassius says :

> Of your philosophy you make no use
> If you give place to accidental ills.

it does not follow that Brutus might not have condemned suicide in Cato.   The teaching of the Stoics on this point is not quite so simple as is generally supposed ;

---

1. Cic. *Brutus*, 31, 120 ; cf. 40, 149 ; 97, 332.   In the *De Finibus*, v. 3, 8, he calls him a follower of Antiochus, the Academician.

nor did they all agree.[1] Their general attitude was that under certain circumstances suicide was permissible or even a duty, but only when to commit the act was more in accordance with reason than not to commit it ; or, as they expressed it, only when the " God within " commanded it. So Cicero: " The God within (*dominans ille in nobis deus*) forbids us to quit our dwelling place without his leave."[2] And there is an interesting passage in the *De Officiis* (i. 31, 112), where Cicero says that a good deal depends on the " personal equation " ; it was right, he says, for Cato to commit suicide, but perhaps would have been wrong for others in precisely the same circumstances, owing to differences of disposition and temperament. It was, in fact, a question of conscience, as we should say. It is clear, then, that even as a Stoic Brutus might have regarded suicide as wrong *for him*, or even for Cato.

The general impression left by Shakspere's Roman plays is that they show a marvellous understanding of and sympathy with antique sentiment. It is surely noteworthy that when he is closely examined on a point of ancient philosophy it is impossible to convict him of any error. In Brutus he has drawn a consummately true picture of the cultured Roman at his best—a man in whom, whether Platonist or Stoic, *gravitas* (dignity and

1. Epictetus and, still more, Poseidonius limited the right of suicide to cases in which extreme physical or mental distress incapacitated a man from living the life of a rational being. Seneca, who is not so strict, yet finds room in his philosophy for a doctrine which is directly antagonistic to suicide ; in the *De Providentia* (i. chap. 1 and 4) he insists, almost like a Christian, that man is made perfect by suffering. "God has a father's rather than a mother's heart for good men ; he loves them without weakness."
2. *Tusculans* i. 30, 74. Compare *De Finibus* iii. 18, 59—61, the chief source of our knowledge of Stoic doctrine on this point.

self-respect) was united with *humanitas* and *clementia* (humanity and mercifulness). Could the poet have penetrated so successfully into the spirit of ancient thought had he been merely the gifted barbarian that he is represented as being?

No. History suggests a very different line of reflection. The most important fact, I take it, in the history of modern literatures is this—that all the names of first rate importance are post-Renaissance. The only exception is Dante, and he too is steeped in the Latin classics. Chaucer had caught the Renaissance spirit in Italy, and among its most prominent representatives are to be numbered Rabelais, Cervantes, Shakspere, and later on Goethe and Schiller. Herein, I take it, lies the ultimate reason why we study the Greek and Latin Classics at all; their study is in reality a study of our own past—our very own—divorced from which all that is most characteristic in the present is only half intelligible. Were it not for this—were it true that the world would be exactly what it is if the Greeks and Romans had never existed, as the late Mr. Herbert Spencer thought and said[1]—then, I confess, I should feel that classical studies could be justified only as a disciplinary study, and for the light that Latin throws upon the vocabulary and syntax of the mother tongue. It is because the precise opposite is true—because modern life is soaked with Greek and still more with Latin influences—that it will always depend for its complete interpretation on a study of the Classics; that is, so long as the landmarks of our present culture remain unshifted.

---

1. See his *Autobiography*, Vol. II. p. 37.

Questions for Discussion

BY

SIR OLIVER LODGE, D.Sc. (Lond.), LL.D., F.R.S.

Principal of the University of Birmingham.

PART I.

THERE are several debatable subjects of general interest which might be debated in an Inter-University organ of this kind. I throw out two as worthy of some discussion, though I wish it to be understood that the ideas are put forward in a tentative and undogmatic fashion, because I perceive clearly that there may be many reasonable objections, and many practical difficulties in carrying them out, even if they were regarded as in principle wise.

First comes a really difficult question, about the time of year when examinations should be held :—whether candidates should be examined directly lectures cease, and before Session ends; or whether they should be given time for revision and digestion, and perhaps oblivion, and be examined just before a new Session commences. My belief is that from an educational point of view the second plan is by far the best : it would give three uninterrupted Terms for College classes and lectures; it would afford an interval during which students might work by themselves (the best kind of work), no doubt often with the help of private tuition, a help which, in many cases, by defect of character or brain power, is really needed; and it would test finally the kind and amount of knowledge which really adhered without blowing off after the lapse of a week. At present the information supplied to the examiner is painfully undigested; and the best students themselves feel that they have no time to supplement and to assimilate the work of the Summer Term. The results could be announced at the beginning instead of at the end of a Session, and a ceremony could be held which would fitly inaugurate it.

Objections to this plan are manifest, and may be considered under three heads.

First, the educative objection, that private tuition during vacation would be liable to degenerate into cram. This should be avoided by wise setting of the questions. The setting of good questions is a most difficult and important and responsible task, and should by no means be done in a hurry and without careful consultation and collaboration. The best questions are those which test real and permanent knowledge of important issues, not those which only test minute and special points, interesting only to the professed scholar, and not likely to remain in the memory or to be of service to anyone else. Broad general features, as opposed to minute technical details, cannot be learnt by cram. Any teaching which results in a broad grasp and understanding of the subject is, *ipso facto*, not cram, but is valuable, whether given by lecturer or by private coach ; and this is the kind of knowledge which a wise examination will test.

A second objection is that the candidates will tend to neglect their work during Term, and work feverishly during vacation, thereby doing away with the value of the vacation.   My answer to this is that if they *have* neglected their work during Term, they do not deserve the vacation, and they will be in a suitable purgatory. On the other hand, if they have worked properly during Term, they will value the time for revision and digestion, and will form reading-parties and employ other sensible methods of combining holiday and work, as Honours students have always done ; and will not run to seed in complete idleness, as some Pass students have been too prone to do.

It may, indeed, be that the delay may be painful to a few nervous individuals ; but nervous individuals who are unable to work for three months by themselves without breaking down, are not very well fitted for ordinary human life, and it is no part of our business to make things much more easy for them than life itself is.

A third objection will come from the point of view of examiners, who may feel that they would rather get the examinations over and done with, at the end of each Session.   This is a point on which I would especially value the opinion of colleagues ; but before deciding it I would ask them carefully to consider the matter.   In many places it is customary to hold examinations in the last fortnight of June, when everybody is rather tired with the work of the Session, and anxious to get away. The result is a certain amount of feverish haste, combined with office difficulty in getting the marks in to time ; and it is rather irksome to have to wait on for the official ceremony at the end of the Session, which is liable to encroach on July, and is often held in very hot weather.

To save this unseemly haste it is, I know, proposed by some to devote the whole month of June to examinations; but, with deference, I suggest that this proposal tends in the direction of attaching too much value and importance to examinations, and that its adoption would shorten the Summer-Term period of teaching unduly, making it extremely difficult to get all branches of the subject properly covered. My own experience is that the loss of even the last fortnight of June makes the lectures of the Summer Term distinctly less satisfactory than those of the other two Terms; and to lose the whole month for examinations would be still worse.

If my proposed scheme were adopted, the method of procedure would be as follows :—Early in the month of June, question papers would be drawn up by the examiners, discussed at Joint meetings, amended, and finally approved ; printed or lithographed by a University Press, and then stored till September. During the last fortnight of September the examinations would be held, at first without the presence of the examiners, being supervised by College officials and by invigilators specially remunerated for that purpose. Towards the end of September the examiners would be returning, ready to take up the work of next Session. They would then look over such papers as were done, conduct such oral examinations as they thought desirable, and, with the help of the office, get the results ready for an Opening and Degree Ceremony fairly early in October.

The reading of papers at this period of the year would, I believe, be less irksome and be better done than during the month of June ; and if it be objected, as it truly might, that the last week in September would thus be cut off from the vacation, and the three months' holiday be so curtailed, I would advocate the cutting off of the last week of June from the Summer Term to balance ; thereby restoring the three months vacation, and liberating for holiday a long-day period of the year which would surely be acceptable to both students and staff. One thing I strongly hold, and that is that the long vacation interval should not be encroached upon : it is in every way necessary for teachers, and it constitutes the one privilege which makes men eminent in scholarship willing to undergo the labours of a Professorial Chair ; it affords scope for fresh learning, as well as opportunity for rest, and the three months' vacation should be jealously guarded. The time for quiet work by themselves would also be of the utmost value to students, if their examinations still lay ahead of them. In fact, I believe that the plan which I have proposed would tend rather towards the safety of the long vacation than its endangerment. One thing, however, would have to be insisted upon by any corporate body which agreed to the change, and that is that every individual examiner should religiously take up his work in the last week of September, and give the time necessary to the reading and marking of papers. If it were found that the staff would not come back, and could only be induced to read the papers before they went away, that indeed would frustrate the scheme.

There is, however, a fourth objection which appears to me more serious than any which I have so far been able to perceive, and specially affects professional candidates in their final year; viz., that students who graduate at a University generally wish to obtain teaching or other remunerative appointments as soon as possible after graduation; and towards the attainment of such appointments the results of graduation must of course contribute. Now it may well be said that since teaching institutions usually begin in September or October, it will be too late to try and seek appointments in October; and that therefore it is desirable to turn out Graduates at the beginning of July, free to depart and seek some opportunity of earning their living. This does appear to me to be a grave objection. It is not one, however, which applies either to Matriculation or to the Intermediate stage; it applies to the Final stage only, but it does apply to that, and it is this difficulty which makes me fear that in spite of what I believe to be the very considerable advantages of the September period for examination, it may not be practical to introduce it. One solution can be suggested, but it is not a very satisfactory one, viz., that the Final Degree examinations only be held in June, and all others in September.

It is desirable, however, first of all to agree upon what is the most ideal arrangement, and then to study how near to that arrangement it is possible actually to go.

So much for the first question; the second question may as well be reserved for another issue.

(PART II. WILL APPEAR IN THE JUNE NUMBER.)

Malaria and a Moral.

BY

MAJOR RONALD ROSS, C.B., F.R.C.S., F.R.S. ; *late* I.M.S.

Sir Alfred Jones Professor of Tropical Medicine in the University of Liverpool.

THE subject of Malaria has been much before the public during the last five years, and most people have doubtless heard of the extraordinary theory of certain scientists— persons who are well known to be much addicted to the chase of wild water-fowl—that the disease is due to the bites of a similar animal, the mosquito. But, though we are duly grateful to the man in the street for condescending to know so much about the matter, I, for one, think that he may as well learn a little more. The subject is one which contains much material for thought—and for action—and one which has its lessons in connection with general education and administration no less than with medical teaching and organisation. These lessons have not yet been fully impressed, and require a more powerful pen than mine to impress them ; but they should not be overlooked at a time when so much is being said and done for the progress of education, knowledge, and efficiency—so that even one of the humblest of the

A SCENE IN FREETOWN, SIERRA LEONE (No. 1).

kind of sportsmen alluded to above, may perhaps be permitted to join in the discussion.

The general importance of the subject is derived from the fact that malarial fever is, perhaps, the most troublesome pest that afflicts humanity. Fortunately, it is not a very fatal malady; but its total prevalence is so enormous that the addition which it makes to the death-roll may possibly exceed that of tuberculosis, cholera, plague and yellow fever put together. Indian statistics show that one-third of the admissions into hospital among the troops are due to malaria; and in many localities in Africa it has been proved that nearly all the native children are infected. Indeed, malaria takes the place in the tropics of chest complaints and rheumatism in temperate climates—where it does not kill, it frequently cripples, or predisposes to other diseases. Moreover, the fact that it tends to abound most in the most fertile countries renders it above all the enemy of civilisation—the great bar of progress in the tropics. I have often thought that Africa has so long resisted the civilisation of Europe chiefly because of its malaria which strikes down the missionary, the pioneer, the soldier, the official, the merchant, who comes to open it up. The growth or many of the most promising colonies has undoubtedly been stunted by it. We should try to imagine what the world might have been without malaria—the tropical and subtropical regions would probably have been as far advanced as the temperate countries now are. To Great Britain especially, into whose hands fate or fortune has delivered the key of the tropics, the subject is of pre-

D

eminent importance; and, in my belief at all events, her tropical empire would have been twice or thrice as large had this disease never existed, or had she taken proper steps to study and control it.

The history of our knowledge of the disease is briefly as follows. The Romans were not only cognizant of it, but also, apparently, of the fact that it is connected with stagnant terrestrial water, and can be reduced by drainage. Many interesting details on this point will be found in North's work on Roman Fever, and also in the writings of Italian physicians on the subject. In the eighteenth century the discovery of the specific action of cinchona bark (from which quinine is made) enabled Torti to discriminate the exact symptoms, especially the peculiar periodic fever; and about the same time Lancisi further emphasised the connection between the fever and stagnant water; but it was not until 1880 that the specific cause of the disease—a minute amœbic parasite living in the blood-corpuscles—was discovered by Laveran, a surgeon of the French army serving in Algeria. This discovery was slowly confirmed by French, Italian, American, and Russian observers, and by one Briton, Vandyke Carter; but the problem as to how the parasites effect an entry into our bodies—that is the problem a solution of which was essential for the purposes of prevention—resisted all such efforts as were made, until it was resolved by a long series of researches carried out between 1895 and 1899. It was then shown that the parasites pass a portion of their life-history in certain kinds of mosquitoes—the insects become infected by biting infected persons, and then, after the lapse of a week or more, inoculate them into healthy human beings. Every stage in the life of the parasites was carefully mapped out, described, and figured by many observers, and healthy birds and human beings were infected under stringent experimental conditions by infected mosquitoes. The long-known connection between malarial fever and terrestrial water was explained by the fact that the malaria-bearing species of mosquito breed in such waters; and in fact all that now remained to be done was to apply the discovery on a large scale to the saving of human life. But though more than five years have elapsed since such a course became practicable, and though decisively successful experiments have been made in a few isolated towns, we still look in vain for any comprehensive or business-like treatment of the subject by those excellent people who are supposed to manage this country and its dependencies.

One of the first questions suggested by this history is why, in the name of reason, was not the old method of drainage more frequently employed against the disease? So far as I can ascertain, the principle was known to the Romans—it has certainly been a sanitary dogma for centuries. Long before the phenomenon was explained by the mosquito-theory, men knew that malaria is connected with stagnant water; and the good effect of drainage is constantly referred to in old medical works. I well remember the prominence which was given to the subject in the lectures delivered to army surgeons at Netley in 1881, and also in certain official proposals for reducing malaria in India published a few years later. But only isolated attempts seem ever to have been made. Nearly every tropical town which I have visited abounded in stagnant ditches, ponds, puddles, rice-fields, and even marshes. When I first saw the old colony of Sierra Leone in 1899—a colony nick-named "the white man's grave," because of its malaria—Freetown, its capital, was full of such waters (see photographs Nos. 1 & 2) of which many were certainly made, not by nature, but by unskilful engineering. Heaven was blamed for the disease, The authorities were not at fault, of course—the "climate" was pestiferous. Yet, if those authorities had chosen to spend a few hundred pounds year by year in removing waste water in accordance with the dogma referred to, thousands upon thousands of lives would have been spared, and the localities would probably have become many times more prosperous than they now are. As for the expense, we must remember that the invaliding of a single soldier costs considerably over a hundred pounds.

But it may be argued that the authorities were not justified in spending any money at all on schemes the utility of which has not been fully proved. This is in fact the stock argument. Logically applied, it would probably put an end to most expenditure. For example, it may be doubted whether the utility of giving each of our petty West African and West Indian colonies a separate and costly government, when each group can easily be administered under modern conditions by one government, has been fully proved. After all, it is only commonsense to suppose that local sanitation has the first claim on the local purse. Moreover, if the utility of drainage had not been fully proved, surely it would have been worth while to make experiments in order to settle the question.

This brings us to another point. It is most remarkable that the malaria problem has been elucidated almost entirely by private persons—medical men who have given up their leisure, and often their money, for the cause, although it was by no means their duty to make the sacrifice. Until quite recently, so far as I remember, no government ever organised more than the most temporary researches on the subject. Yet it is obviously a subject of the most pre-eminent economical importance. Experimental science has existed for centuries, yet no one seemed to have thought of applying it to the study of a disease which retards the civilisation of whole countries. Such trifles are beneath the consideration of politicians. Indeed, at the present moment we can witness precisely the same phenomenon in this country in connection with those humble, but annoying scourges of our homes, scarlet-fever, measles, and—may it even be mentioned?—"cold in the head"; the total amount of public money spent on the investigation of them, would not pay an Under-Secretary. What is our annual expenditure on cancer-research? Yet a cynical man might maintain that the abolition of these diseases would probably be a greater benefit to the country than all which our politicians have conferred upon us during the last two hundred years.

The history of the investigations which have revealed the cause of malaria affords many lessons, pleasant and unpleasant. It is a curious fact that Laveran's discovery of the "germ," although it enabled medical men to diagnose the disease with certainty and also to render their medication more exact, remained almost unused in medical practice for nearly twenty years. No effort was made by the heads of our public medical services to enforce attention to it. Until quite recently, indeed, doctors in the tropics were not even provided with microscopes.[1] I once heard a clever Gascon inveigh against British medical men on the ground that their practice consists of an inspection of the tongue and the prescription of a dose of castor oil. Just possibly the large demand for patent medicines may be the expression of a similar public opinion. Another curious fact is that on several occasions the investigations, far from receiving general assistance, were actually impeded by "professional brethren." On one occasion Drs. Plehn and Rivenburg and myself were practically turned out of a hospital in Calcutta—whither we had gone in order to find cases of malaria suitable for study—and, be it understood, without the shadow of a reason. Colonel King, now Sanitary Commissioner of Madras, was most unmercifully bullied for his researches on smallpox, and Colonel Bruce was frequently interrupted in his investigation on tsetse-fly disease—so that our experience was by no means exceptional. Quite recently a case has come to my

---

1. I have just heard that this remark still applies to one part, at least, of India.

notice in which every possible difficulty has been thrown in the way of two young medical men who are trying to solve a problem almost as important as that of malaria. My readers may think that such stupidity is almost inconceivable—so it is, but it is very common, and, still worse, the perpetrators almost always flourish, and continue to flourish, like the green bay-tree, without ever being cut down, and the nation which allows such a thing, still continues to think that it is going to hold the empire of the world for ever against all comers. The truth is that scientific distinction, and even knowledge, are little considered in the selection of officers for administrative posts in scientific corps. Indeed, it is commonly thought that second-rate men are chosen precisely because they are less likely to urge reforms upon their superiors.

This part of the story is a long one, and though it is important in connection with the organisation of scientific research, cannot be discussed here; but those who are interested in it may possibly learn something with which they are not familiar from my lecture which is now appearing in the "Journal of the Royal Army Medical Corps." I must confess to the fact that my own experiences in research have left me with some most unchristian grudges—which I keep, carefully wrapped in cotton wool in a warm place in my soul, ready for use at the proper moment. My excuse is that the grudges are not on my own behalf, but on behalf of science and humanity. What an amazing thing it is that the last men to receive assistance and the first men to be obstructed, are precisely those who of all men are doing their utmost to benefit others, with the least chance of profit to themselves.

As soon as mosquitoes were definitely proved to be the carrying agents of malaria it became necessary, in the interests of sanitation, to propagate the information as widely as possible among the general public; and this led to many incidents which would be amusing, did they not demonstrate the extreme popular ignorance of science and scientific methods. For years the Press was flooded with letters from people who seemed to resent as a personal injury the refutation of the old hypothesis that malaria is caused by a miasma rising from marshes. They could not be made to see that the old hypothesis was, after all, not far from the truth, but that it is the mosquito, the carrier of the germ, and not the germ itself, which rises from the marsh. One man particularly set himself to "expose" me in the highly respectable pages of a London daily paper, and the only wonder is that I am still alive. Another man gravely informed me that the "theory" could not be true, as there were no mosquitoes in Sierra Leone! A general opinion among officials was that the theory was nothing but the "latest fad of the doctors." It is curious that people who would not think themselves capable of discussing problems connected with astronomy, zoology, or law have no hesitation in contradicting all the doctors in the world. A strong excuse actually put forward for this was that medical opinion cannot be very reliable, because venesection, which was formerly used everywhere, is now everywhere condemned. The public cannot understand that while questions of

A SCENE IN FREETOWN. SIERRA LEONE (No. 2).

treatment are, in the present state of knowledge, largely matters of opinion, questions of pathology are on the other hand often capable of as precise a determination as questions of physics. It is most unfortunate that such an absurd and antiquated name as Medicine should continue to be given to such a large science as that which deals with the nature of disease—the oldest and perhaps the most important of sciences. As well continue the name Alchemy for modern Chemistry. Naturally the man in the street connects the name Medicine with nothing but salts and senna, and attaches as little value to the statement that malaria is carried by mosquitoes as he does to his doctor's diatribes against eating too much meat.

But perhaps the most important lesson taught by the history of malaria, is that our general methods of administration are somewhat obsolete. They are defective in science, energy, and discipline. There is no other reason why the disease should not have been nearly eradicated by this time from most of the principle malarious towns in our possessions. In 1899, immediately after the mosquito-theory was established, I advised, earnestly and repeatedly, that every malarious municipality should at once take steps to drain or fill up mosquito-breeding waters within its limits—at least as quickly as means allowed. Now I can say without vanity, that my advice was, at least, worthy of consideration, because at that time I was certainly the only man who possessed a really intimate personal knowledge of malaria and mosquitoes ; and, withal, I had had an opportunity of becoming very well aquainted with practical tropical sanitation in general. Moreover, the measure which I advocated was merely the old one of drainage, rendered more precise and practical by addenda. Now let it be remembered that the British and colonial taxpayer supports a large and well-paid sanitary staff, which exists in almost every town of note for the special purpose of saving human life from disease by acting on the dictates of science. This staff could easily have been everywhere set in motion by a little persuasion from the head government offices, and in course of time and generally with little more expenditure than the ordinary sanitary budget could afford, waste waters would have been gradually removed and the local health greatly improved. But no efforts of ours availed. I paid several visits to Africa, and even undertook a kind of practical exposition of the subject in Sierra Leone*; but, though such a man as Sir William MacGregor has warmly taken up the scheme, though the French obtained their remarkable victory at Ismailia, and some good work has been done or attempted at Khartoum, in the Federated Malay States, Hong Kong, Madras, the Andamans, and elsewhere, I fear it must be said that nothing approaching adequate general action has been attempted by my countrymen. I do not know whose fault this is. My advice was never asked for, and certainly seldom followed. The head government offices referred to above always express themselves as being most willing to forward the work; but, if so, they are singularly powerless. As a matter of fact—

---

*In association with other members of the Liverpool School of Tropical Medicine

and I have the highest authority for saying so—the
Houses of Parliament, the Cabinet, and all the Secretariats
put together cannot compel a single health officer to put
a barrow-load of gravel into a single puddle. One can
imagine how excellent our system of administration must
be under such circumstances. I fear, however, that it is
a case of lip-service. We have much talk about the
progress and teaching of tropical medicine; mighty
banquets; mutual congratulations over the success of
work which in reality has not yet been commenced, and
so on; but the only effective measure—resolute government action—is, in my opinion, wanting.

Perhaps our reason for the failure lies in the multitude
of councillors. The number of people who have studied
malaria and mosquitoes (in England) is quite large—and
they all have their own schemes. Mine has been
generally condemned, because they say it is impossible to
reduce mosquitoes in a town by stopping their propagation.
Indeed a wonderful experiment, recently made in India,
showed that this process, if anything, increases their
numbers—which is exactly equivalent to saying that the
population of Great Britain would be increased by
abolishing the birth-rate.

The Americans have shown us a very different picture.
In 1901 they proved that yellow-fever also is carried by
mosquitoes ; but instead of spending six years talking
about the matter, they set to work at once and cleared
out yellow-fever, malaria, and mosquitoes together from
Havana, and are now engaged in doing similar work
along the route of the Panama Canal. Recently I had

an opportunity of watching their methods there—much better methods than ours. We as a nation seem to have lost the power of prompt and resolute action; we ponder too much; are too much ruled by vacillating committees consisting of partially informed gentlemen anxious to get home to tea; are too conceited to take the advice of the men of experience; are quite above getting to the bottom of the business; and, above all things, dislike and despise anything of practical utility. If we do not take care we shall follow Spain. At least, that is the moral which the humble writer of these pages has drawn from his experiences in connection with malaria.

The Education of the Citizen.

BY

Professor CHURTON COLLINS, M.A. (Oxon).

I wish the democratic genius of this Country might breathe something of new life into these institutions.—EMERSON.

A REVOLUTION, the nature and extent of which appear to be very imperfectly apprehended by the Academic world has during the last fifteen or twenty years been profoundly affecting the middle and lower sections of society. Those tastes, those studies, those aspirations, which, but a few years ago, were peculiar to a small minority, are now shared by the multitude. There is no quarter of London, there is no city in England in which class-rooms thronged with pupils who, in capacity, energy, and intelligence would compare favourably with the Undergraduates of Oxford and Cambridge, are not to be found. A passion for education, and for education on all its sides and in all its branches, is now as striking a characteristic of the English democracy as the passion for liberty. Nor is this movement of concern only to the people themselves. On every side it has been admitted that what the many are demanding the many must have, advanced instruction, not in Science only but in

Philosophy, Literature, and History; in other words, a system of higher liberal education, so organised and so imparted as to be placed within reach of all who have the energy and ability to avail themselves of it.

But if this movement has its supporters, it has its opponents; and a conflict curiously analagous to the conflicts between the "Greeks" and the "Trojans" and between the Protestants and the Romanists at the Renaissance and the Reformation has been the result. On the one side stand the representatives of scholastic and Academic tradition, the old Universities and all such Institutions as are modelled on the old Universities, in other words, those who draw no distinction between the technical training proper for mere scholars and specialists and the liberal culture proper for the ordinary citizen; on the other side, those who discern the importance of this distinction, and who would bring the Universities and our Academic system generally into touch with modern life. The one party takes its stand on prescription and tradition, and is determined to resist innovation. The other party contends that, as there is no analogy between the intellectual and educational needs of our community as they existed a few years ago and as they find expression to-day, so there is no analogy between the relation in which the Universities once stood to the nation, and the relation in which they ought to be standing now.

But the chief question at issue between the two parties is not simply the relation of the Universities to the State, for the Universities are quite willing, as their attitude to the Extension movement shows, to acknowledge their civil obligations, but the relation of our Academic system generally, as it is now constituted, to the present educational requirements of English citizens. It is not that system as a whole, it is not the Universities as a whole which are impeached. The provision made in them for many branches of study, for Mathematics, for Natural Philosophy in all its departments, for Theology, for Metaphysical and Moral Philosophy, for Political Economy, for Philology, leaves nothing to be desired. But what is justly objected to them is that they regard with indifference those studies which constitute and always must constitute two-thirds of a liberal education in the ordinary acceptation of the term; that they offer, for example, no encouragement to such a study of Ancient and Modern Literature as should enable it to effect as an instrument of culture and discipline what it is of power to effect, and as should enable it, as a subject of knowledge, to inform as it ought to inform; and that what applies to Literature applies also, as a general rule, to History. The one severed from all that makes it vital and influential is degraded into pabulum for Philology, and Cram-work. The other, resolved into mere congeries of facts and separated from Political Philosophy, is degraded into antiquities in theory and into mnemonic tables in practice.

Now. of course, it may be urged that one of the most important functions of Universities is the training of Specialists, and that as Specialists in Philology are and ought to be their peculiar care, no exception can justly be taken to the Institutions referred to. The answer to this is simple. It is not as Specialists in Philology, it is not to undertake the work of Specialists in Philology, that men graduating in this branch of Arts go forth into the world; it is as professors of English Literature, as interpreters of Shakespere and Milton, of Bacon and Burke. It is not as a model for curricula of Philology, it is as a model for curricula of Literature that the provisions of these Institutions practically serve. The instruction they provide, the training they afford,—which, therefore, those graduating in them are qualified and competent to give,—is the sort of training and the sort of instruction that not one person in a hundred thousand requires, or ever, as long as time lasts, will require. But the instruction which they are called upon to impart—for if the Universities confound Philology with Literature, the world without will distinguish them—is the instruction which they have never received. They are called upon to provide instruction in Literature, and to legislate for the teaching of Literature; they have been trained to be Philologists. It is absurd to suppose that taste, tone, temper, sympathy, will not derive their quality and take the ply from the sort of education teachers have received. It would be equally absurd to deny the tendency, the very strong tendency in every man to over-estimate the value of what he has been at great pains to acquire, and to under-estimate the value of what he has been taught to ignore. How far such discipline as institutions like the so-called English Literature School at Oxford and the kindred school at Cambridge provide is likely to qualify a teacher for the duties of an exponent of Belles Lettres, or to enable him to form

any adequate conception either of what constitutes
"Literature" or of the ends at which its interpretation
should aim, is too obvious for comment.

The result of all this is just what might have been
anticipated. Literature regarded as Literature is pronounced to be a subject unsusceptible of "serious"
treatment. In our own Literature all that is worthy of
the attention of "Scholars" is its embryology. As the
expression of genius and art it may be of interest to
Ladies' Schools and to "popular audiences," and serve
to amuse the leisure moments of "Scholars" themselves.
It is useless to contend that Literature, regarded as
Literature, is as susceptible of serious and systematic
treatment and study as any other subject, that to confound
it with Philology is as absurd as to confound Anatomy
with Psychology, and that as long as this confusion is
suffered to continue, so long will our higher education
suffer serious detriment. The answer is always the
same, and the answer is a sneer and a smile. Only
the other day a certain Professor publicly observed of the
University Extension Lectures that they could not be
regarded as satisfactory, or entitled to serious notice, "on
the ground of their teaching not being philological;" no
treatment of Literature, as he was pleased to observe,
could be of an "Academic standard" which was not
"based on Philology."

These, then, are the objections to what may be called
the Academic ideal of liberal education. It confounds the
distinction between technical and liberal education, between
the training proper for those who are in their turn to become

F

the trainers of specialists, and the instruction and discipline proper for those who are intrusted, and that for the benefit of the whole community, with what is and ought to be the chief instrument of liberal and liberalising culture— Literature. And it leads to the confusion of this distinction throughout our whole system of Education. It creates a precedent for totally erroneous conceptions of the proper definition of literature, of the proper organization of literary curricula, of the ends at which literary instruction should aim. Four-fifths of what is excellent in Poetry, all that is of value in Oratory, in Criticism, in Ethical, Metaphysical, and Political Philosophy it excludes and simply ignores. Disassociating the study of Literature from the study of History it deprives it of the key and the commentary without which its development and characteristics must be unintelligible; it separates what is linked inseparably in the relation of cause and effect. Nor is this all. In severing the study of the Literatures of Modern Europe and more particularly of that of our own country from the study of Ancient Classical Literature it establishes a precedent of most disastrous import. No one would deny that, as a counsel of perfection, the basis of liberal education, on the side at least of literary culture, should rest on classical studies. No one would deny that if the Classics of Greece and Rome should lose their vogue among us and cease to be influential, our higher education and what is its expression in result —our literature would suffer serious detriment. There is, probably, no intelligent man in England who, if he has taken the trouble to reflect on the subject, does not perceive that if the languages and literatures of ancient Greece and Rome are to maintain their place in modern education, they can maintain it only by virture of their unique importance.   They cannot maintain it by virture of what they have in common with modern Languages and Literatures, I mean simply by the fact that, as languages, they afford material for philological discipline and as literatures, masterpieces for critical study.   If this be their title to retention, they will be superseded, and ought to be superseded by German, French, and Italian, and nothing can save them.   But what constitutes their unique importance in modern times, lies simply and solely in their peculiar relation to Literæ Humaniores and Philosophy; in their transcendent excellence as the expressions of art and genius, differing, in some respects, importantly, as well in form as in essence, from what has found expression since ; in the fact that, without reference to them, two-thirds of what is best in Modern Literature, and more particularly in our own, is historically unintelligible; and in the fact that for this and other reasons, a thorough acquaintance with them is confessedly indispensable to the equipment and training of a finished critic and professor of Literature.   To set the precedent of disassociating the academic study of the ancient Classics from that of the modern in a School professing, or practically professing, to train literary teachers, and of instituting an honour curriculum of literary instruction based on the assumption that such instruction can be independent of classical studies, is to deprive the Classics of their SOLE

TITLE to retention in modern education. Is it not notorious that what has already half-killed Greek as a factor in our educational curricula, has been its disassociation from the literary side of them, and that where it is alive, it is alive through the efforts of those who are, both as writers and teachers, linking it with the Humanities?

But as a State thrives better under bad laws efficiently administered than under good laws administered inefficiently, so education is likely to suffer less from legislators who know what they want and secure its attainment, than from legislators who, with the best intentions, halt undecided and secure nothing. A system which ought to aim at affording satisfactory literary instruction, and actually affords satisfactory philological and antiquarian instruction is much better than a system which aiming at both affords neither. I am very far from wishing to speak disrespectfully of anything relating to the University of London. As Macaulay observed more than half a century ago, it is, in some memorable particulars, not more a contrast than an example to Oxford and Cambridge. It has always striven to keep in touch with national life. Neither its policy nor its spirit has ever been parochial. Wide and hospitable in its sympathies, it has endeavoured to meet all the educational requirements of our time extending its recognition to subjects not recognised in the older Universities. It has always been in the van where Oxford and Cambridge have been lagging in the rear. But nothing could be more unsatisfactory, or to speak plainly, more ridiculous, than its present regulations for instruction on the side of literature. If they had been drawn up with the special intention of reducing cramming to a science they could not have attained their object more effectually.

And what is the result of these regulations? Precisely the result which they are calculated to produce, and the result which such regulations always will and always must produce. Their appearance each year is followed by a series of cram books. The period of English Literature lying between the prescribed dates is mapped out in divisions and sub-divisions. The principal authors, with their chief works lead-lined, and with the scope and purport of each of these works condensed into a few paragraphs, are arranged in groups. Two or three paragraphs epitomise their biographies, two or three paragraphs their "essential characteristics." The minor poets and prose writers who are of any importance are enumerated and treated, though in a less extended scale, in the same way, with such general or collateral information as is likely to "come in useful," so epitomised and tabulated that it may be taken in at a glance. By methods not less expeditious and, educationally speaking, unprofitable, what is required of Anglo-Saxon and Middle English is made equally easy of attainment. It would be no exaggeration to say that, with the assistance of these mnemonics, any man with powers of memory a little above the ordinary could, in a few weeks, obtain an honour diploma in this examination, so far at least as "Literature" goes. The faculties and energies called into activity by this curriculum begin and end with the exercise, with the mechanical exercise of mere memory.   But this is not all.   The coarseness and vulgarity of feeling and taste, if not actually induced, yet left uncorrected by a system like this often exceed belief.   The study of poetical master-pieces, disassociated from instruction in Æsthetics, foisted into a curriculum two-thirds of which are purely philo-logical, and regarded, as these two-thirds are regarded simply as matter for mark-making, as positive knowledge to be gauged by positive tests, is in truth worse and very much worse than useless.   Well might Matthew Arnold write, as he wrote not very long before he died, " I have no confidence in those who at the Universities regulate studies, degrees, and honours.   To regulate these matters great experience of the world, steadiness, simplicity, breadth of view are desirable.   I do not see how those who actually regulate them can well have these qualifica-tions "—wise words which go to the root of the matter.

What is needed in educational legislation are men who will look at liberal discipline with the eyes of statesmen, and intelligent men of affairs, who will bring to its guidance and regulation " the great experience of the world, the steadiness, the simplicity, the breadth of view" which Arnold desiderated, which Macaulay brought to its guidance and regulation, and which have been brought to the guidance and regulation, both of our Elementary Education, and of Scientific Education.   What is, in the system of our older Universities, either ignored or inex-tricably confused must be defined and distinguished, namely, the instruction proper for specialists; the instruction proper for the liberal discipline of those who design to become teachers and professors ; the instruction proper for the liberal discipline of the ordinary citizen who will pursue other avocations.   The second and third are, of course, essentially identical—differing it may be in degree, as honour standards differ from pass, but one distinction there should be.   Education is a science and education has its history, and its science and history should, therefore, as subjects of knowledge surely hold an important place in the education of those who design to become teachers.   Instruction should be provided in the Languages and Literatures of Greece and Rome, and in those of England, France, Italy and Germany ; and these studies should be co-ordinated, for every encourage-ment should be given to the comparative study of Literature.   A very important place should be assigned to the history of Criticism ; and to Criticism itself, both on its æsthetic and on its verbal side, a place still more important.   Such philosophical works as are not technical and as naturally connect themselves with Literæ Humaniores, such works for instance as the Republic and other Platonic Dialogues, Aristotle's Ethics, The Enchiridion of Epictetus, select portions of Hobbes and Shaftesbury, Butler's Sermons, should be included; and with the study of Literature should be linked insep-arably the study of History, and with the study of History the study of Political Philosophy.

If it be objected that such a scheme is visionary, because it includes too much and expects too much, the reply is, it includes no more than was included in the

famous scheme drawn up by Macaulay for the Indian
Civil Service Candidates, and that it is, like his,
susceptible of all necessary, all expedient modification.
And what is of concern now is not detail but theory, not
accidents but ideas.   The point of importance is the
solution of one of the most pressing problems of our
time—the liberal education of the democracy, of the
average citizen, now mature, now eager for advanced
instruction.   And the education of the democracy implies
the education of its teachers.   The one involves the
other, for what is given must be what has been
received. In other words we have now to exchange
the Academic ideal of education for that civil and
liberal ideal which was upheld by the Ancients,
and which has, generation after generation, ever
since the Renaissance been upheld, now in plea
and now in protest, by the wisest of our countrymen, by
Elyot, More, and Ascham in the sixteenth century,
by Milton, and Locke in the seventeenth, by Chesterfield
and Gibbon in the eighteenth, by Mill, Macaulay, and
Matthew Arnold in our own.

How hopelessly incompatible the Academic conception of Education is with the conception formed of it by
such men as these, and with the conception to which it is
high time that we should conform, requires no further
illustration than a simple comparison will supply.   With
them, the chief end of liberal education was to teach the
citizen to learn *how to live*, both with respect to himself
individually, and with respect also to his fellow citizens and
to the State by the prescription of such studies as should

best afford æsthetic, moral, and political discipline. With our Academic legislators, the chief aim is to impart knowledge, to cram the mind with facts, without reference either to the practical value of the information acquired, or the educational value of the system and methods employed in imparting it. With them, the criterion of the educational value of any given subject, was the importance and usefulness of the knowledge attained, the intellectual discipline afforded by the process of attainment, the moral and æsthetic effect. By our legislators it is estimated purely with reference to the convenience afforded by it for submission to positive examinational tests and for the facility with which, as a subject of study, it can become stereotyped for purposes of mechanical teaching and mechanical acquisition.

If the time has not actually come, it is now within measurable distance, when such a system as I have described will and must be exploded, when those criteria will be applied to the theory and organization of education on its liberal side as have been applied to its theory and organization, both on its elementary side and on its technical and scientific sides, the criteria of common sense, of reason, of expediency. For English citizens know now what they need. The history of such an institution as the University Extension Society, which is directing however imperfectly, the studies of upwards of thirty thousand adult English citizens, has defined it plainly enough. What we want now is a clear conception of what ought to constitute civil liberal education, of the ends at which we should aim, of the means by which those ends may be best attained. And can there be any doubt about either? That the ends are æsthetic, moral and political instruction and culture, the means Literature, Philosophy, and History rationally and intelligently defined and interpreted? That by Literature should be understood the best poetry, the best rhetoric, the best criticism, the best of what is comprised generally in Belles Lettres, to be found in the world; by Philosophy, not those departments of it which are polemical or esoteric and abstrusely technical, but where it bears directly on conduct and life; by History, neither mere antiquities, nor mere chronicles, but philosophy, as Dionysius has so finely described it, teaching by example. Experience has shown that such poems as the Iliad and the Odyssey, the Attic Dramas, the Æneid, the Divine Comedy, and such criticisms as portions of the Poetics, the Treatise on the Sublime and the Laocoon, can be rendered as intelligible and instructive to the many, as they are supposed to be to the few. And what applies to Literature, applies to Philosophy, applies to works like the Republic, the Apology of Socrates, the Crito, the Phædo, the Ethics of Aristotle, the Meditations of Marcus Aurelius, the Enchiridion of Epictetus. Will anyone pretend to say that they are not as susceptible of popular interpretation as the Epistles of St. Paul? That the study of them would not be equally fruitful, nay, that it would not supply a great and increasing popular want? No one who observes with discernment the signs of the times, can fail to perceive that theological teaching as a means of moral culture is more and more losing its hold on the people, or at all events that it is not sufficient, that they need something more, and that that something more is precisely what instruction, under competent teachers, in such works as those to which I have referred will supply.   In the philosophy of the Academy and of the Porch, the ethics of Christianity find at once the best of commentaries, and, what is more, invaluable collateral security.   And to bring, therefore, that philosophy home to all who are capable of profiting from its teaching, as thousands now are, ought to be as much the aim of the legislators of civil liberal education as the interpretation of Doctrinal Theology—the Jewish Scriptures—is the care of the Church.

Not less important is the satisfactory organization of political instruction and culture.   Every encouragement and facility should be given to such a study of History as should be inspiring, as should conduce to the promotion of enlightened views, as should aim at bringing the past into influential relation with the present.   It is not with the eye of the antiquary and specialist, it is not with the object of the antiquary and specialist that the citizen should be taught to regard and pursue this study.   Introduce him to Herodotus, to Thucydides, to Plutarch, to the great classical historians of Rome and of modern Europe, bring them home to him—and you cultivate him ; substitute for minute and detailed study of the history of the Dark and Mediæval Ages a similar study of the history of Europe during the last seventy years, bring home to him what is best in

Political Philosophy—and you instruct him.   Every encouragement should be given to the study of the Constitution of Modern Society, of Modern Institutions, of the rights, of the duties of citizenship.

These, I contend, are the lines on which the education of the adult citizen—the education for which thousands are now ripe, and for which thousands are now eager,— should run.   It represents no new conception.   It is nothing more than the theory on which the work of the University Extension proceeds.   It is what innumerable institutions and agencies all over the kingdom are more or less imperfectly aiming at.   We want now direction, consolidation, system.   We shall not get them from Academic legislators.   We shall not get them from the regulators of such institutions as the so-called School of English Literature at Oxford and the Mediæval and Modern Languages Tripos at Cambridge.   We shall not get them till we have seen the wisdom of doing what every other country in Europe has done—the wisdom of placing the advanced education of our citizens partially, at all events, under the control of the State.   An ideal of education has been practically defined by the instincts of an intelligent democracy, an ideal which differs radically and essentially from that which has from time immemorial been upheld by Academic Bodies; and we must look for its realisation, not to its natural and professed opponents, but to legislators who, being in sympathy with the citizen, are in sympathy with what the citizen needs and demands.

Let us hope that the day has at last come when worthy conceptions of Education will find expression in the constitution of the new Teaching University for London and of our Provincial Universities; when the salutary precedent of the Continent will be followed, and the regulation of studies at the chief centres of study will be controlled not by the upholders of a narrow esotericism but by men—who, with the instincts and temper of statesmen, will realise that a University must be something more than a mere nursery for specialists; that if provision for specialisation be one of its functions, it has more important functions too, namely the definition, regulation, and dissemination of civic liberal instruction and culture,—of education in the sense in which it was understood by Plato, by More, by Matthew Arnold and by Jowett.

Foreign University News.

FRANCE

Communicated by Mons. L. FICHOU, *Secrétaire Général du Bureau des Renseignéments de la Sorbonne, Paris. (April).*

University Developments.

The following interesting statistics have been taken from the official Report issued by the Minister of Education on April 8th, 1905:

Number of Students attending the Universities in January, 1905.

PARIS.

	Men Students.				Women Students.			
	French.	Foreign.	Total.		French.	Foreign.	Total.	Total
Faculty of Law	4703	420	5123	...	17	30	47	5170
,, ,, Medicine ...	2980	251	3231	...	109	119	228	3459
,, ,, Science	1303	147	1450	...	38	117	155	1605
,, ,, Arts	1284	176	1460	...	177	276	453	1913
,, ,, Chemistry .	1168	17	1185	...	50	2	52	1237
,, ,, Theology (Protestant)	42	5	47	...	—	—	—	47
Grand Totals ...	11,480	1016	12,496	...	391	544	935	13,431

Of the total number of foreign students (1560); 83 are of British nationality, distributed as follows: Law, 18; Medicine, 13; Science, 4; Arts, 47; Chemistry, 1; total, 83.

PROVINCIAL UNIVERSITIES.

	Total number of students		Total number of students
Aix-Marseille	1150	Lyon	2551
Besançon	321	Montpellier	1779
Bordeaux	2433	Nancy	1540
Caen	748	Poitiers	888
Clermont	272	Rennes	1257
Dijon	902	Toulouse	2358
Grenoble	769	Alger	1033
Lille	1190		

Total number of men students attending the French Universities = 31,696 (of whom 1676 are foreigners).
Total number of women students attending the French Universities = 1722 (of whom 774 are foreigners).
Grand Total, 33,618.

News and Notes.

The Students' Handbook will shortly be issued by le Bureau des Renseignements. Copies of the Handbook may be obtained on application to the Secretary of the Bureau. The Handbook comprises important University information, and the new edition contains a supplement written in English.

The disturbances which have occurred during the lectures of Mons. Gariel, Professor of Physics in the Faculty of Medicine, have caused the temporary suspension of work in the Faculty until May 1st, although the classes open for foreigners are still held.

An interesting course of vacation lectures on medical subjects has been held in April at the Hôtel des Societés Savantes, Rue Serpente and also at various Hospitals.

The visit of English doctors to Paris is expected to take place on the 10th of May. The visitors will be received at the Sorbonne by Mons. le Recteur Liard, accompanied by Mons. Casimir-Périer (late President of the Republic), President of the "Association des Amis de l'Université."

The Second Congress of School Hygiene will be held in Paris on June 11th, in the large lecture theatre of the Medical School, when Mons. le Professeur Lavisse will preside.

Owing to the success attending the Free Course of Lectures recently given by Professor Beach, (of St. Paul, U.S.A.), he has accepted an invitation to occupy again the Professorial Chair in the coming autumn.

University Extension.

Two very successful lectures have recently been given at the Institute Général Psychologique (13, Rue de Condé, Paris); the first by Professor Charles Richet, member of the Academy of Medicine, on "Personality and the Changes of Personality"; and the second by Professor Yves Delage, member of the Academy of Sciences, on the "Problems of Biology."

At the Université Populaire "La Co-opération des Idées" (234, Rue de Faubourg, St. Antoine) the following lectures have been held: Mons. Charles Gide, Professor in the Faculty of Law on "A New Social System—Le Morcellisme"; and Mons. le Comte Henri de la Vaulx, on "The Utility of Balloons in Science, Warfare and Sport."

At the University (at 157, Faubourg St. Antoine) Mons. Seignobos, Professor at the Sorbonne, recently gave an interesting lecture on

"The French and Russian Revolutions." On April 15th an important address was delivered by Mons. Paul Privat-Deschanel, on "Labour Legislation and Social Questions in Modern Australia"; and on April 25th Mons. Camille Pelletan, late Cabinet Minister, will deliver a lecture on "The Future of Democracy."

At the Foundation Universitaire de Belleville an interesting lecture has been given by Mons. Raymond Reconly, Fellow of the University, on "Impressions and Recollections of the Russo-Japanese War"; and on April 14th Madame Moll-Weiss, Headmistress of the Ecole des Méres, addressed a meeting on the subject of "What ought we to Drink?"

At the Education Sociale de Montemartre a lecture was recently given by Mons. Chartier, Professor of the University, on "Ought Unjust Laws to be Obeyed?"

Recent Scientific and Literary Research.

Madame Lapicque, wife of the eminent Professor in the Faculty of Science, on April 14th presented a thesis for her Degree of Doctor of Science on "The Electrical Excitability of Muscles in Vertebrates and Inverterbrates."

Mons. Albert Demangeon has recently presented two theses for the Degree of Doctor in the Faculty of Arts. The subjects of his papers being the "Beginnings of French Geography in the National Archives" and "The Plain of Picardy, and the Study of Geography on the Chalk Plains of Northern France."

Reform in Orthography.

Among the leaders of the party in favour of a complete reform in Orthography are Professor Paul Meyer, Director of the Ecole des Chartes, and Mons. Louis Havet, Professor at the College of France, and member of the Institute. In the opposite camp, amongst the Conservatives, or at least only moderate reformers, may be mentioned Professor Emile Faguet, whose report has recently been approved by the Académie Française. Professor Faguet is in favour of making changes in only fourteen words, the spelling of which he advises should be brought more into accord with phonetics and commonsense. These proposals are far from satisfying those who have been working for a complete reform in Orthography. The controversy is still being carried on in the columns of the newspapers, in the magazines and in educational circles. Considerable activity is being displayed on both sides. The final decision of the question is in the hands of the Minister of Public Instruction.

New Magazines and Societies.

The first number of a new publication has recently appeared under the title of *La Revue Germanique*. It is published by Alcan, Boulevard St. Germain, and will be devoted to the study of English and German literature.

A number of Professors of the University have recently formed an Association for the Study of Modern Languages and Literature, in order to stimulate and maintain the spirit of scientific research and free discussion in these subjects. It is hoped that this Society may be the means of drawing together many who are now widely scattered, and are in need of such means of inter-communication. Reports will be received from members who are prevented by distance from attending the meetings of the Society, and such communications will be duly considered and published. Meetings of the Society will be held each month. It is not intended to elect a President. The office of Secretary will be held during the coming year by Mons. Charles Audler, Professor at the Sorbonne. Applications for membership (subscription ten francs) should be made to Mons. Ernest Lévy, Assistant Secretary, 6, rue de Cerisoles, Paris.

The following have recently presented theses for the Degree of *Docteur es Lettres :*—Mons. Bazaillas, Professor of Philosophy at the Lycée Condorcet (awarded special honourable mention). Theses: (1) " The Metaphysical Study of Music according to Schopenhauer "; (2) " Individuality, a Study of some Illusions of Objective Perception." Mons. Cousin, late member of the French School of Athens, Lecturer in the Faculty of Arts at the University of Nancy (awarded honourable mention). Theses: (1) (in Latin) " De Urbibus Quarum Nominibus Vocabulum πόλιςFinem Faciebat "; (2) " Cyrus the Younger in Asia Minor (408—401 B.C.)." Mons. Loth, Professor in the College of Tunis (awarded honourable mention). Theses: (1) " Arnoldo Soler, Spanish *Chargé d'Affairs* in Tunis, and his Correspondence (1808—1810) "; (2) " The Growth of the Italian Population in Tunis and Algeria."

Appointments.

Mons. Glasson, Professor of Civil Law, has been appointed Dean of the Faculty of Law for a period of three years, dating from the 24th March, 1905.

The Central Meteorological Office has made the following appointments for one year:—Mons. Bouquet de la Grye, member of the Institute and of the Bureau des Longitudes, to the office of President of the Council of the Central Meteorological Office; Mons. Darboux, Permanent Secretary to the Académie des Sciences, and member of the Bureau des Longitudes, to the office of Vice-President.

The Paris Observatory has appointed for the year 1905:—Mons.

Laussedat, member of the Institute, to the office of President of the Council of the Paris Observatory; Mons. Lippmann, member of the Institute, to the office of Secretary.

Publications.

The following articles of especial interest have recently appeared in the Reviews:—

" Mount Pelée and its Eruptions," by Mons. H. de Lapparent, in *Annales de Geographie.* for March.

"The Axioms of Mechanics and the Principle of Causality," by Mons. Painlevé, in the *Bulletin de la Société française de Philosophie.*

"The Canadian Elections," by Mons. Albert Métin, in *La Renaissance Latine.*

" The Simplification of Orthography," by Mons. E. Faguet; and " The Failure of the Study of Racial Psychology," by Mons. Jean Finot, in the March number of *La Revue.*

" Professor Meyer's Report and the Reform of Orthography," in the *Revue Internationale de l'Enseignement.*

" Mr. H. G. Wells and his Ideas on Education," by Professor Ch. v. Langlois, in the *Revue de Paris.*

" The Simplification of Our Spelling," by Professor Paul Meyer, in the *Revue Pedagogique.*

" Radio-Therapeutics and Cancer," by Dr. P. Desfosses, in the *Revue Générale des Sciences.*

The question of the recruiting of University lecturers and professors is being discussed in the pages of the *Revue Internationale de l'Enseignement.* Professor Picavet, General Secretary of the College of France, has opened an enquiry, aided by the Society of Higher Education, " on the best methods of extending higher education to candidates for public offices, and generally to all those studying for professions that demand the learning associated with an university degree."

Recent Works.

Histoire de la langue française des origines à nos jours. Vol. i. By Mons. F. Brunot, Professor at the Sorbonne. (Published by Colin, 5, rue de Méziéres, Paris.)

Paris sous le Consulat Recueil de documents pour l'Histoire de l'esprit public à Paris. By Mons. A. Aulard, Professor in the Paris University. Two volumes. (Published by Cerf, Paris.)

La démocratie in Nouvelle Zélande. By Mons. André Siegfried, Docteur ès Lettres. (Published by Colin, Paris.)

N.B.—Arrangements are being made for the publication in future numbers of " The University Review," of University information from Germany and the United States of America.

The Universities.

ABERDEEN.

University News and Notes.

" The opening of the Gallery of Sculpture and Art in Aberdeen was happily arranged for the same week as the Spring Graduation, and the interest of both ceremonies was consequently enhanced. The Senatus seized the opportunity afforded by the presence of distinguished foreign representatives to confer the Honorary Degree of LL.D. upon Commendatore Alberto Galli, Director-General of the Pontifical Museums and Galleries, and Mr. Edward Robinson (a graduate of Harvard), Keeper of Greek and Roman Antiquities in the Museum of Fine Arts, Boston, U.S.A. As representing literature the Degree was also conferred upon Mr. Thomas Hardy and Mr. "Maarten Maartens;" while Lord Reay, Professor Bury, of Cambridge, Mr. Haverfield, of Christ Church, Oxford, Mr. J. T. Merz, member of Council of Durham College of Science, and author of the "History of Intellectual Development in the Nineteenth Century," and Mr. John Struthers, C.B., the successor of Sir Henry Craik in the office of Secretary to the Scotch Education Department, received the same honour. The Honorary Degree of D.D. was conferred upon the Revs. Enrico Bosio, Principal of the Waldensian College, Florence; W. R. Inge, Fellow of Hertford College, Oxford; Alexander Miller, and James Wiseman. Mr. Alex. Souter, of Mansfield College, Oxford, obtained by thesis the degree of D.Litt.

Perhaps the most noteworthy feature of the Ordinary and Honours list was the large proportion of women among the graduates in the Faculty of Arts. Of ten students obtaining First Class Honours five were women, and of the other graduates in Arts women constituted about one-third.

The Reception held on the evening of Degree Day, when Principal and Mrs. Lang welcomed the guests, also owed some of its interest to the presence of the visitors. No doubt Mr. Hardy, who seemed to take great interest in the reel-dancing, and

Mr. "Maartens," whose tall, handsome figure was conspicuous in the throng, were the chief objects of interest, but, in addition to the honorary graduates of the day, there was a large attendance of artists, including Mr. Frank Dicksee, Mr. Frampton, Mr. Solomon, Mr. La Thangue, Mr. Leader, Mr. David Murray, Mr. Farquharson, Mr. Coutts Michie, Mr. Noble and Mr. Payton Reid.

The Sculpture Gallery, opened by Sir George Reid, ex-President of the Royal Scottish Academy, though it is not an institution belonging to the University, will prove of great service to our students. Professor W. M. Ramsay has given invaluable assistance in the Greek and Roman Section, which already comprises over seventy casts illustrative of Unycensæan, Lycian, Argire, Attic and Roman Art. There are also sections for Egyptian, Assyrian, Italian, French, German and Celtic sculpture, some of the casts, especially moulded in Rome and Berlin, being the only copies in Great Britain; while many others can be found in this country only at Oxford, Cambridge or London. It is to be hoped that the presence of such a splendid collection will give an impetus to the establishment of a Department of Fine Arts in the University at no very distant date."

At a general meeting of the Aberdeen University Liberal Association, held at Marischal College, recently, the following resolution, proposed by Mr. J. S. Paterson, President of the Students' Representative Council, was adopted:—

"That the Aberdeen University Liberal Association learns with pleasure that the Right Hon. C. T. Ritchie, M.P., has intimated his willingness to become a candidate for the Lord Rectorship of the University for another term of office; and that, in view of his past services to the University and of the able stand he has taken on behalf of Free Trade, this Association joins with the Aberdeen University Unionist Association in giving Mr. Ritchie unanimous election to the office of Lord Rector."

It is stated, however that a number of the students who favour Fiscal Reform are to bring forward the name of Sir Howard Vincent for nomination as Lord Rector.

The spring general meeting of the Classical Association of Scotland was held in the University recently. Profesor G. G. Ramsay, of the University of Glasgow, the President, in the chair. It was resolved to hold the autumn meeting in Glasgow on Saturday, November 25th. Referring to the resolution adopted at the last meeting for the appointment of a Committee to draw up a practical scheme of recommendations on the subject of Latin pronunciation, it was stated that a communication had been received from the Secretary of the English Association, mentioning that they had appointed a Committee for a similar purpose, with instructions to confer with the Committee appointed by the Scottish Association. The President then proceeded with his opening address on the effect which recent educational changes were likely to have upon the higher teaching in country schools. Dr. Marshall, Rector, Royal High School, Edinburgh, followed with a paper entitled " Some Readings and Renderings in the Odes of Horace." In the afternoon, Professor A. W. Mair, Edinburgh University, read a paper on " Suggestions as to the Teaching of Greek."

University Developments.

A curriculum qualifying for graduation with honours in History has now been instituted, and will come into operation in Session 1905–6. It differs in some respects from those of the other Universities of Scotland. British, European, Colonial History, and British Constitutional Law and History are compulsory. Candidates must present themselves for examination in three of the following six subjects, viz., Political Science, Political Economy, Roman Law, Greek History, Roman History and Ecclesiastical History.

The Annual General Meeting of the Aberdeen University Endowment Association was held on April 12th. Mr. Patrick Cooper, secretary, read the report, which drew attention to the desirability of the establishment of a Professorship in Conveyancing. If a Professorship in Conveyancing were established it was probable that lectureships in other branches of legal study at present unprovided for would follow, and the University would then be placed on an equal footing with the Universities of Glasgow and Edinburgh. The report was adopted.

BIRMINGHAM.

University News and Notes.

The Earl of Halsbury, as Warden of the Birmingham University Guild of Undergraduates, will deliver his address to the undergraduates in the large Lecture Theatre of the Birmingham and Midland Institute on Saturday, May 13. Mr. Chamberlain, the Chancellor of the University, will preside.

The annual Huxley Lecture was recently delivered by Professor E. B. Poulton, M.A., F.R.S., Professor of Zoology in the University of Oxford, in the Midland Institute, on " Thomas Henry Huxley and the Theory of Natural Selection."

Arrangements are in progress for the members of the Court of Governors to visit the new University buildings at Bournbrook on Friday, June 30.

The annual meeting of the Association for the Higher Education of Working Men will be held at Birmingham in October, with Sir Oliver Lodge in the chair, and the Bishop of Birmingham and Mr. Richard Bell, M.P., as the chief speakers.

In response to Professor Sir Edward Elgar's appeal for donations to a fund for a University library of music, the University has received (per Mr. Richard Peyton) £500 from Mr. Francis W. V. Mitchell, and £25 from Mr. John Feeney.

A communication has been received stating that the Lord Mayor and the General Purposes Committee of the Birmingham Corporation, in accordance with the directions contained in the will of the late Mr. Thomas Best, have allocated to the University the sum of £20,000.

Miss Annette Harding has given a donation of £100, which at her request has been assigned by the Council to the Faculty of Arts for the purchase of books to be placed in the University library, a book-plate to be affixed to each volume stating that the book was given in memory of the late Mr. Charles Harding.

University Developments.

The School of Brewing is making very satisfactory progress and is now in a most flourishing condition. The buildings, equipment, and annual working cost have all been provided by the Birmingham and Midland Counties' Wholesale Brewers' Association, so that no part of the funds of the University or the Government grant have been used in founding or carrying on the school. Since its establishment some sixty-seven students have completed their course in the Brewing School, and pupils now come from all parts of the country and even from the Colonies. It is now proposed to make additions to the school as a result of a visit made by a deputation from the Board of Management to the Brewing Schools of Ghent, Berlin, Vienna, Munich, and Paris.

A temporary ordinance has been made by the Council assigning the Richard Peyton Chair of Music to the Faculty of Arts for the present.

It has been decided to establish a Professorship of Civil Engineering, and an assistantship to the Chair of History.

University Appointments, etc.

Professor Jordan Lloyd has been elected to represent the Faculty of Medicine upon the Council of the University.

Professor W. R. Phillips, LL.M., of the University of Leeds, has been appointed External Examiner in Commercial Law, and Professor Fynes-Clinton, M.A., of the University College of North Wales, Bangor, External Examiner in Spanish and Italian, for the current year.

Mr. A. D. Imms has been nominated by the Senate to His Majesty's Commissioners of the 1851 Exhibition for election to a Science Research Scholarship.

CAMBRIDGE.

University News and Notes.

The Board of Studies at Cambridge has recommended to the Senate that in 1908 and every fourth year thereafter a Maccoll Lecturer should be appointed to represent the bequest of £500 for the encouragement of the study of the language and literature of Spain or Portugal.

Dr. Sandys, Public Orator at Cambridge, has accepted an invitation to deliver a course of lectures on the Lane Foundation at Harvard. The subject of his course will be "The Revival of Learning in Italy."

Mr. J. F. P. Rawlinson, K.C., and a Commissary of the University, has been selected as a candidate to represent the University at the General Election as a colleague of Sir Richard Jebb. Sir John Gorst, M.P., will probably contest the seat as an independent candidate.

The report of the Cambridge University Day Training College for the last academical year has just been issued. In June, 1904, the College contained 47 students. Of the ten third-year students who graduated last June nine took Honours in Triposes, two of these obtaining a First Class and six a Second Class. The Primary Department of the Training College now numbers 55 students; of these all but one or two are members of Colleges in the University, the others being non-collegiate students. The Training College also includes a Secondary Department for candidates for public school masterships or official appointments who wish to read for the Teachers' Training Syndicate's certificate. There are at present nine secondary students.

University Appointments, etc.

The Vice-Chancellor has announced that the General Board of Studies have appointed Mr. T. S. P. Strangeways, M.A., St. John's College, as the first Huddersfield Lecturer in Special Pathology. Mr. Strangeways has been the University Demonstrator in Pathology, to which appointment he came from St. Bartholomew's Hospital about six years ago, on the occasion of the appointment of the late Professor Durthach to the Chair of Pathology.

Hájjí Mirza Abdul-Husayn Khán has been appointed University Teacher of Persian by the Special Board of Indian Civil Service Studies.

Mr. R. P. Gregory, M.A., of St. John's College, has been appointed Senior Demonstrator in Botany.

Mr. L. H. Courtney, M.A., Hon. LL.D. of St. John's, has been appointed a member of the Board of Electors to the Professorship of Political Economy until February, 1913.

The Governing Body of Gonville and Caius College has, in place of an Assistant Lectureship, established a Lectureship in Modern Languages. Mr. E. C. Quiggin, M.A., has been appointed to the Lectureship.

Newnham College.

The Council of Newnham College, Cambridge, has issued an appeal for funds to endow a number of research fellowships. It is stated that those who lament the present insignificance of the work done by the women's Colleges in the world of science and scholarship scarcely realise how easy it would be to improve the position by means of endowment. "These Colleges, which are dependent for their maintenance almost entirely upon students' fees, cannot be expected to contribute largely to the supply of scientific workers so long as the smallness of their means makes it impossible to hold out encouragements of a monetary and official kind to those who distinguish themselves during their college career. At Cambridge the men's Colleges possess some 400 fellowships, of which a few are in the strict sense research fellowships; the women's Colleges seek to secure for their more distinguished students the advantages which attach to these last." Mrs. Sidgwick, Principal of Newnham College, will be glad to give further particulars concerning the appeal.

DUBLIN.

University News and Notes.

It is stated that the Board of Trinity College have appointed a Committee to inquire into, and report upon, the possibility of improving the systems of teaching and examination now in force there. The Committee is composed of two Senior Fellows, two Junior Fellows, and two Professors. An important part of the Committee's inquiry will have reference to the reform of the Fellowship Course.

Enquiries are being made by the Board of Trinity College with a view to recovering for the Fellows of the College the privilege of electing the Provost. This right was conferred on them by the charter of Queen Elizabeth, but was removed by a charter of Charles I. Since that time the right of nomination of the Provost has belonged to the Crown.

The following statement of the regulations concerning entrance exhibitions in Trinity College has been issued by the Registrar:—

"The Board of Trinity College, Dublin, with a view to co-ordinating Intermediate and University Education, have established exhibitions to be awarded on the result of the yearly Intermediate Examinations without requiring candidates to present themselves at the Exhibition Examination held in the College, and without any restriction as to the schools at which they shall have received their education."

Full particulars as to subjects of examination, conditions, etc., may be obtained on application to the Registrar, Trinity College, Dublin.

DURHAM.

Durham College of Science, Newcastle.

It has been decided by the Armstrong College Council to defer the ceremonial opening of the new buildings until July, August, or September of next year, when it is expected that the King will be able to visit Newcastle to perform the ceremony.

Mr. A. F. Ericsson has been elected a member of the Council.

Messrs. Osbeck and Co. have offered two Exhibitions of £10. 10s. each per annum—one for Mining and one for Metallurgy.

The Newcastle Education Committee has made a grant of £1,200 to Armstrong College, and one of £1,170 to Rutherford College.

EDINBURGH.

University News and Notes.

The Spring Graduation Ceremonial took place in the McEwan Hall on Friday, April 7th. The Vice-Chancellor, Principal Sir William Turner, presided. Honorary degrees were conferred upon the following:—For D.D. degree: The Rev. J. A. Kerr Bain, M.A.; the Rev. R. H. Fisher, M.A., B.D.; the Rev. Alexander Lawson, B.D., Professor of English Literature, University, St. Andrews; and Signor Giovanni Luzzi, Florence. For LL.D. degree: William Watson Cheyne, C.B., F.R.S., F.R.C.S., Professor of Surgery, King's College, London; Sir Arthur Conan Doyle, M.D.; Sir Charles Eliot, K.C.M.G.; George A. Gibson, D.Sc., Professor of Mathematics, Glasgow and West of Scotland Technical College; John Hughlings Jackson, M.D., F.R.S.; the Honourable Lord Kincairney; Augustus D. Waller, M.D., F.R.S., Director of the Physiological Laboratory, University of London; and Colonel Sir Frank E. Younghusband, K.C.I.E. The customary address to the graduates was delivered by Professor Darroch, who took as his subject "The Spirit and Aim of University Teaching."

The University Court has approved of a draft agreement between the Town Council of the City of Edinburgh, the University Court of the University of Edinburgh, and others, arranging for a reconstruction of the Royal (Dick) Veterinary College.

A draft ordinance for the Institution of Degrees in Veterinary Medicine and Surgery and relative regulations has been finally adjusted and approved.

It is announced that Sir John Batty Tuke, M.P., has failed to satisfy the Edinburgh University Free Trade Union in his attitude towards Fiscal Reform, and it is understood that steps will immediately be taken to bring forward a candidate in the Free Trade interest.

Two Spence Bursaries will be open for competition this autumn at Edinburgh University, tenable for two years and of the value of £30 for the first year and £40 for the second year. Candidates must have passed the Preliminary Examination, and have attended one Winter Session or its equivalent in the Faculty of Arts. The Examination will be held in the Examination Hall of the University on Tuesday, 26th September, 1905, and the subjects will be Latin, Greek and Mathematics. Application forms, etc., may be obtained from the Factor, Henry A. Pattallo, 1, Bank Street, Dundee.

The University Court has passed an ordinance providing for the inclusion of geography as a subject qualifying for graduation in Arts, prior to its being submitted to the Senatus and the General Council for their consideration.

On the recommendation of the Senatus, Saturday, 4th Nov., 1905, has been fixed as the date of next Rectorial election.

A joint meeting of the Conservative Association for the Universities of Edinburgh and St. Andrews and local Liberal Unionist supporters was recently held in Edinburgh—Professor Annandale, F.R.C.S., presiding—to consider what steps ought to be taken in view of the recent rumour of opposition in the constituency. Sir John Batty Tuke, M.P. the present member for the Universities, attended, and delivered an address, at the close of which it was unanimously agreed that he be again adopted as the Unionist candidate for the constituency, and that every effort should be made to ensure his return. In reply to the resolution, Sir John said that he gladly accepted the invitation unanimously extended to him, and that in the event of his return being opposed, he was perfectly ready to contest the seat.

Attention is called by the Vacation Courses Council to the special vacation courses in French, German and English, to be held in August next, in rooms which have been placed at the disposal of the Council by the University of Edinburgh. These courses will afford those who are unable to go abroad an opportunity of studying one or both of these two languages in their own country. Each of these two languages, besides English for the benefit of foreigners, will be taught theoretically and practically about three hours daily, during August, by a staff of distinguished French and German professors and lecturers, over 30 in all, phonetics (*inter alia*) being represented by Dr. Henry Sweet, M. Paul Passy, and Professor W. Viëtor. Certificates of proficiency granted by the Council will be recognised by the Scotch Education Department. The complete syllabus and full particulars will be supplied on application to the Hon. Organiser (Mr. A. A. Gordon, C.A.), 128a, George Street, Edinburgh.

University Developments.

The Royal Scottish Geographical Society have issued a circular on the subject of the establishment of a Chair of Geography in the University of Edinburgh. "The claims of the science of geography as a University subject have long been recognised by the leading German, French, and American Universities, and in recent years the Universities of Oxford and Cambridge have also established schools of geography, but as yet there is no special teaching of geography in any Scottish University.   The efficient teaching of geography in our schools and colleges is one of the most urgent needs of our time, affecting the political and commercial welfare of the Empire, and it is believed that the subject cannot be satisfactorily dealt with until our Universities take it up, and provide, in the first place, adequate training for teachers.   Towards this end an important step has been taken by the Senatus of the University of Edinburgh, in approving of geography as a subject qualifying for graduation in the Faculties of Science and Arts, and in response to various representations, the University authorities have given their approval to the proposal for the establishment of a Chair of Geography in the University of Edinburgh. The Councils of the Royal Society, and the Edinburgh Merchant Company, have also expressed themselves as favourable to the object in view, and a Committee representative of these and other bodies has been formed to raise the necessary funds for the endowment of the Chair.   In appealing to the people of Scotland for their assistance in raising funds for this endowment, the Committee feel that the claims of an object so desirable, and so necessary at the present time, are so strong, that the project only requires to be made known to command public support.   The minimum amount requisite to endow the Chair is £15,000, but, in the event of this sum not being immediately forthcoming, a Lectureship might be alternative to the founding of a Chair.   This alternative would, however, be unsatisfactory, and it is earnestly hoped that a sufficient sum will be raised to ensure the endowment of a Chair."   The letter is signed by Prof. James Geikie, Chairman of the Royal Scottish Geographical Society, and by Mr. J. G. Bartholomew, Secretary.

The Edinburgh Dean of Guild Court has granted warrant to the Edinburgh University Court to alter the old High School buildings at the High School Yards (recently acquired by the University from the Edinburgh Corporation), and to adapt them for new laboratories for engineering purposes, with lecture theatre, drawing office, etc., in connection with the University; and to erect an engineering workshop in connection with the classes to be held there, on the ground lying between the old High School and the street known as the High School Yards.

Lord Dunedin, President of the Court of Session, has been formally adopted as Conservative candidate for the Lord Rectorship.

The Right Honourable R. B. Haldane, K.C., M.P., LL.D., has accepted the invitation of the Executive of the Edinburgh University Liberal Association to stand as their candidate at the next Rectorial election.   Mr. Haldane is a graduate of the University.

University Appointments, etc.

Dr. C. G. Knott, Lecturer in Applied Mathematics in the University of Edinburgh, has been appointed the Thomson Lecturer in the Aberdeen United Free College for the Session 1905–6. His subject is to be "Seismology, or Earthquakes and their Bearing on the Theory of the Constitution of the Earth."

The United Free Church of Scotland's Foreign Mission Committee have made the following appointments of Edinburgh graduates:— Rev. David C. Davidson, M.A., assistant minister in Edinburgh, to the Manchuria Mission; Mr. John R. Cuthbert, M.A., to Bombay, for the Wilson College, to be ordained and take charge of classes in Bible Exegesis and Philosophy; Dr. Rutter Williamson, M.D., Ch.B., to Central India, to the Maratha Medical Mission at Bhandara.

Dr. William Fream has been re-appointed Steven Lecturer in Agriculture (Agricultural Entomology) for three years from 29th November next.

GLASGOW.

University News and Notes.

"The members of the University of Glasgow have been much gratified to see that Lord Kelvin, their distinguished Chancellor, has overcome the severe illness from which he recently suffered, which caused so much concern not only to them but to all who appreciate the work of one of the great leaders of modern Science.

The retirement of Alexander Moody Stuart, LL.D., from the Chair of Law, which is about to take effect, removes from the University, after eighteen years of service, at a comparatively early age, a Professor of sound and comprehensive acquirements in his own subject, who taught large classes in Scots Law with ability and success. In the time of his predecessor, the late Sheriff Berry, Civil Law was taught from the same Chair, and this course was followed for some years in the earlier part of Professor Moody Stuart's tenure, but, in accordance with arrangements following on the passing of new ordinances under the Universities Act of 1889, Civil Law has since been taught by a separate lecturer. For some time Professor Moody Stuart has suffered from imperfect hearing, and this is understood to be the chief reason for his resignation. He will carry with him into his retirement the hearty esteem and goodwill of his former colleagues and students, and of many others with whom he came into contact. It is announced that His Majesty the King has appointed Mr. William M. Gloag, B.A., Advocate, to be Professor of Law. Mr. Gloag, who is a son of Lord Kincairney, one of the Judges of the Court of Session, was admitted an Advocate in 1889, and is joint author, along with Mr. Irvine, LL.B., Lecturer on Civil Law in this University, of a standard work on Heritable Securities.

With a view to form an academic centre outside the statutory official bodies, and to promote fellowship among members of the University and others interested in it, steps have recently been taken for the establishment of a College Club in the immediate neighbourhood of Gilmorehill. Premises close at hand have been secured in Hillhead, and these are to be altered and fitted up for their new uses, with a view to be opened about the month of October. The scheme contemplates beginning with about 200 ordinary members and 50 country members. Mr. Allan F. Baird, the Rector's Assessor in the University Court, is acting as Secretary *pro tem.*, and the project is being well supported by members of the University Court, the Senate, and teaching staff, as well as by graduates and prominent citizens.

This year the term of office of the Right Hon. George Wyndham, M.P., as Rector, expires, and the students will exercise their triennial privilege of electing a new Rector. Already the two political parties have chosen their candidates, Mr. Asquith being put forward by the Liberals, while the Conservatives have nominated the Marquis of Linlithgow. The election will probably take place on Saturday, 4th November next."

The report of the Committee on Finance and Statistics of the University, recently issued, states that the revenue of the University for the year, including foundations, amounted to nearly the same amount as last year, £75,000. The expenditure on the General University Account exceeded the revenue on that account by £547. The sums received towards cost of new buildings during the year has been from the Carnegie Trust £6,615, and from the University Equipment Fund £17,000. The Library had for the first time the benefit of a complete year's grant from the Carnegie Trust of £1,000.

A meeting of the Scottish Modern Languages Association was held in the Glasgow University. Mr. Charles Martin, the President, occupied the chair, and there was a large attendance. The Chairman read a paper on " The Mechanism of Speech and its Difficulties." This was followed by a paper in French by M. Leon Pitoy and a discussion on various topics of interest to members.

At the annual meeting of subscribers to and friends of the Glasgow University Students' Settlement Association, held in the University Union, Glasgow, the report on the year's work was submitted by

Mr. William Boyd, Warden. The Settlement, he said, had now attained the age of sixteen, and at the present time was stronger than at any other time in its history. The year's income, which amounted to £390, included £370 of subscriptions and donations, and left a credit balance.

At the close of the last lecture of the recent series of Gifford Lectures Principal Story expressed the sense of gratitude of the University to Professor Boutroux for the way in which he had performed the function of delivering the Lectures. Prof. Boutroux, in acknowledging the references of Principal Story, thanked the University of Glasgow, not only in his own name, but in the name of the Paris University, which warmly welcomed the new tie which united it to the University of Glasgow.

A meeting of the graduates of Glasgow and Aberdeen Universities was held at Falkirk on April 1st for the purpose of hearing Professor William R. Smith, M.D. (Aberdeen), D.Sc. (Edin.), D.P.H. (Cantab), F.R.S. (Edin.), barrister-at-law, of King's College, London, give an address as candidate for the Parliamentary representation of the Universities of Glasgow and Aberdeen. The Professor was thanked at the close, and a local Committee was appointed to promote his candidature.

University Developments.

"The number of students—both men and women—during last Winter Session has been appreciably higher than the average of the last few years, and the number of candidates who entered for the preliminary examinations, and the degree examinations in Arts and other Faculties, also shows an increase. Efforts are being made to provide the needful accommodation for the increasing number of students and for new methods of teaching that are being developed. Following upon other extensions recently completed, large additions to the buildings are in progress, the new accommodation including class-rooms and laboratories for Natural Philosophy, Physiology, Materia Medica, Forensic Medicine and Public Health. It is hoped that the Natural Philosophy rooms may be ready for occupation at the beginning of next Winter Session. When the new buildings are occupied by the various departments for which fresh provision is made, the buildings to be vacated by them will afford means of extension to other departments whose present accommodation is inadequate. The increased provision made in this University as regards laboratories has been very marked in recent years, and this applies not only to buildings but also to equipment and teaching staff. The new erections have somewhat curtailed the athletic ground available for the students, but a movement for the acquisition of athletic grounds of adequate extent in the neighbourhood of the City has been on foot for some time, and is understood to be within measurable distance of a successful issue."

A joint report recently published by the Committees on Educational Policy and Methods and Finance and Statistics on the function that might be discharged by the University in the promotion of commercial education, states that reports and communications the Committee has received point to a growing recognition of the need for specialised instruction sufficiently high in standard and wide in scope to justify the creation of Faculties of Commerce in the Universities. In view of (1) the mass of evidence bearing upon the desirability of improvement in the education of those who mean to follow business careers; (2) the impossibility of effecting this without a supply of specially-trained teachers; and (3) the financial arrangements which must accompany the carrying out of the Scottish Secretary's Minute for the training of teachers for the great variety of work—scientific, industrial, and commercial—now looked for in schools for youths up to 18 years of age—the Committee feel that the time has come when the Council should consider the advisability of the creation of a Faculty of Commerce in the University, and they are glad to observe that this matter has engaged the notice of the University Court.

University Appointments, etc.

As the latest development in the Faculty of Law, the University Court have just instituted a Lectureship on Evidence and Procedure, and have appointed Mr. Robert Lamond, M.A., LL.B., as Lecturer. A course on the subject will be given during the summer session of this year.

Owing to the death of Sir John Neilson Cuthbertson, who had been an Assessor of the General Council in the University Court since 1889, when the Universities' Act allotted four Assessors to the Council, a new election had to be made at the half-yearly meeting of the Council, held on April 5th. The ordinance regulating the election does not allow a poll in the case of an appointment to a casual vacancy where the unexpired period is less than two years, but requires that the election, if not unanimously made, should be decided by a show of hands of the members present at the meeting. The unexpired period in this case being only six months, members could not record their votes except by personal attendance, and as considerable interest in the appointment had been aroused, the attendance was the largest ever witnessed at a meeting of Council, nearly 1,100 being present, including an appreciable number of women graduates. Three candidates were nominated for the vacancy— John Hutchison, LL.D., Rector of the High School of Glasgow; Charles Ker, M.A., a member of a firm of chartered accountants in the city; and the Rev. John Smith, D.D., minister of Partick, and Chairman of the School Board of Govan. With such a numerous attendance many had to find places in the galleries of the Bute Hall after the area had been filled, and the counting of votes was rather a formidable process. Mr. H. E. Gordon, the Chancellor's Assessor, who presided, went over all parts of the hall, taking the show of hands bench by bench, and in little more than half an hour the work was accomplished, and the result of the voting declared as follows:— For Dr. Hutchison, 683 votes; Dr. Smith, 283 votes; Mr. Ker, 123 votes. The Chairman then declared Dr. Hutchison duly elected, and the new Assessor briefly returned thanks.

THE ROYAL UNIVERSITY OF IRELAND.

University News and Notes.

The Executive Committee appointed in connection with the proposed Coyne Scholarship in Political and Social Science has prepared a scheme under which the scholarship should be awarded, which will be submitted to the Senate of the Royal University.

Queen's College, Belfast.

The Examination Hall has been granted for a series of readings by the Belfast Branch of the British Empire Shakespeare Society on the evening of the 28th April in connection with the Shakespearean celebrations which are to take place in the city during the week. Professors Letts and Symington have been re-elected members of the Council for the statutory term of three years.

Mr. John Vinycomb, M.R.I.A., has designed and presented to the College a book-plate for use in the Library.

Professor J. Symington, of Belfast, has been appointed an Examiner in Applied Anatomy and Physiology for the entrance examination to the Indian Medical Service.

LEEDS.

University News and Notes.

In response to the appeal which has recently been made by the University for £100,000, in accordance with the condition laid down by the Privy Council when the University Charter was granted, upwards of £60,000 has already been subscribed. Ordinances dealing with the degrees of the University and the conditions under which they will be presented have recently been adopted by the University Court. Those Ordinances relating to the conditions under which degrees in Arts and Science are to be given have been adopted provisionally in view of the fact that the Boards of the Faculties of Arts and Science are engaged in remodelling the whole programme of studies in these Faculties.

At a congregation of the University held on March 31st, in the Library of the Medical School, the degrees of Bachelor of Medicine and Bachelor of Surgery were conferred on those who had satisfied the examiners in the recent examinations. Before conferring the degrees the Vice-Chancellor (Dr. Bodington) remarked that it was in every way appropriate that the first degrees to be conferred in Leeds, other than honorary degrees, should be degrees in medicine, as the School of Medicine was the oldest of the departments of the University.

It has been decided that the degrees of the University of Leeds shall be as follows:—Bachelor of Arts (B.A.), Master of Arts (M.A.), Doctor of Letters (Litt.D.), Bachelor of Laws (LL.B.), Doctor of Laws (LL.D.), Bachelor of Science (B.Sc.), Master of Science (M.Sc.), Doctor of Science (D.Sc.), Bachelor of Medicine and Bachelor of Surgery (M.B. and Ch.B.), Doctor of Medicine (M.D.), and Master of Surgery (Ch.M.).

The Senate of the University has been empowered by a special Ordinance to recognise courses of study pursued and examinations passed by students of the Yorkshire College or Leeds University at the Victoria University or at the Victoria University of Manchester previous to January 1, 1905, as equivalent to corresponding courses and examinations in the University of Leeds. It also empowers the Senate to make such concessions in exemption from examinations and from attendance on courses of study as may be required to place a past or present student of the University or Yorkshire College who had been admitted before the 1st October, 1904, in as favourable a position in the above respects as if he had become or had continued to be a student of the Victoria University of Manchester. The ordinance also allows that a student of the Yorkshire College who before December 31, 1904, had passed a final examination of the Victoria University or the Victoria University of Manchester for the Bachelor's Degree in the Faculty of Arts, Science, Law or Medicine shall be entitled to be admitted to the Bachelor's Degree of the University of Leeds; and if he has been admitted to the Bachelor's Degree of the Victoria University or the Victoria University of Manchester he shall be entitled to proceed to the higher degrees of the University of Leeds on the same conditions as if he had graduated at the Leeds University.

LIVERPOOL.

University Developments.

" The outstanding feature of the history of the University of Liverpool during the last two years has been the survival of the impetus and the inspiration which created the University. There were many who anticipated that, once the supreme object, a charter of freedom, had been gained, there would be a relaxation of effort for a time, by a natural reaction. In particular, it seemed reasonable to expect that there would be a cessation in the flow of money into the coffers of the University, since £180,000 had been in a very short period subscribed by a city which was simultaneously engaged in raising funds for the erection of a Cathedral. Far different has been the event. Since the grant of the charter additional money has been given for two new Chairs, the Baines Chair of English Language and the Barrow Chair of French, each endowed with £10,000; Mr. E. K. Muspratt, the President of the Council, has just given £10,500 for the erection of a Laboratory of Physical Chemistry, the first of its kind in the United Kingdom; and there have been eight or ten lesser endowments of scholarships, prizes and the like; all this in addition to large new annual grants from the rates in Liverpool, Bootle, Birkenhead, Lancashire and Cheshire. It is evident that the name and idea of a University appeals to the munificence of a modern community as the name of a mere College could never do. It may be taken as brief evidence of the remarkable expansion which is taking place on every side that last term a dinner of welcome was given to over forty new members of the staff. As for buildings, the Johnston Laboratories of Bio-Chemistry and Medical Research, opened two years ago, have been already followed by the magnificent George Holt Physical Laboratories, perhaps the finest of their kind in England, and by the new Medical School; in July there will be opened the spacious new laboratories of Electro-technics, to be shortly followed by an immense zoological building; and in the summer the erection will be begun, at a cost of £20,000, of a large block to accommodate the expansion of the Faulty of Arts, the most numerous but hitherto the most inadequately equipped of all the Faculties.

Far more important than these material signs of growth, there has been a remarkable burgeoning of new ideas on every side—some of which may perhaps be deserving of the fuller attention of readers of this *Review*. The commencement (with no less than sixty students) of the first Veterinary School associated with any British University was an event of the present session. The students are to take an exacting course of five years, and they have already shown that they assimilate readily with other students. The School of Tropical Medicine, already sufficiently well known, becomes daily more vigorous, and attracts students from all parts of the world. The School of Local History, first of its kind in England, has issued an ambitious programme of works for publication. The School of Training for Social Work has very auspiciously opened its first session, and promises to do invaluable social service. The School of Commerce, oldest of its kind in England, is steadily raising the amount and quality of its work. The University Extension Committee is revolutionising our whole conceptions of what University Extension means, and showing us that it covers all those innumerable and fruitful services which the University can perform in the instruction of professions, classes or individuals without its own walls. In the medical world the organisation of the United Hospitals side by side with the Royal Infirmary has for the first time placed substantially the whole of the clinical material of a great city at the disposal of medical students. In various subjects of the secondary schools' curriculum the teachers are being grouped into conferences, which, led by the teachers of the University, discuss with mutual profit the methods and aims which guide them both. The long-established Anglican Theological College of St. Aidan's, Birkenhead, has been affiliated to the University, and will in future send its best students on special conditions to the courses of the University; while the powerful Training Colleges of Edge Hill and Notre Dame have been admitted to somewhat similar privileges, and brought within the sphere and under the influence of the University. Outside, in every Education Committee over a wide area, representatives of the University share in the reconstruction of our educational system, and help to establish the belief, now at last beginning to take root in Northern England, that the Universities are rather the foundations than merely the ornamental pinnacles of the educational structure; the reservoirs from which all the pipes and conduits of the system must be supplied. We begin at last—inside as well as outside of the walls—to realise more fully what the new Universities will mean to England.

But perhaps the most promising and delightful of all the developments to which the inspiration of our new position has led is the rise of a new student life, inspired by a new spirit. All regular students are now included in a Guild of Undergraduates, whose members pay a subscription of fifteen shillings along with their fees at the beginning of each session. This admits every student to every branch of the Athletic Club, to the Debating Society, to the Reading Rooms and Common Rooms, and to one special society selected by the member. Every member of the Guild also receives a copy of every issue of the University paper, *The Sphinx;* while, on production of his membership card, any student will be admitted to the meetings of almost every learned society in Liverpool, or will be able to book a passage on several steamship lines at reduced rates. The Guild is preparing a Students' Handbook or Guide to the University which will shortly be issued; and also a very carefully edited University Song-book, which is expected to be published before July. It is impossible to exaggerate the effect which this new organisation has produced upon the temper and spirit of student-life here: illustrations of it will doubtless be forthcoming in future contributions to this part of the *Review.* But in the meanwhile, all that space permits us to record is that the new vigour which is to be seen in every part of the work of our University, is not least evident among the student body."

University News and Notes.

Sir Alfred Jones, the head of the well-known Liverpool shipping firm of Elder, Dempster and Company, has offered free trips on his various steamers to engineering students at the Liverpool University, in order that they may acquire practical experience in the engine-room.

The skeleton of Ambush II., the King's famous steeplechaser, has now been erected in the Veterinary School of Liverpool University, to which it was presented by His Majesty.

It is announced that the Council of the Institution of Civil Engineers has decided to recognise the ordinary degree of Bachelor of Engineering of the University of Liverpool obtained by passing examinations of that University as exempting candidates from the Associate Membership Examination of the Institution.

A sum of £1,500 has been received to establish a Lectureship in memory of the late Sir William Mitchell Banks, the Memorial

Committee expressing a wish that an annual lecture on some question of medical science should be delivered by a man of distinction.

The Gilchrist Trustees have undertaken to establish a scholarship of £80 a year to enable Liverpool graduates to prepare for teaching modern languages by a period of study abroad.

The Korbach scholarship for the study of German, for some time maintained by annual gifts, has now been endowed with £600 by a donor who desires to remain anonymous.

University Appointments, etc.

Miss Caroline Graveson, B.A., Mistress of Method and Lecturer on Education in the Liverpool University, has been appointed Vice-Principal and Mistress of Method in the Day Training College, recently established at Greenwich by the Goldsmiths' Company.

The Committee of the Liverpool School of Tropical Medicine has appointed Mr. Newstead, F.S.A., as Lecturer in Economic Entomology and Parasitology.

Mr. F. J. Lewis, Demonstrator and Assistant Lecturer on Botany in the University, has been approved for the degree of Bachelor of Science by the University of Geneva; and he has also been awarded the Cuthbert Peck Prize by the Royal Geographical Society for his recent work on topographical botany.

LONDON.

University News and Notes.

The London School of Tropical Medicine has been admitted as a School of the University in the Faculty of Medicine, in Tropical Medicine only.

It has been decided that the donation of £1,000 recently given to the University by four children of the late Mr. William Lindley in memory of their father, shall be devoted to the establishment of a Research Studentship in Physiology.

Mr. Alfred Beit has informed the Honorary Treasurers of the Institute of Medical Sciences Fund that he has decided to increase the amount of his donation to the Institute to £25,000.

The Worshipful Company of Goldsmiths has paid a further sum of £211 in respect of additions to the Library of Economic Literature presented by them to the University.

Dr. E. R. Edwards has resigned his post as Secretary to the University Extension Registrar upon his appointment as Inspector of Secondary Schools under the Board of Education.

Prfessor Walter Rippmann, M.A., has been appointed a Staff Inspector under the University Extension Board in connection with their conduct of the Inspection and Examination of Schools.

An Examination for Entrance Scholarships and Exhibitions tenable at University College, King's College and the East London Technical College will be held by the London Inter-Collegiate Scholarships' Board on June 27th and following days. Entries will close on May 30th. About 20 Scholarships and Exhibitions for Men and Women, ranging in value from £20 to £50, will be offered for competition. Forms of application and further particulars may be obtained from the Secretary of the Board at King's College.

It is stated that Greek, for some time past an optional subject at the Major Scholarships Examinations, has now, on the recommendation of the Intermediate Scholarships Examination Committee, been made optional for that examination also.

The Faculty of Medicine has decided that it is advisable that the pass lists of Bachelor's degrees in medicine should be issued in alphabetical order and without classification.

It is officially announced that the negotiations have now been completed by which, under certain conditions, the higher examination of the Oxford and Cambridge Schools Examination Board and the Oxford Senior Local Examination will be accepted in lieu of the London Matriculation Examination, and the London Matriculation examination will give exemption from Oxford responsions. A similar arrangement has been concluded with Cambridge.

At a meeting of the University of London Liberal Association, Sir Michael Foster, the sitting member, was again adopted as the Liberal representative at the next election. Mr. J. Fletcher Moulton, K.C., M.P., was elected Chairman of the Association on the resignation of Sir William Collins.

Sir Donald Currie has given £500 for the fund that is being collected on behalf of the London School of Tropical Medicine.

Bedford College for Women.

Bedford College for Women—which is a school of the London University, and was the first to offer scholarships and fellowships to women—is making an urgent public appeal for £150,000 to purchase a fresh site and rebuild the College. Not only has it outgrown the present premises, but the lease of an important part of the College buildings will expire in four years, and in other twenty years the leases of the rest of the buildings will also expire, without possibility of renewal. Donations may be sent to Miss Henrietta Busk, Hon. Sec. of the Appeal Fund (at Bedford College, Baker Street, W.), who will be glad to answer all enquiries.

Guy's Hospital.

Guy's Hospital is urgently in need of £100,000 to discharge pressing liabilities, while an additional income of £15,000 per annum is required. Upwards of a third of the money asked for has already been subscribed. The nurses and students of the hospital are collecting subscriptions for the shilling fund which they have started, with the aim of obtaining a million shillings (£50,000). We especially direct the attention of our readers to page 16 of the advertising supplement of this *Review*, where a detailed statement of the appeal is given.

King's College.

At the annual Court of the Corporation of King's College Hospital, Dr. Headlam, the Principal of the College, referring to the removal scheme, said that the site was now nearly all in their hands, and that a Building Committee had been at work for six months evolving the scheme of a hospital on the most scientific and up-to-date model. The Governors had now about £133,000 in hand, including the estimated value of the old site. The Drapers' Company had promised £10,000 on condition that the total amount necessary was raised by the end of the year; and by that time, also, it was hoped that the foundation stone of the new building would have been laid.

The Council of King's College have elected Mr. Peter Thompson, M.D., Ch.B. (Vict.), as Professor of Anatomy; and Professor Arthur Dendy, D.Sc., of the South African College, Capetown, as Professor of Zoology.

Royal Holloway College.

Ten Entrance Scholarships from £50 to £60, and several Bursaries of £30, tenable for three years at the College, will be awarded on the results of an examination to be held from July 3rd to July 8th, 1905. Names must be entered before June 1st.

For forms of entry and further particulars apply to the Secretary, Royal Holloway College, Englefield Green, Surrey.

St. Bartholomew's Hospital.

The Governors of St. Bartholomew's Hospital are issuing an appeal for financial support. The reconstruction and enlargement of the Hospital has become urgently necessary during recent years. The sum of £120,000 is required to meet the cost of erecting the first block of buildings, which will include the Out-Patients' and Casualty Departments. It is earnestly hoped that this famous Hospital will no longer be hampered in the good work it is doing among the suffering poor of London by want of proper accommodation. We trust that the response to the Governors' Appeal will be immediate and generous. We especially desire to draw attention to the appeal which appears on page 18 in the advertising supplement of this *Review*.

South Eastern Agricultural College.

At the last meeting of the Governors of the South-Eastern Agricultural College, Mr. J. Sayer presiding, Mr. F. Escombe's appointment as Professor of Botany, *vice* Mr. A. Howard, who resigned to take up an appointment at the Agricultural Experiment Station at Pusa, was confirmed. The Governors also decided, on account of the increase in number of the students, who now number 91, further to enlarge the College and to lease additional land for farming purposes.

University College.

" The most important recent development in regard to University College and the University of London is marked by the completion of the negotiations for the incorporation of the College in the University, and the Bill to give statutory effect to this incorporation has already been introduced into the House of Lords. Under this Bill the Senate of the University of London will become the supreme governing authority of the College, which will include within it the Faculty of Arts, the Faculty of Laws, the Faculty of Science, the Faculty of Engineering and a portion of the Faculty of Medicine, providing instruction in the preliminary and intermediate medical studies and generally, whether for preliminary or intermediate purposes, in anatomy, physiology and pharmacology. That portion of the Faculty of Medicine which is technically known in the University as the Board of Advanced Medical Studies will be provided with a new building on a site opposite the College, through the generosity of Sir Donald Currie, and will, with the Hospital, form a new Corporation for the purpose of carrying on the Hospital and the School of Advanced Medical Studies. By this means there will at once be constituted in University College buildings a centre for preliminary and intermediate studies to which medical students will be admitted irrespective of the Hospital that they intend to join.

University College Boys' School, which has hitherto formed an integral part of the College organisation, will be removed to Hampstead, and will be constituted a separate Corporation, care being taken to maintain the relationship of the old College Corporation and thus to maintain the traditions of the School. The removal of the School of Advanced Medical Studies from the present College buildings to the new building on the other side of Gower Street, and the removal of the Boys' School to Hampstead, will put at the disposal of the University a considerable amount of space, which will be available for the development and improvement of the existing departments of the College. The great advantage of this incorporation scheme is that it will give to the University direct control over the chief teaching institution of University rank in London, and will enable it as its policy develops to arrange the departments of University teaching and research in the way best suited to the needs of London as a whole. It is to be hoped that some of the more important institutions will follow the lead of University College and enter into closer relationship with the University. If this comes about, and the University of London is provided with adequate funds, its rapid development is secured. At the same time, the traditions of University College are such that the University will be safe in building upon them and in maintaining them.

Of recent appointments the most important are that of Professor A. R. Cushny, of the University of Michigan, U.S.A., to the Chair of Pharmacology, and of Professor Sir Thomas Barlow to the Holme Chair of Medicine, in succession to Professor F. T. Roberts, resigned. Among other important developments of the present Session is to be noted the institution of a lectureship in the department of Fine Arts, to which Mr. D. S. MacColl has been appointed. Mr. MacColl has successfully given his first course of lectures during the current Session."

The last day for giving notice of intention to compete for the Andrews' Entrance Scholarships, Campbell Clarke Scholarship, West Scholarship, Clothworkers' Company's Exhibitions (Chemistry and Physics) has been fixed for May 30th.

Westfield College.

During the past two years extensive additions have been made to the buildings of this School of the University. On June 13th, 1903, Lady Aberdeen laid the foundation-stone of a new Library and Lecture Rooms (costing about £4,000), which were completed and in use by Easter last year.

The College is being still further enlarged by an additional wing (of which the estimated cost is £5,300), planned at the same time as the Library by Mr. Macdonald, the College architect. This consists of one or two more Lecture Rooms and of students' rooms (study and bedroom separate, as throughout the College), bringing the total possible accommodation up to about sixty. These rooms are fast approaching completion, and will be ready for occupation next October.

MANCHESTER.

University News and Notes.

"From a College point of view, April is a month of endings. In University work, it ends the course of the Medical; to the Arts and Science men it brings the strenuous unwilling days of terminals, appreciated only in retrospect from the Easter Vacation —that last oasis before the arid onward march to the June University Examinations. The social activities of the winter draw to a close; the Societies, learned or frivolous, open or exclusive, offer public thanks instead of private criticism as a last injury against their luckless officers; and the Union rooms empty before the invitation of the first strange, warm spring days.

A month of endings, and therefore a difficult subject for the first of a series of monthly summaries. On the side of work, the chief episode, in addition to the examinations mentioned, has been the publication of Mr. D. Knoop's first book, "Industrial Conciliation and Arbitration," a work founded on his Shuttleworth Essay. Mr. Knoop is a member of the Honours School of Economics in the third year of his course.

Among the purely social events of March the most interesting was the "At Home" given by the Women's Union in the Whitworth Hall to celebrate the 21st anniversary of the admission of women to the University. Speeches were made by the Vice-Chancellor of the University, Miss Crompton, Alderman Thompson and Miss H. Johnstone. Dr. Brodsky, the Dean of the Faculty of Music, had arranged an excellent programme of music, and the new College song, *Floreat Victoria*, was sung, under the conductorship of the composer, Dr. Carroll. A souvenir programme, worthy of the event, was issued, containing photographs of Miss Wilson, the late Mrs. Worthington, and the Chairmen of the Women's Union since its foundation, and also an interesting historical review of the progress of the Women's Department in the University.

The whole University shares the regret felt by the Women Students at the continued illness of their Tutor, Miss E. C. Wilson, which has kept her away from College since the beginning of the Session.

On the men's side, the Union has concluded a season of excellent and well-attended debates by a very successful Smoking Concert. The visit to the Pantomime on Shrove Tuesday was the chief event organised during the month by the Students' Representative Council.

As regards games, most of the winter clubs have finished their engagements during the month. Both the football clubs have had successful seasons. One member of the Rugby team, Schulze, has received his Scotch International cap; and with two county men in addition—W. George and H. E. R. Stephens, of Cheshire,—the team has had no great difficulty in bringing home the Christie Shield. The Association team has also won the Christie Cup. Both the women's and the men's Hockey teams have also finished the season with very good records. An interesting game in the programme of the Lacrosse team was that played against the combined Oxford and Cambridge team, resulting in a victory for Manchester by 10 goals to 9."

The Advisory Committee for University Extension at its last meeting unanimously agreed that the present system of University Extension Lectures to Pupil Teacher Centres produces valuable results and that any radical change in the system is to be deprecated. It was also decided that a system of instruction similar to that given by the Universities to Pupil Teachers might with advantage be used as a part of the preparation of acting Teachers.

The Council has given permission for the Educational Exhibit of the University (with one or two exceptions) which was sent to the St. Louis Exhibition of 1904, and awarded a Gold Medal, to be deposited in the Victoria and Albert Museum at South Kensington, for reference by and information of the public.

The Victoria Church Hostel for Women Training Students has been licensed by the University Council as a Hall of Residence for the University, and Professor Tout has been appointed a representative of the University on the Committee.

The Secretary of the University Extension Committee (Mr. Sydney Waterlow) has now issued the General Regulations and List of University Extension Lectures for 1905. This document gives full information as to the arrangement of lecture courses and examinations held in connection with these courses under the University Extension Authority. It also contains a full list of lecturers whose services may now be engaged by individuals or

Extension Centres desirous of arranging for lectures during the Session 1905–6. The subjects in which lectures are offered cover the whole field of the Arts and Sciences, and the lecturers have in each case been chosen not merely for their attainments in particular subjects, but also for their skill and experience in presenting the latest results of modern thought in a form acceptable to popular audiences. Applications and enquiries should be addressed to the Secretary, University Extension Committee, the University, Manchester.

Mr. Capper, Professor of Architecture, is now to take command of the Manchester University Company, which position is to be vacated by the resignation of Captain F. H. Westmacott.

A new magazine for undergraduates has made its appearance at the University, under the title of *'Varsity Opinion*.

By permission of the University Council, a concert recital of Mozart's " Marriage of Figaro " was given in the Whitworth Hall on Saturday, March 25th, by the students of the Royal College of Music. The performance was conducted by Dr. Brodsky, and the orchestra consisted of players connected with the College.

The Joint Matriculation Examination of the Universities of Manchester, Liverpool and Leeds will commence on Wednesday, July 5th, 1905, and will be held simultaneously at the three Universities and in the schools approved by the Joint Matriculation Board. The fee is due on or before June 3. Information as to scholarships awarded on the results of this examination and on other matters may be obtained from R. E. Gwyther, Secretary to the Joint Matriculation Board, the University, Manchester.

The Manchester University Athletic Sports will be held this year at the University Athletic Ground on Saturday, June 3rd.

A proposal recommending that March 12th be set apart annually for the celebration of the memory of John Owens, the founder of Owens College, has recently been agreed to by the Arts Section of the Students' Representative Council.

The first Adamson Memorial Lecture will be given by Professor James Ward, of Cambridge, on June 2nd.

Dr. Ludwig Mond has presented £500 for the extension of the Chemical Laboratories. The Vulcan Boiler Insurance Company propose to found a Fellowship in Engineering.

The Council has instituted a Scholarship of £30, tenable for three years at the University, to be awarded on the results of the next July Matriculation Examination.

A report has recently been issued on the work of the past session in the Faculty of Commerce.   It states that the Faculty is now completely organised and its work in full operation.   The Faculty of Commerce was sanctioned by the University Court in December, 1903, and the regulations were approved by the Council in March, 1904, though work did not begin formally and as a whole until October, 1904.   The number of students who have entered for the degree of Bachelor of Commerce is fourteen.

Miss Catherine Dodd, Mistress of Method at the University of Manchester, has recently published, through Messrs. Smith, Elder and Co., an interesting volume under the title of " A Vagrant Englishwoman," in which she tells of her experiences during her travels, and of her life in a German University town.

University Appointments, etc.

The Council has appointed Mr. Stanley Dunkerley, M.Sc., to the Professorship of Engineering.   Mr. Dunkerley was a student of Owens College, and obtained the B.Sc. degree of the Victoria University with First Class Honours in Mathematics, and in the following year in Engineering.   In 1892 he was elected to a Bishop Berkeley Fellowship.   From 1893 to 1896 he was Senior Assistant Lecturer in Engineering at University College, Liverpool, where he had entire charge of the third year laboratory course and was superintendent in the drawing office.   In 1896 he was appointed University Demonstrator in Engineering at Cambridge.   Since 1897 he has been head of the department of Applied Mathematics in the Royal Naval College, Greenwich.   He has been superintendent of, and, under the Director of Naval Education, responsible for the building and equipment of the new Engineering Laboratory at Greenwich.   He has made various original communications on engineering subjects, for one of which he was awarded a gold medal by the Council of the Institution of Naval Architects.

Dr. Strachan, Professor of Greek, has also been appointed Lecturer in Celtic.   Professor Strachan, whose work in Celtic is well known among scholars, has published (in conjunction with Dr. Whitley Stokes) the Thesaurus Palæohibernicus, a collection of what remains of Old Irish in MSS., prior to 200 A.D.   Professor Strachan's " Selections from the Old Irish Glosses " is in use as a text-book on the Continent and in America, as well as in Ireland.

Mr. G. C. Simpson, B.Sc., has been appointed Lecturer in Meteorology and Assistant Lecturer in the Department of Physics. Mr. Simpson is a graduate of the University, in which he obtained First Class Honours in Physics in 1900, and was elected to a University Fellowship and an Honorary Research Fellowship.   In

1902 the (1851) Exhibition Commissioners awarded him a Science Research Scholarship, which was renewed for a second and a third year. During his third year of tenure Mr. Simpson has conducted an experimental research on the conditions of atmospheric electricity in Northern Norway.

OXFORD.

University News and Notes.

In accordance with instructions left by Mr. Rhodes in his will that the Trustees should dine annually with the Rhodes scholars at Oxford, the first annual dinner was held recently at the Randolph Hotel. Lord Rosebery was unavoidably prevented from attending, and the chair was occupied by Mr. Hawksley. All the scholars at Oxford were present, with the exception of four, the company including Dr. Parkin, Secretary to the Rhodes Trustees, and Mr. F. J. Wylie, of Brasenose College, the Oxford Secretary.

Mr. Frederic Harrison, Hon. Fellow of Wadham College, recently delivered the first Herbert Spencer Lecture, established at Oxford by Pandit Shyamagi Krishnavarma, of Balliol College.

Dr. Fairbairn, Principal of Mansfield College, has recently stated in a letter to the *Times* his views on the government of Oxford. He urges that "it is a primary interest of the University to have its Convocation, or body of graduates, as representative as possible." At the present time the undergraduates at Oxford number 3,572, while Convocation numbers 6,429. If all the undergraduates took the M.A. degree and became members of the University the members of Convocation ought to exceed by at least eight times the number of undergraduates in the University instead of being less than double." Dr. Fairbairn continues : " The charges alike of the University and the Colleges are excessive and out of all proportion to any good promised or any right bestowed. The man who would take his M.A. must pay the University £12 and his College three guineas or thereabouts. If he means to become a member of Convocation the University charges him, if he is under 25, a composition fee of fifteen guineas, and if under 30 of £15. 1s. His College charges him here also a sum, which may be said to vary according to its own needs. In other words, the graduate who compounds pays in all about £41. . . . If a man does not compound he must so long as he lives, say from his 25th to his 70th year, or even later, pay on average £1. 15s. ' per annum ' for a privilege he may never exercise, whether it be the Parliamentary franchise or the decision of some academic question. Is it wonderful, then, that some men find it difficult or even quite impossible to pay so heavily for a remote possibility? And so multitudes neither take their Master's degree nor become members of Convocation."

A letter has recently been published from a number of tutors and lecturers in Modern History in reply to the criticisms of the Oxford Modern History School made by Professor C. H. Firth in the course of his recent inaugural address. It is pointed out that the School was framed and is worked as one of the schools for granting an honours degree in Arts. "The majority of the candidates for the School do not intend to pursue the career of a professional historian, and the University would be false to a paramount national duty if it substituted for a liberal education through history a system and curriculum beneficial only to a very small minority." The writers deprecate any suggestion that the attitude of tutors and lecturers towards research and advanced instruction is unfriendly, and express themselves anxious to strengthen the machinery for promoting it. A number of suggestions are made to this end. Candidates, for instance, might be allowed to offer a written thesis, perhaps in place of one of the special subjects; additional optional subjects, such as Palæography, might be more frequently offered; a Readership in Economic History is approved as soon as the University funds allow it. These and a number of other proposals are made for the advantages of candidates who propose to study History professionally.

The degree of D.Litt., *honoris causa*, has been conferred upon Mr. Edward Arber, Fellow of the Society of Antiquaries, Emeritus Professor of English in the University of Birmingham, and Fellow of King's College, London.

The *Oxford Magazine* has recently published the census for the term. It is shown that the number in residence this term is exactly the same as in Hilary Term last year, in spite of the fact that there are eighty Rhodes scholars up. In 1904 the order of the larger was Christ Church, New College, and Keble; this year New College is first, with 214, then Christ Church with 199, and Non-Collegiate with 179 members in residence.

A scheme is being considered by the India Office for the removal of the Forest Department from Cooper's Hill to the University of Oxford.

An exhibition of historical portraits has been opened in the University Examination Schools, High Street, Oxford, and will remain open until June 1st. The exhibition includes portraits of English historical personages who died between 1625 and 1714, lent by the University, Colleges, Cathedral Chapter, and city; there will

PRINCIPAL JAMES DONALDSON. M.A., LL.D.

Vice-Chancellor of the University of St. Andrews.

also be some portraits of special interest lent by private owners in or near Oxford.

A Committee of the University Council is organising a diploma course in Anthropology, which will be of a similar standard to existing diploma courses in Geography and Economics.

In connection with the forthcoming University Extension summer meeting at Oxford, a camp for working men is being formed, with the Rev. Professor Masterman, of Birmingham University, as Chairman.

University Appointments, etc.

Mr. Charles Grant Robertson, M.A., Fellow and Domestic Bursar of All Souls College, and Mr. Clement Charles Julian Webb, M.A., Fellow, Classical Tutor, and Junior Dean of Arts at Magdalen College, have been elected by their respective societies proctors for the ensuing year.

The Senior Proctor has nominated as his deputies Mr. C. Cookson, M.A., Fellow and Tutor of Magdalen College, and Mr. R. W. T. Günther, M.A., Fellow and Tutor of Magdalen College. The Junior Proctor has nominated as Pro-Proctors the Rev. P. J. Kirkby, M.A., Fellow of New College, and the Rev. H. H. Williams, M.A. Fellow of Hertford College.

Rev. W. H. Griffith Thomas, incumbent of St. Paul's, Portman Square, London, has been appointed Principal of Wycliffe Hall, Oxford, in succession to the Rev. H. G. Grey.

Thomas L. Bullock, M.A., New College, Professor of Chinese, has been elected as a Councillor to represent the University on the Oxford City Council.

ST. ANDREWS.

Presentation to Principal Donaldson.

An interesting ceremony took place at the University on March 29th, when Dr. Donaldson, Vice-Chancellor and Principal of the University of St. Andrews, was presented with his portrait painted by Sir George Reid, R.S.A. The meeting took place in the Library Hall, and the function was attended by a large and representative gathering.

Principal Stewart presided, and called upon the Lord Chancellor to make the presentation. Lord Balfour said that it was with very great pleasure that he accepted the duty which he was

H

now called upon to perform. They had met to honour one who had served his day and generation with very great distinction, and with great profit to the public. Principal Donaldson had served education in Scotland for something like half a century, and in serving education he had, perhaps, chosen the one thing on which it was possible for all Scotsmen to unite in his praise. The Principal would be remembered by his writings, his speeches, his addresses to the University, and from the educational influence he had exercised in Scotland. Those who knew him best would, he thought, remember him longest by the work which he had done for the University for nearly twenty years. During recent years there had been laid the foundation of what he believed would be an ever-widening influence for the old University of St. Andrews.

Principal Donaldson, having acknowledged the gift, handed the portrait over to the University for preservation.

University News and Notes.

The half-yearly statutory meeting of the General Council of the University of St. Andrews was held on March 30th. The Chancellor, Lord Balfour, presided.

It was decided to recommend the acceptance by the Senate of an Ordinance providing for the leaving certificate of the Education Department in Science being accepted by the General Board of Examiners in lieu of the University Preliminary Examination.

At the close of the meeting Principal Donaldson expressed his deep regret that Dr. Scott, who had served the Council so long, had felt obliged to retire from the position of Convener of the Committee on University Legislation, and as an Assessor of the Council in the University Court. He moved that a Committee be appointed to put on record their appreciation of the great services he had rendered to the University. The motion was unanimously adopted.

The annual graduation ceremonial took place on March 28th, in the Library Hall. There was a large attendance of graduates and their friends and of the *alumni* of the University. Principal Donaldson presided, and the graduates were presented by Principal Stewart, Dean of the Faculty of Theology; Professor Lawson, Dean of the Faculty of Arts; and Professor Scott Lang, Dean of the Faculty of Science.

The degree of LL.D. *(honoris causa)* was conferred upon Professor S. Alexander, M.A., Victoria University, Manchester; Mr. George A. Gibson, M.A., D.Sc., F.R.C.P., F.R.S.E., Edinburgh; Mr. Leonard Gow, Glasgow; Professor Josep Kral, Ph.D., University of Prag, Bohemia; Mr. Charles Stuart Loch, B.A., Professor of Economics in King's College, London; Mr. Charles Kincaid Mackenzie, K.C., Sheriff of Fife and Kinross; and the degree of D.D. *(honoris causa)* was conferred upon Professor Franz Overbeck Ph.D., D.D., University of Basel, Switzerland.

Two Bursaries (Spence) will be open for competition this autumn at St. Andrews University. The Bursaries are tenable for two years, and are of the value of £30 for the first year and £40 for the second year. Candidates must have passed the preliminary examination and attended one Winter Session or its equivalent in the Faculty of Arts. The Examination will be held in the Examination Hall of the Edinburgh University on Tuesday, 26th September, 1905, and the subjects will be Latin, Greek and Mathematics. Application forms, etc., may be obtained from the Factor, Henry A. Pattullo, 1, Bank Street, Dundee.

We desire to express our thanks to the Editor of the St. Andrews University Magazine—"College Echoes"—for the kind permission to publish the accompanying photograph of Sir George Reid's portrait of Principal Donaldson.—(Editor, "The University Review.")

WALES.

University News and Notes.

An election of four representatives of the Guild of Graduates on the University Court was recently held at the University College, Cardiff. The following members were elected:—The Rev. R. J. Rees, M.A.; Mr. W. Jenkyn Jones, M.A., Aberystwyth; Mr. Charles Morgan, B.A., Cardiff; and Professor W. Lewis Jones, M.A., Bangor; and the following on the Theological Board:—Professor J. Young Evans, M.A., Trefecca, and Professor J. E. Lloyd, M.A., Bangor.

Special mention should here be made of the recently published "History of the University of Wales" (F. E. Robinson and Co.), by W. Cadwaladr Davies and W. Lewis Jones. To all who are interested in the history of the University movement this volume can be warmly commended. To all past and present students of the University of Wales such a history of their Alma Mater cannot fail to be of especial interest.

The eleventh Matriculation Examination of the University of Wales will commence on Monday, June 26, 1905. Particulars may be obtained from the Registrar, University Registry, Cathays Park, Cardiff. Applications for entry forms must be made not later than Monday, May 29, 1905.

University College of Wales, Aberystwyth.

A meeting of the Court of Governors of the University College of Wales, Aberystwyth, was held at Carmarthen recently, Sir Lewis Morris presiding. Lord Rendel, the President of the College, sent a letter, in which he paid a high tribute to the late Rev. T. Mortimer Green, the Registrar of the College for thirteen years. The Court passed a vote of condolence with the bereaved family, and placed on record its profound sorrow at the loss which it had sustained. Principal Roberts stated that Miss E. A. Carpenter had intimated her intention to resign at the close of the present season the office of Lady Principal of the Hall of Residence for Women Students.

At a recent meeting of the Court of Governors of the University College of Wales, Aberystwyth, Sir Lewis Morris presiding, the following resolution was moved by the Bishop of St. David's:—

"That the Court approve of the steps which have been taken with a view to submitting to the Committee of the Privy Council appointed to determine the place at which the proposed National Library and National Museum are to be established, a proposal that the national Library be established at Aberystwyth. The Court are of opinion that, in view of the priceless collections of books and MSS. already accumulated at Aberystwyth, and of the central situation at Aberystwyth between the northern and southern portions of the Principality, its claim to be selected as the home of the National Library is justified by the aims which a National Library is designed to fulfil, and by the highest interests of Wales as a whole and the wishes of the Welsh people."

The resolution, having been seconded by Principal Prys, Trevecca College, was agreed to unanimously.

University College of North Wales, Bangor.

Representatives of the North Wales University College recently took part in a Conference of local Councils at Carnarvon for the discussion of the question of the site for the proposed Welsh National Museum. A Committee was appointed to issue a statement recommending the claims of North Wales based upon the offers of Carnarvon Castle as the home of the Museum.

A representative meeting of Welshmen was recently held in connection with the fund now being raised to establish a permanent home for the Bangor University College. Mr. Thomas Jones, of Handsworth, presided. The proceedings were conducted in the Welsh language.

University College of South Wales.

"To the members and friends of the Cardiff University College, one predominant subject of interest has long been the greatly needed new College buildings. Plans have long since been prepared and welcomed with universal approval and admiration, but their completion seemed, until recently, to be receding to an indefinitely remote period. It is, therefore, gratifying to be assured that towards the end of June, the foundation-stone will be laid by H.R.H. the Prince of Wales, who will be performing a task which very naturally belongs to him, as the Chancellor of the University of Wales. In conjunction with this ceremony, a Court of the University will be held for the conferring of honorary degrees upon a number of those who have been intimately connected with the College and with educational progress in Wales. We look forward to this event, both as the first-fruits of the realisation of hopes long deferred and as one of the picturesque functions which add so much to the freshness and charm of College life and College memories.

The opening of the term, on April 12th, has found the Professor of Greek, Mr. Burrows, still absent in Athens, whither he sailed, about a month ago, to take part in the proceedings of the Archæological Congress. His return will be eagerly awaited, not only because the College, and, indeed, the town of Cardiff, can ill afford to miss him, but because we are deeply interested in such results of his researches and observations in Greece as he will be able to lay before us. As a competent geographer and investigator of Greek antiquities, Professor Burrows' name is known far beyond the limits of Cardiff, but mention should here be made of his work for the University Settlement, an educational and social institution of modest but ever-widening scope, the business of which is carried on by a band of workers with infinite zeal and self-sacrifice, and with most encouraging results. Both with the establishment and the management of the Settlement, the names of Professor and Mrs. Burrows are closely associated.

One member of the College Staff will be missed at the beginning of next Session, for Professor Raymont has been appointed teacher of Educational Method of Goldsmith's Institute, London. The College, and especially the students of the training department, will take leave of a successful and beloved teacher with deep regret.

Professor Raymont carries with him to London our warmest congratulations, and best wishes for the future.

The Classical Society, which calls itself "The Frogs," may congratulate itself upon a very successful performance which it recently gave of portions of *The Frogs* of Aristophanes, in Greek. Some of the liveliest and most diverting parts of the dialogue and several choruses were so well performed as to amuse and delight a large audience.   Much labour and perseverance must have been devoted to the preparations for such a performance, and the highest praise is due to all concerned.   In particular, we may mention Mr. Ure, the Lecturer in Greek, who inaugurated the plan, and upon whom the main burden of organisation and supervision fell.   Considerable dramatic talent was shown, and the accompanying music was very heartily and pleasingly rendered."

During the Summer Term, 1905, lectures on "Applied Anatomy" will be delivered in the Anatomy Department of the University College, Cardiff, by Mr. E. J. Evatt, M.B., B.Sc.   These lectures will be adapted to the requirements of medical practitioners and senior students.   All those who propose to attend this course are requested to communicate with the Dean of the Medical Faculty.

UNIVERSITY COLLEGES.

Bristol.

The annual report of the meeting of the Governors and of the Council of University College shows signs of continued progress. There are now 1,164 students; the entries for the different classes and lectures—exclusive of medical students—reaches 2,354, a small increase on the record of previous years.   Eight students have been elected to the Associateship of the College.   The changes that have taken place on the staff are few beyond that of the appointment of Dr. Morris Travers, F.R.S., in place of Dr. Sydney Young, F.R.S., who left in December, 1903, to be Professor of Chemistry at Trinity College, Dublin.   To commemorate the long and valuable services of the late Mr. Albert Fry a fund was started to raise a memorial to his memory, £2,000 being collected.   To this was added £500 received from the Local Committee of the Welsh Industrial Exhibition, £400 from the University College Colston Society, and £731 by the trustees of the late Bristol Jubilee Club.   With this sum, amounting to £3,704, the north wing of the College was completed, and the tower christened the Albert Fry Memorial Tower.   The new buildings comprise class-rooms, administrative rooms for the Principal and lady tutor, a common room for women students and an entrance hall. Among other gifts the College again, for the third time, has received an anonymous donation of £1,000, while Mr. F. J. Fry and Mr. P. J. Worsley have subscribed £250 to equip the Electro-technical Laboratory.

On the recommendation of the Faculty of Arts and Sciences, the Council of the College has adopted a scheme whereby Scholarships are awarded on the results of examinations based on the principle that candidates may take such a number of subjects as each may be supposed to be studying in that particular period to which he is eligible. Thus for the Entrance Scholarships candidates are required to take Mathematics, an Essay and four other optional subjects; for the Junior Scholarships they may take any three subjects from the Intermediate Curriculum, and for the Senior Scholarships a principal and a secondary subject. The Chemical and Engineering Scholarships are awarded on the results of examinations in those subjects to candidates who must have fulfilled certain conditions in their first year. The Capper Pass Metallurgical Scholarship will be awarded to post-graduate students.

A new Laboratory for advanced students in the Chemical Department was opened in January last. The question of increasing the accommodation for the teaching of Anatomy and Bacteriology is now under consideration.

A Board of Legal Studies, consisting of representatives both of the College Council and the Law Societies of Bristol and district, has been established. Courses of lectures, primarily intended for law students, have been delivered during the current Session, the subjects being Conveyancing, Equity and the Law of Personal Property. The attendance has been in every way satisfactory.

A course of lectures on " The Problem of the Unemployed " has been delivered under the auspices of the Board of Social and Economic Studies.

Dr. P. Watson Williams will deliver a short course of lectures on " Rhinology," and Dr. F. Richardson Cross will lecture on " Ophthalmology," and give post-graduate demonstrations during the Summer Session.

Reading.

Viscount Goschen, Chancellor of the University of Oxford, has accepted the invitation of the Council of University College, Reading, to lay the foundation stone of the buildings about to be erected on the new College site in London Road, Reading. The ceremony will take place in June.

Sheffield.

It is announced that the Committee of the Privy Council has decided to recommend the King to grant a charter for Sheffield University. A year ago an appeal was made to the Privy Council for a charter. In reply it was stated that when £170,000 had been obtained the petition should be considered. A little more than £100,000 had then been subscribed, and every effort has been made to reach the required amount. There still remains a considerable deficiency, but notwithstanding this the Privy Council has decided to grant the charter.

The Sheffield University Bill dissolves the University College and transfers the property and liabilities to the University to be constituted under a Royal Charter. A clause exempting the University from the rates has been omitted. The Bill has passed its third reading.

The new buildings for administration, and for the Arts, Science, and Medical Departments are rapidly nearing completion, and will be ready for opening by the end of June. They will have cost, when completed, close on £100,000. The extensions in the Department of Applied Sciences have been in occupation since the commencement of the session.

The Iron and Steel Institute is to hold its meetings on the occasion of its autumn visit to Sheffield in the large Firth Hall of the new University buildings.

The Corporation of the City has allowed the telescope presented to the College by Pembroke College, Cambridge, to be housed in Weston Park, and has undertaken to bear the cost of removal. Professor Leahy has been appointed Curator.

An Association of Old Students of the College has been formed. Its purpose is to enable past students to keep in touch with one another and with the College. A re-union and dinner will be held annually, and a Hand-book of old students issued. The President is Mr. Frank Harrison, L.D.S., and the Honorary Secretary Mr. W. Allanach, B.Sc.

Professor Arnold has presented the Bessemer Gold Medal, which he received this year, to the Technical Department of the Sheffield University College. It is to be hung, with the Certificate, in the new Board Room of the Department.

Dr. Addison, late Professor of Anatomy at University College, Sheffield, has been appointed Vice-Dean of the Medical School of Charing Cross Hospital, and Secretary of the Board of Intermediate Medical Studies of the University of London.

The subject for the Gladstone Prize for 1906 is "The Taxation of Site-values." Essays must be sent in to the Registrar according to the directions given in the Calendar before the end of the Michaelmas term of 1905. All students and past students of the College, éxcept such as have already won the prize, are allowed to compete.

It is announced that the Rev. V. W. Pearson, Headmaster of Wesley College, has been appointed Principal of the new Training College, and Mrs. Henry, Head of the Women's Department.

GENERAL NEWS.

Grants to Universities and University Colleges.

A series of papers has been issued detailing the steps recommended by the University Colleges Committee for the distribution of the grants in aid given by the Treasury. As a temporary measure the Committee had last year to provide for a distribution of £54,0000. This was given as follows, the figures comparing with those for the distribution of £27,000 in 1903-4 :—

	1903-4. £		1904-5. £
Manchester	3,500	......	6,000
University College, London	3,000	......	5,000
Liverpool	3,000	......	5,000
Birmingham	2,700	......	4,500
Leeds	2,300	......	4,000
King's College, London	2,300	......	3,900
Newcastle-on-Tyne	1,800	......	3,000
Nottingham	1,700	......	2,900
Sheffield	1,300	......	2,300
Bedford College, London	1,200	......	2,000
Bristol	1,200	......	2,000
Reading	1,000	......	1,700
Southampton	1,000	......	1,700
Dundee	1,000	......	1,000
	£27,000		£45,000

The remaining £9,000 the Committee recommended should be given in grants of £700 to each of the eleven largest Colleges and of £650 each to Reading and Southampton for the purchase of books, apparatus, specimens, etc.

For 1905–6 and following years the Treasury has promised a grant of £100,000. The University Colleges Committee proposes that a moderate sum should be set aside for distribution by way of payment to post-graduate students from the University Colleges who devote themselves for one, two, or three years to special research. To ensure the money being applied most efficiently to the stimulation of individual study the distribution will assume the form of a grant made directly to the student on the advice of some impartial authority. Another portion of the money will be devoted to remedying equipment in books and scientific apparatus, and to increasing the salaries of certain of the existing teachers. The Committee has expressed its sense of the inadequacy of the remuneration of the professors and teachers in some of the Colleges.

Irish Agricultural Department.

The Department of Agriculture of Ireland (Merrion Street, Dublin) offers Scholarships to Irish students in agriculture, tenable for from one to three years, and including cost of board, lodging, books and education. The Scholarships are open to competition amongst Irish-born students, or amongst those who have lived three years in Ireland previous to the date of their offering themselves for examination.

The Carnegie Trust.

The following figures have been taken from the report of the Carnegie Trust for the Universities of Scotland for the year 1904:— The Trustees during the year had for distribution as grants to the Universities and for the endowment of research £59,201. In addition, the income of the Trust included £50,000 to be utilised in the payment of the class fees of students who applied to the Trust and satisfied the necessary conditions. For this purpose £46,000 was distributed. The figures show that out of every hundred students 72 at Aberdeen received fees from the Trust, 70 at St. Andrews, 50 at Glasgow, and 39 at Edinburgh. To the general funds of the Scottish Universities over £38,000 was granted, and £5,000 was distributed for the encouragement of research at the Universities.

The Executive Committee of the Carnegie Trust have framed their scheme of endowment of post-graduate study and research for the academic year 1905–6 on the same lines as that of previous years.

School of Irish Learning.

Scholarships of the value of £10 each have been awarded by the to a number of students to enable them to attend the summer course in Irish philology to be held by Prof. J. Strachan. The Government has assigned a grant of £100 per annum to assist the School in carrying out its programme of publications from Irish MMS. A further contribution of $1,000 has been promised by Mr. Quinn, the editor of the *New York Daily News*, who also offers several scholarships to enable American students to attend the session of the school. Intending students should apply to Dr. Kuno Meyer, the University, Liverpool.

The Management of Voluntary Hospitals.

The Prince of Wales has consented to present a prize of £100, and a silver cup has been offered by Mr. Edgar Speyer, a member of the General Council of King Edward's Hospital Fund, for the best essay on "The Economical Management of an Efficient Voluntary Hospital." Competition is limited to paid secretaries and assistant secretaries of voluntary hospitals in the United Kingdom. The hon. secretary of the King's Hospital Fund, 81, Cheapside, London, will forward particulars.

The Study of Sociology.

Presiding at a meeting of the Sociological Society, Mr. James Bryce, M.P., said it had been suggested, *apropos* of the teaching of Sociology in the London University, that it would be beneficial if the Government were asked to require that those who intended to take up Government employment in certain particular branches should receive Sociological teaching before proceeding to their duties. That was meant to apply particularly to those in the Consular service and in the Colonial and Indian service, the idea being that if those who had to observe men in foreign countries, and the building up of new communities, were imbued with a scientific view of their subject from the first, they would be more useful workers.

Reviews.

SOCIOLOGICAL PAPERS.

By Francis Sutton, E. Westermarck, P. Geddes, E. Durkheim, Harold H. Mann and V. V. Branford, with an Introduction by James Bryce. Published for the Sociological Society by Macmillan & Co., Ltd., 1905.

Only in one British University—that of London—has any provision been made for the systematic study of the science of Sociology. As Professor Bryce points out in his introduction to this volume, it is very much otherwise in most Continental and American Universities where considerable provision is made for social studies. With the formation of the Sociological Society, which is responsible for the volume under notice, it is to be hoped that other British Universities will find means to establish lectureships on Sociology.

The long delay in public recognition of a science of Sociology may be variously explained, though doubtless the chief factor has been hesitation on the part of scientific workers to acknowledge the existence of any body of data or field of work which might properly be left to the science. Even yet the scope of Sociology is a matter on which there is much diversity of view, as is well seen from the discussions which follow the papers contributed by Messrs. Branford and Durkheim. But these papers and discussions are probably those of greatest interest to the average reader, and are certainly interesting and stimulative to thought. It is to be hoped that Mr. Branford, the Secretary of the Society, will find time to pursue his researches in the history of the methodology of the science, which, in spite of a somewhat cumbrous terminology, probably inevitable at the present stage, are always valuable and suggestive. His paper, "On the origin and use of the word Sociology" we would especially commend to the attention of all who are interested in the scope of the science.

Two specialist studies are included in the volume: the first by Dr. Westermarck on "the Position of Woman in Early Civilisation," the second by W. H. H. Mann on "Life in an Agricultural Village in England." The editors describe these papers as "pioneer researches in borderland problems," and both are of value as examples of work which must be undertaken by Sociological specialists.

The paper on "Eugenics" by Dr. Galton, and that on "Civics" by Professor Geddes are classed as Applied Sociology. In these pages we see how the student of social phenomena, after collecting, arranging and classifying his data, proceeds to formulate theories as to social evolution, and to make suggestions as to how that social evolution may be best guided. If other reasons have little weight here surely, is justification for the provision of sociological departments in our Universities. Applied science is recognised in all our Universities, in Medicine, Agriculture, Engineering, to give only a few examples, but hitherto, although it has been expected that those who have studied at our Universities should take a very special part in the work of Government, i.e., in controlling social evolution, no adequate provision has been made for enabling them to engage in social studies. The value, nay more, the imperative necessity of such studies is amply demonstrated in these papers.

T. R. M.

Some Recent Publications.

BIOGRAPHY.

"Robert Browning." By C. H. Herford, Professor of English Literature in the University of Manchester. Edinburgh : William Blackwood & Sons. Price 2s. 6d.

"John Knox." A Biography. By the Rev. D. Macmillan, M.A. With an introduction by the Very Rev. Principal Story, D.D., LL.D. London : Andrew Melrose. Price 3s. 6d. net.

HISTORY.

"History of the Intellectual Development of Europe." By J. W. Draper. New edition in two volumes. G. Bell & Son. Price 2s. net each vol.

"Select Documents Illustrative of the History of the French Revolution." The Constituent Assembly. Edited by L. G. Wickham Legg, M.A. Oxford : The Clarendon Press. Two vols. Price 12s. net.

"A Guide to the Public Records of Scotland deposited in H.M. General Register House, Edinburgh." By M. Livingstone, I.S.O., late Deputy-Keeper of the Records. Edinburgh : H.M. General Register House.

"The Progress of Hellenism in Alexander's Empire." By Professor J. P. Mahaffy, D.D. Unwin. Price 5s.

"Magna Carta." A Commentary, with a Historical Introduction. By W. S. M'Kechnie. Glasgow : J. Maclehose & Sons. Price 14s. net.

"A Student's History of Scotland." By David Watson Rannie, M.A., Oriel College, Oxford. Four maps. London : Methuen. Price 3s. 6d.

"John Graham of Claverhouse, Viscount of Dundee, 1648—1689." By Charles Sanford Terry, M.A., Professor of History in the University of Aberdeen. London : Constable & Co. Price 12s. 6d. net.

LAW AND ECONOMICS.

"Modern Tariff History." By Percy Ashley, M.A., Professor of Economics in the University of Birmingham. Murray. Price 10s. 6d. net.

"Women and Economics : A Study of the Economic Relation between Men and Women as a Factor in Social Evolution." By Charlotte Perkins Gilman. A new edition. Putnam & Sons. Price 6s.

"International Law." A Treatise by L. Oppenheim, LL.D., Lecturer at the London School of Economics and Political Science. Vol. 1. Longmans. Price 18s. net.

LITERATURE.

"Shakespearean Tragedy : Lectures on Hamlet, Othello, King Lear, Macbeth." By A. C. Bradley, LL.D., Litt. D., Professor of Poetry in the University of Oxford. Macmillan. Price 10s. net.

"Plays and Poems of Robert Green." Edited by Professor Churton Collins. Two vols. Oxford : University Press.

"The Temper of the Seventeenth Century in English Literature." By Barrett Wendell, Professor of English at Harvard College; being the Clark Lectures given at Trinity College, Cambridge, 1902–3. Macmillan. Price 7s. net.

NATURAL SCIENCE.

"Morphology and Anthropology." By W. L. H. Duckworth, Lecturer on Physical Anthropology in the University of Cambridge. Cambridge : University Press. Price 15s. net.

"The Cambridge Natural History." Vol. vii., Hemiohordata, by Dr. S. F. Harmer; Ascidians and Amphioxus, by Professor W. A. Herdman; Fishes, by Dr. T. W. Bridge and G. A. Boulenger. London : Macmillan & Co. Price 17s. net.

"The Evolution Theory." By August Weismann. Translated with the author's co-operation by J. Arthur Thomson and Margaret R. Thomson. Illustrated ; 2 vols. Arnold. Price 32s. net.

PEDAGOGY.

"The Principles of Education." By Professor T. Raymont, M.A., University College of South Wales, Cardiff. Longmans. Price 4s. 6d.

"A Visit to American Educational Institutions." By G. S. Robson, B.Sc. London : Sherratt & Hughes. Price 1s. net.

PHILOSOPHY.

"Philosophical Studies." By the late D. G. Ritchie, Professor of Logic and
Metaphysics at St. Andrews University. Edited by Dr. Robert Latta,
Professor of Logic and Rhetoric in the University of Glasgow. Macmillan.

PSYCHOLOGY.

"Physiological Psychology." By W. M'Dougall, Wilde Reader in Mental
Philosophy in the University of Oxford. London: J. M. Dent & Co.
Price 1s.

"The Americans." By Hugo Münsterberg, Professor of Psychology at Harvard
University. Translated by Edwin B. Holt, Ph. D., Instructor at Harvard
University. London: Williams and Norgate. Price 12s. 6d. net.

THEOLOGY.

"The Creed of St. Athanasius." A Lecture delivered at the Divinity School,
Cambridge. By W. Emery Barnes, D.D., Hulsean Professor of Divinity
in the University of Cambridge. Macmillan and Bowes. Price 1s. net.

"How to Preach." By Professor E. Tyrell Green, being a series of Lectures
delivered to Candidates for Ordination at St. David's College, Lampeter.
Wells, Gardner, Darton & Co. Price 2s. net.

"The Historic Martyrs of the Primitive Church." By A. J. Mason, D.D.,
Master of Pembroke College, Cambridge. Longmans. Price 10s. 6d. net.

"The Early Christian Conception of Christ: Its Significance and Value in the
History of Religion." By Otto Pfleiderer, Professor of Theology in the
University of Berlin. London: Williams & Norgate. Price 3s. 6d.

"Cambridge Theological Essays." Edited by Professor Swete. Macmillan.

1.

JAMES   MARTINEAU, 1805–1905

From a portrait by G. F. Watts

The University Review

NO. 2. VOL. I.	JUNE, 1905.

University Settlements

BY

THE REV. CANON BARNETT, M.A. (OXON.),

Warden of Toynbee Hall, Whitechapel, London.

TWENTY-FIVE years ago many social reformers were set on bringing about a co-operation between the Universities of Oxford and Cambridge and the industrial classes. Arnold Toynbee thought he could study at Oxford during term time and lecture in great cities during the vacation. Professor Stuart thought that University teaching might be extended among working people by means of centres locally established. There were others to whom it seemed that no way could be so effective as the way of residence, and they advocated a plan by which members of the University should during some years live their lives among the poor.

Present social reformers have, however, other business on hand. They think that something practical is of first importance, some alteration in the land laws, which would make good houses more possible—some modification of the relation between labour and capital, which would spread the national wealth over a larger number of people. They see something which Parliament or the

A

municipal bodies could do, which seems to be very good, and they are not disposed to spend time on democratising the old Universities or on humanising the working man.

The present generation of reformers claim to be practical, but one who belongs to the past generation and is not without sympathy with the present may also claim that much depends on the methods by which good objects are secured. There is truth in the saying that means are more important than ends. Many present evils are due to the means—the force, the flattery, the haste—by which good men of old time achieved their ends. "God forgive all good men" was the prayer of Charles Kingsley.

Reformers may to-day pass laws which would exalt the poor and bring down the rich, but if in the passing of such laws bitterness, anger, and uncharitableness were increased, and if, as the result, the exalted poor proved incapable of using or of enjoying their power—another giant behaving like a giant—where would be the world's gain? The important thing surely is not that the poor shall be exalted, but that rich and poor shall equally feel the joy of their being and, living together in peace and goodwill, make a society to be a blessing to all nations.

Co-operation between these Universities and working men, between knowledge and industry, might—it seemed to the reformers of old days—make a force which would secure a form not to be reformed, a repentance not to be repented, a sort of progress whose means would justify its end.

The Universities have the knowledge of human things. Their professors and teachers have, in some measure, the secret of living, they know that life consists not in possessions, and that society has other bonds than force or selfishness, and they offer in their homes the best example of simple and refined living. They have studied the art of expression, and can put into words the thoughts of many hearts. They look with the eye of science over the fields of history, they appreciate tradition at its proper value, and are familiar with the mistakes which, in old times, broke up great hopes. Their minds are trained to leap from point to point in thought. They have followed the struggles of humanity towards its ideals, they know something of what is in man, and something of what he can possibly achieve.

If these National Universities, with their wealth of knowledge, felt at the same time the pressure of those problems which mean suffering to the workmen, they would be watch-towers from which watchmen would discern the signs of the times, those movements on the horizon now as small as a man's hand but soon to cover the sky. If by sympathy they felt the unrest, which all over the world is giving cause for disquietude to those in authority, they would give a form to the wants, and show to those who cry, and those who listen, the meaning of the unrest. If they were in touch with the industrial classes, they would adapt their teaching to the needs and understandings of men, struggling to secure their position in a changing industrial system and better acquainted with facts than with theories about facts. A democratised

University would be constrained to give forth the principles which underlie social progress, to show the nation what is alterable and unalterable in the structure of society—what there is for pride or for shame in its past history, what is the expenditure which makes or destroys wealth—it would be driven to help to solve the mystery of the unemployed, why there should be so much unemployment when there must be so great a demand for employment if people are to be fitly clothed and fed and housed. It would, at any rate, guide the nation to remedies which would not be worse than the disease.

" How," it was once asked of an Oxford professor, "can the University be adapted to take its place in modern progress." His answer was "By establishing in its neighbourhood a great industrial centre." The presence, that is to say, of workmen would bring the Universities to face the realities of the day, raise their policy to something more important than that of compulsory Greek, and direct their teaching to other needs than those felt by the limited class, whose children become undergraduates or listeners to an "extension lecturer." A committee of University dons has been described as a meeting where each member is only a critic, where nothing simple or practical has a chance of adoption, and only a paradox gets attention. If labour were heard knocking at its doors, and demanding that the national knowledge, of which the Universities are the trustees, should be put at its service, the same committee would cease criticising and begin to be practical. Knowledge without industry is often selfishness.

Oxford and Cambridge need what workmen can give, the workmen have no less need of the Universities. Workmen have the strength of character which comes of daily contact with necessity, the discipline of labour, sympathy with the sorrow and sufferings of neighbours with whose infirmities they themselves are touched. The working classes have on their side the force of sacrifice and the power of numbers. They have the future in their hands. If they had their share of the knowledge stored in the National Universities they would know better at what to aim, what to do, and how to do it. They, as it is, are often blind and unreasoning. Blind to the things which really satisfy human nature while they eagerly follow after their husks, unable to pursue a chain of thought while they readily act on some gaudy dogma, inclined to think food the chief good, selfishness the one motive of action, and force the only remedy. The speeches of candidates for workmen's constituencies—their promises—their jokes—their appeals are the measure of the industrial mind. How would a parliament of workmen deal with those elements which make so large a part of the nation's strength—its traditions—its literature—its natural scenery—its art? What sort of education would it foster? Would it recognise that the imagination is the joy of life and a commercial asset, that unity depends on variety, that respect and not only toleration is due to honest opponents? How would it understand the people of India or deal reverently with the intricate motives, the fears and hopes of other nations? How would workmen themselves fulfil their place in the future if well-fed, well-clothed, and well-housed, they had no other recreation than the spectacle of a football match? Industry without knowledge is often brutality.

Workmen have the energy, the honesty, the fellow feeling, the habit of sacrifice which are probably the best part of the national inheritance, but as a class they have not knowledge of human things, the delicate sense which sees what is in man—the judgment which knows the value of evidence—the feeling which would guide them to distinguish idols from ideals and set them on making a Society in which every human being shall enjoy the fulness of his being. They have not insight nor farsight and their frequent attitude is that of suspicion. If sometimes I am asked what I desire for East London I think of all the goodness, the struggles, the suffering I have seen—the sorrows of the poor and the many fruitless remedies—and I say "more education," "higher education." People cannot really be raised by gifts or food or houses. A healthy body may be used for low as for high objects. People must raise themselves—that which raises a man as that which defiles a man comes from within a man. People therefore must have the education which will reveal to them the powers within themselves and within other men, their capacities for thinking and feeling, for admiration, hope and love. They must be made something more than instruments of production, they must be made capable of enjoying the highest things. They need therefore something more than technical teaching, it is not enough for England to be the workshop of the world, it must export thoughts and hopes as well as machines. The Tower of London would be a better defence for the nation if it were a centre of teaching, than as a barracks for soldiers! The working class movement which is so full of promise for the nation seems to me likely to fail unless it be inspired by the human knowledge which the Universities represent. Working men without such knowledge will—to say nothing else—be always suspicious as to one another and as to the objects which they seek.

The old Universities and industry must, if this analysis be near the truth, co-operate for social reform. There are many ways to bring them together. The University extension movement might be worked by the hands of the great labour organisations—legislation might adapt the constitution of the Universities to the coming days of labour ascendancy—workmen might be brought up to graduate in colleges, and they might, as an experiment, be allowed to use existing colleges during vacations.

But the subject of this paper is the "way of settlements." Members of the Universities, it is claimed, may for a few years settle in industrial centres, and in natural intercourse come into contact with their neighbours. There is nothing like contact for giving or getting understanding. There is no lecture and no book so effective as life. Culture spreads by contact. University men who are known as neighbours, who are met in the streets, in the clubs, and on committees, who can be visited in their own rooms, amid their own books and pictures, commend what the University stands for as it cannot otherwise be commended. On the other hand workmen who are casually and frequently met, whose idle words become familiar, whose homes are known, reveal the workman mind as it is not revealed by clever essayists or by orators of their own class. The friendship of one man of knowledge and one man of industry may go but a small way to bring together the Universities and the working classes, but it is such friendship which prepares the way for the understanding which underlies co-operation. If misunderstanding is war, understanding is peace. The men who settle may either take rooms by themselves, or they may associate themselves in a settlement. There is something to be said for each plan. The advantage of a settlement is that a body of University men living together keep up the distinctive characteristics of their training, they better resist the tendency to put on the universal drab, and they bring a variety into their neighbourhood. They are helped, too, by the companionship of their fellows, to take larger views of what is wanted, their enthusiasm for progress is kept alive and at the same time well pruned by friendly and severe criticism.

But whether men live in lodgings or in settlements, there is one necessary condition besides that of social interest if they are to be successful in uniting knowledge and industry in social reform. They must live their own life. There must be no affectation of asceticism, and no consciousness of superiority. They must show forth the taste, the mind and the faith that is in them. They have not come as "missioners," they have come to settle, that is, to learn as much as to teach, to receive as much as to give.

Settlements which have been started during the last twenty years have not always fulfilled this condition. Many have become centres of missionary effort. They have often been powerful for good, and their works done by active and devoted men or women have so disturbed the water, that many unknown sick folk have been healed. They, however, are primarily missions. A settlement in the original idea was not a mission, but a means by which University men and workmen might by natural intercourse get to understand one another, and co-operate in social reform.

There are many instances of such understanding and co-operation.

Twenty years ago primary education was much as it had been left by Mr. Lowe. Some University men living in a settlement soon became conscious of the loss involved in the system, they talked with neighbours who by themselves were unconscious of the loss till inspired and inspiring they formed an Education Reform League. There were committees, meetings, and public addresses. The league was a small affair, and seems to be little among the forces of the time. But every one of its proposals have been carried out. Some of its members in high official positions have wielded with effect the principles which were elaborated in the forge at which they and working men sweated together. Others of its members on local authorities or as citizens have never forgotten the inner meaning of education as they learnt it from their University friends.

Another instance may be offered. The relief of the poor is a subject on which the employing and the employed classes naturally incline to take different views. They suspect one another's remedies. The working men hate both the charity of the rich and the strict administration of the economist, while they themselves talk a somewhat impracticable socialism. University men who assist in such relief, are naturally suspected as members of the employing class. A few men, however, who as residents had become known in other relations, and were recognised as human, induced some workmen to take part in administering relief. Together they faced actual problems, together they made mistakes, together they felt sympathy with sorrow, and saw the break-down of their carefully designed action. The process went on for years, the personnel of the body of fellow workers has changed, but there has been a gradual approach from the different points of view. The University men have more acutely realised some of the causes of distress, the need of preserving and holding up self-respect, the pressure of the industrial system, and the claim of sufferers from this system to some compensation. They have learnt through their hearts. The workmen, on the other hand, have realised the failure of mere relief to do permanent good, the importance of thought in every case, and the kindness of severity. The result of this co-operation may be traced in the fact that workmen, economists and socialists have been found advocating the same principle of relief, and now more lately in the establishment of Mr. Long's committee which is carrying those principles into effect. Far be it from me to claim that this committee is the direct outcome of the association of University and working men, or to assert that this committee has discovered the secret of poverty, but it is certain that this committee represents the approach of two different views of relief, and that among some of its active members are workmen and University men who as neighbours in frequent intercourse learnt to respect and trust one another.

There is one other instance which is also of interest. Local Government is the corner stone in the English constitution. The people in their own neighbourhoods learn what self-government means, as their own Councils and Boards make them happy or unhappy. The government in industrial neighbourhoods is often bad, sometimes because the members are self-seekers, more often because they are ignorant or vainglorious. How can it be otherwise? If the industrial neighbourhood is self-contained, as for example in East London, it has few inhabitants with the necessary leisure for study or for frequent attendance at the meetings. If it is part of a larger government—as in county boroughs—it is unknown to the majority of the community. The conseqence is that the neighbourhoods wanting most light and most water and most space have the least, and that bodies whose chief concern should be health and education waste their time and their rates arranging their contracts so as to support local labour. In a word, industrial neighbourhoods suffer for want of a voice to express their needs and for the want of the knowledge which can distinguish man from man, recognise the relative importance of spending and saving, and encourage mutual self-respect.

University men may and in some measure have met this want. They, by residence, have learnt the wants, and their voice has helped to bring about the more equal treatment which industrial districts are now receiving. They have often, for instance, been instrumental in getting the Libraries' Act adopted. They have as members of local bodies learnt much and taught something. They have always won the respect of their fellow members, and if not always successful in preventing the neighbourly kindnesses which seem to them to be "jobs," or in forwarding expenditure which seems to them the best economy, they have kept up the lights along the course of public honour.

There are other examples in which results cannot be so easily traced. There have been friendships formed at clubs which have for ever changed the respective points of view affecting both taste and opinion. There have been new ideas born in discussion classes, which, beginning in special talk about some one subject, have ended in fireside confidences over the deepest subjects of life and faith. There have been common pleasures, travels, and visits in which everyone has felt new interest, seeing things with other eyes, and learning that the best and most lasting amusement comes from mind activity. The University man who has a friend among the poor henceforth sees the whole class differently through that medium, and so it is with the workman who has a University man as his friend. The glory of a settlement is not that it has spread opinions, or increased temperance, or relieved distress, but that it has promoted peace and goodwill.

But enough has been said to illustrate the point that by the way of residence the forces of knowledge and industry are brought into co-operation. The way, if long, is practicable. More men might live among the poor. The effort to do so involves the sacrifice of much which habits of luxury have marked as necessary. It involves the daring to be peculiar, which is often especially hard for the man who in the public school has learnt to support himself on school tradition.

Nothing has been said as to the effect of Settlements on Oxford and Cambridge. There does not seem to be much change in the attitude of these Universities to social reform, and they are not apparently moved by any impulse which comes from workmen. But judgment in this matter must be cautious as changes may be going on unnoticed. It is certain, at any rate, that the individual members who have lived among the poor are changed. If a greater number would live in the same way that experience could not fail ultimately to influence University life.

Social reform will soon be the all absorbing interest as the modern realisation of the claims of human nature and the growing power of the people, will not tolerate many of the present conditions of industrial life. The happiness of the future depends on the methods by which reform proceeds. Reforms in the past have often been disappointing. They have been made in the name of the rights of one class, and have ended in the assertion of rights over another class. They have been made by force and produced reaction. They have been done for the people not by the people, and have never been assimilated. The method by which knowledge and industry may co-operate has yet to be tried, and one way in which to bring about such co-operation is the way of University settlements.

Questions for Discussion.

BY

SIR OLIVER LODGE, D.Sc. (LOND.), LL.D., F.R.S.

Principal of the University of Birmingham.

PART II.

THE second question for our consideration is perhaps even more difficult, namely, the kind of Degrees that should be given by a University, and the kind of curriculum to be encouraged. I used to discuss the matter in a general way with G. F. Fitzgerald, the Professor of Natural Philosophy at Trinity College, Dublin, and my own ideas are not yet thoroughly formed, but I will proceed to state them from the point of view of an advocate, for the sake of clearness; and at present they run somewhat as follows:—
The old English Degree is the B.A., and was intended to signify that the graduate had been properly educated in the knowledge of his time, up to a certain moderate standard. It had no specific reference to any particular kind of Art or Arts, and to this day is employed in many Universities so as to cover a training in almost every variety of knowledge. Recently, since more specially so-called scientific subjects have come into prominence, a few Universities have begun to award a new kind of

Degree, the B.Sc. Now if this is to signify a special professional training in Science, the term is appropriate ; just as, on the other hand, for a specific and professional training in Literature the term B.Lit. would be appropriate. But neither of these trainings is appropriate to the average man who comes for a general education, nor is there any reason why at the outset of his course he should be asked to choose whether he will be trained in Literature or in Science. Indeed, there is every reason for not so asking him. What he ought to want, and at any rate what he should be encouraged to have, is a general education in the knowledge of his time ; and if "his time" happens to include some scientific and some literary knowledge, as well as History and Geography and Grammar and Mathematics and the ordinary everyday subjects of a general education, so much the better. But he need not therefore have a special label attached, as if he was a specially cultivated person in some one branch of knowledge. He should be labelled with the regular general education label, namely, B.A. ; and if, after this, or at the same time, he proceeds to elaborate further his training in some special branch of knowledge, then he may rightly be awarded an additional designation, and be styled B.Lit. on the one hand, if his special subject has been Letters, B.Sc. on the other, if his special subject has been Science ; or possibly some even more exact specification might be employed, such as Engineering, or Fine Art, or Philosophy, or Music.

In this way the general training for B.A. would include some Language, but not necessarily Classics, some

Science but not necessarily Physics, some History and Literature and Mathematics of course, and I should hope also some Art, and several other subjects which I will mention directly ; by all which I mean to indicate a general curriculum such as can be agreed on as adequately representing a broad general education suited for the needs of ordinary life and for the great majority of citizens. If on the top of all this a man can also specialise in some particular direction, and obtain in addition a specific Degree or diploma, he becomes a highly-appropriate product of a University.

But it will be objected that by no means *all* students can be expected to take this general curriculum, to the extent of graduation, before beginning to specialise ; that if they take a general course at school as high as a Matriculation standard, that is all that can be expected of a considerable number of them. This is quite true ; and after Matriculation the avenues for specialisation must be *open*,—the Medical avenue, the Scientific, and the Literary—for those who are intending to take up professionally one or other of these subjects, and have no time for more general education before they can earn a living. For such professional students we have the M.B. and the B.Sc., and as I wish to suggest also, a B.Lit., and *possibly* a Bachelor in Engineering and other subjects. But I would not give to these specifically-trained students the label appropriate to a broad general education or culture. I would suggest the keeping of the old historic B.A. Degree for this latter purpose, and would refrain from giving it to the specialised undergraduates who are

or should be working for the B.Lit.   On the other hand,
I would not ask students who present themselves for
admission without any strong bias towards or necessity
for specialisation, to select one or other of the special
avenues ; I would rather assume that what they wanted
was the general course for the B.A. Degree, and would
leave to the candidate or his guardians the responsibility
for narrowing this down in accordance with supposed
practical exigency.

I believe that there are many subjects that might be
included in such a general course besides those which
occur to everybody.   Some slight knowledge of Agriculture, for instance, is not required only by farmers or
by those who are going to be land-agents ; it is useful
to all who own or occupy land.   Everyone nowadays
who claims to be educated should have some acquaintance
with the general principles of Biology, as well as with the
general principles of Natural Philosophy and Astronomy,
and, I believe, Chemistry and Geology also ; some notion,
too, of what has been done in Philosophy and Ethics and
Logic ; some knowledge of Elementary Physiology; and
some acquaintance with at least the *History* of Art, and
Archæology.

It will be a serious thing for a University if students
from the beginning divide themselves into isolated
groups ; not having common work even for Matriculation,
and separating completely after they have become Undergraduates: one set labelling themselves prematurely
with the name of " Science," another set, perhaps necessarily, partitioning themselves off as " Medicals," and a

third class monopolising to themselves the historic name of "Arts," and looking down upon all the others as more or less uneducated heathen. The advantage of coming to a University should be that one is brought into contact with divers kinds of minds, and thrown into social union with workers in many other subjects. The more that students of different classes can be mixed the better. It would be a great misfortune if the results of our wide range of subjects was to divide students into groups, having very little communication and some feeling of rivalry, perhaps even antagonism, with each other. Half the value of University education will be lost if students of different classes do not mix—mix in their studies to some extent, as well as in their sports; and I can imagine that a general body of B.A. Undergraduates, working at all the subjects equally, might constitute a connecting link, and might indirectly encourage the more special students to take a broader view of their College life, and engraft on their strictly professional training some elements of wider culture. I believe that the University would do wisely to so arrange its regulations as not to leave this solely to unstimulated individual enterprise, but actively to encourage such excursions by recognising them as part of a curriculum: not indeed compulsory, but accepted and rewarded with distinction, so as to afford scope and encouragement to any who have more than average brains and energy, and who would and ought to feel cramped if limited by regulation to their own particular branch of study alone.

There are plenty of young engineers who have *only*

been at some technical school, plenty of young doctors who have *only* been at a hospital. Similarly there are men who have been trained in Theological Colleges and other narrow places where special curricula can be studied. It should be the mark of a University Graduate that he has not been thus limited to one narrow line, that he has attended in some degree to teachings in other branches of knowledge, and that he has mixed with students of every kind and is familiar with their modes of thought. Thus should a University man be distinguished from one who has only received a technical training, and it should be the aim of our regulations to enforce this distinction.

I do not say that it is necessary that every subject should always be lectured upon within the walls of a University building. If there is a good course, on Art or on Music or any other subject, being given at some other institution in the city, then I should say recognise it, throw it open to the students and encourage them to attend. Sometimes we should invite men from other institutions, or men engaged in practical work, to come and give lectures within our walls ; at other times it may be more convenient to utilise them in their own buildings. But our aim should be to take advantage of every teaching institution of adequate rank which can contribute to the general sum of knowledge any portion missing from our own scheme, and to weld them all into a more complete and comprehensive City University.

So far I have spoken as if it might be usual for students to take a general B.A. Degree first, and then specialise on to specific degrees, but I by no means wish to emphasise the order of precedure. It is quite possible for a man to feel the need of a general culture *after* he has had a specific training, and then is the time to encourage him to take up subjects outside his profession; not necessarily first, not necessarily last, but some time in his course ; and if he thus engrafts a wider education on to his special knowledge, and becomes an educated man of whom the University may be proud, I would reward him with the extra distinction of a B.A. or M.A. Degree in addition to his Special Degree. No doubt there are many details of difficulty in carrying out such a plan, some of which I probably do not yet see, but the question again is, first, whether in general principle such a plan as that here sketched can in any sense be approved, or whether it would require extensive modification, or whether it proceeds on mistaken lines altogether.

The Possibilities of Popular Progress

BY

J. A. HOBSON, M.A. (Oxon.).

———

IF we consider the essence of human progress to consist, not in the increasing control of man over his material environment, but in the increasing realisation of reason and justice in the conduct of human affairs, it is not evident to all men that progress is attainable, or that, if it be attainable, the moral aspirations of mankind play any real part in determining its pace or course. The sceptical view is commonly based upon an economic interpretation of history according to which the acquisition and enjoyment of class or personal power based on property is the one continually dominant factor, all social institutions being moulded and directed by economic considerations, all the ideas and sentiments of religions, politics, art, literature, and morals being ammunition in the hands of warring economic interests. The independence of the higher ideal aspirations is but illusory : examine closely the critical events in the history of any nation, their religious reformations, their political revolutions, nay, even the rise and fate of their architecture or drama, these are but aspects of a conflict expressing a disturbance in the balance of economic power.

" If we examine the hidden mysteries of the social mechanism," writes an exponent of this doctrine, " we shall, I think, be free to admit that the sentimental element surrounding all great social revolutions is after all but an illusion."[1]

This mirage of beckoning ideals, reason, liberty, and justice, is indeed needed often to impel the activities of men, but the real ends and the real motor-power lie in the pressure of economic process.

This explanation of progress as the mere drive of a *vis a tergo*—physical necessity, is philosophically—even biologically—untenable.

But it would be idle to deny that it contains a sufficient element of truth, when applied to modern social politics, to cause many to doubt the possibility of achieving popular progress by any form of reasonable concerted action.

So far, at any rate, as the politico-economic structure of Society is concerned, history appears to show that the preponderant possession of property, and the control over the lives of men given by property, passes from one class or order to another, from king to barons, landowner to capitalist, from merchant to manufacturer, from entrepreneur to financier, in accordance with changes in the relative importance of certain economic functions. In English history, it is the scarcity of labour following

1. Loria, " Economic Foundations of Society," p. 285.

the Black Death, the rise in value of work and the debasing of currency under the Tudors, the power of the new merchant class in the Stuart revolutions, the rising power of the manufacturers of the 18th century, the substitution of corporate for individual capitalism, and the growing dominion of finance over industry in our own time—of such nature seem to be the critical events determining ever and anon a fresh shift in the balance of power among the powerful classes a fresh composition of the political and industrial control.   Nowhere are considerations of abstract justice or reason, or greatest happiness of greatest number, real determinants in these changes ; one interest, grown more powerful, asserts itself against another grown more weak : king, pope, barons, squirarchy, capitalists, entrepreneurs, financiers, each uses all the power afforded by new circumstances to obtain the largest control of property, and moulds the forms of political and economic government to further the maintenance and increase of its power.

If any progress in the nature of extended liberty and wider diffusion of material property comes this way, it is incidental and unintended, it is a dole or a concession from the possessing or ruling classes, in no sense a product of the reasonable, intelligent co-operation of the people.   The people cannot help themselves ; the have-nots are powerless against the haves.   If the people possess the name of political power through the forms of a liberal constitution or a democracy, it is because the possessing classes have discovered ways of checking, controlling, and dividing public opinion, which render the forms of popular government innocuous. How can it be otherwise? The class, or classes, in control of the material resources, have leisure to organise methods for conserving their property and power, they can buy men of picked brains or strong bodies to defend their interests with laws or guns, and to confuse or coerce their enemies.

We say that, when the people get education and become intelligent, they will be able to organise and over-power their masters. "Mighty men may thrash numbers for a time; in the end the numbers will be thrashed into the art of beating their teachers."[1] But is this true? The sceptic replies: The means of popular education, the machinery of popular organisation are themselves created, financed, controlled by the possessing classes; the church, the press, the school, the party machinery do not and cannot belong to the people, for each of these educative organs involves the maintenance of a profession and a plant which are not provided out of the pence of the people, but out of the guineas of the well-to-do and the cheques of the millionaires, and those who pay the piper call the tune. How, then, is it possible that the people shall be allowed to get such education as shall furnish the intellectual and moral sinews of an effective revolt against an oligarchy of vested interests?

Is it not always open to the makers of public opinion to curb, direct, or dissipate the forces of popular discontent before they enter politics, or else to employ them in a futile rotatory action inside the machine, as they do in

---

1. Meredith, "Beauchamp's Career."

the democracy of the United States and of Great Britain? or where the popular temper and institutions of a country are refractory before such acts of management, it is always possible to revert to force, to suspend the forms of popular liberty and to reorganise the machinery of government by a *coup d'etat*. This is the interpretation of the history of South Africa during the last decade. In the last resort the armed forces of the nation are at the disposal of the possessing classes, whose political and economic power represents that public order and safety of the commonwealth which it is the function of an army to safeguard.

Or turn from the political to the industrial arena. 'Labour,' we are told, 'is the basis of all wealth. Let the workers organise so as to present a united front to the employing class, they can enforce their demands for their full share in the product of industry.' Can they do this? Is this menace of a general strike a feasible and a logically efficacious policy? In the first place, it may be urged, if the capitalist classes recognise the danger, they can prevent the general organisation of the workers for simultaneous action. By the superior organisation which their smaller numbers, greater ability, and ampler resources furnish they can out-general the workers, harrassing them in detail, corrupting their leaders, sowing dissension between the several trades and localities, buying selected groups by profit-sharing and other preferential schemes of employment, procuring fresh legislation and adjudication favourable to their defence through lawmakers and administrators bound by social and economic bonds of sympathy and interest to support their domination.

But if such a general organisation of labour for simultaneous action were feasible upon a national, or even an international scale, a contingency scarce thinkable, its economic command of the situation is by no means obvious. Were government merely to "keep a ring," preserve public order and leave capital and labour to fight to a finish, the great bulk of the existing stocks of food and other necessaries of life would be the legal property not of the workers but of the employers by virtue of present ownership and command of money: this stock could be increased by the labour of the capitalists and their entourage of servants and unorganised dependants : to this must be added such "free" labour as is in all times available. The straits employers would be placed in would doubtless be serious, but nothing as compared with those of the workers, if these latter kept within the law : for their actual command of food would be infinitesimally small, and they could have no recourse to the machinery of industry to supplement it, for this machinery belongs to the employing class. The whole body of organised workers would be starved into submission—such at any rate is the strict logic of the situation. In no large actual strike have the workers won on the strength of their own saved resources, they have always drawn largely from the funds of other Trade Unions and from the general sympathetic public, from both of which resources they would be excluded upon the hypothesis we are considering.

If it is replied that the workers would not keep inside the limits of the law, but would seize the workshops and instruments of production in order to utilise their labour-power, the struggle at once ceases to be economic and becomes political, or rather, military, a conflict between the armed trained forces of the State defending the interests of capital and an unarmed untrained rabble. About the issue of such a conflict there can be no doubt.

On the assumption, from which we started, that economic interests are the really dominant and, ultimately, determinant factors, it seems as if the sceptics had an impregnable position, and that substantial progress in the sense of an increasing power of reason and justice over the direction of human affairs were impracticable. The progress seems to involve a vicious circle; popular progress is only possible by means of popular organisation, organisation requires intelligent direction, intelligent direction depends upon education, and the machinery of education is in the control of interests opposed to popular progress.

Such is, in large outline, the sceptical position. But is it sound? Is progress really illusory, the progressive forces dissipated by this perpetual movement in a closed circle? The very simplicity of the reasoning is entitled to arouse suspicion. Nowhere else does nature present any instance of purely rotatory movement. Everywhere we are confronted in our analysis with the same apparent antagonism between the *vis inertiæ* of the existing order, the vested interests, and that power which we conceive pulsàting through nature, and seeking to lift some form of matter to a more complex and highly adapted shape through *variation*. All evolution in inanimate and animate nature, is expressed in terms of this conflict, and nowhere does the conflict resolve itself into the futility of mere rotation. Are we to suppose, that when this conflict is raised to the plane of conscious human life and social forces, the result is different? . . . .

'But,' it may be said 'these fundamental considerations are beside the point, no one seriously disputes the reality of progress in general. The question is whether we are not confronted with an *impasse* in that sort of progress which is involved in the realisation of social justice.' We may have every sort of progress that is consistent with the maintenance of a selfish class government in politics and industry, and yet the overthrow of that oligarchy may be unattainable.

But if we test this hypothesis by an appeal to actual history, it certainly appears to break down. Admitting the continuance of class ascendancy in politics and industry in modern civilised states, it is easy to show an expansion in the political liberties of the peoples and a corresponding shrinkage of more direct and forcible control by the political and economic rulers: the life of the average citizen is safer and larger, his command over commodities and services is increasing, his intellectual and moral life freer and better nourished. It may, indeed, be replied: 'These liberties are concessions of the ascendant classes, the old slave and serf systems

no longer pay, the modern domination is subtler and
more direct, it requires a higher standard of material
comfort, a larger circuit of liberty and a higher
intelligence on the part of the helots: but this improvement of the general life of the people does not
really diminish the real subjection in which they are kept
or realise social ideals opposed to the interests of the
master-class.' It is not easy to disprove such a contention.
Yet the argument really contains in itself an admission of
positive progress, for the elevation of the nature and
instruments of domination is itself progress: to enforce
control by laws is an advance upon the use of naked
swords, to govern by working political machines an
advance upon open menace. This is indeed the natural
course of progress; the vicious circle as it first appeared
is no closed circle, but an ascending spiral. The spiral
is rightly accepted as the mechanical symbol of social
progress, implying the natural course of a more powerful
force deflected from a straight upward movement by
resistance meeting it transversely. The spiral form
explains also the illusion of the sceptic who, falsely
identifying the outlook at the several elevations, fails to
recognise the gradual ascent.

The most conclusive evidence of the growing power
of popular ideas and sentiments is the fact that the
vested interests base their defence more and more upon
appeals to the supreme court of reason and of morals.

But do not, therefore, let us be misled into supposing
that the present immediate object of strife, the question of
victory, is higher education or some elevation of the moral

standard of the people.   Before a really effective demand for the higher forms of wealth, the nobler means of life, can be evoked, sufficiency and security of the material basis of personal efficiency must be won.   Economic reforms must take precedence in time: problems of housing and of food, of regular remunerative employment, of access to the land, of greater leisure, of ease and comfort in old age, everywhere stand as barriers to a higher life for the people.   Now the real solution of every one of these practical problems involves a successful attack upon vested interests: economic liberty can only be won by the rasing of the fortresses of monopoly.   The new shift is not an alteration in the objective of the campaign, but in the methods of conducting it.   It is not merely the abandonment of the revolutionary appeals to physical force; the more thoughtful leaders of popular reform perceive that even the weapons of the franchise and legislative power cannot yet be used with much effect.   What the present pressing interests of progress demand is the organisation of the intelligence and moral energy of the people for the definite work of economic reform by the overthrow of vested interests and the establishment of economic equality of opportunity, within the nation.

This enables us to understand the new tactics of defence adopted by the possessing classes.   Their supreme object is to prevent the popular organisation on a basis of intelligent appreciation of the problem of social progress.   There are two chief ways of doing this.

The first is to deny the existence of social-economic

problems and to urge the claims of individual moralisation as the only valid and effectual path of progress. If enough individuals separately win salvation society is saved. The second is to foster the combative competitive instincts of the lower nature of man by urging the necessity and utility of industrial competition within the State and military competition with other States. Thus the moral cohesive forces which would vitalise an organised democracy can be diverted to lower activities and rendered innocuous.

In order thus to divide and degrade the moral and intellectual forces of democracy, an informal sociology is required. Those who watch carefully the influences exercised by the possessing classes over our Universities, churches, political parties, press and even our literature, art and drama, can see how this body of social theory is consolidated for its defensive work. It is not indeed a consciously constructed or consistent system of thought that is evolved, but rather an improvisation of social theory out of the floating ideas and sentiments of the age.

To this sociology of the vested interests Biology, Psychology, Economics, Ethics, Philosophy, Religion, are all made to constitute special aids. But the staple consists in an illicit extension of certain teachings of biology and a falsification of certain premises of economics. Space will not permit me to describe in detail the composition of the sociology, but only to indicate a few of the concepts and formulæ drawn from the several sources.

From biology as the science which first formulated

the modern conception of the evolution of man, the central doctrine of the individual struggle for life as the test of fitness and the means of progress transplanted straight into sociology, has been used to defend the necessity and social utility of individual competition in industry and racial competition in war as instruments of national and international progress. The deep-rooted divergence of species, the strong dominion of heredity, the practical importance of chance individual variations as means of progress, are made to nourish theories of permanent racial and class ascendancy based on superiority, and of individual genius and effort as the instruments of industrial betterment. Progress is represented as the slow orderly play of physical forces pushing from behind, any attempt to alter or accelerate the pace of which is a baneful disturbance of the order of nature. Any proposed activity of the people through legislation or otherwise is held to involve this disturbance and is denounced as interference with nature.

The neglect of the part which mutual aid or conscious co-operation plays in the true biological conception of the struggle for life is a significant feature of the selective method of the class sociology. Nay, even when the suspension of internecine struggle within the group is recognised as a condition of progress, the lesson deduced is that the suspension implies the fiercer and more effective struggle for life between groups, nations, or races. A whole sociology of imperialism is built on this alleged necessity, ignoring the true central teaching of biology that as man ascends above the rest of animal

o

creation his struggles are directed less and less against his fellowmen more and more for the control of his material environment.

But the most impudent abuse of biology consists in the assumption that the methods and formulæ of a science concerned with the individual physical phenomena of man can suffice to interpret the social moral pheno- mena of human achievements, that individual animal evolution constitutes the whole essence of social evolution.

Since the real battle is waged round the fortress of economic privilege, it was only to be expected that the new plastic science of political economy should be moulded and utilised for weapons of defence. And this is indeed the case. That competition secures for the workers in enhanced wages and improved conditions of work the gains of all industrial improvements (in the long run); that the great fortunes secured by entrepre- neurs, capitalists, and speculators, are the just and necessary rewards of the social services rendered by their ingenuity, industry, foresight, and organising power; that capital, the result of thrift, is so mixed up with land values that even rent contains no certain elements of unearned increment; that the workers, as a class, cannot obtain higher wages without increasing their efficiency; that there exists, therefore, no genuine divergence of interests between capital and labour, between employer and em- ployed, landowner and tenant; that all attempts to place increasing burdens of taxation upon capital, or upon the incomes of the rich, will recoil upon the workers by

Checking business enterprise and the demand for labour; that endeavours to restrict private enterprise in alleged monopolies by municipal or state control or management are alike unjust, and injurious to the common good. These are a few of the weapons of defence taken from the arsenal of conservative economics, and directed against movements of reform.

What speciousness these doctrines contain is dependent on two false assumptions, the first, that free competition, as a general practice, actually exists; the second, that the value of anything depends upon the individual conduct of its owner.

The theories about the benefits of competition, individual efficiency, and rights of property, thus selected out of biology and economics, are supplemented by diverse doctrines drawn from other and more elevated studies. Psychology and ethics are summoned to support a theory of social reform, which concerns itself entirely with the education of the individual character, deprecating the dependence upon legislative aids or any artificial sapping of the self-reliance and self-sufficiency of the individual worker, who has always capacity, if he uses his opportunities aright, to obtain for himself the share of the general wealth which is due to him, and represents his earnings. The sole sufficient key to all social problems, according to this school, lies in the assertion of the powers of individual character.

The root fallacy here, of course, lies in the false assumptions that any individual living in a social-economic society is capable of self-support, and that he is endowed with a power of will and intellect competent for the effort which he is supposed to be capable of putting forth. It is bad psychology, for it ignores the reactions of environment upon the springs of individual character, bad ethics, because it ignores the factors of society in forming individual conduct.

Nor do the defenders of "the existing order" disdain such assistance as they can draw from philosophy and religion. For the less cultured man the crude methods of the orthodox churches still suffice; contented with his place in this world let him occupy his thoughts with bright hopes of another; absorbed in the saving of his particular soul he will not worry himself about the safety of the commonwealth, but will leave politics and economics to his betters. For the more cultured a finer brand of quietism and mysticism is furnished, sometimes infused with splendid ritual or subtle esoteric appeals, sometimes a colder and more austere philosophy couched, partly in the authoritative conservatism of Hegelian dogmas, partly in the later determinism distilled out of evolutionary science. These last are the strictly academic contribution to the defences of vested interests, and are particularly calculated to sterilise the liberal sympathies of young intellectuals, so as to deprive the progressive forces of that able generalship which is essential to success. We can observe how the same selective and deterrent influences are brought to bear upon literature, art and the drama, in a boycott of really critical ideas and fundamental social issues, and a saturation of the public mind with commonplace sensationalism, sloppy sentimentalism, and bizarre frivolity. The patronage of the finer and the coarser arts of recreation is expressly directed to foster a combative patriotism, and its attendant forms of animalism, a snobbish reverence for rank, fashion and the valuations of the master class, and a contempt for earnestness, sobriety, and reflections : a debased ideal of chivalry is set up with reckless charity in the place of justice, impulse for reason and passing expediency for principle.

There is indeed no close pattern in the texture of this teaching. It is not deliberately woven as a scheme of defence by "vested interests," but is thrown together by the class instinct of self-preservation. In its higher intellectual form it approaches the dignity of a Sociology, in its lower it is a mere appeal to the passions of the animal self. But it is always and everywhere animated by a common purpose, viz., to check the organisation of a popular movement for the overthrow of common privileges, and the achievement of "reason" in national and international order.

This is no idly speculative analysis. Nothing is easier than to illustrate in detail how modern theories of Oligarchy, Protection, Militarism, Imperialism, Property and Charity, chief buttresses of the present order, are derived from the sources I have named. As the popular movement for economic justice becomes more conscious, and is carried more into intellectual and moral channels, the more urgent will it become for the vested interests to secure these defences. More and more will the instruments of public education, press, platform, pulpit and lecture room, be paid to impose upon the public mind the sedatives, diversions, and distractions which are found serviceable, and the louder and more genuine will be the indignant disclaimers against the imputation of corruption. But though these grave professors, right reverend fathers, right honourable statesmen, and sagacious editors may not know it, the finances which support their institutions are derived from rents, monopoly profits, and other forms of unearned income, and they will fight with such intellectual and spiritual weapons as they can wield for defence of the social-economic order which sustains them.

They will be required to deter and to confuse a clear understanding of the economic and spiritual structure of society, and of the rationalisation of progress dependent on this understanding. As an essential of this defence, they must pretend and believe that their teaching is disinterested and unbiassed, and that their financial dependence does not tarnish their intellectual and spiritual liberty.

Can these defences of the ascendant classes be made effective so as to break or to postpone indefinitely the attack of an organised people? I think not. There is a certain growing irony in the situation. For while the ascendant classes are with one hand building these elaborate moral defences, with the other they are supplying their assailants with the sinews of war. For the very conditions of modern profitable exploitation favour the physical and intellectual solidarity of the people : modern capitalism makes directly for moral democracy. The new methods of industry demand individual intelligence and close complex co-operation among large bodies of workers: the mere machine tender and single-process man is not increasing but diminishing in proportion to the workers whose work involves elements of responsibility and skill. The large-city life imposed by modern industry is at length beginning to bear fruit in a clearer civic consciousness and capacity of co-operation for civic ends. Modern industrialism cannot proceed without increasing co-operation and solidarity of the masses as workers and as citizens: these processes of formal integration cannot fail to generate and feed a fuller and more intelligent popular consciousness. It is this consciousness, enlightened and moralised, that forms the soul of the progressive movement. Upon its growth depends the development of plain popular ideas and sentiments, of a reason and a justice, which will neither be coerced, corrupted nor bemused, by the defences set up by the spiritual mercenaries of the vested interests.

If the struggle were merely one of wits, a sophistical swordplay, it might well seem that the longer purse here, as elsewhere, might buy the better advocates, and so make their defences always adequate. But justice is a great ally. When the struggle is on the plane of brute force, numbers and justice may indeed be overborne, but every elevation of the plane of struggle raises their power. Thus the efficacy of the cause of progress is logically justified, as it is practically demonstrated, by a growing use of spiritual weapons. For the great strength of the cause of the people lies in the substantial justice of its demands for economic equality, and in proportion as the popular intelligence and will are enlightened will they be able to resist the great temptation, to revert to the physical force in which they wrongly imagine themselves superior, and to choose the higher struggle, where reason and justice will befriend them.

Popular progress is not rightly measured in terms of material prosperity, nor does it consist in the destruction of the economic monopolies of the possessing classes, but this levelling of material opportunities is the first essential condition to the free development of the higher life of the people: it is the prime basis of all true liberty, and, once substantially attained, opens a new economy of progress in every field of organised activity.

This methodology of progress, asserting a priority in time for economic reforms, implies no disparagement of intellectual and moral reforms, nor does it revert unconsciously to the narrowly conceived economic interpretation of history rejected at the outset of this analysis. While it is desirable that the main body of our reformatory forces should be at present directed to securing these economic bases of popular advance, this process of direction is itself a spiritual movement, involving a rally and an organised arousal of the latent intellectual and moral energy of the people. While, therefore, in the region of concrete reform work temporal priority must be accorded to economic achievement, or in other words, we must improve the soil before we can hope to grow the fruits of a higher humanity, the actual initiative is drawn for the domain of moral character and intelligence. Moreover, each step in the improvement of the economic environment of a people or a class is only secured so far as it is attended by two results; first, a more or less conscious and, therefore, moral readjustment of the entire economic resources of each group or family, raising the quality as well as the quantity of the "standard of comfort;" secondly, an increased power of assimilating the moral and intellectual opportunities presented in that improved spiritual environment which it is the function of distinctively religious, ethical, and educational reformers to mould, for the satisfaction of the higher human appetites and the transmutation of a rising standard of life.

The Free Churches and the Universities.

BY

THE REV. JAMES HOPE MOULTON, M.A. (Camb.), D.Litt. (Lond.),

Lecturer in New Testament Criticism and Exegesis, in the University of Manchester.

THE present paper is based upon one which was read at the National Federation of Free Church Councils, meeting at Manchester in March, 1905. In adapting it, by request, to the more general audience provided by the readers of this *Review*, I shall, I hope, be free from any danger of uttering an unwelcome pæan in the ears of those who dissent from the Free Church position. Those Churchmen who opposed the advance which I have to chronicle have long ceased to make their protest heard ; and if I suggest that the time has come for the logical completion of this advance, I am not likely to offend, even if I do not convince, those to whom I appeal.

It will be difficult for some to realise that less than fifty years ago conscientious dissent from the theology or polity of the Established Church was an absolute bar to the privilege of a University education in this country. Since this bar affected all who for any reason could not honestly subscribe to the Thirty-nine Articles, it will be seen that the Free Churches, in fighting the battle of freedom, effected a transformation of English University life which has had the most momentous consequences. I am not of course forgetting that London University was giving degrees in every subject but Theology, and demanding a minimum of attainment decidedly higher than that with which Oxford and Cambridge were satisfied in their poll men. But since London only examined and did not teach, my statement remains true. I cannot better bring out the magnitude of the revolution which a single generation has witnessed than by describing the life experience of my father, the late Dr. W. F. Moulton, who was born only seventy years ago, the son and grandson of Wesleyan Ministers. From my uncle, Mr. Fletcher Moulton, M.P., I have received some striking facts as to the progress of the change which came too late for his elder brother to enjoy the privilege of a Cambridge training. Till 1857 no Dissenter could study there at all. For writing a pamphlet urging that this bar should be removed— without a word as to scholarships or fellowships—Bishop Thirlwall was accused by the then Master of Trinity of conduct unbecoming a gentleman! The Act of 1857 removed tests on entrance and on graduating B.A., but left the Colleges a free hand as to tests for scholarships. The son of a Methodist minister could not have gone to Cambridge without a scholarship—though, indeed, my father had the offer of a free education there, on condition that he should study for orders—and the concession, had it come earlier, would therefore have been useless to him.

Gradually the Colleges relaxed their tests, but not till 1871 were fellowships and the M.A. degree thrown open, and "compulsory chapel" stopped. Only five years later, when my father had just come to Cambridge to found the Leys School, the University conferred on him the honorary M.A.; and in the latest years of his life, I am told, there was a serious effort on the part of some prominent men to make him a Theological Professor. Thus the experience of a single lifetime illustrated at once the magnitude of an injustice almost incredible in our day and the rapidity with which the University of Cromwell and Milton strove to wipe out the memory of conditions so unworthy of her own glorious past.

It need not be shown at length that this purely stupid restriction, of which Oxford and Cambridge so rapidly became ashamed, was very little to the advantage of the Church it was meant to protect. A man with a conscience, like Mr. W. S. Aldis, the Senior Wrangler of 1861, might suffer life-long disability, but the pure indifferentist in religion was not likely to forgo a fellowship for the sake of a trifling scruple. There may be a few superficial observers still who lament the disappearance of clerical fellowships, compulsory chapels, and religious tests generally, but no enlightened friend of the Church of England could admit that she has anything to gain from that which puts an obvious premium on hypocrisy. There are, it is true, some results of the new conditions which might suggest a balance of loss. There is an extraordinary drop in the number of clerical dons in residence. During some of the years in which I was on the Special Board for Classics at Cambridge, the Anglican ministers on the Board did not outnumber the Wesleyan. A pessimistic writer in the *Church Quarterly Review* for October, 1904, lamented the decline of theological studies and earnest Churchmanship in Cambridge. I cannot dispute his facts, except that I can witness to the numbers and enthusiasm of the Evangelicals, with whom my own affinities naturally lay. But if anyone draws the inference that the survival of tests would have prevented what decline there has been, I fancy there are few Churchmen of any school who would be disposed to echo his opinion.

I am, however, concerned here with our own share in the effects of the act of Mr. Gladstone's Government, which opened the old Universities to Free Churchmen. Twenty years' residence in Cambridge will naturally prompt me to speak mainly of experience gained there, but I do not believe an Oxford man would have a materially different story to tell. As might be expected, the Nonconformists who have availed themselves of the new opportunities during the first generation have mostly been Honours men : relatively few Nonconformists come up at all if they could only aim at a poll degree. From the first the legislation of 1871 abundantly justified itself. In one year both senior and second Wrangler came from John Wesley's school for ministers' sons; in another, four or five Triposes were headed by Free Churchmen, one of whom had to himself the First Class in Theology. Professors' chairs are filled by earnest Free Churchmen like Dr. MacAlister and Dr. Sims Woodhead. It would be impossible to say how many Fellows would have been excluded by the survival of tests. I might name Professors Peake and Bennett, who were elected at Merton and St. John's respectively for Theology; and I am fain to add a second Cambridge name, that of my friend the Rev. F. W. Kellett, who won a First in three Triposes, and left Indian missions the poorer for his early death. In sixteen years five of Dr. Moulton's pupils at The Leys—not all of them Free Churchmen—were elected to Fellowships at a single Cambridge College (King's). And so I might go on, were it necessary to prove what University teachers most heartily acknowledge. A college tutor, a clergyman, spoke the other day of Nonconformists as the steadiest and best pupils he had ; and in a memorable debate at Oxford last year Professor Bigg described the Mansfield College men as the best prepared of those who entered the theological schools. Nor is it only from the intellectual standpoint that the University welcomes the new element. Coming as they do mostly from homes where religious earnestness has cultivated a high standard of conduct, there must be an unusually large proportion among them of high-toned men ; and the stimulus of honourable poverty which affects so many of them, secures the eager pursuit of the studies for which the University exists. From every point of view the University has gained immensely by the removal of an injustice which the veriest bigot would not dream of reimposing now.

I have not yet referred to the one field in which tests still survive. But before dealing with this part of my subject, I must briefly allude to one very serious corollary of what I have been describing. There is one profession which a large number of these able and sincere Free Churchmen would naturally enter if they found the door really open. But while University education is free from tests, and primary education will certainly be free in a short time, secondary education still interposes barriers which forbid conscientious Free Churchmen from choosing it as their career. I remember a case in which a minister's son, who had palpably lost all interest in religion, secured a mastership at an advanced Anglican school. But a really religious man, to whom the tests mean something, must expect to find nearly every one of the old public schools closed against him. And if he enters the profession in spite of this, and starts with a mastership at Mill Hill or The Leys, he must find by experience that promotion is not to be won by merit alone. There may be no statutory limitation, but sincere religious convictions are found time after time to determine the votes of governors in favour of a rival candidate for a headmastership. The new High Master of the Man. chester Grammar School is the brilliant exception which proves an only too obvious rule. I have no panacea to offer for an evil which many Churchmen will deplore as sincerely as I do; but I feel that the reform will probably start with the Universities, which, in any case, will have a commanding voice in future reforms of our public school system. The spread of enlightenment and toleration has been so remarkable. in Oxford and Cambridge within the limits of a single generation that I confidently hope for the growth of a better spirit through influences radiating from them.

I turn then to Theology, the subject in which the abolition of tests has hitherto proved impracticable at Oxford and Cambridge. It will be remembered that at Oxford the non-resident vote has at least twice defeated reform in respect of theological examinerships. Years ago an invasion of outsiders reversed the tolerably harmless nomination of the Rev. R. F. Horton to examine in Scripture History, or some like subject, in Responsions! And in 1904, when the best teachers in the faculty were agreed in recommending that examinerships in Theology should no longer be restricted to clergymen, the proposal was rejected, after a bitter debate, by the votes of those who could not pretend to represent the working University. The restriction has never existed at Cambridge, and it is quite conceivable that at both Universities the resident vote might any day go in favour of the abolition of tests for theological degrees and professorships. The day of this reform will probably be hastened by the experience of younger Universities. The University of Wales, less than ten years ago, took the first step towards the removal of the crying scandal by which the most learned scholar could not take a B.D. degree in England or Wales unless he were a clergyman of the Established Church. The reconstituted University of London followed suit, and then the Manchester University. I have been connected with the growth of the Manchester faculty from the first, and can chronicle some very instructive experiences. It was confidently predicted that the *odium theologicum* would wreck us before we were clear of port. Nothing could have been more completely falsified. The Dean of the faculty is a Primitive Methodist layman (Prof. Peake), and Free Churchmen are in a decided majority among its members. But no party division enables me to make that statement. In all the delicate questions which abound in the first stages of the building up of a new institution, there has never been a single difference of opinion upon Church lines. It has in fact proved not only possible but easy to treat Theology like other sciences, and establish tests for knowledge alone. Surely the older Universities will learn this ere long? It cannot be to the credit of Theology that men of European reputation like Dr. Fairbairn and Dr. Rendel Harris should be debarred from theological chairs, and even theological degrees, because they are not Anglicans, and Dr. M. R. James and Mr. F. C. Burkitt because they are not clergymen. (That one chair at Cambridge, if I mistake not, is technically free, hardly affects my argument, for the whole system needs changing before the electors can be expected to call up courage to avail themselves of their liberty.) The survival of tests has probably a great deal to do with the unsatisfactory condition of Theology at Oxford and Cambridge. The *Journal of Theological Studies*, the official organ of the faculties in the two Universities, is surely less occupied with really live questions of thought and practice than any journal ever seen. Well may the *Church Quarterly* Reviewer complain of Cambridge

Theology as out of touch with practical life! Christian laymen ask for a lead from those who should be best equipped for defending the faith against present-day attacks, and they get antiquarian learning, mediæval texts, and technical lore generally, which they can neither understand nor even wish to unravel. Make the study less one-sided, less professional, less tied up to one set of opinions, and it cannot but become more practical, and a better training for those whose life-work will be the defence and advancement of Christian teaching. As it is—and I speak as one who tried and deliberately abandoned it— the Theological Tripos at Cambridge is not by any means the best course for men who are entering the ministry; they will get a wider and more truly educative training in courses which demand more thought and less "cram."

But I had a yet wider object in view when I asked the Free Church delegates to consider their relations to the old Universities, and to cultivate more and more assiduously the opportunities afforded by the open door at these great centres of learning. I see here a key to the central problem of English Christianity. This *Review* is not the place in which to discuss the relations of Church and State, or the reasons why Free Churchmen desire the unity and not the corporate union of those who profess the Christian creed. But all its readers will sympathise with any effort to bring earnest thinking men together, without sacrifice of principle, for the common good of all. Disestablishment on the one side, the reimposition of tests on the other, would I believe almost equally exacerbate—at any rate at first—the evils which make English Christianity a sight of sorrow to its truest friends. Must earnest followers of the truth be for ever divided into hostile camps, or at best treat one another with tolerant aloofness? Must mere fashion, social prejudice, or professional advancement count among the motives which determine the choice of a Church among young people with no convictions of their own—unwelcome recruits surely to sincere men on either side? Must we see continued that deplorable incapacity of Established and Free Churchmen to understand one another, to enter sympathetically into the first principles of religion as it appeals to the other side? Can any but the enemies of religion take pleasure in such strife as we still see raging around the problem of elementary schools? The mending of all this is no matter of legislation. Only free intercourse will remove the evil. Till the present generation social and religious forces alike have kept "Church" and "Dissent" in rigidly separated worlds. It is almost comical to see the surprise with which well-bred persons will often make the discovery that a "Dissenter" may be a scholar and a gentleman. In the Universities, more than in any other centre of English life, the discovery has become a commonplace. I could cite innumerable proofs of the mutual respect and tolera-tion which has grown up in the free meeting-grounds of Oxford and Cambridge since the abolition of tests. My father's experience during the twenty years of Bible Revision, and in long association with intimate Cambridge friends like Lightfoot, Westcott, and Hort, would supply abundant evidence for the older generation, and I could add testimony in plenty for my own. But it is naturally the younger men who will show the new influences most powerfully. I believe the abolition of tests has already led the Universities into the van of a movement which will bring together on terms of mutual forbearance and agreement serious men of all schools of thought. Controversy, of course, will go on: it must go on while men continue to care for the things they believe. But nine-tenths of the bitterness of controversy arises from our fighting men whom we only know in print: once create a personal acquaintance between the parties, and the sting of it is withdrawn. As one who in a long experience of the new conditions has seen this approximation markedly growing in a centre of the best intellectual life in England, I plead for the completion of an emancipating policy which has had the happiest results. We expect the old Universities to lead the nation's intellectual and spiritual progress—for what else do they exist that is comparable with this supreme duty? If from them comes forth the establishment of a new era of universal tolerance—the last and hardest virtue that the human mind will learn—it will indeed be the greatest of their services to the country which cherishes with pride the memories of their long and glorious history.

The Study of Local History.

BY

RAMSAY MUIR, M.A. (Liverpool and Oxon.).

*Andrew Geddes Lecturer in Modern History in the University
of Liverpool.*

———

LOCAL history used to be despised—is still despised by
many people. It has been left mainly in the hands of
that type of antiquary whose main preoccupation is to
determine the precise position of the parish pump in 1371,
and in whose eyes any fact is quite as important as any
other fact. The books that these gentlemen have produced—the innumerable parish histories and borough
histories and county histories—are in many cases very
careful and accurate, but in many cases also desperately
dull. They are not narratives, they are disorderly collections of unrelated facts. They are bought by a limited
number of people for reasons of local patriotism, and lie
on their shelves unread. They are sometimes ransacked
by general historians in search of 'local colour.' But
they have done next to nothing to stimulate interest in
the story they so confusedly tell. I imagine there is
scarcely a town or a parish in England where even the
cultivated classes (leaving out the antiquaries themselves)
have any intelligent conception of the story of their
district.

But a change is coming about in the treatment of local history, a change which is due to our changing conceptions of the methods and objects of general history. Now that we have realised that it is the business of the historian, not to confine himself to the rise and fall of dynasties and the marchings of armies, but to tell the life-story of a nation, we are driven to seek a more intimate contact with the actual life of the people than general chronicles or state-papers can give us. It is from local history that this contact can best be obtained. And the most modern school of historians of the Middle Age, led by Mr. Maitland, Mr. Round and Miss Bateson, have taught us that it is from an intimate knowledge of the fortunes of a locality or localities that the great national developments can be most effectively approached. Mr. Maitland bases his study of the mediæval borough upon an intimate knowledge of his own borough of Cambridge; Mr. Round sheds light upon national history from the genealogies of families, or checks the bold generalisations of earlier scholars by detailed studies of the varying and complex conditions shown by Domesday in different parts of the country. Our whole view of national history in the Middle Age is being revolutionised by the results achieved by historians who base themselves upon the actual development of actual parishes or shires. On the other hand, our whole conception of the way in which the history of a locality can be and ought to be treated is being transformed, now that trained historical scholars are bringing their knowledge to bear upon the subject. In short, it is becoming clear that in future national history will have to be written by local historians, and local history by general historians. It would not be a bad law which should lay it down that no historical work should be published by any scholar who had not previously done some work in local history.

It is in the period of the Middle Ages, and for the vexed questions of burghal and manorial organisation, that the illumination of national by local history has been hitherto most marked. But there is even more to be gained in the modern age. We are far from understanding that portentous revolution of the whole social fabric which England has undergone since the middle of the eighteenth century. It is a theme of epical magnitude, and no historian has yet been found bold enough to deal with it as a whole. Nor will any handling of this magnificent theme be satisfactory until it is illumined by an intelligent study of local history. The rise of the the great towns, and the totally new ideas and conditions of life which they imposed, cannot be made intelligible until we have one or two careful studies of the rise of individual towns ; how and why they came into existence, whence they drew their swollen populations ; how they provided for them when they came ; how the old system of burghal government broke down under the strain of the new conditions, and what evils followed from this ; how the new populations gradually learned to organise themselves for religious, political, or economic purposes ; what was the effect of the vast industrial developments of these places upon their intellectual and æsthetic and philanthropic development : these, and a hundred other

questions of equal import, have to be answered from a
detailed study of records in several cities before we shall
begin to understand that vast change, of which the
creation of large towns is only one part. The study, on
these broad lines, of the history of any great modern city,
is surely as worthy a subject as any historian could
desire. It is certain that there can be no historical work
which will do greater public service.

For, quite apart from the illumination which it can
give to national history, local history deserves to be
taken more seriously for other reasons also. We are
accustomed to commend the study of history on the
ground that it fosters a reasonable patriotism. But
there is a patriotism of the city as well as a patriotism
of the state ; and until civic patriotism has been fanned
into a steady glow, we can scarcely hope for any great
result in the struggle for melioration in these vast hives.
Not until a man's city has become a personality to him
will he be ready to think, dream and work for it ; and it
is from an intelligible picture of its past development
that he will most easily obtain a vivid and understanding
knowledge of its present condition. Every city, every
county, therefore, should have a clear popular story of
itself, so written that the ordinary citizen would be able
to read it with pleasure, and to derive from it some
connected and logical ideas. That cannot be said of
the majority of existing local histories. I would go
further and say that there should be school-books on
local history in every school. By the use of local history
in schools we may in the first place hope most easily to

cultivate the historical imagination of children, because the deeds of old forgotten fellow-townsmen in familiar places that can be recognised and visited, are far more easily presented to the imagination than the vague doings of unrealized kings and statesmen. But in the second place we may certainly hope by this means to lay, in the schools, where it can best be laid, the foundations of a reasonable civic patriotism.

But it is not possible to interest either the adult citizen or the child until there have been provided reasonably good books for the purpose, and scarcely any such books exist. They must be clear, vivid, pictorial, with the narrative swing in them. The writers of them must be content to avoid those voluminous quotations of unexplained documents which so conveniently fill up the pages of the ordinary local history; they must escape the temptation to show their expertness in arguing obscure and knotty points, such as the area of the burgage or the survival of heriot in free boroughs. They must realize that they have simply got to tell a straightforward story, and that if it is properly told, their story should be of an enthralling interest.

But these popular books for the use of the citizen, these text-books and reading books for the use of the child, cannot be produced until a vast deal of new work has been done, first in the collection of the abundant materials for local history, and secondly in their interpretation in the light of modern historical scholarship. It is seldom realised how enormous are the stores of material which have as yet been only partially explored. Some towns, which like Cardiff and Leicester have ample records of the proceedings of their own mediæval burghers, have already made known to the world the contents of their archive chests.   But even the most wealthy of these can be reinforced, and in less fortunate places their place can be partially supplied from a variety of sources :—from the national muniments, Pipe Rolls, Patent Rolls, Quo Warranto pleas, records of Assizes, and so forth ; from the Extents and *Inquisitiones post mortem* of the Middle Age ; from the archive-rooms of great territorial families, which usually contain great stores of almost unexplored material ; from the innumerable deeds of transfer of land which survive from a very early date in most parts of the country, either lying unused in library boxes, or stored in the offices of conveyancing lawyers.   And all these kinds of documents (as well as many more which I have not named) are capable of yielding to a patient and expert scrutiny very remarkable results.   Only their investigators must have a double qualification : first, they must know their district ; and, secondly, they must be trained historical scholars, instructed in the art of reading and interpreting documents, knowing the meaning of the technical terms and formulæ of the ages with which they deal, and knowing also, all that the general study of institutions and of social development is able to give them by way of illumination in the study of their sources.   For the modern period, the difficulties are in some ways even greater than for the mediæval period, and so also the need for workers who are trained historical

students.   Here the difficulty arises, not from the paucity
of material, and the necessity of squeezing out of every
scattered reference the last drop of meaning, but from
the opposite defect of over-abundant material.   It is not
possible to read everything, and the student is apt to be
overwhelmed by the volume and particularity of his
information.   Hence it has come about that existing
local histories, which have dealt with the eighteenth and
nineteenth centuries, have become, in these periods,
hopelessly confused and chaotic, without thread or
sequence ; so that instead of showing a culmination of
interest. as marking the conclusion of the long, slow
development of the early ages and their link with ourselves, the story of these modern ages in works on local
history is indescribably dreary, and generally impossible
to read.

There lies before us, then, a vast and only half-
explored field, which can only be dealt with by combined
and systematic effort.   How is that effort to be organised?
Who is to undertake it?   One great and heroic attempt
is now being made by the projectors of the Victoria
County Histories.   Conceived on a very ample scale,
carried out on a uniform and well-devised plan, entrusted
to an army of scholars in all parts of the country, under
the general direction of well-qualified chiefs, the Victoria
County Histories mark an immense advance upon anything that has yet been done, and as a national enterprise
the scheme deserves to rank with, if not above, the
Dictionary of National Biography or the Cambridge
Modern History.   But great and valuable as the enter-

prise is, it does not wholly meet the need. In the first place, the scheme will necessarily do inadequate justice to the modern age, which is, for the great cities at any rate, vastly the most important and instructive. In the second place, not even the projectors of the Victoria County Histories have dared to contemplate an absolutely exhaustive treatment of the vast accumulated stores of material. Nor have they proposed (it is not a part of their object) any means for the proper preservation and treatment of local archives, which are at present in most parts of the country scandalously neglected. A Royal Commission has sat on the subject, and has directed attention to the need of systematic action for this purpose, and discussed several proposals for meeting it: But as yet nothing has been done.

Here, then, is a vast task lying waiting to be performed : the collection, preservation, and interpretation of all the documents bearing upon local history in all parts of the country; the sifting and arranging of them so that they may be easily available for students; the publication in a convenient form, with adequate discussion and elucidation, of the more important of them ; and finally (what is after all the main object of the whole enterprise) the statement of the results attained by all this labour in such a form as to be interesting and intelligible to the ordinary citizen, and to help in stimulating his local pride and patriotism. Every day that is wasted makes the satisfactory achievement of this great enterprise more difficult, because every day the wastage, through neglect and ignorance, of material goes on. For example, old

books of minutes of the early trade unions, which are full
of invaluable evidence not only for the extremely important trade-union movement, but also for social conditions in the revolutionary age at the opening of the
nineteenth century, are being constantly destroyed by
trade union officials, because to them they are of no
further use, and because they cannot solve the difficulties
of storage.   Much material of this kind is irretrievably
lost.   In the same way, such valuable documents as
parish registers are often so carelessly guarded or so
little valued by their guardians that they, too, are gradually
disappearing.   No country is so wealthy as England in
the material for local and social history ; but our wealth
will vanish unless we find some means of banking it.

Who is to undertake this immense and fruitful labour ?
Twenty years ago the problem would have seemed
incapable of a really satisfactory solution.   It would be
no advantage to store all these documents in London,
away from the districts with which they deal, and the
scholars who are most capable of handling them.   On
the other hand, any scheme for instituting in every
county a Record or Archive-house suffers from the
disadvantages first that it would be exceedingly costly,
and secondly that it would not ensure the handling of
the documents there stored by the scholars who were
capable of dealing with them.   But to the readers of
this *Review* there should be no difficulty in finding a
solution.   England is rapidly being dotted over by a
series of provincial Universities ; and among the innumerable services which these institutions will be able to

perform, not the least may be that of solving the problem of dealing with local archives. I have used the term "provincial Universities;" it is a term that to some ears carries a note of contempt. It should rather be welcomed proudly by the new seats of learning; for its real meaning is that they are to be (they are already very rapidly becoming) the foci of all the intellectual interests of the wide *provinces* which they serve. That is the reason of their existence. And in carrying out that aim, the handling of the materials for the local history of their provinces must certainly be one of their earliest attempts.

I should like to see in every provincial University a great archive-room, where all the public archives of the district would be stored, and where private families possessing documents of value would either deposit them on permanent loan, or at least temporarily lend them so that they might be copied. Over every such archive-room should preside a historical scholar of distinction, who should be trained in palæography and diplomatics, and an expert in all questions affecting the preservation . and interpretation of documents. He should be also a teacher of the University. To him would come post-graduate students, some of them men who were devoting themselves to historical research, some of them graduates of the University engaged in teaching or other occupa-tions, but glad to be given a "hobby," and to take a share in a great co-operative scholarly enterprise. He would first train them to handle the documents, then set them defined pieces of work—groups of deeds to calendar or edit for subsequent publication, or the like. To him would also come the best of the students in the honours school of history, to get from him (what the provincial Universities can never give so well in any other way) a lesson in the practical art of historical criticism ; the absence of which from the curricula of most English schools of history forms their gravest defect.

This may seem a large and over-ambitious scheme. It is, however, more economical, and vastly more efficient than any other which has been proposed, for it not only secures the proper handling of the documents, but it also provides a means of making use of them for historical purposes. And it is not wholly untried. In Liverpool there has been working for some four years a school of local history, in which a group of some half-dozen graduates meets weekly to enjoy the voluntary instruction of two scholars in palæography, and to co-operate in transcribing, translating, and editing groups of documents borrowed for the purpose. The work of this school, carried on quietly and without advertisement, has already progressed so far that it is now announcing the proximate publication of an elaborate series of volumes, each consisting of a collection of documents bearing upon some particular aspect of local history, prefaced by a long and full introduction, and fully supplied with indices and critical apparatus. It remains only to provide an archive-room to serve as the centre of this promising experiment; and there is reason to believe that this will be provided at an early date. It is hoped, also, that before very long one result of the enterprise will be the publication of a popular history of the city, in a coherent and connected narrative, capable of interesting the ordinary man of affairs. Clearly this can be no more than a preliminary sketch, for a vast amount of spade-work must be done before a definite history is possible. But at any rate the Liverpool School, while it refuses to palter with the most rigid ideals of scholarship in its immediate work, is penetrated by the belief that the ultimate value of that work will be tested largely by its success in stimulating civic patriotism, and in showing to the community the magnitude of the service which can be rendered to it as well by the humane studies as by the more utilitarian subjects now in such high favour.

THE LATE PROFESSOR S. D. F. SALMOND, D.D.

Principal of the United Free Church College,
Aberdeen

(Reproduced from a photo by kind permission of the
Editors of "Alma Mater")

Memorial Notices.

"Quique sui memores alios fecere merendo."

THE REV. PROFESSOR S. D. F. SALMOND, M.A., D.D.

Principal of the United Free Church College, Aberdeen.

By the death of Principal Salmond on the 20th of April, the theological world has lost one of its most eminent men, and Scottish academical life one of its most characteristic products. It has been the glory of the Scottish Universities that their advantages were open to the poorest in the land, and that their highest prizes were within the reach of the men of brains, irrespective of their rank in life. Stewart Salmond, like many another whose fame is world-wide, had little heritage save his ability and his good home. He was born in Aberdeen in 1838, and was a pupil at the Grammar School when the influence of Melvin was yet alive. Here he gave evidence of his ability, and, on entering the University, he passed through the Arts course with great distinction, especially in Classics. For three years after graduation he acted as assistant to the Professor of Greek. In the Divinity College of the Free Church, to which he transferred himself, he gave great attention to Hebrew, and by spending two summer semesters at Erlangen he laid the foundation of his splendid knowledge of German theology, and became intimate with Delitzsch, with Ebrard, and with Thomasius.

In 1865, he was appointed to the quiet country charge of Barry, near Dundee, and during the eleven years of his ministry there he found time to do much scholarly work. For the Anti-Nicene Library he translated Hippolytus, Caius, Julius Africanus, Alexander of Jerusalem, and others. To the edition of Augustine's works, then being brought out under Dr. Marcus Dods, he gave valuable help. By his contributions to theological magazines, it came to be realised in Scotland that in Stewart Salmond there was a man, not only of most competent scholarship, but of deep spiritual insight. In 1870, he was a candidate for the Hebrew Chair in the Free Church College, in Aberdeen, but in the contest for this he was beaten by one of the most remarkable men of our time, William Robertson Smith. In 1876, he was appointed to the Chair of Systematic Theology in the Aberdeen College, and here he found his life's work.

As a professor, the characteristic of his teaching was its thoroughness. Students realised at once that Salmond had been over the whole field in his own subject, and that he could have taught with almost equal power any other subject in the curriculum. He had not the aloofness from the ordinary interests of human life that made A. B. Davidson almost a prophet to those who came under his spell ; nor had he the fire that causes George Adam Smith to create preachers of the New Testament, while he is aiming only at the exposition of the Old; but he had that entire command of his material which is the first thing students recognise and the last thing they will dispense with. Perhaps it was only when men entered the active work of the ministry that they realised how much Salmond had done for them, His great book, which bids fair to become a classic, on " The Christian Doctrine of Immortality," is entirely characteristic of the man. Nothing has been neglected; the arrangement of the material is the reflex of a mind essentially systematic, its analysis is unsparingly true, and there is throughout a balance of judgement, arising from the complete acquaintance with all that has been written on the subject, that makes us long sometimes for a rash generalisation and a conclusion that can be directly challenged.

The Critical Review was his conception, and was always very largely his handiwork. Along with Driver and Briggs he was editor of the series of International Critical Commentaries in which such remarkable books as Moore's " Judges," Driver's " Deuteronomy," and Sanday and Headlam's " Romans " have appeared. He wrote the commentary on Ephesians in the Expositor's Greek Testament, while, with the hand of death upon him, he put together and arranged in due form the material that A. B. Davidson had left behind him for his " Theology of the Old Testament."

Such a record of arduous work might lead those unacquainted with him to imagine that Salmond must, of necessity, have been a scholarly recluse. Nothing could be further from the truth. He was, in the very best sense of the term, a public man.   When School Boards were yet on their trial, he threw himself into the work of the Aberdeen Board.   For fifteen years he was a member of it, and for six years he was chairman.   He was a most valued member of the University Court in Aberdeen. He was deeply immersed in the life and work of the Church to which he belonged.   The recent judgment of the House of Lords, by which the whole property of the United Free Church, amounting in value to some eight or ten millions of pounds, has been handed over to twenty-seven obscurantist ministers and to a handful of people representing one or two per cent of the total membership, called out in Salmond a passionate indignation and a power of oratory that even his most intimate friends had never credited him with.   Strangely enough, his death took place the day before the issuing of the Report of the Royal Commission appointed to consider the situation.

One prominent feature of Salmond's character was his fine faculty of friendship.   He did not wear his heart on his sleeve.   With this quiet, unimpassioned man no one ever took liberties, but when he gave his confidence he remained always the friend.   In the controversy that arose over the writings of his colleague, Robertson Smith, Salmond took a notable part,   He knew the ground as few men in the country knew it, and, with all his caution in judgment, he saw that in the broad lines of his work, Robertson Smith was right.   The whole-hearted support Robertson Smith received from a colleague so able and respected as Salmond, made the Church understand at once, that however upsetting the Higher Criticism might seem to be, it was not some wild heresy that could be laughed or scolded out of existence, but was a movement commanding the general approval of those who were most able to deal with the questions raised. Salmond's house in Aberdeen was the resort of many a famous scholar, and his home life was singularly happy and beautiful. His knowledge of his students was intimate and tender. With great joy he rejoiced over the student of promise, guided his reading, and followed him with almost a father's care in his subsequent career.

By the death of Principal Salmond, we have lost a representative man. The strength of Scottish theology lies not so much in its exact classical scholarship as in its strong philosophical thought. Scotland does not produce Lightfoots and Westcotts. The classical training has not been high enough. The classical tradition of the best of the English Public Schools, and of Oxford and Cam-bridge is unknown amongst us. But one has only to run over the names of some of our best known men to see where the strength of Scottish theology does lie. Bruce, Salmond, Flint, Fairbairn, Dods, Iverach, Denny, these men are not textual critics. Their power lies in their philosophy. The results of the student of the text and of the student of history are before them, and their question always is "Granted this, what then?" As an exact scholar, Salmond had no mean place. The amount of his learning was extraordinary; but his force lay in the native element, his strong philosophical thought. As student and as professor, Salmond both followed the type and set it. R. BRUCE TAYLOR.

JOSEPH EVERETT DUTTON, M.B., CH.B. (VICT.), D.P.H.

Walter Myers Fellow of the University of Liverpool (School of Tropical Medicine).

DR. DUTTON was educated at the King's School in Chester and at the University College, Liverpool, where he graduated M.B., Ch.B., with Honours, in 1897. During 1897 he held the George Holt Fellowship in Pathology, and in the following year was House Physician and House Surgeon to the Royal Infirmary, Liverpool. In 1899 he was House Surgeon to the Shaw Street Hospital, Liverpool, and studied at the School of Tropical Medicine.

On March 21st, 1900, Dr. Dutton sailed from Liverpool with Drs. Annett and Elliot on an expedition to Nigeria, returning on October 28th, 1900. The expedition published on their return a valuable report on the sanitary measures necessary in that region, and the most complete account of Filariasis yet written. During 1901 Dr. Dutton went to Bathurst in British Gambia, where he made a brilliant discovery which led to the discovery of the cause of sleeping sickness. He also made a careful survey of the district, and embodied his investigations in a report on the sanitary measures necessary to improve the health of the Colony. His discovery of human trypanosomiasis and his subsequent work on the subject have given him a European reputation. In 1902 Dr. Dutton was appointed Walter Myers Fellow. Dr. Walter Myers was a brilliant investigator, who died in January, 1901, aged 29, of yellow fever contracted while studying that disease at Para on the Amazon. The fellowship was founded to perpetuate his memory and to continue the work to which he gave his life.

In 1902, at the request of the French Government,

Drs. Dutton and Todd travelled through Senegambia, and presented a report to the authorities dealing with the public health of the Colony.

In September, 1903, Dr. Dutton, accompanied by Drs. Christy and Todd, went on his last expedition to the Congo Free State, at the request of His Majesty King Leopold. While there the members of the expedition published "progress reports" showing the distribution of sleeping sickness and trypanosomiasis and the relation between the two. They also made important discoveries in relation to tick fever, which have not yet been published. In June, 1904, the members of the expedition were recalled in order to complete their reports and to enjoy a very necessary rest, but with a courage and heroism which must be at once admired and deplored Drs. Dutton and Todd refused to leave their work. They were both subsequently attacked by tick fever, from which however they recovered. But Dr. Dutton was left enfeebled by disease, hardships and privations, and died on February 27th, 1905. It is a sad consolation for his untimely end to hear that his funeral was accompanied by every mark of respect and affection that could be paid to his memory by the natives and authorities of the Congo Free State.

The death of this martyr of science is a loss to the whole world. During the period of not quite five years, during which he had been investigating tropical diseases, he had made for himself a reputation throughout the scientific world. Koch, in Berlin, in an address recently delivered, spoke of Dr. Dutton as an example to be admired and imitated. Laveran, in France, refers to him with respect as " le savant Anglais Dutton."

Personally, he endeared himself to all who knew him. He was slightly built and somewhat pale ; he possessed charming manners and an inexhaustible cheerfulness and and vivacity. His modest and unassuming demeanour gave no hint of the distinction he had won.

The world has need of such men, but yet seems never

able to understand them. We may ask why should a man of such brilliant attainments give up the certain prospect of a life of ease and comfort at home and go out into the wilderness? But the risks and dangers which his chosen work involved did not stop Dr. Dutton from pursuing it, nor will it stop others from following in his steps. The same spirit that drove Sir Galahad into the wilds to seek the Holy Grael must surely animate such men as Myers and Dutton. And others will follow and carry on the work in a climate where no single moment of the day is comfortable, where the average man finds every movement and thought an effort, where the night brings no sleep and every dawn may be the last. In such a climate they will work as few men work at home, conducting difficult and laborious researches, surrounded by savages, and often without proper food or clothing. There is no reward we can give them. We might perhaps use their labours and reward ourselves by improving the health of these great colonies, but as a rule we don't believe in them. We can only build their tombs.

H. H. CLARKE.

■:ᴠNIVᴇᴀꜱITY

RENNES

POITTERS

IS

NANCY

DIJON BES

ƆN

CLER NT

LYON

GRENOB

ƆVSE MO

From a Sketch Map) *(by Miss M. D. Jones*

THE UNIVERSITIES OF FRANCE

Foreign University News.

FRANCE

Communicated by M. LUDOVIC FICHOU, *Secretaire général du Bureau des Renseignements de l'Université de Paris* . . . . *May.*

University News and Notes.

The English doctors who arrived on May 9th were received at the Sorbonne by the University Council and by the "Societé des Amis de l'Université." During the reception cordial speeches were delivered by M. Liard, the Rector of the University; Professor Lyon Caen, Secretary of the "Societé des Amis de l'Université;" Professor Bouchard, President of the French Committee; Sir William Broadbent, President of the English deputation; Professor Clifford Albutt, of the University of Cambridge; and by M. Ogilvie, Director of the French Hospital in London.

On the following day members of the party visited the principal hospitals of Paris and the Medical School at the University. In the evening a reception was held in the Hotel de Ville, and afterwards Professor Bouchard held a reception in the Washington Hall. On May 11th a visit was paid to Chantilly, and in the evening the visitors attended a Soirée at the Automobile Club. On Saturday, May 12th, the deputation visited the English Hospital and the Pasteur Institute, and the visit was concluded with a Banquet at the Grand Hotel.

The Library of the University of Paris has recently made a welcome innovation. It is proposed to publish every month a pamphlet giving a list of all the new books and papers in the Library, affixing to each the number or letter assigned to it in the catalogue. These pamphlets will be supplied to the readers, who will thus be kept constantly informed of all the newest books at their disposal.

By an order recently issued the salary of Professors of the first class in the Provincial Faculties of Law, Medicine, Arts and Science and in the Schools of Pharmacy has been fixed at 12,000 francs.

By the terms of Article 65 of the Budget of 1905 the right of access possessed by all Government officials to their papers is stated as follows:—" All civil and military servants, all employées and workpeople of public institutions have the right of personal and private access to all notes, descriptive papers and all other documents composing their ' dossier ' either before being subjected to disciplinary measures or before losing office or seniority." The effect of this order is that all " informing " will be henceforth excluded from the University.

The Twenty-first Banquet of the General Association of Paris Students was held recently, under the presidency of M. Paul Hervieu, of the French Academy. M. Hervieu, in the course of an interesting speech, declared that the progress of civilisation is characterised by its slow movement. The interplay of conservative and reformative forces holds the world almost stable in equilibrium, or produces at most an almost imperceptible advance.

Many professors and students were present at the banquet. M. Liard, Rector of the University ; M. Bayet, Director of Secondary Education ; Maître Bourdillon, President of the Order of French Advocates ; M. d'Estournelles de Constant, Senator ; M. Hussaye, of the French Academy, were also present.

Financial Statement, 1905.

The following figures have been taken from the annual Financial Statement, showing expenditure and receipts for the year 1904–5 :— The General Budget gives a total of 3,623,053,765 francs, in which is included the sum of 237,014,806 francs for Public Instruction.

The following is a detailed list of the expenditure during the financial year 1904–5 :—

			Francs.
Article	1.	Salary of the Minister and Staff at the Central Administration	1,016,450
„	5.	Awards to Scientists and Literary Men	172,000
„	11.	University of Paris, Staff	3,724,725
„	12.	Provincial Universities, Staff	7,161,586
„	14.	Bursaries for Higher Education, Paris	124,000
„	14a.	„ „ „ Provinces..	256,000
	14b.	„ „ „ Various ...	104,000
„	42.	Staff of the Medical School	54,100
„	44.	Learned Societies	93,000
„	46.	Travels and Missions, Scientific and Literary	324,500
„	52.	National Library, Staff	445,000
„	53.	„ „ Maintenance	274,150
„	64.	National Schools, Boys	4,331,060
„	73.	„ „ Girls	1,214,000
„	90.	Secondary Education	3,254,846
„	91.	Bursaries for Secondary Education	714,800
„	92.	Salary of Staff for Elementary Schools	147,773,835
„	104.	Maintenance of School Buildings, Elementary	8,500,000
„	105.	„ „ „ Secondary..	2,293,500

University Extension.

The following noteworthy lectures have been given during the month :—

At the Université Populaire, Faubourg St. Antoine:

M. Vernes, Director of Education in the Ecole des Hautes Etudes, on " How History Ought to be Taught."

M. Jules Combarien, Professor in the Collège de France, on " Music and Social Work."

Dr. and Mme. Legendre, on " Life in China: The Chinese Temperament."

M. Paul Ghio, Professor in the Collège Libre des Sciences Sociales, on " Agricultural Progress in Italy."

M. Aubertin, Professor in the University of Neuchâtel, on " The Boring of the Simplon."

At the Fondation Universitaire de Belleville:

M. Maurice Alfassa, on " The Political Situation in England."

M. Albert Métin, on " The Labour Deputation to the United States and Canada."

At the Université Populaire " la Co-operation des Idees ":

M. P. Mille, Professor in the Ecole des Sciences Politiques, on " Is the White Race Superior ?"

M. L. Brunschwieg, Fellow of the University, on " The Conditions of Existence of Legislative Power."

Recent Scientific and Literary Research.

M. Chas. Schmidt, former pupil of the Faculty of Arts and of the Ecole des Chartes, Keeper of the Records at the National Record Office, has presented two theses for the Degree of Doctor ès Lettres, the first, entitled " The Grand Duchy of Berg, 1806—1813, a study of the French domination in Germany under Napoleon I."; and the second " The Reform of the Imperial University in 1811."

M. A. Francois has presented a thesis for the Degree of Doctorat de l'Université on the.following subject: " Purism, and the French Academy in the Eighteenth Century."

M. R. de Montessus de Ballore recently presented a thesis for the Degree of Doctor of Science and Mathematics, entitled "Algebraical Fractions."

The following theses have recently been received by the Faculty of Science:—From M. Ludovic Zoretti: 1st thesis, " Sur les fonctions analytiques uniformes qui possèdent un ensemble parfait discontinu de points singuliers;" 2nd thesis, " Deformation des milieux continus; equations de l'elasticité. From M. P. Stœnesco: 1st thesis, " Sur la propagation et l'extinction des ondes planes dans milieu homogéne et translucide, pourvu d'un plan de symétrie; 2nd thesis, " Théorie des mouvements tourbillonnaires."

Appointments.

A Laboratory for General and Experimental Embryology has recently been instituted. M. Loisel, Demonstrator in the Faculty of Science of the University of Paris, has been appointed to the post of Director of the Laboratory. Dr. Louis Hallion, Demonstrator in the Pathological Laboratory at the Ecole des Hautes Etudes, has been appointed Assistant Director.

By order of the Vice-Rector of the Academie de Paris, M. Fernbach, D.Sc., Demonstrator in the Faculty of Science of the University, has been appointed, until March, 1906, to the position of Director of the Lectures on Biological Chemistry (Industry of Metals, subsidised by the Pasteur Institute).

M. Lours-Camille Jullian, Professor of History in the Bordeaux University, has been appointed to the Chair of History and National Antiquities in the Collège de France.

M. Gourand, Doctor of Medicine, has been appointed for six months Chief Assistant in the Laboratory of Clinical Medicine (Hotel Dieu).

University Publications.

In the *Bulletin de la Societé Française de Philosophie:* "Mind and Matter." The article is written by M. Binet, in the discussion which follows MM. Bergson, Darlu, Lachelier, Pécant and Rauh take part.

The *Revue Pédagogique* has an interesting paper on "Recent Researches in Mental Fatigue," by M. Louis Boisso.

In the *Revue Générale des Sciences* "The Teaching of Natural Sciences as a means of Philosophical Education," is the subject of an interesting paper by M. F. Le Dantec.

In the *Revue Philosophique* papers on the following subjects of especial interest have recently appeared:—"The Indirect Morality of Art," by M. F. Paulletan; "The Antagonists of Taine," by M. Maldidier, Professor in the Lycée Janson de Sailly.

In the *Revue Internationale de l'Enseignements* M. Charles Langlois has an important paper entitled "Notes on Education in the United States."

Among recently published works may be mentioned:—

"Les Societés Co-opératives de Consommation," by M. Ch. Gide, Professor in the Faculty of Laws (published by Armand Colin, 5, Rue de Mézières, Paris).

"La Science Géologique," by M. L. de Launey, Chief Mining Engineer, professor in the Ecole Supérieure des Mines (Armand Colin).

"The Philosophy of Fichte; its relations to Contemporary Conscience," by Xavier Léon, Director of the *Revue de Metaphysique et de Morale* (Alcan, Boulevard St. Germain).

University Extension.

The Association to Promote the Higher Education of Working Men.

THE Association to Promote the Higher Education of Working Men, which was founded at Oxford on August 23rd, 1903, hopes to realise its intention, primarily, by means of the extension of University teaching. Its work is defined, in a recently issued circular, as "the adoption of existing means and the devising of fresh means by which working people of all degrees—even the most unskilled and ignorant—may be raised educationally, plane by plane, until they are able to take advantage of the teaching offered by the Universities. It is believed that this work can best be furthered by an associated effort of Trades Unions, Co-operative Societies, Working Men's Clubs, and University Extension Authorities. The basis of the constitution of the Association, therefore, is the joint action of representatives of the workers' organisation and of the Universities of the country."

It is significant of the sympathetic attitude adopted by the Universities that, upon the North-Western Sectional Committee of the Association, the Universities of Oxford, Cambridge, Leeds, Liverpool and Manchester are each represented. This Committee proposes to work "through the University Extension Authorities of the Universities on the one hand, and through local institutions and the local authorities on the other." Its policy will be:—

1. To encourage the co-ordination and correlation of educational work for working men.

2. To bring about, through local institutions and local authorities, continuity of lecturing in each district, and the formation of classes and reading circles to follow up the work done in the lectures.

3. To encourage lectures of an educational value as well as of an attractive type; for example, courses of an adequate length, which are not merely popular, on History, Industrial History, Economics,

and Literature, and to bring about the most suitable arrangement of courses in succession to one another.

It has quickly made its influence felt by the establishment of a strong branch at Rochdale, where a successful University Extension Centre has been at work in connection with the Oxford Delegacy. Local institutions, such as the Pioneers Co-operative Society, the Trades Council, P.S.A.'s, Sunday Classes, Field Clubs, etc., have entered into affiliation, thus ensuring at the outset a broad basis for continued University work. The general objects of the branch will be attained, it is hoped, by :—

> (a) Organising:
> > 1. University Extension and (if thought desirable) other Lectures.
> > 2. Reading Circles and Discussion Classes.
> > 3. Visits and excursions of an educational character.
>
> (b) By encouraging attendance at Evening Classes.
>
> (c) By making such suggestions to the various local educational bodies as, in the opinion of the Guild, may seem desirable.
>
> (d) By sending to its members in the autumn of each year a short calendar of the chief educational fixtures in the district for the ensuing winter.

Bristol University College and the Royal Albert Memorial College are represented upon the South-Western Committee, which defines its policy in terms somewhat similar to those adopted by the North-Western Committee. It hopes to enable the working men of the South-West "to take eventually full advantage of the systematised teaching provided in a University Extension Centre or College."

It is interesting to note the variety of interests represented upon these Committees, charged with the extension of University teaching : Universities, University Colleges, the Co-operative Union, Co-operative Educational Committees' Associations, Trades Councils, the South-Western Federation of Trade Unions, the Women's Co-operative Guild, the National Union of Teachers, Ruskin Hall, and the Parliamentary Committee of the Trades Union Congress (provisionally). This justifies the official claims of both Committees that they are federations of the institutions through which they propose to work.

The local Association at Reading has accomplished useful work during the session just closed. Its educational policy has to a great extent been directed by the Principal of the University College, together with the Secretary of the Local Education Authority, and worked out by representatives of eleven different organisations of the town. An attempt will be made to establish classes in connection with lectures during the coming season.

In the near future the outlying districts of the Metropolis will begin to reveal an attitude of expectancy towards the University of London. Ilford, a rapidly growing township of 60,000 inhabitants, cherishes a local ambition that it may one day be a University outpost. To this end it has established a local Association, which has set itself to secure a fortnightly course of University Lectures on the English novel, to secure recruits by means of popular lectures upon aspects of Literature, and to establish a class for advanced students under the University. A Literature course has been adopted in view of the fact that the town has recently decided to establish a Free Library.

The recently issued Report of the Education Committee of the Co-operative Union indicates work which, if properly developed, will help to bring workpeople into connection with the Universities to a marked extent. Every year the Committee sends several of its most successful students to the University Extension Summer meeting. Almost without exception these students return to their respective localities charged with enthusiasm for liberal education. In looking down the list of successful teachers in the Co-operative Movement, one is struck by the number of them who are ardent extensionists. This justifies the remark of Mr. J. A. Dale, in the April *St. George*, when he said " that the influence of University Extension upon the teachers of the working classes is considerable." It is, moreover, not generally known that the Co-operative Movement has two Scholarships (tenable at Oriel College, Oxford) to offer to its young men. Some eight or ten Co-operative scholars have graduated. In very many towns the University Extension lectures are financially supported, and in some cases are entirely managed, by the Co-operative Societies. These latter are not the least successful of the Centres.

A. M.

Inter-Universities Students' Congress.

THE first British Inter-Universities Students' Congress is being held in London this year, and the London University Students' Representative Council is now actively engaged in making the necessary arrangements. The Students' Representative Organisations of almost every University in the United Kingdom have promised to send delegates. The meetings of the Congress will be held on the mornings of June 28th, 29th, 30th, and July 1st. Of the many interesting subjects that have been chosen for discussion may be mentioned:—

1. The question of the establishment of a system of mutual recognition among the Universities, by means of which work done at any one University may count towards a Degree at any other University.

2. The position of Women in Universities; and the advisability of establishing a separate University for Women.

3. The educational value of mixed Arts and Science Degrees.

4. The encouragement of physical training among students by the educational authorities.

5. The propriety of Universities granting Degrees as a source of revenue.

6. The advisability of having a minimum age for obtaining Degrees.

F

7. The possibility of forming an Inter-Universities Appointments Board to facilitate the obtaining of appointments by University students.

8. Universities and the Training of Teachers.

9. The work of Municipal Educational Institutions.

10. The claims of the Universities for State Support.

It is hoped that many of the delegates will arrive on Tuesday, 27th inst., in time to attend the annual Sports of University College. On the afternoon of June 29th, the members of the Congress will be invited to hear the Foundation Oration at University College, which will be delivered this year by Dr. A. B. N. Kennedy, F.R.S.

Arrangements have been made for the women members of the Congress to reside at Bedford College during their visit.

Among the social functions already arranged we may mention the Conversazione, which is to be given in honour of the Congress in the University buildings, South Kensington, by the Chancellor, the Vice-Chancellor, the Principal, and the Senate of the University. A Smoking Concert will be held on the evening of June 29th, when the women delegates will be entertained by the Women's Union Society of University College. A Garden Party at the Royal Holloway College, Englefield Green, Surrey, is being arranged, and a Conversazione is to be given on Wednesday, June 28th, at University College by the President, Council, Teaching Staff and Union Society of the College.

Several other important arrangements are pending which, it is hoped, will add very considerably to the interest and importance of the Congress.

The Universities.

ABERDEEN.

University News and Notes.

At a meeting of the Court of the Aberdeen University, held on May 9th, a resolution was adopted expressing the Court's sense of the loss it had sustained by the death of Principal Salmond, and alluding to his ability as a scholar and theological writer, his long and faithful service to the cause of education, and his unflagging interest in his alma mater.

The Court acquiesced in the nomination by the Senatus of Professors Harrower and Baillie as representatives of the University to co-operate with St. Andrews University in a scheme for the celebration of the 400th anniversary of the birthday of George Buchanan.

At a recent meeting of the Aberdeen Students' Representative Council it was resolved not to take any action with regard to the proposed George Buchanan quater-centenary celebrations to be held in St. Andrews next year.

BIRMINGHAM.

The Visit of the Warden.

The Lord Chancellor (Lord Halsbury), as Warden of the Guild of Undergraduates of the University, delivered an address on Saturday, May 13th. Mr. Chamberlain (Chancellor of the University) presided, and among those present were Lady Halsbury, Mrs. Chamberlain, the Lord Mayor, Alderman C. G. Beale (Vice-Chancellor), Lord and Lady Avebury, Mr. R. B. Haldane, K.C., M.P., Mr. Austen Chamberlain, M.P., Mr. and Mrs. Henry Birchenough, Sir Oliver Lodge (Principal), the President of the Guild (Mr. H. P. Pickerill).

The Lord Chancellor delivered an interesting address, in which he congratulated the undergraduates upon the constitution of their Guild. He felt that such an institution as the University of Birmingham would add very considerably to the amount and value of the intellectual cultivation in the world. He regretted to notice that there was no Chair of Greek in the University. He hoped that this great need would not long remain unsatisfied. Mr. Chamberlain, in proposing a vote of thanks to the Warden, said the Lord Chancellor's address was a defence of the whole scheme of these modern Universities, which have been growing up so rapidly in this country. He himself would not be satisfied until similar Universities had been placed in every great and populous district. In the afternoon the Lord Chancellor visited Bournbrook and inspected the progress of the new University buildings.

University News and Notes.

The reconstruction of Queen's College, Birmingham, was commemorated on Saturday, May 6, when a distinguished company inspected the new buildings, and subsequently lunched together. Among those who attended were Lord Windsor, who presided at the luncheon (which was preceded by a short service in the College chapel), the Bishop of Birmingham, the Lord Mayor (Alderman C. G. Beale), and Sir Oliver Lodge, Principal of the University. The toast, " The City and University," was proposed by the Chairman, and responded to by the Lord Mayor and the Principal of the University. In the absence of Mr. Chamberlain through illness Mr. E. Parkes proposed the toast of " The College," to which Bishop Gore and the Rev. Professor J. H. B. Masterman, Warden of the College, replied.

The Queen's College, in addition to providing accommodation for the training of candidates for Holy Orders, will serve as a hostel for some of the students of the University.

Dr. James Kerr, Medical Officer to the Education Department of the London County Council as Ingleby Lecturer at the University, recently delivered the first of his addresses on the subject of mentally defective children.

A course of four lectures has been given during the month of May by Professor Fiedler, Dean of the Faculty of Science, on " Phonetics, with Special Reference to the Teaching of Living Languages."

A meeting of the University Engineering Society was held on May 11th, at the University, when the Principal (Sir Oliver Lodge) delivered his annual lecture to the members.

Alderman C. G. Beale, Vice-Chancellor of the University, has been elected by the City Council, Lord Mayor of Birmingham for the remainder of the year in the place of the late Mr. R. H. Berkeley.

Two Harding Scholarships in German of the annual value of £50 each, tenable for three years, are offered to students entering the School of Modern Languages next Session. At the close of the third year Travelling Scholarships of £100 each, tenable at a German University for one year, may be awarded to these scholars, provided that they have taken the M.A. Degree in the School of Modern Languages. Entrance Examinations to the School of Modern Languages will commence on Monday, June 19th, 1905, and September 18th, 1905. Applications for admission to the September Examination must be received by the Registrar on or before August 30th. Further information may be obtained from the Dean of the Facutly of Arts (Professor H. G. Fiedler), at the University.

CAMBRIDGE.

University News and Notes.

The Drapers' Company has offered a grant of £5,000 towards the buildings required for the Agriculture Department of Cambridge University, provided a like sum is raised by voluntary contribution before 1906.

The University accounts for the year 1904 have recently been published. It is stated that the total receipts of the University amounted to £42,679. 2s. 1d., and the expenditure to £44,350. 1s. 2d.; the excess of expenditure over receipts being £1,670. 19s. 1d. As compared with 1903 the total receipts show a falling off amounting to £1,201. 10s. 5d.

The following Degrees have been conferred during the year:— D.D., 8; LL.D., 6; M.D., 18; Sc.D., 5; Litt.D., 1; B.D., 3; M.A., 364; . LL.M., 4; M.C., 2; M.B., 5; B.C., 78; B.A., 718; LL.B., 43.

Mr. E. S. Roberts, Master of Gonville and Caius, Dr. Adam, Mr. S. H. Butcher, and Mr. G. H. Hardy, Trinity, have been elected additional members of the Syndicate appointed to consider what changes, if any, are desirable in the studies, teaching and examinations of the University.

The report of the Non-Collegiate Students' Board states that 231 non-collegiate students have taken the B.A. Degree during the 14 years commencing October, 1891. Of these 60 have taken Honours. Forty-eight out of the 90 undergraduates now in residence are in their first, 23 in their second, and 19 in their third or fourth year.

The sum of £630 subscribed by the friends of the late Sir Leslie Stephen for the endowment of a Lectureship in Literature has been gratefully accepted by the University.

Mr. M. R. James, Litt.D., Fellow and Lecturer of the College, has been elected to the Provostship of King's College in place of the late Rev. A. Austen-Leigh. Dr. James was educated at Eton and King's. He graduated in 1885, taking the highest Honours in both parts of the Classical Tripos. As an undergraduate he obtained the following University distinctions:—Carus Greek Testament Prize, Bell University Scholarship, Craven University Scholarship, Jeremie Septuagint Prize, first Chancellor's Medal for Classical Studies. He was elected to a Fellowship at King's, and was appointed Tutor, which position he resigned soon after his appointment as Director of the Fitzwilliam Museum. Dr. James is the 33rd Provost since the foundation of the College in 1441, and is the first layman who has held the office of Provost since 1675.

The sum of £150 offered to the University by the former pupils of the Misses Fletcher, late of Upper Hornsey Rise, for the purpose of founding an annual prize, to be called the Fletcher Prize, for success in Latin and Greek at the higher local examinations, has been gratefully accepted.

It is stated in the *Cambridge Review* that the number of members of the University in residence during the present term is 3,507. At Girton and Newnham there are 342 residents.

Research Studentships.

The Master of Gonville and Caius College gives notice that by the operation of new statutes and in consequence of recent benefactions there will henceforward be several post-graduate Research Studentships tenable at this College, subject in general to the condition that the student elected must have kept not less than nine nor more than fifteen terms of residence at the College. These Studentships are:—

(1) The Frank Smart Studentship, restricted to Botany, £100 a year for one, two or three years.

(2) The Shuttleworth Studentship, given by preference for Zoology or Physiology, at present £110 a year for one, two or three years.

(3) The Ramadge Studentship, for Legal History (or, failing qualified candidates in that subject, then for Theology, Languages, Archæology or other literary study), £100 for one year in alternate years.

(4), (5) Two Studentships of £120 a year tenable for one, two or three years, which are not restricted as to subject and may be given either for literary or for scientific research.

(6) A Studentship, at present of £80 for one, two or three years, given by preference for research in some branch of literature or arts.

DUBLIN.

University News and Notes.

A meeting of the Senate was held on April 29th for the purpose of conferring Degrees. The occasion caused special interest by reason of the large number of women students, who have already obtained the Tripos Certificate of Cambridge University or its equivalent from Oxford, who presented themselves. The University Caput consisted of the Right Hon. Mr. Justice Madden, LL.D., Vice-Chancellor of the University, the Provost of Trinity College, and Mr. George L. Cathcart, M.A., F.T.C.D., Senior Master Non-Regent.

Seven women students from Oxford University and seventy-nine from Cambridge presented themselves for the B.A. Degree, and of these sixty-seven proceeded to the M.A. Degree. Miss Ethel Gertrude Skeat, in addition, presented herself for the Degree of Doctor of Science.

At the conclusion of the ceremony the ladies were entertained to lunch by Trinity College; the Vice-Chancellor and Mrs. Madden, the Provost and Mrs. Traill and Miss Gwynn, Lady Registrar, being amongst those present.

Since last June 146 women have presented themselves for the Degree of B.A., and of these 101 have also proceeded to the M.A.

In commenting on this ceremony, the Dublin correspondent of *The Times* remarked:—"The system (of conferring Degrees on women graduates of Oxford and Cambridge), which was introduced last year, is defended on the plea of financial necessity." But the Provost, in reply to this, has stated that there is no foundation for this statement, as the University is not in any financial straits whatever, as is sufficiently proved by the fact that the University has already expended upwards of £1,500 in making preparation for the education of women students in one branch alone—that of Medicine, and that no expense will be spared to put them in every way on an equality with men.

The death of the Very Rev. Hercules H. Dickinson, Dean of the Chapel Royal, Dublin Castle, has aroused feelings of deep regret on all sides. After a long and trying illness, which forced him to resign a few years ago a number of positions which he held in connection with the Church of Ireland, Dean Dickinson passed away on May 17th, at the age of 77. For ten years he held the Chair of Pastoral Theology in connection with the Divinity School of the University of Dublin, and as an author his "Lectures on Prayer," "Scripture and Science," and "Work in the Church" were very widely read. He was a musician of no mean order, and displayed keen interest in the production of the authorised version of the Hymnal and its Appendix, which is in use in the Church of Ireland. With his death the Deanery of the Chapel Royal—a pre-Disestablishment office—becomes extinct.

The Board have appointed Mr. Harold Lawson Murphy, B.A., to be Assistant to the Professor of Modern History in the University.

The Board have elected Dr. Luncas White King, C.S.I., Indian Civil Service, to the Chair of Arabic, Persian and Hindustani.

University Developments.

Building operations have been commenced on the new Physical Laboratory, the erection of which will cost £16,500. This amount has been generously subscribed by the Right Hon. Lord Iveagh, K.P., while the capital necessary for the maintenance of the Laboratory (£350 per annum) has been subscribed by members and friends of the University, including the Earl of Rosse, K.P., Chancellor of the University; the late Rev. George Salmon, D.D.; John Jameson, M.A., D.L.; Frederick Purser, M.A., F.T.C.D.; E. P. Culverwell, M.A., F.T.C.D.; and R. Mackay Wilson, M.A. It is expected that the Laboratory will be completed in the course of twelve months, and that it will be devoted to the general study of Experimental Science. Great attention has been paid to the details, both of construction and utility, no pains being spared to insure its being up to date in all its requirements.

The Science Schools Committee hold out hopes of very soon being in a position to proceed with the erection of the new Botanical Laboratory, at a cost of about £7,000, also the munificent donation of Lord Iveagh. The want of this Laboratory has been very much felt of late, and its erection will greatly facilitate the proposed School of Agriculture, which many friends of the University are seeking to establish in Trinity College.

Hitherto the education of teachers in the University has only consisted of two Examinations—one for the Special and Ordinary Certificates in the Theory and History of Education, and the other for the First and Second Class Diplomas in the Practice of Teaching—but the Board of Trinity College, recognising the importance of the question in view of present day requirements, has now founded a Chair of Education in connection with the University. They have elected Mr. Edward P. Culverwell, M.A., F.T.C.D., to the Professorship for a period of five years, and a full curriculum of lectures in the Theory, History and Practice of Education will shortly be drawn up. These courses in Education will be open to men and women alike.

Mr. Culverwell has always taken great interest in educational questions, and has been University Examiner in Educational Theory, History and Practice for some years. Last Michaelmas Term he gave a very successful series of lectures on Education, including a highly interesting one on Japanese Educational Problems.

The Honour Courses in Modern History and Political Science have been materially changed and improved. In both the Freshman years Honour Examinations have been instituted in Hilary and Trinity Terms, while the subjects for the Michaelmas Prize Examinations have been altered so as to make the course continuous.

In the Junior Freshman year the period to be studied is from 1598 to 1815, and in the Senior Freshman year from 476 to 1598. As regards the Sophister years, the Honour Examinations in the Senior Sophister year for Hilary and Trinity Terms will be discontinued, while in the Junior Sophister year the Honour Courses for Hilary and Trinity Terms and the Prize Course for Michaelmas Term have been altered and enlarged so as to include Economic History and Political Science. These Courses and Examinations will come into force in 1906. Lectures in both Freshman and Sophister years will be delivered in future, beginning with next Michaelmas Term by Dr. Bastable, Professor of Political Economy, Mr. J. H. Wardell, M.A., Professor of Modern History, and Mr. Murphy, Assistant to the Professor of History.

DURHAM.

University News and Notes.

The Rev. Dawson Walker, Theological Tutor and Censor of the unattached students in the University of Durham, was recently presented for the Degree of Doctor of Divinity at a Convocation of the Senate of the University of Oxford. Upon Dr. Walker's return to Durham he was met at the railway station by a band of students and escorted by a torchlight procession to his residence.

The number of undergraduates at Durham this term is considerably greater than it has ever been before, and is six times larger than it was in 1861.

At a convocation held recently at the Castle Hall the following Degrees, among others, were conferred :—

M.D. *ad eundem :* Sir Isambard Owen, M.D., Anthony Bourchier, Annie T. Brunyate, John W. Caton, Thomas M. Clayton, Flora Murray, Alfred H. P. Oswin.

M.A. *ad eundem :* Arthur Dolphin, M.A., Oriel College, Oxford.

EDINBURGH.

University News and Notes.

At the recent half-yearly meeting of the General Council of the University draft ordinances in regard to instruction in Geography, and a Degree in Forestry in the University, were approved.

A motion approving of the proposal to form a Philological Society, and recommending it to the favourable consideration of the members of the Council was adopted by a large majority.

The total invested funds of the University now amount to about three-quarters of a million sterling, about one-tenth of which belongs to the General University Fund, which is the only free and unfettered fund existing in the University.

The number of matriculated students shows that the increase of the last three years is being well maintained. The total figure is now just over 3,000, which is the highest since 1893-4. In Arts there is a slight falling off in numbers, but this is more than counterbalanced by the increase in Science. Divinity, Medicine, and Music all show a satisfactory increase. In Law there has been a decrease from 388 of last year to 344 in 1904-5, a figure lower than any since 1876-7. In addition to the 1,487 matriculated medical students, there are 105 non-matriculated women students of Medicine in attendance at classes in Edinburgh and qualifying for graduation.

At a recent meeting of the University Court leave of absence was granted for the remainder of the current Session to Dr. R. M. Johnston, Lecturer on Diseases of the Larynx, Ear and Nose, and the arrangements were approved under which Dr. A. Logan Turner will act as Dr. Johnston's substitute. The arrangements whereby Professor J. Bretland Farmer will act, in connection with the July examinations, as substitute for Professor Marshall Ward, Additional Examiner in Botany, during his absence, were also approved by the Court. On the recommendation of the Senatus, Professor M'Intosh, (University of St. Andrews), was appointed an Additional Examiner of a thesis submitted for the Degree of D.Sc. It was decided to recognise the Army Medical College, as an institution where two months' practical work in Hygiene and in Pathology may be taken by candidates for the Degree of B.Sc. in Public Health. The Court approved of special courses of instruction being instituted for candidates for the public medical services. The Chancellor of the University has reappointed Lord Stormonth-Darling as his Assessor on the University Court. The Principal has been reappointed the University's representative on the Carnegie Trust. The Court approved of the conditions on which the War Office authorities were prepared to grant the use of bridging material to the University in connection with the courses of instruction given by the Lecturer on Military Subjects.

The Edinburgh University Free Trade Union have adopted Mr. J. St. Loe Strachey, editor of *The Spectator*, as Free Trade candidate for the joint constituency of Edinburgh and St. Andrews Universities in opposition to Sir John Batty Tuke. Mr. St. Loe Strachey was born in 1860, and was educated at Balliol, Oxford, where he took a First Class in History. Since 1884 he has been a journalist in London. He was editor of the *Cornhill Magazine* from 1896 to 1897.

(A Review of " Twenty-one Years of Corporate Life at Edinburgh University," by Mr. J. I. Macpherson, M.A., LL.B., will appear in the July number of " The University Review.")

GLASGOW.

University News and Notes.

On Monday, 22nd May, on the eve of the meeting of the General Assembly of the Church of Scotland, a portrait of the Very Rev. Dr. Story, Principal of the University, painted by Sir George Reid, R.S.A., was presented to the Church, in the offices, 22, Queen Street, Edinburgh. Lord Balfour of Burleigh made the presentation, remarking on the long and distinguished services the Principal had rendered to the Church and otherwise, and mentioning that their movement had been so successful that more than enough had been provided to enable this portrait to be presented to the Church, and to allow of a second one being presented to the University of Glasgow. It is expected that the presentation of the portrait to the University will take place in the course of the coming autumn.

With the opening of next Winter Session the teaching staff in Medicine and Science will be augmented by the inauguration of the Grieve Lectureship in Physiological Chemistry, funds for the endowment of which were bequeathed by the late John Grieve, M.D., of Glasgow, a graduate of the University. The University Court have appointed Edward Provan Cathcart, M.D., as the first Lecturer on the foundation. Dr. Cathcart graduated as M.B. and Ch.B. in this University in 1900, and, after acting for a year as Resident Physician and Surgeon in the Western Infirmary, proceeded to Munich, where he prosecuted further studies in Bacteriology and Physiological Chemistry, subsequently working in the University of Berlin, where he continued the study of Physiological Chemistry, and also devoted special attention to the clinical application of Chemistry. In 1903 he was appointed a research student in Pathological Chemistry in the Lister Institute of Preventive Medicine,

London, and in February of this year was appointed Assistant Bacteriologist in that institution. In 1904 he graduated as M.D. with Honours, and carried off a Gold Medal for eminent merit in his thesis for the Degree. It is intended that the Lecturer should give a short course on Physiological Chemistry to form part of the instruction for students of Medicine and Science, that he should have charge of the Laboratory for Physiological Chemistry, and that he should conduct original researches in that subject, and assist students and others who may be doing higher work in the department.

The recent appointment of Alexander R. Ferguson, M.D., to the Chair of Pathology and Bacteriology in the School of Medicine at Cairo, Egypt, has removed a well-known member of the teaching staff, who for a number of years has been Senior Assistant to the Professor of Pathology, and also Assistant Pathologist to the Western Infirmary. Dr. Ferguson graduated in 1892, with high commendation, as M.B. and C.M., and ten years later obtained the Degree of M.D. with Honours, gaining a Gold Medal for his thesis. It is worth mentioning that another Glasgow graduate—Douglas Dunlop, M.A., LL.D.—holds a distinguished position at Cairo in the Egyptian educational system, being Secretary-General of the Department of Public Instruction.

Scottish University Government.

At a recent meeting of the University Court a Committee was appointed to consider the question of simplifying the procedure in obtaining amendments on the ordinances regulating graduation and other academic matters. The questions involved are of considerable interest, both from a constitutional point of view, and otherwise. The objection to the existing procedure rests, perhaps, on a somewhat theoretical basis, but in some quarters a belief has grown up that the Scottish Universities are less free than others to effect reforms, and that greater freedom of individual action would be beneficial. It will be interesting to see the outcome of this movement, and, as the present procedure is prescribed by Act of Parliament, any modification of it would of course require Parliamentary sanction.

LEEDS.

University News and Notes.

The interesting announcement has been made that a Committee of the Court of Governors of the University is arranging for the establishment of an Observatory in connection with the University. The building is to be erected on Woodhouse Moor, and is to be called the "Cecil Duncombe Observatory," after the late Hon. Cecil Duncombe, whose son, Captain C. W. E. Duncombe, has recently presented to the University a powerful telescope which belonged to his father. The site of the Observatory has been granted by the Leeds City Council.

The Council have appointed Mr. James Gilchrist, B.Sc., to the Lectureship in Civil Engineering which became vacant on the death of Dr. George Wilson. Mr. Gilchrist is a graduate in Science of the University of Edinburgh, with First Class Honours in Engineering.

The University has recently sustained a great loss through the death of its Treasurer, Sir John Barran, who was for many years a Governor of the Yorkshire College. Sir John Barran took the greatest interest in the establishment of the University of Leeds, and at the Inaugural Congregation of the University, held in October last, the Honorary Degree of LL.D. was conferred upon him.

We have received a copy of the special issue of *The Gryphon*, the journal of the University of Leeds, which has been published as a momento of the recent Inauguration of the University. The production is worthy of the highest praise, and will be found of considerable interest, not only to past students of Yorkshire College, but to all who are interested in the University movement. Among the contents may be mentioned an interesting article on the "Beginnings of the Yorkshire College," by Professor L. C. Miall, F.R.S., and another on "Medical Student Life in Leeds Sixty Years Ago," by C. G. Wheelhouse, D.Sc. A new poem, written by the poet Laureate appears under the title of "The Primacy of Mind." The number is illustrated by upwards of fifty photographs of the Honorary Graduates, the Officers and Senate of the University, the University Buildings, etc. Copies may still be obtained (price one shilling each) from the Secretary of the University Union, Leeds.

LIVERPOOL.

University Developments.

At a meeting of the University Court, held on May 20th, several important pieces of academic legislation were approved. A Degree in dental surgery (to be called B.D.S.) has been instituted, and also a Diploma in the same subject (L.D.S.). The Degree course will extend over five years, the Diploma course over four years. To regulate the courses and examinations in this new school a special Board has been instituted, reporting to the Medical Faculty.

The second important ordinance submitted to the Court was a

revised form of an ordinance passed some six months ago, and establishing evening courses leading up to the Degree of B.A. The institution of these courses forms a novel and interesting experiment. It is meant to meet the needs of that large class of students, to be found especially in the teaching profession, whose circumstances have precluded them from taking the ordinary courses for the Degree, or who had begun their professional work before the new university movement began. The only opportunities hitherto provided for this class of students have been the open examinations of London and of the Royal Irish University, but no University has organised regular instruction for them. In Liverpool a demand for such instruction was put forward at the first meeting of the Court after the establishment of the University, and received strong support; and the University felt it was bound to take up the question. A course was therefore worked out in Latin, French, Modern History, Economics and English Literature, to extend over five years, the hours of attendance exacted being in all not less than those required from day students. The fees charged are the same as those for the corresponding day classes, to prevent the possibility of students being tempted to transfer from the day classes; while the subjects of instruction are the same, and the two sets of students will be examined on the same papers. To this scheme the sister Universities of Manchester and Leeds took exception, on the ground that it was likely to divert students from the day course, a result which everybody would deplore. To meet their views an age limit, below which students would not be admitted to these courses, was fixed; and their objections were withdrawn. The courses will be initiated next October, with probably about forty students. It will be interesting to find whether students of maturer years are able, in evening work after a day's labour, to attain the standard of regular day students. There is no doubt that these courses will meet a real need, and will give help to a very deserving and hardly used class of students. But there is no one—not even the most ardent supporter of the scheme—who does not hope that the need will be only temporary. With the development of the educational system and the multiplication of scholarships, the defects which have brought this class into existence should gradually disappear, and with the disappearance of the class special provision for their needs will cease to be required. In the meantime the duplication of courses in the subjects concerned will involve an increase of the staff of the University in these subjects.

While these acts of the Court represent the culmination of movements which have been for some time in progress, the month has been marked by considerable activity in other directions. A modification of the regulations for the Degree of B.A. has been made, so as to render possible a course more particularly suited for students preparing for business life. This course will include two modern languages, Modern History, Geography, Economics, the Practice of Commerce and certain other optional subjects. The scheme scarcely goes so far as the Commercial Degrees of the Universities of Manchester and Birmingham. But a more detailed examination of the nature and objects of the scheme may well be left to a later issue of the *Review*. A reshaping of the Degree courses in Architecture is also under consideration, and in this connection the proposals of the Royal Institute of British Architects on Architectural Education will probably have great weight; but here again the time is hardly ripe for comment. Our University School of Architecture, almost the first of its kind in Britain, has been, since its foundation in 1894, intimately associated with a school of the fine arts and crafts maintained by civic funds in the University grounds. This school has recently been incorporated with the second great art school of the city, which has just come under the control of the Corporation. It is as yet too early to predict on what lines the combined school will develope. But those who are most deeply interested in art teaching hope and expect that at all events the more advanced sections of the combined school will be kept in the most intimate relations with the University, and will ultimately perhaps develope into a Faculty of the Fine Arts. A Faculty of the Fine Arts would be a novelty in a British University, but this is the age of academic experiments, and our long experience of the value of intimate relations between the Fine Arts and the more commonplace subjects of the University has taught us to feel that both sides would lose immeasurably by severance; that the wholeness of knowledge, which a University should represent, demands the inclusion of the Fine Arts just as much as the art of literature or the practical science of engineering.

The Guild of Undergraduates.

Another important piece of legislation submitted to the Court was an Ordinance definitely constituting the Guild of Undergraduates, giving full self-governing powers to the elected Council of the Guild, and imposing a compulsory subscription on all its members. The subscription is at present fixed at 15s., which gives the Guild an annual income of something like £500. This ordinance may be said to be the first overt act of the University in the attempt to organise student activities. The note struck at the outset is thus that of the most complete student self-government. In moving and supporting the adoption of the ordinance, Mr. B. S. Johnson and the President of the Council (Mr. Muspratt) seized the opportunity to make a strong plea for the creation of a Club-house or Union to be a centre of student activities. This plea has been strongly supported by leading articles in the local press, and it is probable that the erection of a large Union will be the next step forward in this University: a Committee, consisting of representatives of the Council, the Senate, the Old Students' Association, and the Guild of Undergraduates, is now engaged in drawing up a scheme, which, it is hoped, will be definitely launched before many months have passed. As the leader-writer of the *Daily Post* observed, the University has now more or less completed for the moment its external organisation of buildings, staff and degree regulations, and has now leisure to turn to the not less important question of encouraging and developing student life. The students have already fully earned all that can be done for them by the self-reliance and energy with which they have worked their independent institutions since the establishment of the Students' Representative Council thirteen years ago; and it is time that external aid should come to their assistance in providing the means for a still more active development of the corporate spirit.

To turn to student activities, perhaps the most important feature of the month has been the completion of the first draft of the new University Song-book, which is now almost ready to go to press. It is dangerous to boast in advance; but those concerned are confident that our song-book will have many features which will distinguish it from its predecessors, and will make it popular far beyond our own bounds. It was at first hoped that the book would be published in time for the Degree Ceremony in July, which is always made the occasion for elaborate festivities among both students and graduates. This hope has now been abandoned, but it is intended to issue a selection of some sixteen songs, words and music, before that date. This little collection will include several new songs, and several new translations or adaptations of German student-songs not hitherto accessible in English.

University News and Notes.

Mr. Percy E. Newberry, who is attached to the Institute of Archæology of the University of Liverpool, has been invited by the Egyptian Government to write the official account of the magnificent discoveries of Mr. Theodore Davis, which form perhaps the most important discoveries ever made in Egypt.

At a recent meeting the Council granted leave of absence, for the Lent Term of 1906, to Mr. Ramsay Muir in order to enable him to accept an invitation of the American Society for University

Extension to undertake a lecturing tour in the United States under their auspices during that term.

The Liverpool School of Tropical Medicine has just published, through the University Press, its fourteenth memoir, consisting of a report, by Professor Boyce and Drs. Evans and Clarke, on " The Sanitation and Anti-malarial Measures in Practice in Bathurst, Conakey and Freetown."

Mr. E. Brown, M.Sc., Lecturer in Applied Mechanics, has been elected to an Associate Professorship of Engineering in McGill University, Montreal. Mr. Brown was a student and graduate of the University of Liverpool, where he had a distinguished career.

LONDON.

The Work of the University.

Presentation Day was celebrated on May 10th at the University of London, South Kensington. The Vice-Chancellor (Dr. Pye-Smith) occupied the chair in the absence of Lord Rosebery, the Chancellor. Before the presentation of candidates for Degrees and Honours the Principal (Sir Arthur Rücker) read his annual report, from which the following statements have been taken:—

Some of the preliminary work which has been done since the reorganisation of the University, has begun to bear fruit in the academic year which is now approaching its termination, and the activity of the University has been extended in several directions.

The gathering of the various Colleges round the University as a centre is being followed by the beginnings of a corporate life among the students.

The number of students matriculating at the University has been well maintained.

The actual entries into the University have increased from 1,854 to 3,434, or by 85 per cent. The total number of internal students is now 2,590—an increase of about 10 per cent. above the figure for 1903–04. The classification of the students is somewhat difficult, but a careful census has lately been made from which it appears that the total number of those who, in the Session 1903–04, either pursued a regular course of study in the Schools of the University, or attended in other institutions approved courses under teachers recognised by the University, was 11,730, of whom 2,344 were technically internal students. These students were instructed by 1,338 teachers, of whom 745 were recognised by the University.

Last year the Degree of M.A., or of Doctor in one or other of the Faculties, was conferred on 128 candidates.

The transfer of the Goldsmiths' Institute at New Cross to the University has recently been completed, and to this magnificent gift the Worshipful Company of Goldsmith have added a subvention of £5,000 a year for five years, with a further £5,000 for the current year to enable the University and the London County Council to carry on the Evening Classes. The institution has been renamed the " Goldsmiths' College," and will be opened in September as a Training College for Teachers. Mr. William Loring, M.A., late Fellow of King's College, Cambridge, has been appointed Warden of the College, and Mr. Thomas Raymont, M.A., Professor of Education in University College, Cardiff, and Miss Caroline Graveson, B.A., Mistress of Method and Tutor of Education in the Day Training College of the University of Liverpool, have been appointed Vice-Principals of the Training College and Master and Mistress of Method respectively.

The principal gifts received by the University during the past year have been as follows:—

	£
London County Council (annual subvention)	10,000
Goldsmiths' Company—	
The site and buildings of the Goldsmiths' Technical Institute, New Cross.	
Grants in aid of work at the Goldsmiths' College ...	10,000
Grants in aid of Library (about)	1,000
Drapers' Company—	
Payment of debt of University College	30,000
Grant in aid of Department of Applied Mathematics	1,000
Mercers' Company—	
Grant in aid of Department of Physiology in University College	1,000
Donations towards Institute of Medical Sciences—	
Mr. Alfred Beit (additional)	20,000
Lord Howard de Walden	3,000
Fishmongers' Company	1,050
Earl of Rosebery	1,000
Lord Iveagh	1,000
Mercers' Company	1,000
Other donors...	350
Mr. Francis Galton for Research Fellowship in Eugenics	1,500

Amounting to a total of £81,900, exclusive of the site and buildings of the Goldsmiths' Institute, on which about £100,000 had been spent by the Company.

Bedford College for Women.

The Council of Bedford College held the usual reception at the College on Commemoration Day, May 10th, at which 500 guests were present. The guests were received by the Principal (Miss Hurlbatt, M.A.), Mrs. Leonard Darwin, Mrs. James Bryce and the other members of Council. Thirty-one students of the College were presented to the Vice-Chancellor of the University, two for the Degree of M.A., ten for first Degrees in Arts, eight for first Degrees in Science and nine graduates in Arts or Science for the Teachers' Diploma. Miss K. Shepherd, B.A., was presented for the George White Studentship, and Miss C. H. Harding for the Reid Trustees Scholarship. Two Scholarships, of the value of £10 each for one year, are offered for the course of Secondary Training, beginning in October, 1905. The Scholarships will be awarded to the best candidates holding a Degree or equivalent in Arts or Science. Applications should reach the Head of the Training Department not later than July 7th, 1905.

Royal Holloway College.

On Friday, May 5th, a Greek performance of Sophocles' " Antigone " was given by the students of the College in the Picture Gallery. The entertainment was a great success, and was attended by a large and appreciative audience. Mendelssohn's music was used for the choruses. The honours of the evening rested with A. K. Elliot as Creon, and the title rôle was taken by D. Seaton with much dignity.

On May 11th Dr. E. A. Wilson, the naturalist of the " Discovery," gave a most interesting lecture—illustrated with numerous lantern slides—on the recent Antarctic Expedition. The lecture was open free to all students of London Colleges. After the lecture a large number of water-colours were exhibited in the Museum, showing the wonderful colour effects produced by the clearness of the atmosphere of the Polar regions.

The College Athletic Sports were held in the College grounds on Saturday, May 13th. A cup was offered for the winner of the greatest number of points. In five out of the seven principal events, which included flat races, jumping, hurdles and throwing the cricket ball, D. Hunter and C. Tyas each scored an equal number of points. To meet the difficulty the Principal kindly presented a second cup. The afternoon closed with the distribution of prizes by the Principal.

The Tennis fixtures for the remainder of this term are as follows:—June 10th, Old Students; June 15th, Girton College; June 20th, Somerville; June 24th, London School of Medicine for Women. All are being played at R.H.C., except the match against Somerville, which will take place at Oxford.

The School of Tropical Medicine.

The London School of Tropical Medicine, which has recently been admitted a School of the University of London in the subject of Tropical Medicine, owes its origin to the Right Hon. Joseph Chamberlain, who, while Secretary of State for the Colonies, with the object of affording instruction in Tropical Medicine to Medical Officers in the Colonial Service, invited the Committee of Management of the Seamen's Hospital Society to establish a School in connection with their Hospitals. In accepting Mr. Chamberlain's invitation, and with the view of still further increasing the usefulness of the School, the Committee resolved to throw it open to all medical graduates who might wish to avail themselves of the exceptional facilities it affords, together with their own hospitals, for the study of this particular branch of Medicine. There are a number of diseases peculiar to tropical and sub-tropical regions—of which examples are never seen in this country except at the great seaports—requiring special methods for diagnosis and treatment, while the hygiene of the tropics is very different from that at home. It was to afford instruction in these tropical branches that the School was founded. The School is situated at the Seamen's Hospital Society's Branch Hospital, near the Royal Victoria and Albert Docks, E. No more suitable spot in Great Britain could have been selected, as, at the Docks, ships arrive from all parts of the Tropics in large numbers. The proximity of the Hospital and School to the Docks allows of immediate admission, thus affording ready opportunity for the treatment of patients and for the observation and study of Tropical diseases. From the student's point of view a more central position for the School would have been desirable, but as Lascars, Negroes, Chinese, and all other coloured natives, object to be taken far away from the ships they arrive in, and regard removal to a distance from the Docks, with suspicion, if not with actual fear, it was necessary, in order to secure the presence of the " native " class of patient, to sacrifice to some extent the convenience of the student. Originally providing accommodation for 20 students, the School premises have recently been enlarged, and at present there is space for 40 students. The buildings consist of a large general laboratory, a private room for the medical superintendent, a lecture theatre, a museum, a library and a dark room for photography. There is in addition a large research laboratory for the prosecution of research work in protozoology and helminthology, with the necessary adjuncts—mosquito house, etc. Residential quarters, with mess and common commons, are also provided for 12 students, and luncheon and tea are available for all at a moderate tariff, and thus the School comprises a complete collegiate system—admittedly a not unimportant part of a true University education. In this connection it may be mentioned that the Senate of the University of London has recently decided to admit a sixth branch of study—tropical medicine—in which candidates may graduate for the Degree of Doctor of Medicine.

The adjoining Hospital, with 50 beds, provides the necessary accommodation for patients suffering from tropical diseases, and the curriculum includes both laboratory work and clinical instruction. The funds for the foundation of the School have been provided (1) by a banquet presided over by Mr. Chamberlain; (2) by a mission to the East by Sir Francis Lovell by which a sum of £9,000 was collected, of which £6,666 was contributed by a Parsee gentleman, the Hon. Bomanji Petit, and (3) by contributions from certain Colonial Governments. These contributions, however, still left a debt of £6,000, and in order to clear this off and to provide for endowment (for which £100,000 is required) another banquet, presided over by Mr. Chamberlain was recently held (May 10th), at the Hotel Cecil. Mr. Chamberlain on this occasion, in proposing the toast of the London School of "Tropical Medicine," directed attention to the munificence of the citizens of Liverpool in supporting their own School, and expressed the hope that London would not lag behind in so good a cause. He also paid a tribute to Sir Patrick Manson, the senior member of the staff, to whose initiative schools of Tropical Medicine, both here and abroad, are due. Subscriptions and donations to the amount of over £10,000 were promised.

Since the foundation of the School, six years ago, 503 students have passed through it, and many important researches have been conducted by its members, e.g., on the mosquito-malaria theory and malaria prevention, on the mosquito transference of filariasis, on beri-beri, on sleeping sickness, etc. Research has been stimulated by the Research Scholarships of £250 given annually for some years by Sir John Craggs, M.V.O., who now presents a prize of the value of £50 every year for the best piece of original work carried out by a past or present student of the School. Recently the Government, through the Colonial Office, has endowed for a period of six years, chairs, primarily for research, in the subjects of protozoology and helminthology. In order to make these permanent, to promote additional research and to remunerate the staff of lecturers and teachers, further endowment is urgently needed—a sum of £100,000 being none too much for this purpose. The School so far has been able to meet current expenses, but only through the self-sacrifice of the staff, who have given their time and services for most inadequate remuneration.

University College.

THE UNION SOCIETY. The following is a brief account of the formation and development of the Union Society of University College : Owing to the unsatisfactory condition of the Athletic Clubs in University College in 1893, it was proposed to amalgamate them into a Union, which should exercise a common financial control. A general meeting of the men students was therefore called, and it was decided to form a Union Society, which should include all the Athletic Clubs and a Debating Society, and at the same time absorb the three social Clubs then in existence, namely, the Common Room, Reading Room, and Smoking Room Societies. The main objects of the amalgamation was to make it possible that the payment of one subscription to the Union should render a member eligible to take part in any of the associated Clubs, and at the same time have the use of the Common Rooms. In order to enable the Medicals at the Hospital to participate in inter-hospital competitions, it was agreed to run separate Football and Cricket Clubs for both the Hospital and College, under the auspices of the Union. As time went on new Clubs were formed, and certain outstanding clubs were amalgamated, until at the present time all the men's Clubs have been absorbed with the exception of certain departmental associations, such as the Medical and Engineering Societies. The Union now includes the following Clubs :— Chess, Racquets, Hockey, Lawn Tennis, Hospital Association Football, College Association Football, Hospital Rugby Football, College Rugby Football, Hospital Cricket, College Cricket, Boxing and Gymnastic, the Athletic Club and the Debating Society. An Athletic Ground at Acton has been obtained by the Union, of which all Union Athletic Clubs have portions allotted to them. There are two classes of subscriptions :—(1) Full subscription, which entitles members to participate in all of the associated clubs; members paying this subscription have two votes at the general meetings of the Union. (2) Room subscription, which includes only the right to use the Union Rooms, together with the membership of the Chess Club and the Debating Society. Members paying this subscription have only one vote at the general meetings.

The Union also, soon after its inception, took over the publication of the *College Gazette*. Recently this journal was re-organised under the title of *The Union Society Magazine*, and is now the recognised organ of the Union. The College authorities use this magazine as a means of publishing items of official news of interest and importance to the students and staff. The magazine contains each month articles of general interest, and notes from the different College Faculties. Considerable success has attended the new publication.

The government of the Union is vested in the General Committee, which is constituted as follows:—(1) The Officers, consisting of the President, two Vice-Presidents (one of whom must be a medical), the Treasurer and the Secretary. (2) Ordinary Members; each associated club elects a representative to serve on the Committee, and for each club member there is one supplementary member; all the supplementary members are elected by a general meeting of the Union. (3) The Editor of the Magazine.

At the first Committee meeting of the year a number of Sub-committees are elected to deal with certain specified matters, such as the Union Rooms and the Athletic Ground. It is the duty of all the Sub-committees, and also of all the associated clubs, to present from time to time reports of their doings and financial requirements.

The financial control is exercised as follows:—At the beginning of each Session each club secretary submits to the treasurer an estimate of expenditure for the running of his club for the Session. The treasurer then prepares his budget, which he presents to the Committee and wherein he reports upon the financial status of the Union, and, if necessary, recommends a revision of these estimates. In this way control is exercised over all the clubs. The treasurer also submits an interim budget in March, and finally, at the end of the Session, the balance-sheet is prepared and presented to a General Meeting. A money grant is made by the Committee only upon the presentation of an account by a club representative or an authorised committee-man after it has been passed by the treasurer.

The Union Society plays a very important rôle in connection with the student life of the College and Hospital, more especially on account of its being officially recognised by the College authorities. It is not difficult to understand how much benefit accrues to the men students as the result of the active and energetic part played by the Society in their corporate life.

MANCHESTER.

University News and Notes.

The need for new Union buildings, recognised for several years, is at last finding expression which seems likely to produce practical results. The Chairman and the Committee, in conjunction with the officials of the Women's Union, have definitely formulated their requirements, and trust that at the beginning of next session they will be able, with the support of the University Authorities, to take steps towards raising the required fund.

The Cricket Eleven and the Tennis Team have opened their

seasons successfully, and prospects seem promising in both games. The first of the Inter-'Varsity matches—that against Liverpool— gave Manchester a fine victory. On the same day, the Tennis Team defeated the Leeds University representatives.

Dr. F. V. Darbishire has been appointed Assistant Lecturer in Chemistry at the Agricultural College at Wye, and has therefore resigned his Demonstratorship in Chemistry.

Dr. W. A. Bone, Lecturer in Chemistry, has been elected a Fellow of the Royal Society.

Miss Mary Bateson will deliver two lectures under the Warburton Trust in the Michaelmas Term of next session, her subject being "Law in the Mediæval Boroughs."

A meeting of the Court of Governors of the University was held on May 11th. In the report of the University Council submitted by the Chairman, Sir Frank Forbes Adam, C.I.E., reference was made to the great loss sustained by the University through the deaths of Mr. Edward Behrens, Mr. Alderman King, Mr. Oppenheim, and Mrs. Worthington. The report comments upon the satisfactory nature of the negotiations which had preceded the division of the assets of the Victoria University between the three Universities of Manchester, Liverpool, and Leeds, the fair division made, and the adjustment of the claims. The general financial position of the Manchester University was stated to be sound, though more money is still required for many desirable extensions.

It was resolved:—" That the Court considers that with the growth of the University increased accommodation for the residence of students in proper halls of residence is urgently needed, and has heard accordingly with great satisfaction of the proposal of the Governors of the Hulme Hall to build a new hall with increased and better accommodation for the residence of students, and trusts that the required support will be received to enable the scheme to be carried out."

The Court authorised the conferment of the Degree of M.A. on Mr. Sydney Chaffers (Bursar of the University), Miss C. I. Dodd (Lecturer in Education and Mistress of Method) Mr. Edward Fiddes (Registrar), and Miss Edith C. Wilson (Tutor for Women Students). Conferment of the Degree of M.Sc. *in absentia* was also authorised in the cases of Mr. R. S. Baker (Burmah), Mr. R. R. Cormack (Egypt), and Mr. A. G. F. Napier (India).

The terms of the Fellowship founded by the Vulcan Boiler and General Insurance Company are as follows:—" The Fellowship is of the annual value of £120, and will be awarded by the Senate. The object of the Fellowship is the encouragement of advanced study and research in mechanical and electrical engineering, and every

Fellow will be required to devote the whole of the time during which he continues to hold the Fellowship to the pursuit, under the direction of the Professor of Engineering, of such study or research in the University or, if a graduate in the University of Manchester, either in the University or other place sanctioned by the Senate. The Fellowship is open to graduates of the Victoria University of Manchester or of other Universities who can furnish satisfactory evidence of being able to pursue original research.

University Appointments Register.

Perhaps the most important event to be recorded this month is the establishment of a University Appointments Register. The feeling has long been general that some systematic medium is needed, through which members of the University desiring appointments, and corporations and individuals seeking suitable candidates for vacant posts, may be brought together. The Appointments Register is intended to satisfy this need.

The Universities of Oxford and Cambridge have for some years past done very useful work by means of their Appointments Board and Appointments Committee. These organisations have been found of great assistance to students desirous of obtaining employment at the end of their academic career, and it has now become possible to supply the need, which has long been felt, of a similar organisation in connection with the University of Manchester. The task, on the one hand, of finding employment for students, and on the other of selecting suitable men and women in response to the enquiries of employers, has hitherto been discharged unofficially. The Council of the University of Manchester has accordingly established an Appointments Register, which is intended not to supersede these private activities, but to supplement and co-ordinate them by collecting information as to vacancies and by recommending to employers such candidates on the books as may seem suitable. It is intended not so much to make a new departure as to systematise existing practice.

The Register will include the names of members of the University who desire to obtain appointments in works, business houses, the teaching profession and other occupations. The Secretary (Mr. Sydney Waterlow) will be glad to supply information as to the qualifications and character of candidates to persons, governing bodies and authorities who wish to obtain the services of suitable men and women who have had a University training.

No fees are charged for information and advice supplied.

OXFORD.

The Martineau Centenary.

The centenary of Dr. Martineau's birth was celebrated recently at Manchester College, Oxford. The proceedings began on May 1st, when a special service was held in the College Chapel, and an address was given by the Principal, Dr. Drummond. On May 2nd a representative company lunched at the Randolph Hotel. The Rev. S. Alfred Steinthal, President of the College, occupied the chair. The Rev. J. Estlin Carpenter, in proposing " In Memoriam," referred to the many years of service Dr. Martineau had devoted to Manchester College. For 16 years he had been its Principal, and had held the position of Lecturer in Philosophy for 46 years. The President proposed the toast of " Prosperity to Manchester College," to which Principal Drummond replied. In the evening there was a largely attended reception at Manchester College, at which Professor Henry Jones, LL.D., Professor of Moral Philosophy at the University of Glasgow, delivered an address on " The Philosophy of Martineau in Relation to the Idealism of the Present Day."

University News and Notes.

Full term began on April 30th, but, as usual, the Colleges began to assemble on the previous Friday, and the majority of lectures did not start until the middle of the following week. The first item of University news which greeted the returning undergraduate was the Class List in Honour Moderations, which Balliol headed with eleven Firsts, an almost unprecedented performance. It is interesting to note in this connection that two of these Firsts were obtained by men who took the examination in their first year under the new regulation concerning graduates from other Universities. One of them, Mr. Rose, is a Canadian Rhodes scholar.

A promising event in University finance is the publication of the Accounts of the Curators of the Chest on May 9th. Increased taxation has resulted in the reduction of current liabilities by one-half, and it is possible that at the end of the present year this deficit will be cleared off. It will then be possible for projects of expansion to be entertained. This is an encouraging prospect, but persons of an optimistic temperament may still be permitted to hope for a reconstruction and consolidation of the whole body of College and University revenues, which should make it possible for Oxford to be relieved from the stress of poverty without extraneous assistance.

It is seen in the financial statement that the total receipts for the year amounted to £70,746. 9s. 5d., and the total expenditure to £67,631. 1s. 10d., giving a balance on the side of income of £3,115. 7s. 7d., which reduces last year's deficit to £2,876. 3s. 6d.

On May 13th Mr. H. W. Wolff delivered a lecture for the Drummond Professor of Political Economy on " Co-operation in Banking as a Remedy for Agricultural Distress and a Help to the Poor."

Among recent literature emanating from this University one of the most important works is the first volume of Dr. Greenidge's " History of Rome." It is the publication of books of this nature which is the best refutation of the old lament that Oxford is a place of education but does nothing for learning. Dr. Greenidge's work, when complete, will undoubtedly take rank among the most notable scientific histories, and the author is more particularly to be thanked because he gives his authorities and so provides the material by which he may himself be judged. It is his neglect in this respect which has so much impaired the value of Mommsen's great work to the scientific student, and especially to the student who adopts the " Oxford Point of View " in historical research.

The Second Exhibition of Historical Portraits is still open, and represents in a compendious form the historical wealth and artistic poverty of England between the reigns of Charles I. and Anne. To the lover of " Art for Art's sake," these exhibitions are necessarily disappointing; but to the student of the history of English painting they cannot fail to be of great value, while to the general public they are striking evidence of the intimate connection which has existed—and we may hope still exists—between Oxford and the national life.

In the sphere of University journalism a new periodical, *The Protean*, has made its appearance, but it will need considerable improvement if its existence is to be prolonged. Eights Week is to see the usual crop of papers, including one new issue *The Parasol*. The most interesting contents-bill is that of *The Barge*, which is to be edited by Mr. Guy Thorne, and will contain contributions by many well-known writers. The week begins on May 25th, and the arrangements for it include concerts at Balliol, Brasenose, Exeter and St. John's, and the annual Conversazione of the Junior Scientific Club.

The subject of the Romanes Lecture which is to be delivered by Professor Ray Lankester on June 14 will be " Man and Nature."

Mr. Arthur L. Smith, Fellow of Balliol College, Ford's Lecturer in English History, will take as the subject of his lectures, " Sidelights on English history in the thirteenth century."

The officers for the Union Society this term are:—President, Mr. A. Shaw; Junior Treasurer, Mr. A. Paterson; Librarian, Mr. H. Paul; Secretary, Mr. E. M. C. Denny.

The first number of the *Oxford Magazine* contains an interesting suggestion by Mr. Hubert Reade to affiliate the Union Society and other Oxford Clubs to similar institutions in the Colonies. By this means emigrants from Oxford would be enabled to find an easier footing in the country of their adoption and a closer tie might be established between the students of the Empire.

It is interesting to note that it is proposed to confer the Degree of D.Litt. *honoris causa* on Herr Gerhart Hauptmann. It is strong testimony to the growth of a more liberal spirit when so uncompromising a representative of the "modern" movement is selected for such a distinction in this home of tradition and mediævalism.

The Board of Electors to the Beit Professorship has been constituted as follows:—The Vice-Chancellor, the Regius Professor of Modern History, the Chichele Professor of Modern History, the Colonial Secretary, the Provost of Oriel, Mr. John Doyle (All Souls'), and Mr. Herbert Fisher (New College).

WALES.

University College of North Wales, Bangor.

The celebration of the Twenty-first Anniversary of the establishment of the College, which is to take the place this year of the usual closing ceremony, will be held on the afternoon of Saturday, July 1st. There will be a Public Meeting and the formal presentation of the Deed of Gift of the new site by the Corporation of Bangor, followed by a Garden Party.

The Annual General Meeting of the Welsh Language Society was held recently at University College, Bangor. Sir Isambard Owen was elected President for the ensuing year and Sir Marchant Williams Vice-President, and Professor Lloyd, Treasurer. The meeting discussed a scheme for universal compulsory teaching of Welsh in elementary schools of the Principality, and was of the opinion that compulsory teaching of Welsh, even in English-speaking areas in Wales, should be generally enforced, having at the same time due regard to educational efficiency. An Executive Committee was appointed to consider the whole question, including the existing official regulations and examinations, and was empowered to take immediate action.

University College of South Wales, Cardiff.

Sir Marchant Williams has been re-elected Warden of the Guild of Graduates of the Welsh University. The question of the publication of a Welsh Dictionary is being considered by the Guild, and it is hoped that arrangements will soon be made for the immediate publication of the first portion of the Dictionary.

The following arrangements have been made for the forthcoming visit of the Prince of Wales to Cardiff:—His Royal Highness will leave Paddington at 11 a.m. on June 28th for Cardiff, and on arrival will lunch at Cardiff Castle with the Marquis of Bute, after which he will lay the foundation-stone of the new buildings of the University College of South Wales and Monmouth. At 5-30 His Royal Highness, as Chancellor of the University of Wales, will confer a number of honorary degrees. On the following morning His Royal Highness will visit the Cardiff docks, and will afterwards receive the freedom of the borough of Cardiff.

UNIVERSITY COLLEGES.

Bristol.

The Board of Education has authorised the establishment of a Training Department for men teachers. Preliminary steps have been taken towards securing premises for a tutorial house, which will be placed under the control of the Master of Method, Mr. T. S. Foster, M.A., formerly of St. John's College, Battersea. The Department will open in the autumn with a full complement of 30 students. In the following year the number will be increased to 60.

By the erection of handsome iron gates and boundary railings, the gift of the University College Colston Society, the west front of the College has now been completed. With the exception of the Botanical Garden the whole of the College land is now covered by buildings which are fully occupied. It will be necessary to secure space for extension at an early date.

A very successful Conversazione was held in the College on the 19th May. About 1,200 guests were received in the Great Hall by the Chairman of the Council (the Right Hon. Lewis Fry), the Principal (Professor C. Lloyd Morgan, LL.D., F.R.S.) and the Dean of the Faculty of Medicine (Professor E. Markham Skerritt, M.D.). The whole of the departments were thrown open and demonstrations by members of the staff were given at intervals during the evening.

During this Summer Term a Field Class in Geology will pay visits to localities of interest in the neighbourhood.

In the Department of Oriental Languages the newly-appointed Reader in Burmese, Mr. L. Alan Goss, is giving a course of lectures.

Reading.

Viscount Goschen, as Chancellor of the University of Oxford, has arranged to visit Reading on Wednesday, June 7th, to lay the foundation stone of the new buildings of University College on the site given by Mr. Alfred Palmer, High Sheriff of Berkshire. The estimated cost of the new buildings is £80,000. Contributions have already been received of £10,000 each from Lady Wantage and Mr. George W. Palmer, £6,000 from Messrs. Sutton and Sons, £3,000 from Mr. J. H. Benyon (Lord-Lieutenant of Berks), and £1,000 each from the Hon. W. F. D. Smith, M.P., and Mr. G. H. Morrell, M.P.

University College is affiliated to the University of Oxford, and receives support from the Board of Education, the Board of Agriculture, the Royal Agricultural Society, and many other public bodies.

Sheffield.

The arrangements made at University College, Sheffield, to promote the general social life of the College are mainly performed by two societies, the Students' Union and the Athletic Club, to both of which all fully-registered students belong, the subscriptions of students to these Clubs being defrayed by the registration fee, while the funds of both Clubs are assisted by subscriptions from members of the College staff and others.

The Students' Union arranges for debates in which all subjects other than theological are permitted; it also organises two " Social Evenings," one at the end of the Christmas and one at the end of the Lent Term. Tea is provided before each of the debates, as well as at the social evenings, and every encouragement is afforded to enable all classes of students to meet on these occasions.

The Athletic Club makes all arrangements for Cricket, Football and Hockey; it also assists Lawn Tennis, Swimming and other Clubs affiliated to it by grants of money as its funds permit. Both Clubs are managed by committees on which all classes of students are fully represented; the Students' Union also makes special arrangements for the representation of past members of the College.

In addition to these Clubs there are also several Societies of a more sectional nature; the medical students have a special Union of their own, and several departments possess societies specially connected with the subjects in which they are interested, such as the Biological, Chemical, Clinical, Engineering, Literary, and Physical Societies. There is an official College Magazine, and independent Magazines of a less official character occasionally make their appearance.

It has been announced that through the generosity of manufacturers in the east end of the city of Sheffield—all of whom have made contributions of £1,000 and upwards to the fund for establishing the new University—and of other donors, the University of Sheffield is now practically established from a financial point of view.

Correspondence.

The Royal University of Ireland—A Correction.

To the Editor of "The University Review."

SIR,—

In the very interesting introductory note which Mr. Bryce has prefixed to the first number of the *University Review*, there is an error which I ask your leave to correct.

On the map of the Universities and University Colleges of the United Kingdom the only institutions mentioned in Ireland are the University of Dublin and the three Queen's Colleges of Belfast, Cork and Galway, and it is said in the note that these Colleges " constitute the Royal University of Ireland," of which there is no mention in the map.

That statement is inaccurate. It is quite true that these Colleges did constitute the Queen's University which gave its degrees only to students who had attended the courses of one or other of the Queen's Colleges. But the Royal University has no constituent colleges: it gives its degrees to all students who pass its examinations, irrespective of the manner in which they may have acquired their knowledge. It may, perhaps, for that reason be held not inaccurate to describe the Royal University as an " Examining Board," but, if so, the description applies also to the University of Dublin, which gives its degrees yearly on examination alone to many students who have never attended a lecture in Trinity College, or in any other College. I hold that the Royal University is much more than an " Examining Board."

University College, Dublin, which is quite ignored in your map, has held for many years the foremost place in the examinations of the Royal University, its students winning a larger number of First Class Honours and Prizes than those of the three Queen's Colleges taken together. The teaching work at that College is carried on mainly by 15 Fellows of the Royal University, who are appointed and paid by the Senate of the University under the express condition of teaching in University College, and who are called on yearly to give a return to the Senate showing the subjects and number of their lectures, and the number of students attending their several classes; and, therefore, as far as University College is concerned, the Royal University, which maintains it, is to all intents and purposes a teaching University, much more, in fact, than the University of Dublin is in relation to Trinity College.

I am, Sir
Your obedient servant,
WILLIAM DELANY,
President.

University College,
Dublin, May, 1905.

(We desire to express our regret for the error pointed out by Principal Delany.—Editor, "The University Review.")

"Universities and Examinations."

To the Editor of "The University Review."

SIR,—

Professor Schuster's article on "Universities and Examinations" in your first issue emphasises some points which are very necessary to be remembered. His main thesis, that training in original work is of far greater importance than the accumulation of facts, and that this should be recognised in our degree courses and tests is especially valuable. But I am sure Professor Schuster will be interested to learn that what he has propounded as an ideal to aim at was carried out, nearly two years ago, in the Faculty of Arts in the University of Liverpool. In Liverpool, exactly as Professor Schuster urges, the honours course in Arts, has been divided into two parts. During his first two years the student covers the general subject, and passes at the end of the second year what corresponds to Professor Schuster's "qualifying examination." The results of this are published in alphabetical order and without discrimination; and the student who shows no promise of good work is turned back to read for an ordinary degree. In the third year the students devote themselves to a piece of special work, and write a dissertation, on which mainly the final award is made. The scheme has now been two years in operation. It has worked extremely well, and there is no doubt in the minds of either students or teachers that it constitutes a training infinitely superior to the old examinational system.

Yours, etc.
LIVERPOLITAN.

Liverpool University, May, 1905.

with

uding

with apparatus
of the Country

From a photo)   *(by C. H. Park, Fleet Street*

THE JOHN HARVARD MEMORIAL WINDOW
In the Cathedral Church of St. Saviour, Southwark

The University Review

NO. 3. VOL. I.   JULY, 1905.

The Training of Architects.

BY

C. H. REILLY, M.A. (Cantab.), A.R.I.B.A.

Roscoe Professor of Art (Architecture) in the University of Liverpool.

DURING the last few years, many signs of discontent have shown themselves in the architectural world, some of which may have been noticed by the world outside. It is, of course, not an uncommon thing to find the members of any profession complaining of their want of recognition by the general public, and with those who practice an art in England there is, in general, good reason. But while the history of other professions, of the law and medicine for example, show a steady but continuous increase in the estimation in which their members are held, there is no doubt about the decline of the architect from the days of his greatness during the Italian Renaissance to the days of his subordination to the amateur enthusiast of the Gothic revival, and to the business speculator of to-day.

The result is, that to the majority of people, he has become a rather mysterious person, with very ill-defined

A

functions, whom a rich man may employ occasionally but a poor man never. He has consequently to suffer from inroads into his province in all directions, from the engineer in one, from the tradesman-decorator in another. In addition, the large change of patrons he has been forced to undergo, due to economic causes far removed from his art, has still further added to his degradation, because, on the whole, his new employers have not yet realised the dignity of their own pursuits, and that the place of business, for instance, may represent as worthy an idea for the architect to express as the nobleman's house. Municipal bodies, who in past centuries have been among the best and most powerful supporters of the art, are fast failing in England to understand their responsibilities in this respect, so that we too often find their surveyor, their expert in land purchase, in road-making and drainage schemes, employed on architectural projects of the first magnitude.

For the architect, then, these are signs of the times which he cannot afford to disregard. Many remedies are suggested. A large number of architects are anxious to be labelled for the benefit of an undiscerning public, if not as artists, at least as safe constructors, to whom the public may entrust their lives. Others, including most of the leading men in the profession, (whose position is best assured,) reply that an architect's only claim to recognition should be through his work, in the way that a sculptor or painter makes his, and that the only question, therefore, for him to look to is that his work be good enough. To the young and struggling architect in a provincial town, who has every reason to doubt whether his public as a whole knows or cares anything whatever for the art he practices, this is a hard saying, and it is little to be wondered at if we find his attitude to his art, after a few years, undergoes some rapid changes, admits the introduction of one or more branches of surveying, and finally ends in his appearing to the plain man of affairs as differing in no way from any other business man, except perhaps in the smallness of his turnover and the poorness of his prospects.

Both parties, those who seek for improvement from without and those who seek it from within, are then willing to admit, as indeed is evident to all, that there is at the present time a vast and preponderating amount of the work executed by persons styling themselves architects, which is vulgar and absurd through sheer ignorance of first principles, while leaving out of account altogether the larger portion of the buildings executed in the land for which no architect at all is employed. Therefore, while safeguarding the inherent right of genius to break all rules in its own way and at its own times, it is at least highly desirable, as a first step, to find some means of making mediocrity as respectable and sober in its architecture as it generally manages to be elsewhere. Better education, then, on sounder principles, if they can be found, whether it is to be achieved by compulsory registration or by the initiative of architects themselves, emerges at once as common ground on which all parties can unite.

Such an agreement has recently taken place and has

resulted in the creation, by the Royal Institute of British Architects and other bodies represented, of a very strong board, entitled the Board of Architectural Education. This Board, which includes most of the leading men in the profession, has deliberated for more than a year, has received suggestions from advisory members, representing the Universities and other bodies interested in the training of architects, and has issued a report, which, though still under revision, is sufficiently public property for its suggestions to be reviewed.

These, it may at once be said, are of an epoch-making character as regards architectural training; firstly, because there is authoritatively laid down a sound general principle, by which in their work masters, teachers, pupils, and public alike can thread their own way through the quicksands of fashion and caprice, and reach solid ground in so-called "matters of taste," and, secondly, because there is suggested, for universal acceptance, a method of training, which in England has only been very partially attempted up to the present time, though in common practice abroad.

The general principle referred to, and clearly enunciated in the report, is the old but little regarded one, that construction is the basis of architecture. To lay minds this may at first sight seem a difficulty in dealing with an art, but architects will at once recognise its significance, even if their own training did not emphasise it. To construct, with the beauty born of directness, simplicity, and suitability, is the first step to fine architecture. It is the strict observance of this vital relation of construction to actual needs and conditions which can alone prevent copyism and the revival of forms, which have long lost their meaning, such as mainly distinguished the architecture of the middle portion of the nineteenth century. It is, therefore, essential that from the first the student should be familiarised with the actual building materials and processes, the use of which is the technique of his art. With these he should be set to solve constructional problems of gradually increasing complexity, but of strictly practical application. That he may do this in forms of æsthetic value, the report points out, the architecture of the past must be laid before him, as the solution of a similar series of problems under other conditions, social and material, with which he should be acquainted. He will then be able to realise how certain forms were evolved from the conditions in which they were used and were proved efficient. The mere accidents of style and ornaments, so precious to the learned amateur, will sink to their proper level in his mind, and the temptation to copy be lessened. He will learn to design as a practical constructor, who knows how to handle and proportion the masses of his building as well as the details, and to make them result in forms of abstract beauty. For this after all is the function of the architect, and if it were patent to everyone that he is an artist skilled to do this, less would be heard of his want of recognition.

Having then laid down this method by which the study of architecture should be approached, so that it may be from the beginning a living art, and not a mere branch either of engineering on the one hand or of archæology on the other, the report strikes two further blows. The first is at the old pupilage system, as it has existed from time immemorial and in England to the present day, and the second is at the system of examinations apart from teaching, whereby the Institute, for the last ten years, has sought to determine the minimum of architectural ability to be expected in its members.

In order that among other advantages a right attitude towards construction from an architect's point of view, as already explained, may from the first be achieved by the student, the report lays down, that, at the commencement of his technical education, he should attend for two years or more at some properly equipped architectural school, which it is stipulated should contain, not only a museum of architectural models and materials, but a laboratory or workshop, where a student can, by experiment and demonstration, be brought into contact with actual building processes.

In France and America, where I think most architects would admit that the general level of executed work is much higher than it is here, the pupilage system only exists, where it does at all, in a very modified form. The school, as for instance the École des Beaux Arts in Paris, is all powerful, with result, it may justly be argued, that to a certain extent individuality has been sacrificed to uniformity. If the ordinary Beaux Arts student can produce a big scheme for the "lay out" of large public buildings at the end of his four years' course, an achievement it would be hopeless to expect from an office-bred English pupil of similar standing, the schemes so produced bear a remarkable similarity one to another, especially in detail. I for one, however, would not encourage anything else in students' work. Detail, and ornament particularly, should be very sparingly used by a beginner; the first business of the student is to learn to handle his masses. The encouragement of premature originality of detail has led to most of the absurdities of the Art Nouveau. But the greater individuality, which may be supposed to distinguish our best English architecture, if it has been maintained by the pupilage system, by students working in more or less isolated groups in contact with one man immersed in his own work, will still be cherished by the schemes of the new board. Pupilage is not to be entirely abolished as it has in the medical profession. The report lays down a four years' course, the first two of which are to be spent in a recognised school of architecture, and the latter two in an office as an articled pupil or in some other capacity, but during these, the student is still to keep in touch with his school and to be directed in certain of his studies from it.

This seems at once to be a very excellent compromise largely combining the advantages of both systems, and to be entirely suited to English characteristics. At his school of architecture, which it may be hoped will generally be situated in the midst of other schools at Universities, the student from whom some minimum of general education has been enacted, will, from the very outset, be given a wider view of his art than it is generally possible to put to him in an office.   He will be shown by the great examples of the past what are the possibilities that lie before him, how the best architecture has in every age preserved the vital relation I have mentioned, to human life and thought, and that it will be his mission to perpetuate in stone or brick for the world at large what is most worthy of perpetuation in modern life.   Such views will be given him before the necessary drudgery of office routine can disgust him.   He will then, in these first two years, either have his enthusiasm fired or he will be advised, let us hope, to try something else.

This at once removes a great practical difficulty in the present system, where a youth is bound for three or five years, more often than not the latter, and a large premium is paid for him in advance.   The parent in such cases is naturally anxious for some return for his money, and is not very ready to admit a mistake has been made.   How common such mistakes are every teacher well knows. They are only to be expected from the reasons many parents give for the fond hope and belief that is in them that their sons can be fashioned into architects.   An elementary proficiency in drawing at school, an auctioneer uncle at home, sickness in childhood and need of a supposed outdoor life, these are among the more usual. Therefore, any system which allows a certain time for the student to find his feet and to see the direction he is moving in, before he irrevocably decides the course of his whole career, is preferable, on this count alone, to one that does not.

Having gained then in his first two years, some idea

of the scope of his future work, both theoretically and technically, the student will be able to exercise, to a limited extent no doubt, his judgment in the choice of the master he is to serve under.   With the present system, where the pupil's whole outlook on his art is in the first instance through the eyes of his master, this all-important step is generally taken in complete darkness alike by parent and pupil.   For those who are fortunate enough to find themselves in the office of a master, who is an enthusiastic artist, loving his work in all its details, the five years' personal relationship to such a man are probably as good a training from all points of view, except perhaps in breadth of outlook, as any system that could be devised.   But these masters are few and the premiums the best architects deservedly obtain prohibit many of those most fitted to profit from finding a seat in their offices.   This inequality will be redressed then by the shortened period of articles and by the continuance during them of direction and tuition in the school.   The personal relationship, however, of pupil and master, a much closer one than can generally exist between pupil and professor, still remains, and can be made, as it has often been in the past, one of the most delightful possible to human nature, in the best cases capable of affording the most lasting influences a man can receive.   It may even be extended, for it is not so probable that a student will go elsewhere after two years to become an assistant as after five.   But in the worst cases, and it is for the purpose of raising the general level of architectural education that the present board exists, the student will

certificate that is offered and the degree, this course has for some time been successfully persued, and the Institute has accepted it in lieu of its own intermediate examination.

If this scheme of training, which has been sketched out, and which is being promoted by a representative body including many of the best architects in the country, should attain the universal acceptance which is hoped for,—and I see no valid reason why it should not,—the important question at once arises as to the part the Universities are to play in relation to it. They would seem to be the natural centres in which the new schools of architecture may be placed. Have not most of them grown up round similar schools for other professions to the great profit of the Universities and professions alike? Why should not the architectural student have the same advantages of intercourse and training which other classes of technical students enjoy, at least in the newer Universities? It seems difficult to deny them it, except on the ground that as students of an art their standards of work and achievement are not so easily commeasurable as in other subjects. This, however, is a theoretical difficulty rather than a practical one, as those who have had to judge the work of architectural students will readily admit. Although architecture is an art, like sculpture, dealing with abstract form, its technique of building construction includes a very definite range of facts to be scientifically studied, and without a due appreciation of which we have seen it cannot make much headway. As far as its technique is concerned there is little more difficulty then in including it in the accepted academic categories than the various branches of engineering. Degrees in surgery offer a still closer parallel. Even in the æsthetic application of the facts of construction, which must proceed concurrently and from the first, if they are viewed in a sober and conservative spirit, there is no very real difficulty. It has not been felt in America, where large architectural schools doing good work are to be found attached to most of the Universities, the good influence of which is to be seen in much of the best recent American building. Nor does the experience of the Liverpool school differ. It is hoped, therefore, that a subject which so vitally affects the life of everyone, and success in which till now has always been a distinguishing mark of a great people, will soon be included in the recognised courses, not only at our newer Universities, but also at Oxford and Cambridge. Indeed it seems to me that the sister arts of sculpture and painting might well be included too, and, in fact, must be if the sympathetic relationship between them and architecture is to be maintained and strengthened. That so large a branch of human activity as fine arts cover can be excluded, makes the term "University," as at present used, a somewhat misleading one. Degrees and certificates are matters of detail, which may or may not present a difficulty. They are certainly not essential to the teaching of an art. What is desirable and even necessary in an University is that all branches of study and all legitimate activities be represented.

For such Universities then as already possess architectural schools, the more practical question is the amount of general and liberal study that can be infused into a technical curriculum. If the example of Harvard is to be followed, a student reading for a degree in architecture would, in general, be required to graduate with a B.A. degree first. This is no doubt the best of all plans. Such a student rapidly overtakes those who have started earlier, and, as a rule, surpasses them. In England we have experience of this in the increasing number of architects who have graduated at Oxford or Cambridge before signing articles, and who have afterwards come to the front in their art. The latest architectural associate at the Royal Academy, and one of the secretaries to this new Board of Architectural Education is an excellent example. Such a course though, involving five years at the University, three for the B.A. and not less than two for the technical curriculum, even if best in the long run, will mean too great an expense for the average student. To meet such, it might be possible to permit a portion of their technical subjects to count, according to their nature, towards either a B.A. or B.Sc. degree, so that their purely technical course afterwards, whether leading to a degree in architecture or to the proposed certificate of the Board, could be of less duration. Beyond these again, there will always be the students, who, from some gap in their general education, in their mental, or even their pecuniary equipment, cannot tackle a B.A. or B.Sc. course, but who may yet make excellent artists, and who must be provided for in the schools. These are the students who will start at once on the technical course for degree or certificate, which degree or certificate, under proper safeguards, the Board should recognise in the case of properly equipped Universities in lieu of their own. The Board then, in this suggested arrangement, would throughout the land settle the minimum of training to be required from each student, while the various Universities would offer courses in slight variation or in excess of it, according to their local needs and opportunities. In this way, the architectural degrees or certificates of the Universities would each attain its own standing and weight, as the various medical degrees have done long ago.

There is a very important but indirect effect which should follow the formation of architectural schools within the Universities. It is the stimulus that might be given to scientific research into the whole field of building materials. In the laboratories of engineering, physics and physical chemistry, which bulk so largely at the newer Universities, it should be possible to resolve many of the problems pertaining to such ordinary materials as Portland Cement and concrete, which the architect has to face in actual work, but for which at present he has very insufficient scientific data to go upon.

There is one further point. For these suggested diplomas and degrees to maintain their proper value among architects, as well as for the training given in the schools to be real and vital, it is essential that the teacher, in every case and every degree, should be a practising architect, devoting a very considerable portion of his time to the design and superintendence of actual building operations. It is only in this way that archæological pedantry and doctrinaire views can be avoided in the teachers themselves, and suitable men be selected for the posts. No architect with any real interest in and love of his work,—and only such can teach effectively, however highly paid,—will forego all chance of seeing his creative work carried out. But it is not only, or chiefly, from his point of view that this is necessary. His students will not have that respect for him as an artist, which is essential, unless they know and see the actual work he is doing and the good that is in it. But if they can study, under his guidance, the buildings he is erecting, these will become for them, in every stage of their construction, a series of practical experiments carried out under the most advantageous circumstances and the best laboratory in which an architectural student can work.

The American Professor and his Salary.

BY

HERBERT W. HORWILL, M.A. (LOND.), B.A. (OXON).

MANY teachers on this side of the Atlantic will have read with considerable surprise the announcement of Mr. Andrew Carnegie's recent benefaction. Is it not a work of supererogation to spend ten million dollars on improving the condition of professors in American colleges and Universities? Nowadays, America is so commonly held up to us as an example in educational matters, especially in whatever concerns financial support, that one's first impulse is to interpret this gift as an instance of the principle, "To him that hath shall be given." The prevailing impression that the American professor is one of the most fortunate members of the educational profession is not, however, borne out by facts.

It is, perhaps, desirable to preface a discussion of this subject by a few words on the use of the title "professor" in American institutions of higher education. In the larger colleges the professor proper comes into contact with the more advanced students only. He is assisted by associate professors and assistant professors, while a large body of instructors is responsible for the more elementary work. In the smaller colleges every teacher is called a professor. Accordingly, if an Oxford or Cambridge tutor, who holds no University chair, visits America as a representative at an academic celebration he is always reported in the papers as Professor So-and-so, receiving the title that would be enjoyed by an American teacher of the same functions and status. Custom also gives this distinction to the head-masters of secondary schools, but this eccentricity need not, of course, be considered here. In the official reports of the U.S. Commissioner of Education the total number of "professors and instructors of Universities and colleges for men and for both sexes" is given as over 15,000, in colleges for women as over 2,400. In the schools of technology, which are included in the benefits of Mr. Carnegie's gift, some of which, like the Massachusetts Institute of Technology, are of high educational rank, the professors and instructors number nearly 1,500.

The Commissioner's reports do not supply material for an estimate of the average salary of a professor, but a recent article in the New York *Evening Post* from a special correspondent at Cambridge, Mass., gives particulars relating to the most distinguished place of higher education in America. According to this statement, the average salaries at Harvard are as follows: Full professors, 4,000 dollars; associate professors, 3,500 dollars; assistant professors, 2,160 dollars; lecturers, 781 dollars; instructors, 999 dollars; and assistants, 328 dollars. In translating these figures into English currency it must be remembered that, according to the experience of Englishmen living in America, the purchasing power of a sovereign here is very much greater than that of its nominal equivalent, five dollars, there. Another important factor in international comparisons is suggested by the same authority when he adds, on the strength of the above statistics: "Thus it is seen that a large part of the teaching force at Harvard College is composed of men who receive salaries that would not tempt men to become conductors and motor-men on a street railway." He points out also that the salaries of teachers at Harvard have not kept pace either with the expenses of living or with the increased incomes of other professions. "A professor in 1839 with a salary of 2,000, or one in 1868 with a salary of 3,000 dollars, could afford to occupy a house in the same street with lawyers, physicians, and bankers, and could live comfortably with such neighbours. The professor of to-day, lucky indeed if he has 4,000 dollars a year, finds this a serious proposition. . . . Anybody who is competent to be a full professor at Harvard is capable of securing several times the income of his professorship in some other line of work."

The *Evening Post* correspondent expresses the opinion that "Harvard is probably better off than any other American College." If he means that the Harvard professor or instructor is better paid than any professor or instructor elsewhere, his generalisation is open to a few exceptions. There are one or two of the newer Universities, established by the large endowments of millionaires, which are commonly reported to have offered unusual inducements to certain of the most distinguished members of their faculties. But on the whole the situation at Harvard is far more comfortable than at the majority of American Universities and colleges which have a much more modest endowment to depend upon, but which at the same time feel themselves compelled in the competition with other institutions to spend more and more on the material equipment for a type of education far more expensive than the old-fashioned curriculum. In frequent instances an institution which is doing excellent work in its own field suffers from such constant straitness of means that its president has to occupy a great part of his time in soliciting help from wealthy friends to avoid retrenchment or bankruptcy. In the home of many a professor in such colleges there is being waged to-day a struggle hardly less wearing to body and mind than that revealed by Mrs. Harriet Beecher Stowe's reminiscences of a professor's household in a former generation.

Some striking testimonies have recently been given of the dangers to which American higher education is exposed by this state of affairs. Three in particular may be noted : one from a visiting English scholar; another from a German, who has held for the last ten years an important professorial chair in America ; and a third from a native American. Last October, Sir William Ramsay, in a speech given at Brooklyn at the close of a visit to the United States, warned his hearers that the under-payment of the professors in their leading colleges and Universities involved a serious risk to their national prosperity. Unless it were soon remedied, the scientific chairs, he predicted, would be filled by three classes only : (1) Enthusiasts willing to make a sacrifice for science' sake; (2) Men of independent means : (3) Men of third-rate quality. The first and second classes would necessarily be small in number. The salary received by a professor—and this remark applied, according to Sir William Ramsay, not only to science, but also to medicine, law, and theology—was so much less than could be obtained by professional practice, that only those who had reason to doubt their capacity to rise in their profession would elect a professorial career. This would inevitably react upon the training of professional men in general, for students trained by third-rate teachers could not them-selves reach the front rank. Sir William noted that the large gifts and bequests made to American educational institutions had generally been applied to the erection of buildings, and suggested that prospective donors might use their money more fruitfully by increasing the emolu-ments of professorial chairs.

The next significant evidence to be quoted is that of Dr. Hugo Münsterberg, Professor of Psychology at Harvard. In his " American Traits," he fills several pages with an indignant protest against the damaging effect produced by the low salaries of professors upon productive scholarship in America. He advocates a rise in salaries, not only that the professor may be free from financial cares and may have an opportunity for research, but for a further reason, which holds for America alone. In spite of the absurdity of much that has been said about "the worship of the dollar," it remains true that in America, to an extent far greater than in any other country, excellence is tested by a financial standard. Those who observe how the American instinctively gauges the value of a thing by what it costs, and of a person by what he gets, will understand the force of Professor Münsterberg's contention when he adds : "We need high salaries, because at present they offer the only possible way to give slowly to productive scholarship social recognition and social standing, and thus to draw the best men of the land." This judgment is the more valuable because accompanied by the confession of a change in his own opinion. When he came to the country, he was shocked at hearing an English visiting scholar declare that America would not reach the highest rank in scholarship till every professor in the leading Universities had a salary of at least 10,000 dollars, and the best scholars 25,000 dollars ; the American was not anxious for the money itself, but money was, to him, the measure of success, and, therefore, the teaching career needed the backing of money to raise it to social respect and attractiveness, and to win over the finest minds. "My English acquaintance," comments Professor Münsterberg, "did not convince me at that time, but the years have convinced me ; the years which have brought me into contact with hundreds of students and instructors in the whole land ; the years in which I have watched the development of some of the finest students, who hesitated long whether to follow their inclination towards scholarship, and who finally went into law or into business for the sake of the social premiums."

But low salaries not only tend to keep highly qualified men out of the educational profession, they also tend to the deterioration of the work of those actually engaged in it. "The great majority of American professors seek money-making opportunities that have a varnish of scholarship but no pretence of scholarly aims." It is a financial situation in which America's best scholars "are so poorly paid that they feel everywhere pushed into pursuits antagonistic to scholarship." The professor or instructor "deceives himself by all kinds of compromises— writes popular books here, and articles for an encyclopœdia there; makes schoolbooks and writes expert's testimonials; works in University extension, and lectures before audiences whose judgment he despises." "American Traits," from which these opinions are taken, was published in November, 1901. In a later book, "The Americans," issued in November of last year, the same writer recurs to this question, and repeats his lament over the injury to scholarship resulting from "the fact that the scholar is tempted, by high social and financial rewards, to give scientifically unproductive popular lectures, and to write popular essays." The nature of these temptations may be appreciated from the illustrative statement that "in a state like Massachusetts, every little town has its woman's club, with regular evenings for lectures by outside speakers; and the condition of the treasury practically decides whether one or two hundred dollars shall be paid for some drawing speaker, who will give a distinguished look to the programme, or whether the club will be satisfied with some teacher from the next town, who will deliver his last year's lecture on Pericles, or the tubercle bacillus, for twenty dollars." Professor Münsterberg is ready to admit that this popularization of knowledge may rightly become the life-work of men who have a special talent for exposition, but he maintains that this "easy way for the ready speaker, perhaps, of doubling his salary from the University" does serious harm to many. "Their popularization of knowledge diminishes their own scholarship. They grow adapted to self-educated audiences; their pleasure and capacity for the highest sort of scientific work are weakened by the seductive applause which follows on every pretty turn of thought, and by the deep effect of superficial arguments which avoid and conceal all the real difficulties."

Our third witness is Dr. George Trumbull Ladd, one of the leading American psychologists, and, until his recent resignation, the head of the philosophical department at Yale. "The Degradation of the Professorial Office" is the title of a scathing article contributed by him to the *Forum* of May, 1902. He declares point blank that "the office of teacher in our colleges and Universities is being subjected to influences which are bringing it down to a relatively low level of appreciation and reward. . . . The motives, character, and culture of the average college professor are undergoing a species of decline. The average man of this professional class is not so much of a man, not so much of a gentleman, not so influential a member of society or of the commonwealth, and not so much respected and looked up to by the public as he was one generation or two generations ago." Several reasons are given in explanation of this change, and prominent among them is "the quite inadequate salaries of our college professors." Dr. Ladd dismisses as "always partly specious, and, in some cases, almost hypocritical" the plea that colleges which have hundreds of thousands of dollars to spend on magnificent buildings cannot afford to increase these salaries. He continues: "When the current American way of regarding the values of men and of their services is taken into the account, how is it possible to expect that this state of things will not contribute to the degradation, in the popular estimate, of the professorial office?" Even the professor himself cannot, without many a painful struggle, retain his self-respect. "His dentist takes a whole day's pay from his salary for a single hour of dental work. The plumber is as well rewarded for his time as he." For this and other reasons the present-day professor, though ahead of his predecessors in technical equipment and comparing favourably for intelligence and character with any other class in the community, shows a degeneration from earlier standards in general mental and moral training, and in strength and dignity of character, nor has he retained the same ideals of his life-work.

It would be easy for a diligent reader of the best American journals to collect numerous confirmations of these testimonies. To what cause or causes are we to attribute the conditions which they describe and deplore? Certainly not to any deficiency of the financial resources of the country, nor to any stinginess in the application of these resources to educational purposes. The American public is so accustomed to huge benefactions from its multi-millionaires that when the morning paper reports another gift of a million dollars to a University no more excitement is aroused than if it had been another big railway accident. But these large contributions, whether gifts or bequests, are devoted as a rule to equipment, especially in the form of buildings. An American usually prefers his generosity to have a visible result. You can show a visitor your library or your laboratory, but you cannot take him on a personally-conducted tour around the salaries of your professors. The stimulus to an ex-penditure that is capable of being displayed is increased by the rivalry between colleges, or rather the rivalry between localities. If there is competition between Oshkosh, Wis., and Kalamazoo, Mich., or between Rome, N.Y., and Athens, N.Y., to obtain the finest city hall, it is not surprising that local patriotism should be stirred with the ambition of possessing the most costly, and therefore the finest, educational apparatus also. How naturally an American's ideas of educational progress turn to edification in the literal sense was curiously illustrated the other day in a newspaper interview with President W. R. Harper, of the University of Chicago. "The University," he said, "is moving steadily forward, and is not only laying its foundations broadly, but is building permanently, and with an eye constantly to the future." One would naturally expect to hear, in exposition of this text, something impressive and statesmanlike concerning methods, curricula, and the like. But this is how Dr. Harper continues: "Of the twenty-nine buildings now on the campus, only two are brick—all the others are of stone. Seven new buildings that have cost between 1,500,000 dollars and 2,000,000 dollars have just been completed and put into commission." It happens that in the case of Chicago, the erection of magnificent buildings has left a sufficient surplus for the adequate remuneration of the teaching staff, but in the majority of colleges the placing of such emphasis upon the outward and visible signs of the higher education leads to the starving of those energies which are necessary to produce its inward and spiritual graces.

Unfortunately, there is not much that can be said in answer to the question : What is being done to remedy the present situation? Early in the present year, a movement was set on foot among Harvard graduates to raise 2,500,000 dollars before Commencement Day this summer, for the permanent increase of the salaries of professors and instructors in their *alma mater*. Possibly, similar enterprises have been started elsewhere, but have not been made generally known. The recently established Carnegie fund will do much to help professors who are approaching old age, but will not greatly relieve the present distress of younger men, whose problem is to make the two ends meet this week. And this fund will not apply to State Universities and colleges, or to denominational institutions. No satisfactory improvement can be expected until there comes a revival of earlier traditions of American education, now regarded as old-fashioned and behind the times. There was a period when the personality of the teacher counted for more than the expensiveness of his apparatus. Those were the days of the strong men of American educational history— of Eliphalet Nott, whose fame it was that he took the sweepings from other colleges and turned them out pure gold; of Mark Hopkins, of whom it was said, I believe by his pupil, President Garfield, that a log of wood with Hopkins at one end and a student at the other was enough to make a college. During the last few years, I have many times seen this definition of a college quoted in the American press, always in a tone of ridicule or contempt. It gravely underestimates, no doubt, the value of finely tempered tools to the skilled workman, but it seems to me to rest upon a sounder philosophy than the theory which makes much of the tools and sets little store by the workman. Although we live in the twentieth century, it is still true that man is more than machinery.

The Pronunciation and the Teaching of Greek

BY

J. GENNADIUS, D.C.L. (Oxon.).

IN a letter which appeared in *The Times* of April 25th, on the Archæological Congress at Athens, the well-known correspondent of that journal refers to the production of the *Antigone* of Sophocles in the restored Stadion by undergraduates of the University, and goes on to make the following observations:—

"The play was given in the original text with, of course, the modern Greek pronunciation, which, undoubtedly, is nearer the ancient than any of the arbitrary systems adopted in Central and Western Europe. The accents, for which the Alexandrine grammarians devised written symbols in accordance with the pronunciation existing in their time, have never changed, and their use in the iambic dialogue of the play never for a moment obscured the metrical rhythm. Even the changes from the iambic to the anapestic measure, or *vice versa*, were immediately noticeable, the rhythm being even more marked in the anapestic lines. The fact will not surprise anyone who has heard a passage from Homer recited by a cultivated Greek, and it must be remembered that in Greek, as in French, the accent is much weaker than in English, in which the unaccentuated syllables of many words are almost lost in ordinary conversation. Nevertheless, no educated Englishman, in reciting the poetry of his own language, would alter the accent of a word because, as often happens, the accent ran counter to the rhythm, or pronounce the word 'disobedience' with two accents, because it forms a double trochee in the first line of 'Paradise Lost.' Pronunciation 'according to quantity,' if it ever existed in the past, can only have been employed in musical recitative, in which certain syllables lent themselves to production or contraction as in modern music. Those who still insist in discarding the Greek accents, which have been preserved from antiquity, would do well to hear a Greek play recited by Greeks. With regard to the pronunciation of the vowels the sound of the Italian *u* or English *oo* given to the diphthong ου (undoubtedly the pronunciation of antiquity, as shown by the Latin transliterations) was an immense improvement on the hideous 'ow' sound with which we are familiar, and which is all the more unbearable owing to its frequent repetition in genitives, and in such words as οὗτος and οὐ or οὐκ. On the other hand the 'itacism,' or frequent recurrence of the *ee* sound (probably a corruption in the case of the vowel *v*), was a blemish, but infinitely less objectionable than the perpetual 'ow' of English recitation."

These remarks appear to merit some special attention, coming, as they do, from one who, both by reason of his familiarity with the mode of teaching Greek in English schools and Universities, by reason of his own scholarly attainments, and by his experience of local conditions, is particularly well qualified to judge. Moreover his verdict is given after the severest test to which any kind of pronunciation can be subjected, namely, the delivery of dramatic verse from a stage in the open. To me it does not seem surprising that one so well equipped should have added his weighty vote to that of all Englishmen of education and culture whom I have known express an opinion on the subject, after some residence in the country and a familiar acquaintance with its spoken tongue. The Rev. J. Lowndes, author of the first Modern Greek and English lexicon; the Rev. Leeves, translator of the Septuagint into Modern Greek; the Rev. J. H. Hill, Chaplain to the British Legation for some thirty years; Sir Thomas Wyse, British Envoy, and Mr. Merlin, British Consul General in Athens; Sir George Bowen, some time Secretary to the Lord High Commissioner in the Ionian Islands, and others, whom it would be too long to enumerate, whatever their academic prepossessions may have been before residing in Greece, were all converted to the same views as those so pithily expressed by *The Times* correspondent. Sir Mount-Stuart Grant Duff in his delightful "Notes from a Diary" (ii. 93) relates that during his visit to Athens in 1892 he took lessons in Greek pronunciation, and he adds: "Need I say that every day and all day I heap curses on the heads of the pedants who wasted my youth, and that of all my contemporaries. Any intelligent boy of fifteen who knew the alphabet, applying himself to the study of Greek in Athens for three years, could read, write, and speak Modern Greek by eighteen with perfect facility, and translate a hitherto unknown passage from an ancient prose author quite as well as the average Ireland scholar—all this without intermitting a reasonable amount of attention to other things."

Now, as regards the methods employed in the tuition and the study of Greek—a question which was again debated at considerable length of late in the columns of *The Times*—I would venture to affirm that the adoption of the traditional pronunciation would insure, to those who must needs devote valuable time to the study of the classic language, the almost simultaneous acquistion of a living tongue at no additional labour. That the literary form of Greek of the present day—the Greek of the Church, the educational establishments, the newspaper press, the language of official documents, of parliamentary debates, of cultivated converse—is, to all intents and purposes, as pure as the Greek of the New Testament, is admitted by all those who have inquired into the subject.[1]

---

1. "The literary language has been greatly purified during the present century by the expulsion of foreign words and the restoration of classic forms. The Greek of the newspapers now published in Athens could have been understood without difficulty by Demosthenes or Plato. The Greek language has thus an unbroken history, from Homer to the present day, of at least 2,700 years." Professor W. Goodwin's "Greek Gram.", 1883, p. 3.

The difference between this literary Greek and the Greek of Demosthenes is less pronounced than that between the English of Chauser and of Tennyson.[1]   The opinions of such authorities as the late Professor E. A. Freeman, John Stuart Blackie, Sir Richard Jebb and others, are set forth in an article which I contributed some time ago to *The Forum*, on "The teaching of Greek as a living language," and in which I referred to the material advantages to be secured by the reintroduction of the traditional pronunciation.

I speak of *reintroduction* advisedly.   For one of the most astonishing circumstances in connection with this matter is the persistent disregard, in certain quarters, of the fact that Greek was first taught in England, as well as in the rest of Europe, in accordance with the traditional pronunciation.   Not only this is ignored, but there seems to prevail a wilful forgetfulness of the very peculiar, indeed, ludicrous circumstances in which the so-called Erasmian pronunciation was invented and introduced.   So that, as things are now, the students are imbued with the conviction that they are being tutored in the delicate modulations, and the niceties of sound, which emanated from the lips of Pericles and Plato.

When Greek was first taught in England by the great Greek Archbishop of Canterbury, Theodore of

---

1. "Chauser's English (500 years ago) we master by dint of good solid application, and with considerable help from a glossary ; and King Alfred's English (1,000 years ago), which we call Anglo-Saxon, is not easier to us than German." Wm. Whitney. "The Life and Growth of Language," 1883, p. 33.

Tarsus (668-690), the traditional pronunciation was used.[1] So later (1240) also, when John Basing assisted Robert Grosseteste in reviving the study of Greek. Basing had journeyed to Athens, and was there taught the language by Constantina, the talented daughter of the Archbishop of that city. Alexander of Hales, Richard Middleton, William Ockham, Walter Burley, Thomas Bradwardine, and others between 1245 and 1349 transmitted to their successors whatever Greek they possessed in the only known and only used pronunciation at that time—the traditional pronunciation. During the revival of letters we find that the first Englishman who then taught Greek at Oxford, William Grocyn, had studied under Demetrius Chalcocondyles in Italy, along with his countryman Thomas Linacre, the famous founder of the College of Physicians. Linacre had been elected a member of Aldus's *New Academy*, in which Greek, as spoken by the Greek friends and fellow-workers of the great printer, was the exclusive and obligatory language. About the same time William

---

1. A psalmbook of Pope Gregory the Great (590-604) contains the Greek text of the first psalm in Latin letters: *Macharios anir os uk eporefthi en buli asebon ke en odo amartholon uk estike*, &c. The last leaf of "King Æthelstan's Psalter" (Br. Mus. Cotton MS. Galba A. xviii.) contains certain prayers in Anglo-Saxon characters. The words are wrongly divided, proving that the scribe himself was ignorant of Greek, and was writing under dictation; but the rendering of the pronunciation is to the point: *diatus staverusu* = διὰ τοῦ σταυροῦ σου; *os senu uranu keptasgis tonartonimon tonepi ussion* = ὡς ἐν οὐρανῷ καὶ ἐπὶ τῆς γῆς· τὸν ἄρτον ἡμῶν τὸν ἐπιούσιον, &c. This MS. is ascribed to the end of the eighth or the beginning of the ninth century. Luitprandus Ticynensis, an historian of the tenth century (Pertz, *Monumenta Germaniæ*), writes, in Latin characters, *tis ptochias* = τῆς πτωχείας, *igoumenon* = ἡγούμενον, *wasileu* = βασιλευ, *chrisotriclinon* = χρυσοτρίκλινον, *athei ke asevis* = ἄθεοι καὶ ἀσεβεῖς, &c. In all these instances the pronunciation rendered is identical with that of the Greek of to-day, except here and there, where the nearest available Latin consonant is necessarily used.

Latimer was a pupil of Mussurus at Padua; and William Lily, the first High Master of St. Paul's School (1512), taught Greek as he had learned it during his sojourn in the Island of Rhodes.   The tradition which these great men had brought over with them was confirmed by Calpurnius, a native Greek, who first held the readership of Greek founded by Cardinal Wolsey in 1519 at Oxford. As regards the sister University, Erasmus, who had been the pupil in Greek of Grocyn (1488), first taught at Cambridge the little he ever knew of that language, according to the "Erotemata" of Chrysoloras and the traditional pronunciation.   He had not yet invented the pronunciation of the Lion and the Bear.

As long, therefore, as active intercommunion with the fountain-head was maintained, as long as Italy and France and, in a minor degree, England also, were visited by those noble and learned Greeks who had fled before the Turkish deluge, the correct pronunciation of Greek remained unimpaired and unquestioned.   But with their gradual disappearance, the precise and pure sound of the Greek letters became uncertain among local teachers, and doubts and disputes as to the exact sound value of those letters were frequent.   In the confusion which thus prevailed, the difficulties naturally experienced by Englishmen, Germans, and Dutchmen in mastering the peculiarly mellow sounds special to Greek became more apparent.   Consequently, considerable variations of pronunciation began to creep in, deviating in each case towards the mother tongue of the local teacher who, in self-justification, naturally maintained that his was the right way of pronouncing, and that, no doubt, Greeks so pronounced.

It was at this precise juncture, and in these very circumstances, that Erasmus's famous "Dialogue" made its appearance. We shall see that it was the result of a hoax suggested by his own vanity and want of critical acumen. That such was the origin of the "Dialogue" is passed over in discreet silence by latter day Erasmians; but the facts are recorded in great detail by no less an authority than Gerard Jan Voss, through whose instrumentality, be it remembered, the new pronunciation was made compulsory in Dutch schools. Thus he was an advocate of that pronunciation; but, with commendable frankness, he devotes a considerable part of a chapter of his "Aristarchus, sive de Grammatica" to the narration of the pitiable incident which engendered the "Dialogue." In order fully to appreciate the circumstances, let us not forget that Erasmus had taught Greek, as all his predecessors and contemporaries had done, in the traditional pronunciation. Moreover, in his "Familiar Colloquies," he makes Echo respond to *epi*SCOPI by κότοι, to *eruditi*ONIS by ὄνοις, to *fame*LICI by λύκοι, etc., which can only serve when uttered according to that pronunciation. Furthermore, in a letter to Janus Lascaris, referring to the newly founded college at Louvain, he says: "There are many here who seek for the Greek professorship; but my opinion has always been that we should send for a native Greek, from whom the students might acquire the *genuine* pronunciation." And he requests Lascaris to recommend such an one for the post. It is a curious coincidence that it was at Louvain, and at that very college that the hoax related by Voss, an indisputable authority, was perpetrated upon Erasmus. Henricus Loritus, of Glarus (Glareanus),[1] poet Laureate to the Emperor Maximilian, and a man of keen humour, on arriving from Paris, dined with Erasmus at the college, and told him "a story he had made up on the journey, inasmuch as he knew Erasmus to be inordinately fond of novelties and wonderously credulous. He said that some native Greeks had reached Paris, men of marvellous learning, who made use of a pronunciation of the Greek tongue entirely different from that generally received in those parts; for instance, they called β, instead of *Vita*, Beta; and η, instead of *Ita*, Eta; αι, instead of *æ*, ai; οι, instead of *i*, oi; and so on. On hearing this, Erasmus wrote soon afterwards the "Dialogue" on the right pronunciation of the Latin and Greek tongues, in order to appear himself the inventor of the matter (ut videretur hujus rei ipse inventor). . . . Erasmus, however, having found out the trick [practised upon him], never afterwards used that method of pronouncing, nor did he direct those of his friends, with whom he was more familiar, to follow it." Voss goes on to add, in proof of this, that he had in his possession a copy of a *later* scheme of Erasmus for the pronunciation of Greek, "which in no way differed from that which learned and unlearned use everywhere for that language."

---

1. Heinrich Loriti (1488—1563), one of the most famous scholars of his time and the author, among other works, of ΔΩΔΕΚΑΧΟΡΔΟΝ, *seu Tractatus de Cantionum Musicarum Modis*, Basiliae, 1447. He was, therefore, well qualified to appreciate matters of rymth and pronunciation.

Such was the astonishing genesis of the much-lauded treatise, which was first published by Froben at Basle in 1528. It is couched in the grotesque form of a dialogue between a sapient lion and an erudite bear, who, after putting their heads together, come to the conclusion that both Greeks and Latins pronounced the letters of their respective alphabets as the Dutch did their own. When we consider Erasmus's very meagre knowledge of Greek we are not surprised to find that, evidently having doubts about his premises, he hedged, with characteristic subtlety, against contingencies, and had recourse to this ponderous kind of humour, so as to allow the dialogue to pass, if need be, as a mere literary squib. Indeed, his more benevolent biographers tell us that it was only "a sporting production," a *jeu d'esprit*. As a matter of fact, it is neither humorous, nor clever, nor weighty. It is a superficial attempt, devoid of philological research or acumen, resting upon untenable assumptions, abstract surmises, and gross casuistry, inferior in these respects even to Ignatius Donelly's notorious Baconian crypto-gram, and far less convincing than the humorous gravity of Archbishop Whately's inimitable brochure on "Historic Doubts relative to Napoleon Bonapart." Its hollowness and shallowness is well summed up by M. Egger ("L'Hellenisme en France," i. 452), when he says of it: "Rien n'est plus loin d'un traité dogmatique, soit pour le fond, soit pour la forme." Yet rooted prejudice and vested interests are so powerful, even in the world of letters; they exercise so blinding an influence, even on men of the highest attainments, that a scholar like

Professor Blass does not hesitate to declare: "I shall disregard practice, and keep to scientific discovery; for as such, and a very great discovery, I regard the achievement of Erasmus." Fortunately for German scholarship a compatriot of Dr. Blass is of a contrary opinion. Dr. E. Engel ("Die Aussprache des Griechischen," Jena, 1887) believes that a more general and more precise acquaintance with the contents and character of the *Dialogue* would soon render the phrase "Sie sind ein Erasmianer" a term of reproach.

What is certain is, that the " Dialogue " was never put forward as a serious argument in favour of the change which was then being wrought, principally in England, imperceptibly and, so to say, automatically, by the force of the circumstances already alluded to. The exponents of Greek thought and Greek speech were no longer the illustrious refugees from Byzantium; and those who now learned Greek did so no longer from the living word. There was no one to give the true note, the pure sound of a pronunciation which presents peculiarities of its own, and requires considerable training, especially for an English mouth. The difficulty of keeping undefiled a pronunciation strange and alien, beset with perplexities, and consequently distasteful to those who had now to learn Greek from books only, engendered an opposition which sought justification in philological doubts as to the authenticity of the traditional sounds. Consequently the gradual adoption of a more or less arbitrary mode of giving voice to a language which was considered dead, was thus sanctioned. For the human mind is only too prone to espouse, on merely plausible arguments and in the absence of all proof, that which seems to respond to some prevalent disposition, to satisfy a vague desire, and to confer a delusive advantage.

It was in this frame of mind, induced by the circumstances just set forth—not any serious scientific research, nor any philological evidence—which brought about, in England more especially, the abandonment of the traditional pronunciation. That this was so is placed beyond doubt by a close examination of the movement then initiated in the University of Cambridge. The main incidents of the famous dispute (1535-1560) between Sir John Cheke and Sir Thomas Smith, Professors of Greek, on the one side, and Bishop Gardiner, Chancellor of the University, and its senior members on the other, are known to all English scholars. But I doubt whether certain important facts, which alone explain the inner character and significance of the movement, are as fully admitted or appreciated. Yet without the admission of those facts, which are attested to by the disputants themselves and are recorded by Strype ("Lives" of Cheke and Smith and "Ecclesiastical Memorials"), no reliable estimate of the question can be formed. They are briefly the following:—

(*a*) That the exact sounds of the Greek alphabet, as practised by native Greeks, had been obscured, if not entirely lost among English Grecians, and that, while condemning the traditional pronunciation, they were in constant doubt as to its precise character. It was now more than a generation since the last Greek had lectured at

Oxford and, therefore, it is not surprising to find that the examples of the pronunciation criticised by Cheke in his letters to Gardiner are inaccurate. Moreover, he admits that having met a Greek ecclesiastic, he could not understand him, and he was equally unable to make himself understood in Greek. Likewise, Sir Th. Smith, after propagating the new system, went about the Continent endeavouring to ascertain what was the pronunciation he had already condemned; and in an interview with a learned Greek in Paris, he had to fall back upon French and Italian in order to converse with him.

(*b*) That both Cheke and Smith were zealous advocates of spelling reform and of the phonetic rendering of the English language. They were the first to devise a complete scheme to that end,[1] and they pressed that reform simultaneously with their new pronunciation of Greek. In other words, they sought to alter the spelling of English, the pronunciation of which they could not possibly modify; and to introduce a fanciful pronunciation of Greek, the orthography of which was beyond their power to recast. In the the first of these attempts they failed, not because it was more irrational than the pronunciation they invented, but because it proved as vain to press it upon Englishmen, as it would have been hopeless to prevail upon Greeks to adopt the new-fangled

---

1. Dr. Johnson in the Grammar prefixed to his Dictionary (Todd's Ed. 1827, p. 106) gives an account of the system of Smith, to whom he refers as to one "much practised in grammatical disquisitions." Cheke adopted his new orthography in some of his own writings.—See pp. 18-19, of "The Gospel according to Saint Matthew . . . translated into English from the Greek, with original notes by Sir John Cheke; with an introductory account by J. Godwin," Cambridge, 1843.

pronunciation.   In the second they succeeded, after a time, because, as it is positively recorded, it offered relief to the undergraduates, who consequently supported the proposal with acclamations as uproarious as they were undiscerning.

(c) Sir Thomas Smith states that both he and Cheke were young men of twenty when they conceived and initiated these vast projects—projects which, failing a genius not claimed for them by their admirers, should have been matured by a long preliminary research and a many-sided erudition, which they certainly did not bring to the consideration of the subject.   They avow that they were simply puzzled because several vowels and diphthongs convey the same sound in Greek; and yet they had before them the undeniable fact that similiar consonances occur in almost all written languages, and that in English, more especially, there are no fewer than a dozen vowels and combinations of vowels representing the sound i (Italian).   On that account, they pleaded that "they found it difficult to teach this (Greek) tongue well"; and they set about groping for a solution of the imaginary difficulty.   Erasmus's "Dialogue" was already in their hands; they could not adopt the advice of the Lion of the Low Countries to read Greek like Dutch, so they accepted the manifest conclusion that they should read it like English in England.

(d) Strype's narrative establishes beyond dispute the fact that the reform was first introduced, not as a "scientific discovery," but surreptitiously and by insinuation.   Mullinger also ("The University of Cambridge,"

p. 55) positively states that Smith, "without giving any intimation of his design, commenced . . . an occasional use of his own method—to quote his own expression—*lapsu linguæ*, as it were." When, finally, Smith and Cheke had made sure that their idea took with the undergraduates, they determined to stand by it, and they set about evolving *ex post facto* arguments for its support. The most powerful incentives to the adoption of the reform were considerations of expediency, not scruples as to philological accuracy. The latter were invented afterwards to lend respectability to the former. Moreover, the philological pleadings, if good in regard to Greek, were equally applicable to Latin. Yet no attempt was made to reform the pronunciation of Latin, so long as the Church of Rome was dominant, and communications were active with Italy. Nevertheless, English sounds had already began to supersede automatically, so to say, the traditional Latin pronunciation, exactly as they had done the Greek.

The struggle for prevalence was long and obstinate. The undergraduates, as may be imagined, were all for the "reform," which they "received with much applause and commendation,"—naturally enough, considering the facilities it afforded them. But with the senior members it was otherwise.[1] Ratcliff's disputations with Cheke occasioned riotous scenes. Roger Ascham's vigorous opposition at the outset was appeased as soon as he was appointed Greek reader, when he espoused the cause

---

1. "At the celebration of Divine Service in the Colleges Latin and Greek began now to be read differently, after the new way. But this was looked upon as very odd by the older sort that heard it."—Strype, p. 577.

with the ardour of a convert—without ceasing, however, to protest his humble admiration of Gardiner.   John Caius was an opponent of very different mettle.   He held scientific truth above personal considerations.   And his science in Greek was esteemed so highly that he was invited to lecture on Aristotle at Padua in 1539, when that University was one of the foremost seats of learning in Europe.   In opposing, therefore, the new method he was well qualified to affirm that "Greek itself became barbarous thus clownishly uttered, and that neither France, Germany, nor Italy owned any such pronunciation" (Fuller's "Hist. of the Univ. of Camb." vii. 7). During his sojourn in Italy he examined carefully all available data and ascertained the opinions of the most eminent scholars; so that on his return to Cambridge he was able to declare most authoritatively in favour of the traditional pronunciation.   His treatise, "De pronunc. Gr. et Lat. linguæ," published subsequently in London, 1574, is by far the most profound and weighty contemporary document relating to that dispute; for which reason it is discreetly ignored by Erasmians.   The struggle continued to wage fiercely up to the death of Gardiner (1555); nor does the new pronunciation seem to have been firmly established at Cambridge until after the accession of Queen Elizabeth.   As regards Oxford, it is certain that as late as 1561 it was not received there.   For in a letter dated April 16th of that year Richard Cheny, afterwards Bishop of Oxford, informs William Cecil that in a discussion with some of the heads of the Colleges there the authority of the traditional pronunciation was upheld.

On the Continent the adoption of the Erasmian theory was no less slow. Scaliger the elder, Melancthon, Œcolampadius, and their immediate successors, recognised the tradition as the only normal and legitimate rule. As late as 1608, Joseph Scaliger seems to take a malicious pleasure in relating to Stephen Ubertus (Ep. ccclxii.) his encounter with certain Englishmen and their Erasmian Latin: "Anglorum vero etiam doctissimi tam prave Latina efferunt, ut in hac urbe, quum quidam ex ea gente per quadrantum horae integrum apud me verba fuisset, neque ego magis cum intelligerem, quam si Turcice loquutus fuisset, hominem rogaverim ut excusatum me habebit, quod Anglice non bene intelligerem. Ille qui cum ad me deduxerat tantum cachinnum instulit ut mea non minus intefuerit pudere, quam ipsius ridere." Similar must be the vicissitudes of English-spoken Greek at the present day. For although the Erasmian method has now prevailed all over the Continent, each country has adapted the pronunciation of its own language to that of Greek, all claiming to have thus revived the exact sounds of the time of Plato and Demosthenes, yet each differing from all the others, and all agreeing to differ in various degrees and modes from the traditional practice. So that Gardiner's warning to Cheke that his method would inevitably lead to a confusion worse than Babel itself, has proved prophetic; and Dr. Giles may well say, in the "Life" which he prefixed to his edition of Ascham's Works, that Cheke's innovation is "a system which is not only barbarous in itself, and irreconcilable with all known theories of language, but has separated the English as much in the power of communicating in speech with other nations, as they are separated physically from their neighbours by the Straits of Dover."

It would be an error to suppose that the mischief ended there. When Strype, in innocent admiration, exclaimed that by Smith and Cheke's achievements, "never to be forgotten by posterity, was the noble Greek tongue, restored to itself, as it was spoken in the times when Greece flourished and brought forth Plato, Dionysius, Plutarchius, Demosthenes and Thucydides," he had but little notion of the difference which certainly existed in the pronunciation of Greek between the times of Plato and of Plutarch, and less foreknowledge of the wide divergence which was bound to ensue between the "only true and genuine pronunciation" evolved by Smith and Cheke, and the one now in use with their successors. The pronunciation they invented has been undergoing, since their time, changes parallel with the modifications introduced into the pronunciation of English itself. Precisely in a similiar manner the German pronunciation of Greek has been changed since the Erasmian theory was first introduced into Germany, *pari passu* with the mutations which have supervened in the sounding of the letters of the German alphabet. So also in France. For the articulation of neither English, German, nor French remained during this space of time immutable. In England, Mullinger (p. 95) says, "in the course of the seventeenth century, this (Cheke's) method was, in turn, abandoned for the method now in use, which differs alike from the Erasmian and that by which it was preceded."

Not only this, but later again a fresh change in the pronunciation of Greek and Latin was introduced into English schools. Entirely different systems prevail now in Scotland and Ireland, in Protestant and Catholic schools ; while in the United States a dozen various systems contend for supremacy—a perfect "chaos," as Professor Godwin confesses. The inevitable result of these conflicting and contradictory systems—admittedly mere pretences and makeshifts—is the periodical appearance of fresh and strange proposals, each one of which claims to have finally established the only really "ancient" pronunciation—how ancient, whether Homeric, Platonic, or Plutarchian; of which particular form of Greek, whether of Attic, Ionic, Æolic, or Doric ; of which precise Greek locality, whether of Attica, Laconia, Doris, Bœotia, Crete, Sicily, Cyprus, or Ephesus—and we know that at such different times and places the pronunciation varied perceptibly—of these minutiæ, the discoverers take no heed. But they all differ among themselves. The latest discovery,[1] as far as I can remember, was vigorously debated in the *Academy* of January and February, 1896. In these circumstances, the verdict with which Mr. A. J. Ellis ("The Eng. Dionys. and Hellenic pronunc. of Greek") sums up his able examination of the matter, appears anything but harsh or exaggerated : "The efforts of Cheke and Smith were alone instrumental in imposing the conjectures of Erasmus into school use. These conjectures did not represent the pronunciation of Greek at any period, but gave sounds which were not difficult to

---

1. "The restored pronunciation of Greek and Latin with tables and practical explanations," by E. V. Arnold and R. S. Conway, Cambridge.

Englishmen of the sixteenth century.   Such sounds then
could be used by schoolboys, and learned more easily
than Hellenic sounds, to which they had previously had
to submit.   Greek and Latin in this way became, so far
as pronunciation was concerned, a part of English speech,
without any separate individuality in a learner's mind ;
just as our boys at present, when they spout Homer, have
little or no notion that they would be utter barbarians to
the Greeks of all time.[1]   Hence the sound given to the
Greek letters changed with the change of the pronunciation of English . . . Such a result is not very creditable
to scholarship."

It would, therefore, appear not unreasonable to
maintain that if any attempt is to be made towards
remedying the existing confusion, by the adoption of
some more rational pronunciation of Greek, the first step
should be the wider knowledge and recognition of the
facts recorded in the foregoing pages.   At present they
are systematically ignored and passed over in silence, for
the very reason—one is constrained to believe—that they
are inconveniently true, quite unanswerable, and absolutely destructive of the fiction on which the present
system, or want of system, is based.   And here I must

---

1. In confirmatory contrast to this may be noted a case which came within
the personal knowledge of Sir Reginald Cust, and was referred to by him in an
address to the London Central School of Foreign Tongues. A son of Greek
parents established in London, was sent to an English school. ''The unfortunate
boy was at once compelled, in spite of his urgent protests, to read his Greek
lessons in the English fashion. He endeavoured loyally to acquire the art of
doing so, but from time to time his memory failed him, and he lapsed from the . . .
well established classical pronunciation of the English school into more euphonious
but less orthodox accents which he had inherited from his mother. The consequence was, that the poor boy became the object, not of admiration, but of
derision by his schoolfellows. who regarded him as an ignorant young barbarian ;
and his sufferings were such, that his parents were obliged to remove him from
the school."—*The Journal of Education*, July, 1895.

add at once that no Greek, whose opinion is of any weight, pretends that we pronounce Greek exactly as it was spoken during the different epochs and in the various localities alluded to above.   Such a pretension would have been as absurd as the alleged discovery of "the only true and genuine" pronunciation.   Our contention is as moderate as it is reasonable aud unassailable: it is that we have maintained unbroken the living tradition, which is the only safe guide and norm in respect to the pronunciation of all languages.   It is so with English, German, and French, in which languages changes in sound, much more material, have taken place; and that within an incomparably shorter space of time, than in Greek.[1]   But no one has yet made, so far as I know, the Quixotic proposal that Chauser, the Niebelungenlied, or the Chanson de Roland, which are now read with all the mannerisms of latter-day pronunciations, should in future be delivered according to some newly discovered method, supposed to render the slight variations of sound, the niceties of speech, and the modulations of voice which may, or may not, have prevailed when those works were composed.   Such niceties and modulations can no more be "discovered," than they can be represented by the

---

1. The pronunciation of English has changed considerably even within recent times.   Pope's verse will not rhyme in all cases according to the pronunciation of the present day.   Pitt the elder provoked a general titter in Parliament when he pronounced sugar as "shagger," but he only conformed with a slightly antiquated usage.   Lord John Russell was one of the last who habitually said "an 'voman," "cowcumbers," "laylocks," "obleeged," &c.   W. D. Whitney (ut supra, p. 33) is of opinion that "if we were to hear Shakespeare read aloud a scene from one of his own works, it would be in no small part unintelligible, by reason especially of the great difference between his pronunciation and ours."   "The French of Canada has preserved peculiarities which were recognised at the time of Molière, but have long vanished from Parisian French.   If Canadians pronounce loi and roi like loué and roué, so did Molière, nay, so did Lafayette so late as 1830."—Max Müller, "The Science of Language," i. 78.

D

inanimate, and fixed symbols, which go to make up an alphabet. They vary with time, and are modified by circumstances, fashions, and surrounding influences. When, however, the living tradition remains unbroken, we are compelled to admit that the pronunciation, in its essential features, has been maintained unimpaired, in spite of the slight, and, for the matter of that, the considerable modifications which time and usage have sanctioned. Such modifications are legitimate; and one cannot go back upon them. This rule, which holds good in all languages, applies especially to Greek, the continuity in which tongue is not disputed; no Erasmian has ever pretended to have discovered a point of time in the history of Greek, at which the continuity of tradition was broken. On the contrary, even Erasmians allow that there is no perceptible difference in the pronunciation of Greek since the third century B.C., as the evidence in the Septuagint and other documents satisfactorily establish. Which language, which pronunciation can claim as venerable a record, as noble a pedigree? Taking, therefore, into account the considerable local variations and modifications known to have existed in classic times, we are authorised in maintaining that the pronunciation has been handed down to us from generation to generation practically unimpaired. We are strengthened in this especially by the fact that the tradition has been scrupulously preserved by the most conservative of Christian Churches. But we can adduce even stronger proof. We have the irrefragable evidence of inscriptions of the best times, in which we meet with words engraved, either designedly or by error, in a phonetic rendering; and such rendering tallies absolutely with the present day manner of pronouncing those words and letters.   There is nothing to be opposed to evidence of this description.   On the other hand, there are local variations of pronunciation sufficient to enable a Greek to distinguish between natives of Attica, Corfu, Epirus, Constantinople, Trebizond, Cyprus, etc., exactly as this was the case in classic times; but these variations are in no instance as marked as those which exist between the pronunciation of a Piedmontese and a Neapolitan, a Hannoverian and a Viennese, a Highlander and a Virginian.[1] Nevertheless, to a Greek of no matter what locality or time, Greek pronounced according to the various systems in vogue in the West, is absolutely incomprehensible.   Of this, I had personal experience on a Speech Day in an English educational establishment. I was asked what I thought of it, and I had to confess that I had understood the English, French, German, and Italian recitations, but, alas, not the Greek!

Finally, I will endeavour to deal briefly with the very reasonable remarks of *The Times* correspondent anent the *ee* sound of η and υ—the so-called "iotacism."

---

1. If anyone imagines that a precisely identical pronunciation could have prevailed among a people like the Greeks, inhabiting tracts of country and islands widely apart, he should consider the variations noticeable in England, and even more marked in other English speaking communities. Mr. Lowell has placed on record how Gloster, if he were an American, would have pronounced the opening lines in *Richard III.* :—

> Neouw is the winta uv eour discontent
> Med glorious summa by this sun o' Yock,
> An all the cleouds that leowered upon eour Heouse,
> In the deep buzzum o' the oshun buried.
> Neow air eour breows beaund 'ith victorious wreaths.
> Eour breused ams hung up fer monumunce,
> Eour stan alarums changed to merry meetins,
> Eour dreffle marches to delightfle masures.

Although it can be proved satisfactorily that the sound *ee* is less frequent in our pronunciation than in that of the English language, yet we admit that the ancient sounds of these two vowels have undergone considerable modification. But this admission is made with important reservations. We can show, on the one hand, that this gradual assimilation in sound dates from very ancient times; while, on the other hand, we adduce evidence of present-day local usage, according to which the υ is still sounded in certain words, as *u* (French)[1]—ἄχυρα, σκύλος, θύρα, &c.; and the η as *e* (Italian)—σίδηρος, κηρίον, ξηρός, &c. Now it is a remarkable fact that in classic Greek both ξηρός and ξερός occur. The natural inference is, therefore, that such special sounds of those two vowels, as well as of some diphthongs, were confined, even in classic times, to certain words, and, perhaps, also to certain localities only. Nor should it be forgotten that the very delicate sound *u* (French) has a natural tendency towards attenuation; witness the German fünf, pronounced as *finf* locally. And this is one of the many unanswerable remarks made by Bishop Gardiner in his correspondence with Cheke: "Vide quæso apud nos in nostra διαλέκτῳ utrum osculum jam *kusse* dices, vel *kysse*, quod exemplum ideo tibi propono, ut videas apud nos sonum literae υ Graecae, quae antiquioribus et rudibus sonabat *u*, urbanitate quadam loquendi in sonum ι literae extenuatum."

As a matter of fact, nothing has more effectually disposed of the empiricism, the crudities, and the caprice

---

1. Yet the French are content to name the twenty-fourth letter of their alphabet "y greo," and to pronounce it, in words derived from Greek, as a mere i.

of Erasmians than the phonetic laws and principles established by the new science of language. " Different languages have different phonetic tendencies . . . each language has phonetic laws and phenomena peculiar to itself" (Sayce, "Introd. to the Sc. of Language," i. 231). " Each language has its own phonetic idiosyncracy " (M. Müller, "Sc. of Lang.", i. xiv.). It is this idiosyncracy of the Greek language which the Erasmians have failed to grasp, and without its comprehension and admission they will never find their way to a reasonable and true solution of their difficulties. As long as they are content to declare *ex cathedra* that the traditional pronunciation is "corrupt and barbarous," and continue to speak Greek "every man in his own tongue," so long will the delivery of the one appear strange to the other, and all of them remain quite incomprehensible to those for whom Greek is a mother tongue, not dead, but very much alive and stirring. The anecdote which the late Sir George Bowen used to relate with much humour is to the point. An English official in Athens sent home his son, who had been born and bred in Greece, to qualify for holy orders. At his examination he did not make much headway, but was on the point of collapsing, when he was taken over his Greek Testament. In this, he showed considerable proficiency ; whereupon the examining Bishop said to him approvingly: "You are doing much better now, Mr. M—; but *where* have you acquired that *strange* pronunciation of Greek ? " —" In Athens, my Lord," was the prompt reply. The Bishop's reflections are not recorded.

Universities, Schools, and Examinations.

BY

P. J. HARTOG.

———

In the opening number of this *Review*, Dr. Schuster put forward cogent arguments for the devotion of the third year of University study, not to the "acquisition of knowledge," but to the "working out of some problem which contains some novelty and requires some originality."[1]   In the second number of the *Review*, Sir Oliver Lodge suggests that in a general course for the B.A. degree, our young men and women should become acquainted with the general principles of Biology, Natural Philosophy and Astronomy, Chemistry, and Geology; that they should further "obtain some notion too of what has been done in Philosophy and Ethics and Logic; some knowledge of Elementary Physiology; and some acquaintance with, at least, the History of Art and Archæology"[2]—a list only more modest than that prescribed by Milton himself.

---

1. *University Review*, " Universities and Examinations," p. 20.
2. *University Review*, " Questions for Discussion," Part II., p. 146.

The average reader may well feel bewildered between these apparently conflicting ideals of intensive and extensive University culture.   I venture to submit, in all humility, that the problem of University education, as presented by these two distinguished and critical writers, is not a determinate one.   And it is indeterminate for a reason of fundamental importance.   I mean because of the extraordinarily indeterminate and unsatisfactory character of secondary instruction in England.   The word unsatisfactory slipped from my pen.   I shall come to that later.   It is on the indeterminate meaning necessarily attached in this country to the term secondary instruction that I desire first to say one word.   A German boy, a French boy, a Swiss boy, an American boy, a Hungarian boy, when he has passed, at eighteen or nineteen, the school-leaving examination, or *baccalaréat* of his country, which is his passport to the University, has a certain amount of acquired information on which his University teachers can fairly count.   Now the standard reached by these foreign boys on the literary and historical (and in some cases on the mathematical) side is far higher than that of our own University entrance examinations, and, in some cases, higher than the standard of an English intermediate examination.   The foreigner coming into our University classrooms for students (except the classrooms in experimental science) in their first and second years, at once exclaims, "higher secondary education."   The Englishman going into the higher classes of a French *lycée* or a German gymnasium at once realises that the character of the teaching (often given by specialists of international reputation) is of a kind which no English University would disown. It would seem, at the first blush, as if English University education must, owing to the insufficiency of our secondary teaching, necessarily be distinctly less advanced than Continental University education.

In many branches, and in many individual cases, it undoubtedly is so. Our inferiority is saved from being glaring by the exceptions. For many English boys, trained in exceptional schools, or by exceptional effort on the part of their teachers, enter our Universities with a knowledge and power immensely in excess of the minimum required, and are pointed to later as model specimens of University students. The second year senior wranglers, of whom Dr. Schuster speaks, may be quoted as a case in point. Against these how many may we not set who scrape through the University preliminary examinations in a state of unculture, which I will not further define? Everyone knows that at any examination the standard is not wholly determined by the ideals of examiners. It depends on what can reasonably be expected from candidates having gone through the average course of training available for them. And when the average course of training in secondary schools is low, the minimum standard of the test for admission to the University must necessarily also be low. The chief object of this article is once more to draw the attention of University teachers (1) to the fact well known to specialists, that our secondary instruction is deplorably behind secondary instruction abroad, and (2) to the consequence, that if the

University teachers wish to improve University education as a whole they must use every effort as individuals and as members of a University to improve secondary education. And first of all the Universities must make up their minds what they want in a far more definite and complete way than they have done hitherto.   The tremendous explosion on the Greek question, the question as to whether boys should or should not be made to learn as much Greek as can be got up by scholarship holders in six months, revealed the singularly one-sided view of secondary education taken by many members of the older Universities.   As for the newer Universities they have not yet made up their minds as to whether the normal age for entry should be sixteen or eighteen.   It need hardly be said that the whole University curriculum depends on the choice.   In London what is, I believe, an increasing number of students come each year to the University at eighteen, having already passed the intermediate examination.   It is an excellent sign, and one cannot but hope that it points to a day when our secondary schools shall no longer fall short of continental ideals.   When that day arrives surely we shall be in a position to demand of the schools that general conspectus of things which Sir Oliver Lodge would have taught at the University.   I feel that in the interests both of secondary and of University education, Sir Oliver's demand should be resisted to the utmost.   The "old English degree of B.A.", to which he refers as a model, was taken not by men but by boys, in the days when it was forbidden to play marbles on the

Senate House steps at Cambridge. I believe the majority of science men, at any rate (and I include among science men the historians and the philologists), would agree with Dr. Schuster that during the years from eighteen to twenty-two a student should begin to do something in which his original faculties have free play, and that if you do not give him the time necessary, you may in those years sterilise his original faculties utterly. The attitude of continually working to please other people, instead of working to please and satisfy one's own mental requirements and critical power, is the attitude systematically encouraged at the present day by English secondary and University education, taken as a whole. In time the desire to please vanishes, and we get the perfunctory performance of duty which is inefficiency itself.

Dr. Schuster tells us indeed plainly that in his proposal he has "chiefly kept in view the student of good ability who intends to do his work in life with pleasure to himself and profit to others." But to what percentage of the "professional schoolboys," characterised by his fellow writer as "intellectually dull, apathetic, and indolent,"[1] who leave school to enter the University, will his scheme apply?

Some time since, in connection with a former essay of Dr. Schuster's on University Education. I drew attention to the fact that the extremely large proportion of distinguished amateurs in this country

---

1. Sir Oliver Lodge, "School Teaching and School Reform," p. 9.

pointed to some sterilising influence at our Universities.[1]
May I now suggest that the remarkable efficiency and
superior power of initiative displayed by the officers
of the navy, all of whom have escaped ordinary school
training from the age of 15 or earlier, points no less to
sterilising influences in our secondary schools?

The training for the navy, like the life on the veldt,
gives an element in education which is lacking at present
in our schools.

If the reader desires to obtain evidence as to the lack
of culture, and of capacity and desire for individual effort
induced by secondary training at present, he may be
referred to the report of Mr. Akers-Douglas's Committee
on preliminary training for the army.

On the reasons for the intellectual deficiencies of
our secondary education, it is hardly possible to do more
than touch in the present article.   But there are two
main reasons which are fairly obvious.   Our secondary
teachers are only in the rarest cases men who have
made any contribution to the subject which they teach;
their ideal, as a rule, is still the mediæval ideal of learning.
They are underpaid; their hours of work are so long that
they can scarcely hope to find time or energy for personal
work; and their tenure is precariousness itself.

The English Universities and the public seem unable
to realise how vitally important it is that the secondary
preparation for the highest University training should be
made adequate, and that to attain this the teachers should

---

1.   In an article published in the "Special Reports on Educational Subjects
of the Board of Education."   Vol. 11.

be chosen from those in touch with the University, and of individual power of such a calibre, that in many cases they will naturally come back to the University.

For the inadequacy of the staff of secondary schools, the Universities can scarcely be said to be directly responsible. But there is one way in which, as many authorities have realised recently,[1] the Universities have exercised an evil influence on secondary education. I mean through the bad side of examinations, and I say expressly through the bad, because I believe we may, if we are not careful, forget in the near future that they have another side. If you take a very big thermometer to test the temperature of a little water, you will lower the temperature of your water perceptibly before you get your reading. Now, our examinations have lowered very perceptibly indeed the temperature of the education they were intended to test. That is, however, a reason perhaps rather for improving than for abusing or throwing away our thermometers altogether, and there is one possible improvement in the examination thermometer to which I desire to draw attention.

"The power of applying knowledge," Dr. Schuster tells us (*loc. cit.*,p. 11), "cannot be tested satisfactorily by examination. We should recognise that examination serves its legitimate and very necessary purpose when it tests the existence of knowledge."

Now, one can surely test by means of an examination whether a student can translate a piece of a foreign

---

1. The "School-leaving" examinations, instituted by a number of Universities.

language, whether he can summarise, understand and analyse a long statement (such as might be contained in a three or four page quotation from a historical, scientific, or philosophical memoir), whether he can solve a triangle with the help of trigonometrical tables, or integrate an expression, or investigate the equation of a curve not previously seen, or determine the refractive index of a piece of glass, or analyse qualitatively and quantitatively a mixture or a compound. Are these to be regarded as tests of the "existence" or of the "application" of knowledge? I should feel inclined to call these tests of the *application* of knowledge (as well as of its existence, of course), while I should say that only the *existence* of knowledge was tested by such questions as the following : " Describe Joule's experiments on the mechanical equivalent of heat." "Relate the chief events in the reign of Edward I." " Write out the 47th proposition of Euclid." " What is the only French masculine word ending in *-ence*?" (I choose as a last example one of the most favourite and inept).

As in the case of all distinctions (*teste* Mr. Alfred Sidgwick) there will be a borderline where the distinction drawn above ceases to be sharp; but it is valuable in spite of that, and especially valuable in dealing with the question of minimum marks for a pass examination. Dr. Schuster points out (in another connection) that examiners set as a rule papers that are too difficult and then fix too low a standard for a pass (*loc. cit.*, p. 15), and later he adds (p. 22) "A minimum of knowledge is required. Let that minimum of knowledge be tested properly or even severely.'

The present minimum (in the examinations of different Universities with which I am acquainted) varies from thirty to fifty per cent., according to the University and the examination. It seems to me that while such a minimum may be reasonable in testing knowledge of facts, it does and must yield results that are futile in testing the power to apply knowledge. I will take the simplest possible of cases. You wish to test a boy's power of doing "tots" and of multiplying. Either he can add and multiply correctly or he cannot. To allow him to pass if he gets thirty or forty per cent. of his answers right is to give a certificate of competency to an incompetent person.

Similarly a person either can or cannot solve a triangle, when given the necessary data and a table of logarithms. If we leave the region of mathematics (the only one in which marks and merit have anything like a rigorous relation) the case becomes more difficult. Nevertheless I believe we should have no hesitation in a given instance in saying whether a boy can or cannot give the sense of a piece of unseen French or German, whether he can or cannot analyse or summarise a piece of prose, &c. Now, if we give a proper allowance of time for reflection, there is no reason why in such tests of the power to apply knowledge we should not make the minimum pass standard eighty or ninety per cent.[1] instead

1. I do not say 100 per cent. in order to allow for chance errors, which time for checking would correct. In certain cases the minimum might certainly approach 100 per cent. The suggestion has been made already by M. Lippmann, Member of the French Institute, in his evidence before the French Parliamentary Commission on Secondary Education of 1899. ("Enquête sur l'Enseignement secondaire," t. 1, p. 35.)

of 30 per cent.   It is no longer a question of the testing of the memory, but of powers which have or have not been acquired.   I would suggest therefore that pass papers might, in many cases, be divided into two parts, the first testing chiefly the "power to apply knowledge," the second, memory.   In the first portion the minimum for a pass would approach reasonably near to 100 per cent., in the second we might retain the 30-50 per cent. standard of to-day.   It is obvious that the carrying out of such a proposal as I have sketched in outline would raise difficulties of detail, but I believe these could be met.

To set papers in which essentials and unessentials figure on an equal footing, and to allow a candidate to pass who obtains 30 or 50 per cent. of the marks on the whole is a procedure which has had serious effects on school education, and for which our examining bodies themselves, in the end, pay very dearly.   It is one which they have it in their power to amend.   Indeed, the whole subject of examinations appears to me to be in urgent need of investigation by an absolutely independent body, such, for instance, as a committee of the British Association, including representatives of all grades of teachers and examiners.   The object of such investigation should be not to discover past delinquencies, not to produce a Blue Book of horrors, (and it would be easy to compile one) but to test and improve our methods, with an eye constantly on the watch for the probable effects of methods of examining on methods of teaching.

Such an investigation is a debt that we owe to our

secondary schools, to our University students, and to the country.

I hope that the secondary schools will, in future, do the work which Sir Oliver Lodge would impose on the Universities. I hope that they will enable the students coming from them to carry out work on the lines recommended by Dr. Schuster. The key to University reform lies in the reform of our secondary teaching.[1]

---

1. I would refer the reader interested in the subject to Professor M. E. Sadler's brilliant essay on "The Unrest in Secondary Education"; to Mr. Twentyman's article on the New Prussian Curricula, and various other articles on Foreign Secondary Education, which have appeared in the "Special Reports on Secondary Education"; published by the Board of Education; and also to the "New Curricula for French Secondary Schools."

THE LATE CANON A. S. FARRAR, M.A., D.D.
Professor of Divinity and Ecclesiastical History in the University of Durham.

Memorial Notice.

"Quique sui memores alios fecere merendo."

The Rev. A. S. FARRAR, M.A., D.D., F.R.A.S., F.G.S.

Canon of Durham, Professor of Divinity and Ecclesiastical History in the University of Durham.

DR. FARRAR, who was descended from an old Wesleyan family, received his early education at Liverpool Collegiate Institution. Born April 20th, 1826, he matriculated in 1844 at St. Mary's Hall, Oxford; and obtained a first class in *Literæ Humaniores* and a second class in Mathematics in 1850. In 1851, he won the Arnold Prize with an essay on "The Causes of the Greatness and Decay of the Power of Carthage." In 1852, he was elected to the Michel Fellowship, Queen's College, and was ordained by the Bishop of Oxford. In 1853 and 1854, he obtained the Denyer Prize with essays on "The Doctrine of the Trinity" and "Original Sin." He was appointed Mathematical Moderator in 1854, and Classical Examiner in 1856. At this time, he became a tutor at Wadham College, and in 1858 he was appointed to be one of the preachers at the Chapel Royal, Whitehall; and in 1861 to be Bampton Lecturer. In 1864 Dr. Jenkyns vacated the Divinity Professorship at Durham, and Dr. Farrar—he received the degree of D.D. in that year— was appointed by Bishop Baring Professor of Divinity and Ecclesiastical History in the University of Durham. In 1878, Dr. Farrar succeeded to the Canonry of Dr. Jenkyns.

During this—the Oxford—portion of his career, Dr. Farrar published, in 1856, a pamphlet of *Hints to Students in Reading for Classical Honours in the University of Oxford;* in 1859, a volume of sermons entitled *Science in Theology;* and in 1862 his Bampton Lectures, *A Critical History of Free Thought in reference to the Christian Religion.*

During his twenty years at Oxford, he touched life at many points ; and on which he would finally settle, could hardly be foreseen. A classic, a mathematician, a divine, a Fellow of the Royal Astronomical Society and of the Geological Society, a traveller who had compassed the whole of Europe and part of Asia Minor, and who knew the military topography of every place he visited ; he had before him a wide variety of choice. But on going to Durham, he renounced everything for the work to his hand—his work as Professor. The renunciation was great, but it was not without its reward ; if he gave himself up to his lectures and his pupils for forty years, he reaped the harvest of admiration and affection to which he was entitled. Those who had not the opportunity of attending his lectures could only form some idea of the learning with which they were furnished, if they were fortunate enough to hear him converse freely. But all who chose to attend Cathedral when he preached, had an opportunity of appreciating the lucidity, learning, and literary grace of his utterances. And behind the intellectual qualities was the generous heart: "Few," said Dean Kitchin, in his reference in Cathedral to the loss of Canon Farrar, "few were aware of the great kindness of heart which characterised him to those who had need and wanted help in the time of trouble.

F. B. JEVONS.

Foreign University News.

FRANCE

Communicated by M. Ludovic Fichou, *Secrétaire Général du Bureau des Renseignements de l'Université de Paris* .... June.

REFORM IN MEDICAL STUDIES.

The Minister of Public Instruction has recently issued a circular to the Rectors of the University inviting them to consult the Faculty of Medicine on the following points:—

1. The reorganisation of the teaching of medicine so as to secure better co-ordination and to ensure the progressive instruction of students.

2. A more complete, systematic and efficient organisation in practical work, so that it may be possible to give students some recognition of their share in the work done.

3. Whether to keep to the present Examination Regulations, or to restore the system of examinations at the end of each year or to group them at the end of the second or fourth years.

The results of this enquiry are to be communicated to the Minister before January 1st, 1906.

FOREIGN ASSISTANTS IN LYCÉES.

In order to facilitate the appointment of a sufficient number of foreign assistants, duly qualified to teach modern languages in these schools, the Minister of Public Instruction has invited all heads of such schools to inform the Archiviste du Musée Pedagogique (41, Rue Zay-Lussac) if they wish to engage assistant teachers for the year 1905-1906, and for what language—English, German, Italian. Teachers at present holding such posts may be retained for another year.

TRAVELLING SCHOLARSHIPS.

Two Bursaries of 7,500 francs each have recently been offered to women possessing a University Degree who can show a practical knowledge of a foreign language and who will devote this sum to making a tour in Europe and the United States in one year. It is required of the holders of the Scholarships that they should travel together. The donor desires to remain anonymous.

NEWS AND NOTES.

A banquet was held to celebrate Dr. H. de Rothschild's nomination to the "Legion d'Honneur." As founder of the surgery which bears his name, and Treasurer of the League that has been formed for the prevention of Infantile Mortality, he was warmly congratulated by Professors Dieulafoy, Budin, Poirier and Huchard.

On his return from his expedition to the South Pole, Dr. Charcot was received at the Sorbonne by the University and by the Geographical Society, under the presidency of M. Le Myre de Villers, Deputy. Dr. Charcot has been promoted to the rank of "Chevalier de la lègion d'Honneur."

The second Congress on School Hygiene and Physiological Pedagogy was held recently in the Medical School, M. Lavisse, Director of the Ecole Normale Supérieure, acting as President.

A Geographical Excursion to Switzerland (Lausanne, Valais, Gemmi, Interlaken, Oberland, Bernois) was organised from June 10th—16th, under the direction of Professor Ch. Vélain, of the University of Paris, and Professor Lugeon, Dean of the Faculty of Science at Lausanne.

University Extension.

Among recent meetings we may mention the following:—

At the Education Sociale de Montmartre (7, Rue de Trétaigne):

"Sociability as the Origin of Religions," by M. S. Reinach, member of the Institute.

"The Duration and the Hygiene of Work," by M. Blancheville, Director of the Ministry of Commerce.

At the Union Mouffetard (76, Rue Mouffetard):

"The Union of Nations," by M. le Baron d'Estournelles de Constant, Senator.

At the Fondation Universitaire de Belleville:

Maurice Barre's new book, "In the Service of Germany," by M. Robert de Beauplan, of the Ecole Normale Supérieure.

At the Université Populaire (157, Faubourg St. Antoine):

"The Origin of Life," by M. Zaborowski.

"The Philosophy of Herbert Spencer," by M. Kownacki.

"The Cultivation of Originality," by M. le Pasteur Wagner.

At the Université Populaire "La Corporation des Idées" (234, Faubourg St. Antoine):

"The Poetry of Peace," by Professor Ch. Richet, of the Academy of Medecine.

"Education of Mentally Defective Children," by Dr. Legrais, Principal of the Asile de ville Evrard.

"The Separation of Church and State," by M. Gide, Professor in the Faculty of Law.

Recent Literary and Scientific Research.

The following theses for the degree of Docteur ès Lettres have been received:—

By M. Dhaleine: (1) "A Study of Tennyson's Idylls of the King"; (2) "Life and Works of Hawthorne."

By M. Hanappier, Professor at the Lycée de Caen: (1) "Realistic Drama in Germany"; (2) "The Development of Rhythm in German Lyrics."

By M. Merland, Professor at the Lycée of Brest: (1) "Classification of the Works of Sénancour"; (2) "The Personal Novel from Rousseau to Fromentin."

By M. Cirot, Director of the Lectures on Spanish at Bordeaux: (1) "General History of Spain from Alphonso X. to Philip II."; (2) "Mariana, the Historian."

At the University of Lyons. By M. Russier: (1) "Transportation and Penal Colonisation"; (2) "The Division of Oceania."

At the University of Paris. By M. Humbert, Professor at the Lycée de Bordeaux: (1) "The German Occupation of Venezuela in the 16th Century"; (2) "Venezuelan Origins."

By M. Roger, Professor at Lycée Carnot: (1) "The Teachings of Classical Learning from Ausone to Alcuin."

For the degree of Docteur ès Sciences the following theses have been received:—

By M. Nicalardot: "Research on the Sesquioxide of Iron."

By M. Gonmy: "Research on the Buds of Fruit Trees."

By M. Y. Chautard: "A Study on the Physical Geography and Geology of Fonta Djallon, and its Eastern and Western Approaches."

By M. de Daniloff: "A Study of the Physical Geography of the District of Yalta (in the Crimea)."

By M. Edm. Bordage: "Anatomical and Biological Research on the Origin and Development of Arthropodes."

By M. Th. Solacolu: "The Influence of some Mineral Foods on the Functions and Structure of Vegetables."

By M. Sarton: "Experimental Research on the Anatomy of Allied Plants."

Appointments, etc.

NATURAL HISTORY MUSEUM. M. Perrier, member of the Académie des Sciences, Professor of Comparative Anatomy at the Natural History Museum, has been appointed Director of the Institute for a fresh period of five years.

FACULTY OF MEDICINE. M. Castex, Doctor of Medecine, has taken charge of a supplementary course at an additional surgery for diseases of the throat, ear and eye.

FACULTY OF ARTS. On account of his services and advanced age, M. Monod, Professor of the History of Civilisation and Institutions of the Middle Ages at the Faculty of Arts, University of Paris, and President of the Practical School des Hautes Etudes, has applied for, and has been granted, a retiring pension, dating from June 1, 1905. M. Monod has been appointed Honorary Professor.

ACADEMY OF FINE ARTS. M. Allar has been elected to succeed the late M. Guillaume in the Department of Sculpture.

University Publications.

The following articles of interest have recently appeared in the Reviews:—

"Religious Teaching in Schools," by M. Appühn, in the May number of The Bulletin de la Societé de Philosophie, followed by a discussion in which the following take part: M.M. Belot, Blondel, Brunschwig, Chartier, Darlu, Dunan, Halevy, Jacob, Lauson, Malapert, Pécaut.

"Morality and Immorality," by M. A. Fouillée, member of the Institute, in the Revue Bleue (May).

"The Ritualistic Movement in the Anglican Church," by M. Thureau-Dangin, of the Académie Française, in the Revue des deux Mondes.

"German University Libraries during the Last 39 Years," by M. Leblong, in the Revue Internationale.

"Morals and the Science of Manners," by M. Lévy Bruhl, Professor at the Faculty of Arts. (Published by Alcan, Paris.)

"Moral Experience," by M. Rauh, Professor of Philosophy in the Faculty of Arts. (Alcan, Paris.)

"General History of Plastic Art," by M. Reinach. (Hachette.)

" The Teaching of Social Science," by M. Hauser, Professor in the Faculty of Arts at Dijon. (Pichon, 20, Rue Souffert.)

" Studies on Education and Colonisation," by M. Maurice Courant, University of Lyons. (Pichon.)

" True Religion According to Pascal," by M. Sully Prudhomme. (Alcan).

N.B.—Catalogues and programmes of the courses of work 1905-1906, with general information on French University work and organisation, can now be obtained from the Secretary of the Bureau des Renseignements at the University of Paris.

GERMANY

THE UNIVERSITY OF GÖTTINGEN.

(From a Private Correspondent.)

University News and Notes.

The record of the present Summer Semester shows the largest attendance since the foundation of the University. According to the recently published " Official Syllabus of the Staff and Students of the Royal George-August University at Göttingen, Easter to Michaelmas, 1905," the figures are:—1,779 matriculated students, 114 authorised to hear lectures, and 71 women students; total, 1,964. The division, according to the different faculties, is as follows:—

	Students.
In the Theological Faculty	113
In the Law Faculty	443
In the Medical Faculty	174
In the Philosophical Faculty	1049

The last-named is thus constituted, according to its various departments:—

History and Philology	477
Mathematics and Natural Sciences	368
Chemistry	84
Finance	22
Agriculture	40
Pharmacy	25
Dentistry	18
Other Departments	15

According to nationality there are 1,313 Prussians, and 356 other Germans. Of 110 foreign students 40 are Russians, 20 Austrians, 18 Americans, 8 Englishmen, etc.

The Teaching Staff of the University at present consists of 149 members, thus divided:—

In the Theological Faculty:—
7 ordinary professors, 2 special professors, 3 lecturers.

In the Law Faculty:—
10 ordinary professors, 1 special professor, 4 lecturers.

In the Medical Faculty:—
12 ordinary professors, 7 special professors, 16 lecturers.

In the Philosophical Faculty:—
42 ordinary professors, 17 special professors, 23 lecturers.

University Appointments.

As compared with the Winter Semester of 1904–5, the following changes are to be noted:—the Chair of Pathological Anatomy—Prof. N. Borst, M.D., in place of Prof. H. Ribbert, M.D., who has removed to Bonn; the Chair of Physical Chemistry—Prof. Fr. Dolegalek, Ph.D., in place of Prof. W. Nernst, Ph.D., who succeeded Prof. Landott in Berlin.

The Director of the Institute of Experimental Therapeutics in Frankfort-on-Main, Paul Ehrlich, Secretary of the Board of Health, was appointed Ordinary Honorary-Professor of the Medical Faculty.

The following have recently been appointed:—

H. Walsmann, LL.D., in the Faculty of Law, with a trial lecture upon "The Formal Enforcing of the Creditors' Right of Disturbance."

R. Birnbaum, M.D., in the Faculty of Medicine, with a trial lecture upon "The Significance of the Corpus-luteum in its Anatomical, Physiological, and Pathological Relations."

C. Carat Léodory, Ph.D., in the Philosophical Faculty of Mathematics, with a trial lecture upon "Volume and Superficies"; and E. Pfuhl, Ph.D., has been appointed for Archæology with a trial lecture upon "Circular Building among the Ancient Italians and Greeks."

Student Organizations.

Interesting information is furnished with regard to Student Organisations in the "Calendar of the University of Göttingen," published by the University Book Agency of Dieterich (20th edition, Summer Semester, 1905). According to the Calendar there are 40 organizations (Corps, Students' Associations, Gymnasiums, Vocal

Societies, etc.) and Unions (Scientific, Sporting, Stenographic, etc.) existing at the University. In addition, there has recently been organised a branch of the *Finkenshaft*, that is, the Society intended for the benefit of students who belong to none of the recognised Unions or Corporations, but who also select representatives to serve on the Students' General Committee.

The question of the Students' Organisations has received special attention in consequence of the so-called "Fight for Academic Freedom," which, since the beginning of the present year, has been waged in the different Prussian Universities and technical high schools; and concerning which the Press has furnished full reports. The Senate of the University of Göttingen took up the question at the point where the discussion turned upon the maintenance of certain old traditions concerning a definite measure of self-government on the part of students, particularly in the associating together of corporations, etc. The whole matter was dealt with by Prof. V. Ehrenberg, LL.D., of Göttingen, at a Conference of Rectors which was held in the Prussian Ministry of Instruction in Berlin from May 15th to 19th. (Compare the report in the official *Norddeutschen Allgemeinen Zeitung*).

Prize Distribution.

The University of Göttingen celebrates annually two Festivals, viz., that of its foundation, which is transferred to the birthday of the Kaiser and King of Prussia; and the Festival of the so-called Prize Distribution on the 4th of June, the birthday of George III., the founder of the prizes in the year 1784. The latter consist of a sum of gold given for the best answer returned to four prize questions yearly set by each Faculty. This year one prize was distributed in the Philosophical and half a prize in the Theological Faculties.

The Prize Distribution is also made the occasion for the Pro-Rector of the University,* elected in the preceding September, to deliver his Inaugural Address, and also for one of the professors to contribute an Address of Invitation. The former was this year delivered by Professor E. Schwarz, Ph.D.—"De Pionio et Polycarpo."

Open Session of the Society of Sciences.

The Open Sessions of the Royal Society of Sciences, which are held twice a year, and whose members consist for the most part of representatives of the Philosophical Faculty, while not actually

---

* The Rector of the University of Göttingen is Prince Albrecht of Prussia Regent of the Duchy of Brunswick.

festivals of the University, cannot be allowed to pass unmentioned here, in view of the reports that are made on these occasions concerning an important part of the scientific labours of the University of Göttingen.

The Summer Session was held this year on the 13th of May. The President of the Society, Prof. E. Ehlers, Ph. D., delivered the report, according to which fourteen sessions have taken place during the preceding half-year. Owing to death the Society had lost a number of foreign, i.e., corresponding members, also an ordinary member, Prof. Meissner, professor of Physiology, concerning whom his successor, Prof. M. Verworn, M.D., Ph.D., gave an obituary notice. Prof. W. Voigt, Ph.D., spoke of the deceased physicist, Prof. Abbe, of Jena; while Prof. F. Frensdorff, LL.D., referred to the deaths of the historian, Höhlbaum, of Giessen, and Hoppmann, of Bostock. The report further mentions that the first volume of the "Thesaurus Linguae Latinae," of the Academies of Berlin, Göttingen, Leipsic, Munich and Vienna, is ready, and that the second volume is almost completed. During Whit-week a session was held, under the presidency of the Austrian Minister of Instruction, von Hartl, wherein Prof. Leo, LL.D., of Göttingen, took part, and spoke concerning the further continuation of the work.

Of the works of C. F. Gauss, published by the Society of Sciences, 40 sheets of vol. 7 have been printed.

"The Encyclopædia of Mathematical Sciences," published by the Academies of Göttingen, Leipsic, Munich and Vienna, has made considerable progress during the past year. In the week before Whitsuntide there took place in Leipsic, in connection with the Encyclopædia, a *Kartellsitzing* of the above-named Academies, at which also the editors were present. There are some parts ready for early publication, especially a first part of the volumes "Geodasie" and "Astronomie."

The Observatory for Seismological and Magnetic Appearances, erected by the Society of Sciences in Apia, Samoa, will, through the support of the Imperial Government, be maintained until the year 1909. The observer is Dr. F. Lincke, Ph.D., formerly assistant at the Physical Institute in Göttingen. The Special Commission, appointed by the Society of Sciences for purposes of supervision, consists of Prof. H. Wagner, Prof. E. Riecke, and Prof. E. Wiechert.

The labours of Prof. P. Kèhr (now Director of the Historical Institute in Rome), with respect to the Old Pupil Records, are concluded so far as Italy is concerned.

(Further correspondence from the University of Göttingen will be published in the next number of "The University Review.")

THE UNITED STATES OF AMERICA.

(From Special Correspondents.)

Columbia.

A NEW SCHEME OF COLLEGIATE STUDY.

The Faculty of Columbia College has adopted a new programme of studies, which takes effect on July 1st, 1905.

Students will hereafter be received in Columbia College as candidates for the Degree of Bachelor of Science as well as for the Degree of Bachelor of Arts. Candidates for the Degree of B.S. will not be required to offer any ancient language at entrance or to pursue the study of an ancient language in College. Such students will be required to give to the study of the natural and physical sciences the time given by candidates for the Degree of Bachelor of Arts to the study of an ancient language and its literature.

The proportion of prescribed and elective studies in the College programme will include courses in English, French or German, History, Latin, Mathematics, Philosophy, Physical Education and the Natural and Physical Sciences, and must be completed, so far as practicable, during the first two years of the student's college residence.

The standard of attainment for the Degrees of B.A. and B.S. is no longer fixed in terms of years of college residence, but in terms of work accomplished. A total number of 124 points—a *point* signifying the satisfactory completion of work requiring attendance one hour a week for one-half year—will be required for graduation. Therefore, the student who takes work amounting to 15½ hours a week for each half-year would complete the requirements for the Degree in four years of residence. Students may, however, take as many as 19 points in any half-year, or an even greater number with the consent of the Dean. No student may take work amounting to less than 12 points in any half-year.

A new principle is introduced in the programme by the provision which gives increased credit for high standing in a course, and attaches a penalty for low standing. The student who obtains the mark A (Excellent) in any two courses in one half-year will be entitled to receive one point of extra credit, provided he has not fallen below the mark B (Good) in any of the courses pursued by him during the half-year. A student who receives the mark D (Poor) in two or more courses in any half-year is to be given credit for but one of these courses.

By the terms of this new programme of studies, Columbia University will hereafter offer a curriculum of liberal studies in the arts and sciences, without the ancient classics, leading to the Degree of Bachelor of Science, as well as the existing curriculum including the ancient classics and leading to the Degree of Bachelor of Arts.

It will be possible for the well prepared student who makes a very good record in College to complete the requirements for a Degree in three or three and one-half years.

It will be possible for the student of Law, Medicine or Technology to secure both a College Degree and a professional Degree in six years. It will be possible for the student who looks forward to teaching, or to work in the fine arts, to combine professional studies in those subjects with his ordinary College studies. In either case the student will have the benefit of a carefully considered and well organised two-year curriculum in the arts and sciences. It will be found to the advantage of the student of engineering in any of its branches to enter the Schools of Applied Science through Columbia College, rather than direct from the secondary school.

Provision is made in the new programme whereby elective courses chosen by students must bear some relation to each other, and whereby some one subject must be pursued for a sufficient length of time to gain genuine educational discipline from it.

The new programme removes the emphasis from time spent at College, and places it upon work done in College, and penalises the poorly prepared or negligent student. Students will not be permitted to spend their time wholly upon either unrelated or elementary courses.

Harvard.

Harvard has just received two gifts of money—one of $100,000 to be used as a fund for the development of a department of ethics of the social question, and one of $55,000, the income of which is to be used for sending a Harvard excavating expedition to Palestine yearly.

Enrollment in American Universities.

The accompanying table of statistics concerning the registration of students in the principal Universities and Colleges of the United States has been taken from *The Michigan Alumnus*. The interesting figures have been compiled by Dr. Rudolph Tombo, Registrar of Columbia University. It is shown that while there has been an increase in attendance in the majority of the Universities, the total growth of the combined institutions has not been as great as it was a year ago. This falling off Dr. Tombo attributes to the late economic condition of the country.

	California	Chicago	Columbia	Cornell	Harvard	Illinois	Johns Hopkins	Leland Stanford, Jr.	Michigan	Minnesota	Pennsylvania	Princeton	Syracuse	Yale
College Arts, Men	505	604	527	672	2005	351	188	884	729	470	510	645	1068	1286
College Arts, Women	948	784	363		407	325		447	624	775	604			
Scientific Schools*	789		663	1479	528	909		†	970	560	305	628	370	774
Law	91	115	342	224	745	111		187	830	532	547		130	227
Medicine	106	114	560	391	307	629	291		417	283	182		154	140
Graduate Schools	194	388	709	193	366	132	194	89	100	135		92	61	335
Agriculture	89			184	22	338				750				
Art	198										362		60	36
Dentistry	90				108	153			108	141				
Divinity		170			43									93
Forestry									12					60
Music			35			96					29		595	79
Pharmacy	80		435			147			64	65	155		†	
Teachers' College	†	154	627								82			
Veterinary				103		42	71				164		45	
Other Courses	42		13	135										
Deduct Double Registration		(141)	(218)	(17)	(15)	(103)	(2)	(187)	(187)	(40)			(84)	(25)
Total	3130	2218	4056	3364	4516	3233	740	1420	3667	3671	2940	1385	2419	2995
Summer Session	913	2237	961	774	1007	239		18	647	215	137		59	16
Deduct Double Registration	(305)	(420)	(184)	(275)	(131)	(103)		(14)	(314)		(50)		(28)	(3)
Grand Total, 1904	3738	4035	4833	3833	5392	3369	740	1424	4000	3886	3027	1385	2452	3008
" " 1903	3690	4146	4557	3438	6013	3239	694	1370	3926	3550	2944	1434	2207	2990
" " 1902	3676	4296	4156	3281	5488		669	1378	3764	3505	2549	1345	2020	2804
Officers	330	184	551	451	534	365	156	130	270	197	330	114	201	330

* Includes schools of engineering, chemistry, architecture, mining and mechanic arts,

† Included in college statistics,

Inter-Universities' Athletics.

Cornell, for the first time in her athletic history, won the championship of the Inter-Collegiate meet at Franklin Field, Philadelphia, Saturday, May 27, by scoring 30½ points in the thirteen events. Yale was second with 28 points, and Harvard third with 20½. The other contestants scored as follows:—University of Pennsylvania, 19; Princeton, 11; Amherst, 8; Syracuse, 8; Colgate, 8; Stevens, 3; Swarthmore, 2; Haverford, 1. The following are the chief events and times:—

One Mile: Won by Munson, Cornell. Time, 4 min. 25$^1/_5$ sec.

Quarter Mile: Won by Hyman, Pennsylvania. Time, 49$^2/_5$ sec.

120 Yards Hurdles: Won by Amsler, Pennsylvania. Time, 15$^3/_5$ sec.

Two Miles: Won by Hail, Yale. Time, 9 min. 50$^3/_5$ sec.

Half Mile: Won by Parsons, Yale. Time, 1 min. 56 sec. (being a new Inter-Collegiate record, previous best, 1 min. 56$^4/_5$ sec.)

High Jump: Won by Marshall, Yale. Height, 6 feet.

Long Jump: Won by Simons, Princeton. Length, 23ft. 2½in.

Yale.

The following official valuations of the more important of the University buildings appear in the grand tax list of exemptions at the office of the New Haven Board of Assessors, the valutions not including the land on which the buildings stand:—Vanderbilt Hall, Academic, $750,000; Woolsey Hall, $400,000; Dining Hall and Memorial vestibule together, $450,000; East Divinity, $164,250; West Divinity, $117,500; Gymnasium, $216,065; Law School, $185,500; Byers Hall, $100,000; Medical School, $78,000; Kent Laboratory, $100,000; Sloan Laboratory, $125,000; Peabody Museum, $350,000; Osborn Hall, $200,000; Art School, $250,000; Chittenden Library, $15,000; Old Library, $175,000; Battell Chapel, $125,000; Sheffield Laboratory, $112,500; Winchester Hall, $112,500; and Sheffield Hall, $112,500. The valution of all the buildings reaching a total of considerably upwards of five million dollars.

The Yale Commencement Week this year is being held from June 23rd to 28th. Twenty classes will hold re-unions during the week, with an estimated aggregate attendance of 1,400. The earliest class planning a re-union is the Class of 1850. From that year up to the Class of 1902 all classes due for re-unions will hold them.

The Yale Corporation at a recent meeting decided upon the erection of a new library on a site adjoining the present library. The scheme contemplates equipment sufficient for the next 25 years, making stack room for 700,000 volumes. This is approximately twice the present capacity.

University Extension.

The Oxford Summer Meeting.

The University of Oxford Delegacy for the extension of University Teaching has arranged for the annual summer meeting to be held in Oxford from August 4th to 28th.

The main courses of the Lectures will be as follows:—

1. History (the period of the Renaissance and the Reformation).

2. Literature (to illustrate the Literary Movement of the 16th Century in England and abroad).

3. Painting, Architecture, Applied Arts and Music (including lectures upon the Painters of the Italian Schools, and upon the Architecture and Applied Arts of the Renaissance).

4. Natural Science (introductory lectures upon the Scientific Method of Investigation and the Scientific Analyses of Thought, followed by lectures illustrating the application of the Scientific Method).

5. Social Economics (lectures on the Problem of the Poor, treating the subject both historically and practically.

Among those who have consented to take part in the meeting are: The Vice-Chancellor of the University; Lord Crewe; Lord Lytton; Mr. George Wyndham, M.P.; Sir Richard Temple; Father Gasquet; Professors Walter Raleigh, A. C. Bradley, W. F. R. Weldon, Sherrington, Flinders Petrie, and Churton Collins; Mr. W. L. Courtney; Mr. Sidney Lee; Rev. Dr. R. F. Horton, and Mr. Herbert Paul.

The price of tickets for the whole meeting is £1. 10s., or for either of the two parts (August 4th to 16th, and August 16th to 28th), £1. 1s.

Application for tickets and all enquiries in connection with the Summer Meeting should be addressed to the Secretary, Mr. J. A. R. Marriott, M.A., University Extension Office, Oxford.

News and Notes.

At Paisley during last month it was reported that a number of co-operative students had been examined and certified as class teachers under the Oxford University Extension Delegacy. A suggestion made, during the discussion on the Education Committee's report, to the effect that the Co-operative Movement welcomed this connection with the University met with approval. It was also emphasised that the sending of successful students to the University Summer Meetings was in every case a good educational investment for the Movement.

The Association to Promote the Higher Education of Working Men proceeds apace. During the past month successful meetings have been held at Darwen and Torquay, each resulting in the establishment of local associations. It has been decided to issue an appeal for a central office fund of £500 per annum maintained over a period of five years. So far the draft appeal has been signed by Mr. Thomas Burt, M.P., the Bishop of Birmingham (Dr. Gore), Canon Barnett and Professor Michael E. Sadler, each of whom recognises the urgent necessity of a successful issue. The Bishop of Birmingham and Professor Sadler have each, with others, guaranteed £5 for five years. Copies of the appeal and details of the Association can be obtained from Albert Mansbridge, 198, Windsor Road, Ilford, Essex.

The Universities.

ABERDEEN.

University News and Notes.

A meeting was held on May 30th at the close of the General Assembly of the Church of Scotland for the purpose of promoting a memorial of the late Principal S. D. F. Salmond, D.D. Principal Rainy, the Moderator, presided. The Rev. Dr. Whyte moved a resolution that some memorial, such as a portrait, of Principal Salmond should be produced and gifted to the College where he did such splendid work. The motion was cordially adopted, and a provisional committee was appointed.

Dr. Iverach has been appointed Principal of the United Free Church College, Aberdeen.

Professor Hay has been re-elected for a further period of four years as one of the Trustees on the Carnegie Trust.

Mr. Arthur Lord has resigned the offices of Lecturer in Political Science and University Assistant in Moral Philosophy on his appointment to be Professor of Philosophy and History in the Rhodes University College, Grahamstown, South Africa.

The Professor of Natural History has announced the donation to the Museum, from Mr. W. S. Bruce, leader of the Scottish Antarctic Expedition, of two skins of the very rare Weddell's seal from the Antarctic.

A handsome brass tablet has been placed in the parish church of Glass by Lady Geddes, in memory of the late Principal Geddes. The tablet bears the following inscription:—"In memory of Principal Sir William Duguid Geddes, M.A., LL.D., D.Litt.; from 1855 to 1885 Professor of Greek; and from 1885 to 1900 Principal and Vice-Chancellor in the University of Aberdeen. Born 21st November, 1828, in the parish of Glass. Died 7th February, 1900, at Chanonry Lodge, Old Aberdeen."

BIRMINGHAM.

University News and Notes.

The fifth Degree Congregation will be held in the large lecture theatre of the Birmingham and Midland Institute, Paradise Street, on Saturday, July 8, at noon. The Vice-Chancellor (Alderman C. G. Beale, M.A., Lord Mayor of Birmingham) will confer Degrees. In the afternoon Alderman Clayton (the Pro-Vice-Chancellor) will give a garden party in the Botanical Gardens, Edgbaston.

The Dean of the Faculty of Medicine (Professor Barling) has presented to the University a portrait of Dr. John Tomlinson Ingleby, in memory of whom the Ingleby Lectures and Scholarships were established by the Rev. Charles Ingleby, his son.

The Students' Club House, which is being built at a cost of about £6,500, is well-nigh completed, and will soon be ready for furnishing. The students have recently initiated a movement to provide a fund for the furnishing of the building. It is estimated that the sum of £1,500 will be required for this purpose.

By special invitation, Professor Fiedler, Dr. Sandbach, and a party of twenty students in the German Department of the Birmingham University visited Oxford to attend the ceremony of conferring the Honorary Degree of D.Litt. on Gerhart Hauptmann, the famous German dramatist.

It has been decided to invite Sir Archibald Geikie, LL.D., F.R.S., to deliver the Huxley Lecture in 1906.

Mr. E. T. Borlase has been appointed Demonstrator in Metal Mining.

Mr. Guy Ricketts has resigned the Demonstratorship in Metallurgy.

The Council has approved a scheme for the establishment of a Department of General Analytical Work in connection with the School of Brewing.

A provincial sessional meeting of the Royal Sanitary Institute was held recently in the University of Birmingham, when Dr. John Robertson, Medical Officer of Health for the city, read a paper dealing with various aspects of the housing problem.

CAMBRIDGE.

University News and Notes.

Mr. E. A. Beck, M.A., Master of Trinity Hall, has been re-elected Vice-Chancellor for the academical year beginning on October 1.

The Senate has appointed a special Committee for the direction of the studies of the increasing number of students in the University requiring instruction in living Oriental languages, other than Indian. The Committee is to be called the Foreign Service Students' Committee, and will consist of Dr. Peile, Master of Christ's College; Mr. W. Durnford, King's; Mr. H. G. Comber, Pembroke; Mr. F. C. Burkitt, Trinity; Professor Giles; and Dr. A. W. Ward, Master of Peterhouse.

The University of Queen's College, Kingston, Ontario has been adopted as an institution affiliated to the University of Cambridge.

Mr. W. R. Sorley, M.A., of King's College, Knightbridge Professor of Moral Philosophy, has been approved by the General Board of Studies for the Degree of Doctor in Letters.

There are now fifty students attending the courses in Agriculture at the University.

A syndicate has been appointed to consider the desirability of establishing in the University a Diploma in Forestry.

Colonel Sir Francis Younghusband delivered the Rede Lecture on June 10th, his subject being "Our True Relationship with India."

The Degree of M.A. *honoris causa* has been conferred upon R. Stephenson, late Chairman of Cambridge County Council; H. G. Aldis, Secretary to University Library.

The terminal election of officers at the Union has resulted as follows:—*President*, W. W. Harris, St. John's College; *Vice-President*, H. L. Fosbrooke, Clare; *Secretary*, N. C. Sampson, Trinity; *Librarian*, Dr. Rogers, Caius.

The Hon. W. Everett, M.A., formerly of Trinity College, Mr. H. T. Bovey, of Queen's College, and Mr. R. G. Moulton, M.A., formerly of Christ's College, have been appointed to represent the University on the occasion of the installation of E. J. James, Ph.D., as President of the University of Illinois, in October next.

The University Press announces for publication in October the first number of the *Modern Language Review*, a quarterly journal devoted to the study of mediæval and modern literature and philology. The *Review* will be edited by Dr. J. G. Robertson, Professor of German in the University of London, assisted by an Advisory Board consisting of Dr. H. Bradley, Professor Brandin, Dr. Braunholtz, Dr. Breul, Professor Fiedler, Professor Dowden, Mr. Fitzmaurice-Kelly, Mr. W. W. Greg, Professor Herford, Professor Ker, Professor Kuno Meyer, Professor Morfill, Professor Napnier, Professor Priebsch, Professor Skeat and Dr. Paget Toynbee.

Honorary Degrees.

A special meeting of Congregation was held on June 14th for the conferment of Honorary Degrees, the Vice-Chancellor, the Master of Trinity Hall, presiding.   The recipients of Degrees were as follows : —

DOCTORS IN LAW.

The Right Hon. Sir Edmund John Monson, Bart., G.C.B., G.C.M.G., G.C.V.O., late Ambassador to the French Republic.

Sir Robert Bannatyne Finlay, G.C.M.G., K.C., M.P., Attorney-General.

Paul Vinogradoff, Professor of Jurisprudence in the University of Oxford.

DOCTORS IN LETTERS.

The Right Hon. Lord Reay, G.C.S.I., G.C.I.E., President of the British Academy.

Samuel Rolles Driver, D.D. (Oxford), Regius Professor of Hebrew in the University of Oxford.

Father Ehrle, S.J., Prefect of the Vatican Library.

Basil Lanneau Gildersleeve, Professor of Greek in the Johns Hopkins University, Baltimore.

Frederic Harrison, M.A. (Oxford), Honorary Fellow of Wadham College, Oxford.

DOCTORS IN SCIENCE.

Commander Robert Falcon Scott, R.N., C.V.O.

Sir Francis Edward Younghusband, K.C.I.E.

University Appointments, etc.

Mr. H. A. Roberts, of Gonville and Caius, has been appointed Secretary to the Board of Indian Civil Service Studies.

Mr. L. A. Borradaile, M.A., of Selwyn College, has been appointed Assistant Secretary for Lectures to the Local Examinations and Lectures Syndicate (University Extension).

Mr. A. P. Goudy, M.A., has been appointed University Lecturer in Russian until Michaelmas, 1910.

Mr. E. T. Whittaker, M.A., Trinity College, has been appointed University Lecturer in Mathematics for five years.

Mr. Benjamin Benham, M.A., of King's College, has been appointed Assistant Registrary, Mr. E. G. Swain, M.A., having resigned the post.

Sir Edward Maunde Thompson, Director of the British Museum, has been elected Sandars Reader in Bibliography for the ensuing year.

The following University appointments have been renewed for five years:—Dr. Baker, St. John's, Lecturer in Mathematics; Mr. G. F. C. Searle, M.A., Peterhouse, Lecturer in Experimental Physics; Dr. Shore, St. John's, Lecturer in Physiology; Mr. G. H. F. Nuttall, M.A., Christ's, Lecturer in Bacteriology and Preventive Medicine; Dr. Marr, St. John's, Lecturer in Geology; Mr. J. Gollancz, M.A., Christ's, Lecturer in English; Dr. Haddon, Christ's, Lecturer in Ethnology. Shaykh Muhammad Asal has been reappointed University Teacher of Arabic for the Michaelmas term.

DUBLIN.

University News and Notes.

This term the new regulations regarding Sizarships come into force, and the efficacy of the changes which have been made by the Board is well shown by the greatly increased number of candidates who have presented themselves. Eighteen Sizarships will be awarded in the following subjects:—Mathematics, Classics, Experimental Science, Hebrew and Irish. The Sizarships in Experimental Science are a new institution this year, and are being keenly contested for. In future the Sizarships will only be awarded to non-matriculated students who are under nineteen years of age.

The University of Durham is about to confer an Honorary Degree upon the Very Rev. J. H. Bernard, D.D., Dean of St. Patrick's Cathedral, and Archbishop King's Lecturer in Divinity to the University of Dublin.

The College Races were held on June 16th, in the presence of a large and fashionable gathering, and were favoured by fairly good weather. The standard, both as regards entries and performances, showed a marked improvement on previous years, and the University contingent may be relied on to give a good account of themselves at the Irish Championships. The 100 Yards Scratch, for the President's prize, was won easily by H. Thrift in 10$^4/_5$ sec.; while S. C. Armstrong, a promising runner, secured the Freshmen's Half Mile. The Silver Cup, presented by James H. Campbell, K.C., M.P. for the University, for the Two Miles Flat, was won by G. C. Duggan. The Silver Cup, presented by the Right Hon. Mr. Justice Madden, Vice-Chancellor of the University, for the best performance at the Races in the opinion of the judges, was awarded to G. N. Morphy for his effort in the Half Mile Handicap. Starting from scratch, he soon had his field in hand, and finishing strongly he timed 1 min. 57$^2/_5$ secs., thus beating the Irish record by $^4/_5$ of a second.

A good deal of stir has been caused by the annual elections of officers in the various College Societies, which take place this term.

Mr. H. L. Murphy (Sen. Mod.), B.A., the auditor-elect of the College Historical Society, has had a distinguished academic career. He has recently been appointed Assistant Professor of Modern History in the University of Dublin. He has held the offices of Librarian, senior member of Committee and Treasurer of the "Historical," and has gained the Society's Silver Medal for Oratory.

Mr. T. J. D. Atkinson (Mod.), B.A., B.L., J.P., the President-elect of the University Philosophical Society, graduated at Trinity College in 1903 with a Silver Medal in Legal and Political Science, and in the same year obtained first place in the Reid Law Scholarship Examination.

A meeting of Fellows has been summoned to consider the draft King's letter referring to changes in the mode of election to Fellowship.

Mr. Ernest Henry Alton, M.A., has been elected Fellow of Trinity College. The Madden Prize of £400 and a Fellowship Prize of £60 have been awarded to Mr. Robert Malcolm Gwynne.

The festival of Trinity Monday was observed by the customary Evensong in the College Chapel. There was a large congregation present. The Rev. Canon L. A. Pooler, D.D., was the preacher, the sermon being in memory of the Rev. Edward Hincks, D.D., some time Fellow of the College, and afterwards Rector of Killyleagh, a well-known Egyptologist and Assyriologist, who died in 1866.

Honorary Degrees.

A meeting of the Senate of the University was held on June 17th, for the purpose of considering the Honorary Degrees to be conferred on July 6th. In consequence of a ruling of the Vice-Chancellor the proceedings were conducted in private. The following Honorary Degrees proposed to the Senate by the Provost and Senior Fellows were agreed to:—

LL.D.: Margaret Byers; Henrietta Margaret White; Sir Thomas Drew, President of the Royal Hibernian Academy; Right Hon. Sir Arthur Wilson, B.A., K.C.I.E.

M.D.: Sir Richard Douglas-Powell, Bart., K.C.V.O.; Henry Rosborough Swanzy, M.B.

Sc.D.: Edward A. Schäfer, Professor of Physiology, Edinburgh; Sydney Young, Professor of Chemistry, University of Dublin.

Litt.D.: William Graham, M.A., Professor of Jurisprudence and Political Economy, Queen's College, Belfast; Hon. Emily Lawless.

Mus.Doc.: Michele Esposito.

Great interest is being taken in the Lectures which are to be delivered at the end of June in the Experimental Science Lecture Theatre by Mr. B. P. Grenfell, Litt.D., Fellow of Queen's College, College, Oxford, on "Oxyrhynchus and its Papyri" (illustrated by lantern slides), and the new "Sayings of Jesus."

EDINBURGH.

University News and Notes.

Professor H. M. Gwatkin, M.A., Dixie Professor of Ecclesiastical History, Cambridge, began on May 30 the second course of Gifford Lectures, continuing his consideration of the subject to which he devoted his addresses last year—"The Knowledge of God," and dealing on the present occasion more particularly with the historical part of his theme.

Professor Waldeyer, Berlin, delivered an address on June 14 to the members of the Royal Society of Edinburgh on the subject of the present position of the Neuron doctrine. Sir John Murray, K.C.B., Vice-president of the Society, was in the chair, and there was a large attendance.

Professor A. R. Simpson has made application to the Court for permission to retire from the Chair of Midwifery as at 31st August next.

The University Court's draft ordinance for the regulations for the degree of bachelor of science in forestry has been finally adjusted and approved.

On the recommendation of the Senatus the University Court has approved of a proposal by the Professor of Divinity to divide the class of Divinity into two classes—junior and senior.

Professor Eggeling has been appointed Curator, and Mr. Alexander Anderson, first assistant of the University Library.

The visit of some faith-healing missionaries to Edinburgh has been the means of provoking a somewhat serious disturbance, ending in a conflict between a large body of students from the University and the police.

The University Court has approved of the plans submitted for the proposed extension of the University Students' Union.

The University Calendar for the ensuing year 1905–6 has recently been published by Mr. James Thin, Edinburgh.

The following is the text of a petition to the House of Commons by the Senatus Academicus of Edinburgh University in favour of the Education (Scotland) Bill, 1905:—"Your petitioners observe with satisfaction that the Lord Advocate of Scotland has introduced into your honourable House a Bill to amend the laws relating to education in Scotland, and for other purposes connected therewith.   Your petitioners desire to express their approval of the principles of the Bill, which, if it becomes law, will greatly conduce to the efficiency of national education in Scotland.   Your petitioners cordially welcome the proposals in Part III. of the Bill to establish Provisional Councils for Education in Scotland, in connection with the four Universities, and on which the Universities of Scotland are to be represented. They believe that through the powers entrusted to these Councils the Universities will be brought into closer connection with the teachers and schools of the country, and that to the advantage alike of schools and Universities the cause of education will be promoted.   And your petitioners will ever pray, &c."—Signed for and on behalf of the University of Edinburgh, Wm. Turner, Principal; L. J. Grant, Secretary.

(The Editor regrets that the review of Mr. J. I. Macpherson's "Twenty-one Years of Corporate Life at Edinburgh University," announced for publication in the present issue, is unavoidably postponed.)

GLASGOW.

Proposed Extension of the Session in Arts.

A Conference, attended by nearly twenty delegates from the four Scottish Universities, was held here on Thursday, 15th June, with a view to considering the proposal made by this University about four years ago for an extended session in Arts.   The Conference lasted about two hours; the various aspects and bearings of the change were discussed, and it is understood that the general opinion was decidedly in favour of extending the session.   The various delegates will report the result of the Conference to their respective University Courts, and it is believed that some progress will ere long be made towards the realisation of the scheme.

For many years there have been comments on the short and condensed nature of the session in Arts and the undue length of the vacation, but, notwithstanding the comments, the tendency has been still further to curtail the teaching session.   In the days when Adam Smith and Thomas Reid taught at Glasgow there was a session of nearly, if not quite, eight months, lasting from 10th October till the early days of June.   Down to 1810 the session did not close till about 15th May, but in 1811 it was resolved to close on 1st May, and the closing day suffered little change till the passing of the

Act of 1889. Long before this, however, probably about 1844 or earlier, the session had been shortened at the other end, and the date of opening postponed till 1st November or a few days later. The Commissioners under the Universities Act of 1858 found that the session in Arts in the several Universities extended over 23 to 25 weeks, and, though they were not quite satisfied with this, they considered that the compulsory introduction of any great change from long-established usage might involve serious risks.

The Commissioners under the Act of 1889 were empowered to make regulations, *inter alia*, for regulating the length of the academic session or sessions, and they ordained that the winter session should extend to at least twenty teaching weeks, and that the University Court should institute a summer session of ten teaching weeks in such subjects qualifying for graduation in Arts as they should determine upon, after consultation with the Senate. At Glasgow a beginning was made with a summer session in a few Arts subjects—mostly Latin, Greek and Mathematics—two summer sessions of ten weeks, with a yawning gulf between them, being held equivalent to the attendance for one winter session which qualifies in a particular subject for the ordinary Degree. A summer session on this footing went on for some years without any very notable success; and as a desire was shown for some more effective and widely applied arrangement, the Faculty of Arts of this University, under the guidance, it is understood, of the late Professor Adamson, proposed that the separate summer session should be discontinued, and that an extended session should be introduced, and they seemed to indicate a preference for its being divided into three terms with intervals of two or three weeks between. It was urged that under such a system, instead of students having to attend daily lectures in all their subjects, and being too often led to regard the lectures as a condensed summary of all they need know in a particular branch of study, they would then have instruction given to them at a slower rate, and would find time for reading and independent work in the subjects in which they were attending lectures. About four years ago the University Court of the University of Glasgow opened communications with the other Scottish Universities regarding this scheme, and though discussion and negotiation have moved somewhat slowly, a hopeful view seems now to be taken of the prospect of securing an extended session.

Quater Centenary of George Buchanan.

The proposal to hold a celebration at St. Andrews in April, 1906, of the four hundredth anniversary of the birth of George Buchanan has evoked considerable interest in this University, with which the distinguished humanist had many ties, though he did not study or graduate here. The Senate have appointed Principal Story and Professors Ramsay, Ferguson and Latta to represent them on the General Committee for organising the celebrations, and the University Court have appointed for the same purpose Dr. David Murray, Dr. John Hutchison, Mr. R. M. Mitchell and Mr. A. E. Clapperton. Buchanan's name appears as one of the witnesses to the *Nova Erectio* or new Charter for reconstituting and regulating the University of Glasgow, which was granted by the Regent Morton during the minority of James VI., in July, 1577; and he is believed to have had a hand in drawing up the Charter and procuring its issue. About the same time he presented to the library of the University a number of books, amounting to twenty or more volumes. They included the works of Plutarch, Plato, Demosthenes, Aristophanes, Euclid, Strabo, Commentaries on Aristotle, etc., and were marked in the library catalogue of the time as "*Omnes ex dono viri optimi et doctissimi Georgii Buchanani, D. N. Regis Magistri.*"

That the administrators of Glasgow College felt themselves to be under special obligations to Buchanan is shown by a lease which they granted in February, 1578 (1579), of certain lands in Dumbartonshire to a member of the clan Buchanan, and probably a kinsman of the great scholar. The lease runs: "Be it kend till all men" that the Principal (Melville) and Regents of the College, with consent of the Rector and Dean of Faculty, "for the singular favour that ane honorable man Maister George Buchannan, teachar of our Souerain Lord in gude lettres, hes borne and shawen at all tymes to our College, to hawe sett to our weilbelouit Jhone Buchannan, present occupyar of our landis of Ballagan, and to his airis and assignais, our saidis landis and stedding of Ballagan in the parochin of Kilmarnock, for the space of nyntein yeiris nixt following: payand tharefor yeirlye ten bollis gude and sufficient ait meil, laying the samyn in to our College of Glasgow." For several generations the Buchanans continued to possess Ballagan as tenants of the College. More recently the administrators of Glasgow College, in January, 1837, testified their regard for the memory of Buchanan by voting a sum of twenty pounds for repairing and upholding the monument sum of twenty pound for repairing and upholding the monument erected to him at Killearn.

The Physiological Department.

The Physiological Department has been further strengthened by two new appointments by the University Court. Dr. Walter Colquhoun, the present Muirhead Demonstrator in Physiology, has been appointed to be Lecturer on the Physiology of Nerve and Muscle.

This office means that Dr. Colquohoun will have chief charge of what may be called the physical side of physiological teaching and research. His qualifications are specially adapted for the post, as, after graduating as M.A. in 1886, he was for several years a teacher of higher mathematics, and he has paid special attention to physical science. In the new buildings he will have charge of the rooms set apart for experimental physiology. The Court have also appointed Dr. George H. Clark, D.P.H., who graduated in Medicine in 1901, to be the Muirhead Demonstrator, and he will be largely occupied with the teaching of Histology. In the new laboratories, which are quickly approaching completion, Professor McKendrick will be able to carry out his ideal of what a physiological department of a University should be, indeed must be, in modern days. Each of the three divisions of Experimental Physiology, Physiological Chemistry and Histology will be under the care of men specially qualified to deal with these subjects, while the Professor will be the chief teacher and the Director of the whole Department. In addition it may be mentioned that in the new laboratories there will also be a laboratory for physiological psychology, a branch of science forming an all important link between physiology and philosophy.

University News and Notes.

Four representatives from the University of Glasgow—Professors Ramsay and Latta representing the Senate, and Mr. Copland and Dr. Hutchison representing the University Court—formed part of the deputation which waited on the Secretary for Scotland and the Lord Advocate in Edinburgh, on Saturday, 17th June, to urge the importance of safeguarding the position of Endowed Schools under the Education (Scotland) Bill now before Parliament, and of having the Bill passed during the present session.

Professor Stewart, D.D., has been re-appointed as the representative of the University on the Carnegie Trust for four years from 1st August next.

The summer session here is of much greater importance in the Faculty of Medicine than in any other, and towards its close there comes the final professional examination to test the fitness for graduation and admission to the medical profession of candidates who have completed the curriculum of five years and passed the earlier examinations. The number of candidates who have entered for the present examination is 133, including 11 women students. The examinations extend from 15th June to 10th July. Candidates will learn their fate on 11th July, when the results are to be declared.

LIVERPOOL.

The Institute of Archæology.

Liverpool is distinguished among other modern Universities by the possession of an Institute of Archæology which, though yet young, is in a very thriving condition. We have just welcomed the return, after six months' work, of an expedition sent on behalf of the Institute to make excavations in Upper Egypt under the direction of the Reader in Egyptian Archæology; the funds for the expedition were provided by a group of munificent benefactors. Good results are reported. The site at Esna which was conceded to the expedition for the season proved to be of great interest, belonging to the little known "Hyksos" period (before 1600 b.c.), and much new archæological information has been obtained by the excavators. The antiquities which fell to the lot of the expedition fill ninety cases, thirty of which are being presented to various public institutions at home and abroad, while the remainder will be exhibited in the Institute during the present summer. We shall hope to give some account of this exhibition in the next issue of this *Review*.

The Institute itself was founded last year for the encouragement of teaching, study and research in connection with the Faculty of Arts. It is managed by a special Committee, including a large number of representatives of the University. The patron is H.R.H. Princess Henry of Battenberg, and the Presidents are Lord Stanley and Lady Alice Stanley. The Vice-Presidents are for the most part the benefactors of the Institute and the patrons of the excavations. The munificence of several citizens of Liverpool has enabled the Committee to establish several posts in the Institute, which already includes a group of specialists in the main fields of archæological research. The subjects already represented are Assyriology, Classical Archæology, Egyptian Archæology, Egyptian History and Numismatics. Each of these posts is, or will soon be, held by a scholar of distinction. The Rankin Lecturer in the Methods and Practice of Archæology (a post recently endowed by the generosity of Mr. John Rankin) is the Organising Honorary Secretary. In a future issue of this *Review* we shall hope to give a fuller description of the organisation and work of this Institute, which is almost unique in England, and may be expected to produce great results. In the meantime it must suffice to say that the temporary premises of the Institute comprise two houses, suitably reconstructed, within a couple of minutes of the main buildings of the University; and include a museum of Comparative Archæology (at present mainly Egyptian) chronologically arranged, together with a library, a lecture-room and private rooms for the staff. Courses of lectures have already been given as the various subjects covered by the Institute; and an extended programme is contemplated for next session.

The Liverpool Institute of Tropical Research.

The latest development in Liverpool is one which, if it obtains the success it deserves, is likely to be of inestimable importance and value, not only to the University and the city, but to the kingdom and the Empire at large. Under the title which heads this paragraph there is being founded a powerful organisation, intimately linked with the University, whose objects are officially defined as follows:— "To collect and systematise information of a scientific nature concerning the Tropics, and more particularly all branches of the Physiography, Meteorolgy, Geology, Botany, Zoology and Ethnology of those regions; to organise and maintain research and exploratory expeditions to tropical countries; . . . . . to collect and tabulate statistics and other information on these subjects; to establish and maintain in Liverpool a bureau of scientific and technical information and research concerning the Tropics," etc., etc. The programme is ambitious, but it is being entered upon with enthusiasm and with every prospect of success. An annual income of £1,000 for four years has been already guaranteed; and the first research expedition will leave Liverpool in October next, under the leadership of Viscount Mountmorres, who is to be the Director of the Institute. We are glad to be able to publish an early account of this remarkable and significant development, and hope to deal with its organisation and progress more fully in later issues of this *Review*. Meanwhile we would tender to Lord Mountmorres our heartiest welcome on the initiation of his work, and our warmest wishes for the success of the immense and fruitful task which he has undertaken.

University News and Notes.

On July 8th Sir Joseph Swan will formally open the latest addition to our rapidly growing buildings. The new laboratory is designed and equipped on the most ample scale, but it must be confessed that while in most of our buildings we have not allowed ourselves to be harassed by too zealous a striving after external effect, in this, the latest of all, we have been content to imitate the flaunting simplicity of the factory.

"Degree Day" (which this year falls on July 8) is always an occasion for a good deal of celebration. This year's functions will be enlivened by the appearance and use of "Twelve Songs for Students selected from the Liverpool University Song Book." This small collection will include two new songs, "The Liverpool 'Varsitee" and "Our Alma Mater on the Hill," and four or five new translations or adaptations from the German; the list being completed by such inevitables as "Gaudeamus" and "Integer Vitæ," and by one or two old English songs, and "The Yeomen of England," of which Messrs. Chappell have generously granted us the use.

Among the most interesting events of the present term was the visit of our cricket and tennis teams to Birmingham on June 6th. Owing to the approach of the examinations we were not able to take our best teams; but, judging by the form displayed by our Birmingham friends, we should have had a hollow thrashing whatever teams we had taken. We were sorry that we could not give a better game, but we enjoyed immensely the opportunity of meeting the Birmingham men, and nothing could surpass the cordiality and hospitality with which we were received. It was an excellent beginning to an interchange of relations which we hope will continue with increasing vigour. Next session we hope to welcome at Liverpool representatives from Birmingham, Manchester, Leeds and Sheffield at a great combined debate.

The summer term is usually a quiet one in student politics, for we are all in the shadow of approaching exams. But the Union Committee has been active, and has drawn up and presented to the University Council an ambitious and well-thought-out scheme, which we hope to see realised during next session.

LONDON.

University News and Notes.

Sir Edward Busk, M.A., LL.B., has been elected Vice-Chancellor for the year 1905–6.

The best thanks of the Senate have been accorded to Dr. Philip Henry Pye-Smith for the services which he has rendered to the University during his tenure of the office of Vice-Chancellor.

The Lister Institute of Preventive Medicine has been admitted as a School of the University in the Faculty of Medicine for the purpose of Research in Hygiene and Pathology.

The Senate has approved Archæology as a subject for the Honours Degree of B.A. and B.Sc. and for the Degree of D.Sc. for both Internal and External Students; also for the Degree of M.A. for Internal Students.

By the recent constitution of a Faculty of Law the University now possess its full complement of eight Faculties, viz., Theology, Arts, Laws, Music, Medicine, Science, Engineering, and Economics.

Central Technical College.

The Old Students' Association of the College has recently instituted a scheme of hon. year-secretaries, whose duty it will be to keep in touch with the men of their own year, and so obtain interesting personal information for publication in *The Central*—the excellent magazine belonging to the Association. In the March issue many interesting notes of the whereabouts and doings of past students are recorded.

City and Guilds of London Institute.

The yearly meeting of the Institute was held on May 31st, Sir John Wolfe-Barry (Chairman of the Executive Committee) presided in the absence of the Lord Chancellor (the Chairman of the Council).

In their annual report the Council call attention to the diminished income of the Institute. The total income for the past year, including donations for special purposes, amounted to £43,432, of which the Corporation and the Livery Companies contributed £23,308, the remainder coming from fees and other receipts. In the previous year the income was £46,829, of which the Corporation and Livery Companies contributed £29,385.

The Chairman, in moving the adoption of the report, spoke of the proposals for the federation or co-ordination of all the teaching institutions which were gathered round about South Kensington, with a view to bringing them into more intimate connexion with the University. It was felt that a system of this kind would be a very great benefit not only to the general teaching which was given, but also to post-graduate teaching, which would be largely developed in the future.

Royal Holloway College.

In the way of sports, this term has been mainly divided between tennis and cricket. Four tennis matches have been played. The first, against Bedford College, resulted in a victory for Holloway. The second was played on Old Students' Day, and was a victory for Present Students. In the match against Girton College, played on June 15th, the representatives of Holloway were defeated. The match against Lady Margaret's had to be abandoned owing to bad weather. One cricket match has been played, in which Holloway was successful against S. Quentin's.

On Saturday, June 3rd, a large party of girls from the Lambeth Factory Girls' Club were entertained by the College. On June 17th a party of twelve crippled boys from St. Crispin's Workshop, Southwark, spent the day here.

We hope to entertain the delegates of the University Congress on Wednesday, June 28th, when it is expected that about eighty representatives of the Universities of England, Ireland, Scotland and Wales will be present.

A most interesting Lecture was given by Mr. Bullock Workman on Tuesday, May 30th, on " Recent Exploration in the Himalayas."

At the end of this term two changes are taking place in the staff of the College. Miss Strachey, Assistant Lecturer in French, is returning to Cambridge as a member of the staff of Newnham College, and Miss Mason, who for the past year has been Assistant Lecturer in Classics, is also leaving us. Their places will be taken by two past students of the College—Miss Honey and Miss Ghey.

The term ends on July 1st.

South Eastern Agricultural College, Wye.

"This College may be taken as an example of the modern agricultural college of the best type. It was founded to supply such training in agriculture and the sciences applied to it, as is indispensable to all future occupiers of land, whether as owners, tenants or agents, either at home or in the Colonies, and, at the same time, to give outdoor instruction upon the College farm, in order to give the students that practical experience upon which all successful farming depends.

The College buildings were originally erected by Cardinal Keayse about the year 1470 for the accommodation of twelve young priests. They have been greatly enlarged and adapted to suit the requirements of a modern scientific institution. The College farm at present consists of about 230 acres, of which 130 acres are arable and the remainder pasture, but an adjoining farm has recently been acquired and will be taken over at Michaelmas. The chief idea in the management of the farm has been to make the work interesting and instructive to the students and to carry out agricultural research.

Being situated in the fruit and hops district, considerable prominence is given to the growth of fruit and hops on the farm. The hop garden is six acres in extent, and much valuable work has been, and is being, done with experiments on the effect of manuring, cultivation, fertilisation, etc. There are two fruit plantations, one mainly occupied by young stock and used for instruction in bedding, grafting and other methods of propagation; whilst the other is laid out for experimental purposes to test various systems of manuring, the effects of stocks, planting and pruning, etc. Other branches of the practical side of the College work are forestry, poultry keeping, dairy work, bee keeping and farriery.

The course of instruction is arranged to cover a period of three years. During the first year of the course attention is chiefly given to the purely scientific subjects which form the necessary foundation of agricultural science—Chemistry, Botany, Veterinary Anatomy and Physiology, Zoology, Geology, Mechanics, etc. At the same time, instruction in agriculture is commenced, both by lecture and demonstration, on the farm. The lectures in the second year deal more particularly with the application of the sciences to agriculture— Agricultural Chemistry, Veterinary Medicine, Diseases of Crops, Insect Pests, Land Surveying and Levelling, etc., etc.

The third year's course is specialised according to the requirements of the student, who may devote the bulk of his time to such matters as Advanced Agriculture, Agricultural Chemistry, Agricultural Botany, Agricultural Entomology, or Estate Management and Surveying.

On the completion of two years' residence, a diploma is granted to those who pass the qualifying examination, and on the completion of a third year honours may be awarded in any of the subjects just mentioned in which the student may have specialised.

Students are also prepared for such external examinations as the National Diploma in Agriculture, the Diploma in Agriculture of the University of Cambridge, the examinations for Associateship and Fellowship of the Surveyors' Institution, and, most important of all, the Degree of Bachelor of Science (Agric.) of London University. For the purposes of this Degree the South Eastern Agricultural College was constituted a School of the University in Agriculture by the Commissioners appointed under the University of London Act, 1898. There is a board of Studies in Agriculture, and most members of the College Staff are recognised as teachers of the University. Students of the College who pass the Matriculation Examination become internal students of the University. The College has steadily grown. Opening in November, 1894, with 13 students, there are now 91 students in residence."

University College.

It is stated that "University College, London (Transfer), Bill" has passed all the necessary stages in the House of Lords, and was on

G

June 5th read for the second time in the House of Commons without opposition.

The Council of University College, after consultation with the Senate of the University of London, have decided to institute a chair of Roman-Dutch law, and will shortly proceed to make an appointment thereto.

MANCHESTER.

University News and Notes.

Professor Schuster has been nominated by the Council of the Royal Society as one of their representatives on the Committee of Management appointed by the Treasury for the Meteorological Office in London.　He has also been elected as a representative of the Council of the International Association of Academics.

The Chancellor of the Duchy of Lancaster has accepted the resignation of Sir Samuel Hall, K.C., as Vice-Chancellor of the County Palatine, on the ground of ill-health.　Mr. Alfred Hopkinson, K.C., Vice-Chancellor of the Manchester University, is acting as Deputy.

A brass tablet in memory of the late Professor Withers was unveiled at Isleworth College on Saturday, June 11th, by Mr. S. Watson, Chairman of the College Committee.

The Lancashire Veterinary Medical Association has voted the sum of £20 as a subscription to the equipment fund of the new Public Health Laboratories in York Place.

It has been decided that the Professor of Pathology at the University shall be appointed a member of the honorary staff of the Manchester Royal Infirmary if and as soon as the necessary change can be made in the rules.

The Manchester University Sports were held on Saturday, June 3rd, at the University Athletic Ground.　The Inter-University quarter-mile was won by H. F. Renton (Leeds University).　The Christie Challenge Cup and the Milnes Marshall gold medal for the championship of the Sports was won by J. Green.　The prizes were presented by Mr. S. J. Chapman.

The Chancellor has appointed Mrs. Rylands a member of the Court of Governors.

The Langton fellowship has been awarded to Mr. A. H. Baker, late University scholar.

Mr. W. J. Goodrich, M.A. (Oxford), has been appointed junior assistant lecturer in classics.

The Council has appointed Mr. Cyril Atkinson, LL.D., B.C.L., Lecturer in Jurisprudence and Roman Law.

The first Adamson Lecture which was founded recently in memory of the late Professor Adamson, as a biennial lecture, upon some subject of philosophy, literature or science, was delivered on June 9th to a large audience in the Whitworth Hall by Professor James Ward, of Cambridge, upon " Mechanism and Morals: the World of Science and the World of History."

A Garden Party is to be held at the University Athletic Ground on Degree Day, July 8th, by the invitation of the University Council.

The resignation is announced of Miss Edith C. Wilson, M.A., who has been for so many years the head of the Women's Department. Her recent illness has rendered necessary a prolonged holiday for recuperation. The news of Miss Wilson's departure has been received with very real regret throughout the University.

Miss Jessie D. Clarkson has been elected Chairman of the Women's Union for the Session 1905-6.

The Manchester University Settlement.

The Council of the Manchester Art Museum and University Settlement has recently presented the annual report of the year's work. There has been a steady development in the many branches of the Settlement. The registered members of the clubs, classes, and societies (adults and children included) now exceed 1,500. During the past year the Settlement has manifestly strengthened its happy relations with the district. The connection of the Settlement with the University has grown closer this year, the students, since the establishment of their representative council, having come in greater numbers than ever before to learn and to help in Ancoats. From the members of the University staff the Settlement received, as ever, much valuable and ready help in the leadership of their education classes. Mr. J. W. Graham, the Treasurer, reports that financial aid is urgently needed. During the past year about £800 has been received in subscriptions and donations—about £40 more than was received in the previous year,—but the expenditure was £1,200. A sum of £800 has been given by Mrs. James Worthington, and by that means the work has been kept going. Mr. T. C. Horsfall, the President of the Settlement, and Canon Barnett, Warden of Toynbee Hall, also spoke of the valuable work done by University Settlements.

OXFORD.

University News and Notes.

The term is now drawing to its end, and like all summer terms it has been full of activity, but except in the case of those people whom Sir Oliver Lodge would rescue from the pressure of the examination schools the main interest of the term cannot be said to have been academic.

The annual " Robert Boyle" Lecture was delivered recently under the auspices of the Junior Scientific Club by Sir Victor Horsley, who chose as his subject the Cerebellum. In the course of his address he traced back the history of our knowledge of this portion of the brain to the experiments of Robert Boyle himself and of his friend Wallis at a time when Oxford was the centre of great activity in the sphere of natural science.

This same phase in the history of the University was strongly insisted on by Professor Ray Lankester in the Romanes Lecture which he delivered in the Sheldonian Theatre on June 14th. His subject was "Man and Nature," and his main point was that the human race had set itself in opposition to the law of the survival of the fittest, and that unless this opposition was maintained by means of scientific research man would fall a victim to the forces against which he was contending. He took the opportunity of applying his main thesis to the University of Oxford in particular, and attacked the classical tradition with great vigour. He even denied that it was a tradition at all, and asserted that it was an invention of the eighteenth century. Before that time, as was shown by the activity of Robert Boyle and his associates, Oxford was not dedicated to the "humanities" alone, but was the centre of research in every department of learning.

A further portion of the Oxford English dictionary containing the words from Pargeter to Pennached has been issued, and the Goldsmiths' Company have generously contributed £5,000 towards the sixth volume of the work.

During Eights Week the annual Conversazione of the Junior Scientific Club was held at the University Museum, and met with its usual success. Lectures were delivered by Professor E. B. Poulton and Dr. Tutton, and there were various exhibits and demonstrations by members of the Club.

Among University papers there are two new publications to be recorded—*The Mosaic* and *L'Auréole*. Both are somewhat more ambitious than the majority of such periodicals. *The Mosaic* possesses somewhat æsthetic tendencies, and *L'Auréole* is the first French review which has appeared at Oxford. For Commemoration

From a Water-colour Drawing)   *(by Henry Tamb*

THE TOWER AND FIRTH HALL, SHEFFIELD UNIVERSITY.

(June 15th, 1905)

week a new paper of a somewhat more frivolous nature—*The Umbrella*—is announced. In addition to these publications we may notice an excellent book of parodies, appropriately called "Misfits," by Mr. G. E. Forrest.

A recent number of the *Oxford Magazine* contains an account of what is probably one of the least known possessions of the University. This is the "Ruskin Reserve," a piece of ground near Basselsleigh, which was presented by the late Mr. Willett to the Ashmolean Natural History Society, with the stipulation that it should be kept as a Natural History Reserve. Three acres have since been added by purchase. The Reserve contains two small shallow pools, which are full of a pondweed which is not known elsewhere in the region of the Upper Thames, and is remarkable for the variety of its vegetation. It forms a pleasing combination of woodland, water and marsh, and should prove a delightful as well as a useful hunting ground for the natural historian. Cambridge boasts a similar possession in a portion of Wicken fen, and it was the gift of this to "the other place" which suggested the idea to Mr. Willett of doing the same service to Oxford.

Mr. Robert Bridges has now consented to the publication by the Clarendon Press of his masque "Demeter," which he wrote last year for the members of Somerville College, and was acted by them on the occasion of the inauguration of their new buildings.

The thanks of the University have been accorded to Mr. Vernon J. Watney, M.A., New College, for his munificent gift of £500 to the general fund of the Bodleian Library, an amount larger than any donation for a quarter of a century.

It is proposed to establish a delegacy to superintend the instruction of candidates for the Indian Forest Service, and for granting diplomas in forestry. This step has been rendered necessary in view of the fact that the Indian forestry students hitherto trained at the Cooper's Hill Engineering College, are in future to receive their special training in forestry at Oxford. Such candidates will be required to have passed Responsions or an equivalent examination. They will study for two years at Oxford, and in their third year will have practical instruction, visiting Continental forests under suitable supervision.

It has been decided to raise the emoluments of the Professor of Physics to a potential £800 per annum. At the same time the stipend of the Demonstrator is to be raised by £100 a year, to make provision for the training of advanced students not only in term time, but also in vacation.

The electors to the Beit Professorship of Colonial History will proceed to an election in October. The professor will be elected for a period of seven years, and will be entitled during that period to the annual income of £900, arising out of Mr. Beit's foundation. It will be the duty of the professor to lecture and give instruction on the history of the British dominions and possessions over the seas, excluding India and its dependencies, but including the history of the American colonies before their separation from the mother country.

On the invitation of the Provost of Oriel, Professor Andréades, of the University of Athens, recently gave an interesting address to members of the University interested in the Macedonian question.

A pension of £150 per annum has been voted by Congregation to the Rev. W. D. Macray, M.A., Hon. D.Litt., Fellow of Magdalen College, upon his retirement from the Bodleian Library, where he has rendered valuable services for many years as sub-librarian and special assistant.

Mr. Andrew J. Herbertson, M.A., Ph.D., non-collegiate, has been appointed University Reader in Geography.

Mr. W. Tyrrell Brooks, M.B., M.A., Christ Church, has been elected Litchfield Clinical Lecturer in Medicine.

The Union Society.

The election of officers for the Union Society for next term had the following result:—*President:* Mr. M. H. Woods, Trinity. *Librarian:* Mr. E. M. C. Denny, Jesus. *Junior Treasurer:* Mr. R. C. Bonnerjee, Balliol. *Secretary:* Mr. G. T. C. Rentoul, Christ Church.

The chief event at the Union has been the visit of Sir Henry Campbell-Bannermann, who spoke in favour of a motion directed against the present Government. The house was crowded, but despite Sir Henry's speech the motion was lost. This result was somewhat unexpected, recent debates having shown a majority against the Government.

Among the other debates the most interesting was that in which three prominent members of the Cambridge Union Society took part, for it afforded an opportunity of comparing the styles of debate at the two Universities. The visitors showed considerable knowledge of the facts, and displayed them in a clear and methodical manner, but there seemed to be a lack of humour and brilliance in their speeches. If one may be permitted to generalise from a single instance, it would appear that Cambridge rhetoric is going through a period of what we might call the "historical method." Oxford speakers, on the other hand, are only too ready to sacrifice argument and conviction to rhetorical effect. This contrast, moreover, seems to be in intimate relation with a similar contrast in other spheres of academic life.

SHEFFIELD.

The University Charter.

The charter ordaining the foundation of the University of Sheffield was granted by the King in Council on Wednesday, May 31st.

The historic document was brought from London on June 3rd by Mr. George Franklin, the Pro-Chancellor, and its arrival was made the occasion of a demonstration by the students of what has hitherto been University College. Alderman Franklin was welcomed on his arrival by a large crowd of students, who escorted him in procession to the University Hall. All along the route there was a liberal display of flags and decorations of the University colours, yellow and black. At the University the Pro-Chancellor formally handed over the charter to the Vice-Chancellor (Dr. Hicks, F.R.S.), and congratulatory speeches were made on the successful termination of an effort which has enlisted the loyal support of the whole city. The first Chancellor of the University is the Duke of Norfolk, who telegraphed to the Vice-Chancellor from Arundel:—" My heartiest congratulations to you and all connected with University on reception of our charter, and earnest best wishes for a glorious future of good work for Sheffield.—(Signed) NORFOLK."

The Visit of the King.

The arrangements for the visit of the King and Queen to open the new University buildings are now complete. It has been decided that their Majesties will arrive in Sheffield at one o'clock on July 12th. They will be welcomed at the station by the Lord Mayor and Lady Mayoress, and the Duke of Norfolk, the Chancellor of the University. After luncheon the Royal visitors will proceed to the University buildings on Western Bank. The opening ceremony will take place in the quadrangle in the presence of some 4,000 spectators. In Western Park there will be a reception and garden party organised by the University authorities. Their Majesties will pass through the Park and down to the parish church, where they will unveil a memorial to the men of the York and Lancaster Regiment who fell in the South African war. Their Majesties will leave Sheffield at five o'clock by their special train, and will proceed direct to Knowsley.

ST. ANDREWS.

University News and Notes.

The summer session in the "Oxford of the North" which has just closed, has been a pleasant one. It is an unwritten law, that no classes except those in laboratories may be held later than two o'clock, so that the afternoon may be left free for out-door exercise. But in the laboratories of Botany, Zoology, Chemistry, Geology, Anatomy and Physiology, there have been many busy workers all day long. Even for these enthusiasts, the long bright evenings of our northern summer give opportunities for a "round" of the links or several games of tennis before the dark.

For the fifth time, a special course of lectures and demonstrations on the nervous system and the senses has been given in the Physiological Department by Dr. D. Fraser Harris, and has been well attended, notwithstanding that it has been held *post meridionem*.

The Council of the University of Paris has accepted the invitation of the University of St. Andrews to send representatives on the occasion of the fourth centenary of George Buchanan's birth.

On May 26th, Mr. A. G. Barry (St. Andrews University) beat the Hon. O. Scott (Royal North Devon) in the final round of the Amateur Golf Championship at Prestwick by three holes up and two to play.

WALES.

University News and Notes.

The University of Wales some time ago resolved to confer its Honorary Degrees upon the Chancellors of all the Universities of the United Kingdom, at whatever time they might find it convenient to attend. At the Degree Ceremony on June 28th the Right Hon. Joseph Chamberlain, M.P., received a Degree as Chancellor of the University of Birmingham. The other names on the list were:—Lord Tredegar, a notable benefactor of the College; Sir John Williams, the eminent physician; Dr. J. Gwenogfryn Evans, perhaps the greatest living authority on Welsh Mediæval Palæography; and Professor Henry Jones, of the University of Glasgow, another of the Principality's most distinguished sons.

A special meeting of the Court of the University of Wales was held at Shrewsbury on June 9th. The Senior Deputy-Chancellor, Sir Isambard Owen, presided. The Registrar announced the resignation of Mr. W. Edwards, Mr. R. E. Hughes, Mr. D. E. Jones, and Mr. T. W. Phillips, four of His Majesty's Inspectors of Schools, of their seats on the Court. A resolution was passed expressing deep regret at the simultaneous loss of so many active members of the Court, and intimating that if the resignations were due to instructions received from the Board of Education, the Court desired to express its great surprise that the Education Board had deemed it necessary to take such a step on the eve of an important meeting of the Court, and at the fact that no notice whatever had been given to the University.

Two alternative schemes for the future administration of the University were considered by the Court. It was agreed that in order to admit of further consideration by the Court of the question of the appointment of a salaried head of the University—(1) The University grant the present Registrar a pension of £200; (2) That a Registrar with academic qualifications be appointed at a salary of £500 a year.

University College of South Wales, Cardiff.

The Council of the University College of South Wales and Monmouthshire have issued an appeal for subscriptions to the fund for the new buildings, the foundation stone of which was laid by the Prince of Wales, Chancellor of the University of Wales, on June 28th. It is estimated that the whole building scheme will cost £234,000, to which is added £46,800 for maintenance and £10,000 for furnishing and fitting. In view of this heavy outlay it is proposed to defer the construction of the great hall included in the plans. In this way the proposed expenditure will be reduced to £251,500. The site, which is valued at £25,000, was given by the Corporation of Cardiff. The buildings are planned in several departmental blocks, and it is proposed to proceed at once with the erection of the block devoted to arts and administration, which, it is expected, will cost £106,000. The actual amount in hand at the present moment exceeds £92,100. In a letter to the *Times* Dr. E. H. Griffiths, Principal of the College, says: "May I ask all friends interested in the promotion of higher education in this important part of the Principality to assist us in our efforts to secure the additional £14,000 required. I would call attention to the fact that the block now to be erected contains ample provision for a research laboratory and that a satisfactory start has been made with regard to the provision of suitable apparatus. Donations may be made in a single sum or spread over intervals of three or five years. Communications should be addressed to the Hon. Treasurer, Mr. H. M. Thompson, University College of South Wales, Cardiff.

Some disappointment was naturally felt in Cardiff at the location of the Welsh National Library in Aberystwyth. Those, however, who are best acquainted with the country will admit that it cannot have been easy to decide between so many conflicting claims. Under the circumstances, the decision is probably as satisfactory on the whole as any other would have been; and we may expect the arrangement thus effected to become, with the lapse of years, gradually more familiar and acceptable.

University College of Wales, Aberystwyth.

Miss H. M. Stephen, Warden of the Hall of Residence for Women Students of the Victoria University of Manchester, has been appointed by the Council of the University College, Aberystwyth, Warden of the Alexandra Hall of Residence.

The University College of North Wales, Bangor.

In addition to continuing for another session the Entrance Scholarships and Exhibitions awarded in 1903 and 1904, and amounting in annual value to £540, the Senate have made several new awards for 1905-6.

UNIVERSITY COLLEGES.

Queen's College, Belfast.

Professor F. C. Boas, M.A., has resigned the Chair of English Literature, as from 5th October next, also the office of Librarian, on being appointed a Divisional Inspector of Higher Education under the London County Council.

A meeting of the subscribers to the fund for the better equipment of the College was held last month. Sir Otto Jaffé, J.P., ex-Lord Mayor of Belfast, presided. A report was submitted by Professor Symington, F.R.S., one of the Hon. Secs., giving an account of the working of the fund during the four years of its history. The total amount received has been £30,040. 17s. 8d.

The following additions to the equipment of the College have already been made by the help of the fund:—

1. The "Musgrave Chair of Pathology" has been founded by Government, the necessary endowment having been provided by the late Sir James Musgrave, Bart., D.L., and the College statutes having been altered for the purpose by a King's Letter.

2. The "Purser Studentship" has been founded for the promotion

of teaching and research in Mathematical Science, in memory of the late Professor John Purser, LL.D., the funds for the purpose having been provided by Professor Frederick Purser, M.A., F.T.C.D.

3. "The Riddel Demonstratorship in Pathology and Bacteriology" has been founded by means of moneys contributed by the Misses Riddel, Beechmount, Belfast.

4. A large, well-made, and well-enclosed playing field for the students has been provided, Sir Daniel Dixon lending valuable help in this important work.

5. "The Mitchell Organ," presented in memory of the late Mr. W. C. Mitchell, J.P., by his family, has been erected in the Examination Hall.

6. A Lectureship in Music has been founded, in connection with which classes are held in harmony, counterpoint and musical form.

7. A Library of Music has been established, and is largely used.

8. An Assistant in the Department of Botany has been provided.

9. A Lecturer in History has been provided.

10. Three tubes of radium, containing in all 60 milligrammes, have been presented by Sir Otto Jaffé, J.P., ex-Lord Mayor of Belfast.

11. A scheme for the establishment of a Faculty of Commerce in the College has been drawn up by the Belfast Chamber of Commerce, after conference with the College authorities, and several munificent subscriptions have been promised in connection therewith, and although it has not been found possible to proceed with it without further help, it is most earnestly hoped that this very important project will ere long be carried out.

12. A grant has been made towards providing a much-needed Assistant in the Department of Modern Languages.

13. An admirable and completely fitted Biological Laboratory, for part of the cost of which the fund made itself liable, has been erected.

14. Several minor, but by no means unimportant, grants have been made by the Allocation Committee.

An appeal for further help was made. In moving the adoption of the report the President of Queen's College, Belfast (the Rev. Thomas Hamilton, D.D., LL.D.) said they had many things yet to do, and it would be a great matter if the College could continue to feel that it had behind it the confidence, sympathy and support of the people of Belfast and the North of Ireland. Its doors were open, without let or hindrance, to men and women of every creed and every class, and he was happy to say that its class-rooms contained men and women belonging to all the creeds which prevailed around them. Even the breath of slander had never whispered that there had ever been the slightest attempt on the part of the College, or of anyone within its walls, to tamper with the faith of the students, or to weaken the convictions implanted in them from childhood. On these lines the College had always gone, and on these lines it would always proceed. These lines were, he thought, approved of by the people of the North of Ireland, and so long as they maintained them, and knew no object save to maintain there a school of research and higher learning, he thought they might ask and claim and expect the support of the people to such a great fund as that, the object of which was to maintain there a College worthy of Belfast and worthy of the great purpose for which it was placed there by the Government.

The resolution was seconded by Sir Robert Lloyd Patterson, D.L., and among other speakers were Professor Gregg Wilson, Sir James Henderson, D.L., Sir William Whitla, M.D., LL.D., and the High Sheriff of Belfast.

University College, Bristol.

The photograph of the College, which is reproduced in this number of the *University Review*, is taken from the Bristol Grammar School grounds. The building on the right is the Medical School. Next in order to the left is the great Hall and Library, behind which is the Engineering wing. The Chemical and Physical Departments find space in the centre of the building, and Arts is accommodated in the building on the extreme left. The open space next to the College, and adjoining it, is used as an experimental garden.

After twenty-nine years' association with the College, Professor James Rowley has retired from the Chair of History and Literature. Professor Rowley was one of the two Professors appointed by the Council of the College when it was established in 1876. Professor Rowley has exercised a great influence in the College, and his work has gone far to spread its reputation as the centre of higher literary education in the West of England.

The Council have decided to invite applications for the Chairs of Modern History and English Literature and Language. The appointment will probably be made before the close of the session.

Mr. O. C. M. Davis, B.Sc., Lecturer in the Faculty of Arts and Science, has been appointed Lecturer on Materia Medica and Practical Pharmacy in the Faculty of Medicine.

Dr. Newman Neild has been appointed Lecturer on Pharmacology and Therapeutics.

Professor Morris W. Travers, F.R.S., has been invited to deliver the Inaugural Address at the opening of the Session 1905-6.

The Executive Committee of the Council have approved of plans for the extension of the Anatomical and Bacteriological Departments. The dissecting room will be enlarged and reconstructed, and accommodation will be provided for embryological work. The large laboratories with rooms for sterilisers, etc., will be provided for the teaching of bacteriology.

The general prospectus and calendar for the Session 1905-6 will contain a short article setting forth the history of the College and its present aims.

Queen's College, Cork.

Arrangements have now been completed for affording a complete course of training for teachers in this College, commencing in October next. The College has also secured recognition by the Board of Education in England for the purposes of section 3 (2) i. of the Teachers' Registration Regulations, this College being the first institution in Ireland to have secured this recognition.

The courses of lectures in this College will be given by Mr. McSweeney, Headmaster of Blackpool Schools, "History of Education;" Miss Martin, Headmistress of Cork High School for Girls, and late Mistress of Method, Whitelands College, Chelsea, "Methods of Teaching and School Management;" and Professor Stokes, M.A., "Psychology."

The course will be opened by a public lecture by the President on "The Recent History of Secondary Education in England."

During the session special lectures will be delivered on "The Teaching of English Literature," "Recent Methods of Teaching Modern Languages," and "Nature Study," by the Professors of English Literature, Modern Languages and Biology respectively; and additional lectures will be delivered on "School Hygiene," by Dr. Donovan, Lecturer on Hygiene at the College, and Medical Officer of Health for the City of Cork.

The practical work will be carried on, under arrangements with the head teachers and governors in certain schools in Cork. Arrangements have already been completed with the following:— The Grammar School; the High School for Girls; Ladies' School, South Place.

University College, Reading.

An important ceremony took place at Reading on Wednesday, June 7th, when Viscount Goschen laid the foundation stone of the new buildings of University College, which are to be erected on an extensive site in the London Road, the gift of Mr. Alfred Palmer, J.P. It is proposed to proceed at once with the erection of the College Hall and the buildings for art, physics, botany, chemistry, zoology, agriculture, and manual work. The foundation stone, which was set in the north wall of the College hall, bears the following inscription: "This stone was laid by the Right Honourable Viscount Goschen, D.C.L., F.R.S., Chancellor of the University of Oxford, vii. June, MCMV." During the proceedings it was announced that Mr. G. W. Palmer had offered a sum of £50,000 to the College, to be called the George Palmer Endowment Fund, after his father. The King, through Sir Deighton Probyn, wrote that he continued to take the warmest interest in the College.

Hartley University College, Southampton.

Under the name of "The London Society of Old Hartleyans" an association is in the process of formation for the benefit of all past students of the College who live in and around London. The scheme has been received with enthusiasm. A Sub-Committeee, under the presidency of Miss Fage, has been elected to draw up a scheme for the constitution of such a Society.

The first general meeting of the Society will be held in London next September. The time and place of the meeting will be announced later. It is of extreme importance that all past students of the College now in London should co-operate in this movement. All those who desire to join this Society are asked to communicate at once with Mr. F. J. Hemmings, 12, Pearcroft Road, Leytonstone, N.E., who, acting in the capacity of Secretary, *pro tem.*, will gladly forward full particulars respecting the proposals which have so far been made. Students are asked to send in the names and addresses of any past students of the College who are likely to join, and who are now in London.

Notes and Comments.

The Harvard Memorial Window. *(See Frontispiece.)*

The memorial window recently presented to the Cathedral Church of St. Saviour, Southwark, by Mr. Choate, the late American Ambassador, in memory of John Harvard, the founder of the Harvard University, was unveiled by the donor on May 22nd. Among those present at the ceremony were the Archbishop of Canterbury, the Bishop of Rochester, Canon Thompson, the Master of Trinity College, Cambridge, and Mr. James Bryce, M.P. The window is placed in the ancient Chapel of St. John the Divine, shortly to become the Harvard Memorial Chapel, and depicts the baptism of Christ. Upon the bottom panels is the following inscription :—" In memory of John Harvard, founder of Harvard University in America, baptised in this church 29th November, 1607." The window was designed and executed by Mr. J. La Farge, of New York.

In the course of a brief speech Mr. Choate said he had presented the memorial from a desire to signalise his long residence in England by an appropriate gift, which should be in itself emblematical of the friendship which united England and the United States. As a loyal son of Harvard he thought nothing could be more fitting than a permanent memorial of the principal founder of Harvard University.

John Harvard was born in Southwark, and was educated at Emmanuel College, Cambridge, where he spent eight years. He then emigrated to Massachusetts, where he died within two years of his arrival. Finding the infant colony without means to establish a College he bequeathed to its foundation his library and the half of his fortune, which amounted in all to about £1,900. "And now, after the lapse of three centuries, the little College in the pathless wilderness has become a great and splendid University, strong in prestige and renown, rich in endowments, and richer still in the pious loyalty of its sons."

University Halls of Residence.

We have received a copy of the report of the Halls of Residence Committee appointed at the first English and Welsh Inter-Universities Students' Congress, held at the Manchester University in June, 1904. It is a very interesting document, and represents the first attempt that has been made on so large a scale to collect statistics and opinions on the important question of students' residence in the new Universities. We hope to notice this report at some length in an early number of the *Review*. Meanwhile we offer our congratulations to the Secretary of the Committee (Mr. A. C. Ward, Leeds), whose energy has resulted in this excellent piece of work. Miss Manning (London) and Miss Mitchell (Aberystwyth) are also deserving of praise for the interesting particulars they have collected of the residential accommodation for women in British Universities and Colleges.

The Southampton Record Society.

As if by way of comment on Mr. Ramsay Muir's article in our last issue,* we have received a pamphlet describing the foundation of the Southampton Record Society for the publication of select documents from the valuable archives of the great southern port. It is proposed, in the first instance, to publish the records of the Court Leet, which extend from 1550 to 1905, in about ten volumes of some 150 pages each. The series will be under the general Editorship of Professor Hearnshaw, of Hartley University College, Southampton, to whose energy the foundation of the Society is primarily due. Professor Hearnshaw has already done admirable work in stimulating the interest of Southampton in its own history, and he is to be congratulated very heartily upon the example which he has set to the Professors of History in other Colleges and Universities. The youngest of the University Colleges is showing its elder sisters what can be done, in one important sphere, for the service of the community in which it is established. The publications of the new Society will not, however, be of purely local interest ; Southampton has so long and full a history that its records will be of great value to all students of English mediæval history ; and we are sure that there are many of our readers who will desire to take advantage of the new Society by becoming subscribers to its publications. Full particulars may be obtained from Professor Hearnshaw, Hartley University College, Southampton.

---

* " The Study of Local History," *University Review*, June, p. 181. .

the

with
of the Country

7,

From a drawing   *by Henry Lamb*

DR. NICHOLAS MURRAY BUTLER,
President of Columbia University, New York.

The University Review

| NO. 4 VOL. I. | AUGUST, 1905. |

Questions for Discussion.

No. III.

BY

SIR WILLIAM RAMSAY, K.C.B., F.R.S.

I HAVE read with much interest the article on Degrees* by my friend Sir Oliver Lodge. Like him, I, too, had the privilege of discussing such questions with Professor George Fitzgerald; and I have no doubt Sir Oliver has rightly interpreted his ideas. The plan of crowning a general education with a degree such as that of B.A. is, nevertheless, no new one. It was the plan in the Scottish Universities for many years, and has been altered only recently, and, as many think, not for the better. The degree was, however, termed Master of Arts. It was gained in the following manner: For the first two years the classes attended were Latin, or "Humanity," as it was (and is still) called, and Greek. If a lad knew no Greek, he entered the junior class; if he had studied some Greek at school, the middle Greek class. At the end of two years' study, the student presented himself for examination in Classics. It is not to be inferred that he was not frequently examined during his curriculum, but

---

* "Questions for Discussion," Nos. I. and II., *University Review*, pp. 42 and 146.

A

these were class examinations, and, so far as I know, were not taken into account in the final verdict. The examination consisted of passages for translation from classical authors, questions on Grammar, and on the history and antiquities of Rome and Greece. The next year was usually given to Mathematics, and to Logic and Rhetoric; the fourth to Moral Philosophy, Mathematics, Natural Philosophy, and English Literature. The examination was held in two divisions, Logic and Moral Philosophy on the one hand, and Mathematics and Natural Philosophy on the other. To obtain a degree, therefore, four years' study were necessary, with attendance at the requisite classes. The instruction was given almost entirely by lectures; and as the earlier classes began at 8 a.m., by 1 p.m. the day was finished. The rest of the day and evening were available for reading and digestion of the subject-matter. And it was none too much. However, the curriculum was too narrow. Many subjects of great general interest were omitted, and in my own case, for example, I drifted away into the chemical laboratory. My case was by no means an isolated one; many students left without graduating. Indeed, to graduate was perhaps on the whole exceptional; it was customary for men of business to give their sons a couple of years at the University, as a preparation for their business career, even though, from a practical point of view, this training would have no tangible result.

Of course such a method does not lend itself to any deep acquaintance with any one subject. At best the youth obtains only a smattering. Still, a smattering of

Hamilton, of Locke, of Mill, of Hegel, and of Kant is not to be despised. I should say, that the student learned how much there was to learn, and, even if he never went further, a new field was opened to him, so that he could say that he knew to some extent what had been said and done in the domain of the subjects he had studied.

There was no "spoon-feeding." It was left to the student to make use of his opportunities. And I am convinced that this is best. For, if a student finds that he can get his thinking done for him, in well-arranged text books, he will not learn to think. I thoroughly believe that the chief object of education, after school years, is to teach men to teach themselves, and the Scottish system lent itself admirably to this. It was not faultless; sometimes one felt amused at the peculiarities of the teacher; often the teaching was not good; but the food was there, and if the man had an appetite he consumed it, and digested it. There were few, if any, set tasks; it was counselled that certain books be read; and essays were prescribed on their subject-matter, calculated to draw out all the ideas which the young man could form.

Surely, too, lads were more mature in those days than in these. It was by no means uncommon for boys of fourteen to sit side by side with what we took to be old men, probably of five-and-twenty. For the ploughman was a not infrequent student, and a right good fellow he usually was. I remember, in the junior Latin class, having on my left a man from Inverness-shire, who spoke English perfectly, though his accent betrayed him; and on my right, a red haired Celt, whose knowledge of English was scanty; and I have often listened to whispered conversations in an unknown tongue, when the odes of Horace were apparently being rendered into Erse for the benefit of the Gael. Incidentally, there was a good deal of moral training and *savoir-faire* to be gained by association with men much one's senior in age and experience.

These reminiscences, however, are rather beside the mark. The point which I wished to make is that, in Scotland we had such a general education as Sir Oliver Lodge counsels. Personally, I should be disposed to admit of a wider choice of subjects; let Chemistry, Zoology, Botany, or Geology be allowed as alternatives to Physics; let French and German be equivalent to Latin and Greek, assuming that these names imply a study of Romance and Teutonic languages; and let rudiments of Law and Political Economy replace Logic and Moral Philosophy, if desired. The power to make such substitutions would be valued, and would tend to widen the scope of education.

In my opinion, far too much stress is laid, now-a-days, on what is called "practical work." To take my own subject, it is possible to have quite an intelligent idea of Chemistry, without ever having handled a test tube or touched a balance. Lectures on Chemistry may be well illustrated experimentally, and the necessary theories demonstrated by the lecturer. Of course, that will never make a chemist; but we are not talking of making chemists, we are discussing the best way of giving a general education, and I maintain that to spend several hours a day in practical work is, if not a waste of time, at least a work of supererogation.   The lad who has heard lectures on Chemistry, and seen experiments, will, if he has it in him, become a chemist.   He will enter a laboratory will-he nill-he.   The lad who intends to be a lawyer will be all the better for a smattering of Chemistry ; of having gained a survey of the subject.   But the real difficulty which faces the proposal of Sir Oliver Lodge is, that while such a course of study might be very well suited for a gilded youth, who has not later to gain his own livelihood, it necessitates the passing three or four years in work which is not a direct preparation for making money.   Suppose a lad enters the University at sixteen, he will be nineteen or twenty before he commences professional work.   As the average age of entry is more commonly eighteen, he will be twenty-one or twenty-two before that point is reached.   That, indeed, is what is common in American colleges, where such a general education is ordinarily given, before "University work" starts.   But it certainly postpones entry into life to a late date.   Now in Germany, education in "Gymnasia" is prolonged till-eighteen or nineteen, and many of the subjects which appear in the curricula of our Universities and University colleges are taught in such secondary schools.   In Scotland, the early age of entry to the University made it possible for a young man to graduate as M.A. at nineteen, and afterwards to start his professional studies.   But the raising of the age of leaving school has naturally raised the age at which professional studies can begin; and it is a serious thing for many parents to have to support their sons till the age of twenty-five or twenty-six, for if a B.A. degree cannot be taken before twenty-two, professional studies will take, at least, three or four years more.

The question, as Sir Oliver Lodge says, is a difficult one; difficult, because of the length of time required for general and special studies. There can be no doubt of the advantage of the course he urges; but unless earlier entry to the University or college is sanctioned, it must remain impracticable, I am afraid, for most of those for whom such courses would be an advantage.

THE LIBRARY AND READING ROOM, BEDFORD COLLEGE FOR WOMEN.

Bedford College for Women

(University of London.)

BY

THE HON. MRS. BERTRAND RUSSELL, A.B.

(Bryn Mawr College, Pennsylvania),

Member of the Council of Bedford College for Women.

THE great development in education of the last fifty years by the extension of the old Universities and the creation of new ones has done much for men, but it has done everything for women. Before 1850, it was almost impossible for a woman to obtain a good education, nor indeed was it thought necessary for a woman to be more than superficially instructed. It was considered ample education for a girl to be taught at home for a few years, and then at thirteen or fourteen to be sent to a finishing school for a couple of years. She returned to her father's house at about sixteen, finished, knowing nothing thoroughly, and with not even enough knowledge to make her desire more. She saw her brothers at that age, or older, pass out of their schools and begin a three years' course at one of the Universities, and from that time she ceased to be able to talk on the same subjects, or to sympathise when they turned their thoughts and energies to any specialised branch of learning.   But now, any woman may obtain practically the same education as her brothers.   She may take the same examinations, and, in the case of the newer Universities, she may bear away the same degree.

One of the pioneers in the higher education for women was Bedford College, founded in Bedford Square, in the autumn of 1849, by Mrs. Elizabeth Jesser Reid.   It was her desire that colleges for women should be established to provide a thorough and liberal education, and to include all the higher branches of study in various departments. With this intention, Bedford College was founded on the broadest and freest principles, offering education without any theological test, but with the highest moral and spiritual aims.   One hundred and ninety-three students entered the College during the first session, taking, for the most part, single classes, and the time table offered four or five lectures a day, beginning at 9-20 a.m., closing at 3-30 p.m. in time for the then fashionable 4 o'clock dinner.   Drawing, Elocution, and Music were naturally on the time table, but when George Eliot was a pupil, it also included Latin and Mathematics, Moral Philosophy and Natural Science, as well as Modern Languages and History, Ancient and Modern.

Many middle-aged ladies, married as well as un-married, took advantage of this mode of supplementing their earlier education, but as younger pupils presented themselves, it was found that they were insufficiently trained to benefit by the professors' lectures, and in 1853 a school where they could be prepared was established in connection with the College, and was only closed in 1868, when many good schools for girls had become available.   In 1856, to assist those who wished not only to attend a class or two, but to receive a really systematic education, a college course was arranged which extended over three or four years.   Gradually the standard of work was raised, and in its thirty-first session the College offered fifteen lectures and classes a day instead of five.   This was in 1879, the year when the first Matriculation Examination at the University of London was open to women, when several present and several former students presented themselves, and all passed.   Now, in its fifty-sixth session, the College provides over thirty lectures and classes a day, also laboratory practice, and the lectures of the Training Department for Secondary Teachers, and the Hygiene Department, and classes in the Art School.   The courses of study include :—

1. A University Course in Arts or Science : Pass or Honours.
2. A College Course : General or Special.
3. A Professional Training in Teaching.
4. A Course of Scientific Instruction in Hygiene.
5. An Art School.

In addition to honours and post graduate courses arranged by the College, students attend University and Inter-Collegiate lectures, which do not appear in the College time table.   These courses are held at the various schools of the University of London, including Bedford College.   Out of its 260 students, 173 are reading for degrees, and of these 41 are in residence. The residential side of the College is, indeed, one of its most important features. Early in its history a boarding house was opened for girls whose parents lived in the country, and when the College was removed to York Place, Baker Street, in 1874, the upper floors were utilised for residence. The students in residence form a nucleus for the development of that *esprit de corps* and that spirit of corporate collegiate life which are such important factors in a University Education.

The spirit of college life is fostered among the students in various ways; there is a common room, and there are clubs and societies, both recreative and instructive, including boating, hockey, lawn-tennis, swimming, gymnastics and fencing clubs, and architectural, classical, debating, impromptu-debating, natural science, musical, photographic, Reid literary, Shakespeare reading, and sketching societies, and a students' association of past and present students which holds meetings at least twice each year.

London is cosmopolitan, and the College benefits by the large proportion of colonial and foreign students who become either resident or day students. During the last session six colonial students have been in the College, one from South Africa and two from New Zealand taking the scientific hygiene course, another from South Africa the intermediate science course, while two students from South Australia and Canada took one the B.Sc. course, the other a general course. There have been in residence students from India, Cape Colony and the Orange River

Colony, while students from Newfoundland, Singapore, Canada, the United States, India, South Australia and New Zealand attended the College daily.

Bedford College offered the first Scholarships to women in 1851, and founded the first Scholarships for them in 1860. In 1893 it offered, jointly with the Reid Trustees, the first Fellowship for women. There are now eight endowed Scholarships, four in Arts and four in Science, two of which are offered annually. The Reid Trustees, who administer funds bequeathed by Mrs. Reid, founder of the College, award annually two Scholarships. A former student of the College, living in India, is now maintaining two "Deccan" Scholarships in Science. All these Scholarships cover the fees for degree courses. Small Scholarships are also offered to reduce the fees for Secondary Training; and small Bursaries to reduce the fees for residence. There is a loan fund available for students of the Training Department, and for other students completing their college course. The London County Council in return for a grant of £800, nominate twenty-five free Scholars. These Scholarships are open to the daughters of London residents of two years standing, with maximum income of £400. Students holding Scholarships under the following County Councils are now attending the College; Hertfordshire, Kent, Lancashire, Glamorganshire, Norfolk, Nottinghamshire, and Salop. St. Dunstan Scholars and Gilchrist Scholars are also among the students of the College.

Prizes are offered annually by the Early English Text Society, and biennially by the Gladstone Memorial Trustees.

The Library, originally started with many of Mrs. Reid's own books, has gradually grown until it contains some 11,000 volumes used for reference and study, housed in four adjacent rooms. The funds available for books are unfortunately small and uncertain, but from time to time special bequests and donations have helped to supply the pressing wants of various departments. Lately a special Treasury grant of £300 has made it possible to obtain some expensive books, otherwise beyond the power to purchase. Gifts of books of great value have been presented, including from Dr. Furnivall an original second folio Shakspere, and a *facsimile* (Clarendon Press) first folio. Students have the use of the library from ten to six daily, and under certain regulations may take out books during term and vacation.

It was at Bedford College that teaching in practical Science was first put within the reach of women. In 1860 Dr. W. J. Russell, F.R.S., who for forty-three years was associated with the College as Lecturer in Natural Philosophy and Chairman of the Council, held his first class for practical laboratory work. Now the College has special laboratories equipped for the teaching of Chemistry, Physics, Botany, Physiology, Zoology, Bacteriology, and Geology, all in constant use. A special block of buildings, the Shaen wing, was erected as a memorial to Mr. William Shaen, Chairman of the Council, 1880-1887, containing the present lecture rooms and laboratories for Chemistry and Physics respectively. This building was opened in 1891 by the late Empress Frederick of Germany.

The Council recognised years ago that special openings in public service, for which women would be specially adapted, were those in the Department of Public Health. Acting on this conviction Bedford College started the first really scientific hygiene training course for women, and this course still remains the best and the most complete, being comparable with the course given to men for the diploma of public health. The course includes lectures and practical work in Hygiene, Physiology, Bacteriology, Chemistry, Physics and Meteorology: visits are paid to various places of interest, such as filter-beds and works of water-companies, model dwellings, dairy farms, insanitary areas, sewage works, all from a public health point of view. This special department of the College deserves to be widely known; the definite object is kept in view of gaining full knowledge of the laws governing personal and public health.

The College has altogether had no fewer than 4,500 students since its foundation, and of these many have distinguished themselves in after life in literature, medicine, public work, and in the teaching profession. Miss Anna Swanwick was an early pupil, as well as George Eliot, and in later years Miss Beatrice Harraden, Miss Lawrence Alma Tadema, and Miss Alice Zimmern read here for their degrees.

Of the eight women Factory Inspectors, two are from Bedford College, and others of the Hygiene students are engaged as Sanitary Inspectors and Lecturers in various parts of the country. Among the past students of the College were also Miss Traill Christie, to whom was entrusted the responsible duty of plague investigation in India, and Miss Humphry and Miss Kelly, who, through their researches and discoveries in Chemistry, have earned the distinction of Doctor of Philosophy at Zürich and Leipsig. Among those who have entered the Teaching profession, there are Mrs. Bryant, D.Sc., Miss Ainslie, B.A., and many other head mistresses, besides an ever-increasing number who leave the College and Training Department to take up School work.

In its early days there were associated in the administration of the College Lady Romilly, Lady Belcher, the wife of the great traveller; Lady Bell, the wife of Sir Charles Bell; and the wife of Barry Cornwall; and among other distinguished women connected with the College were Miss Eleanor Smith, Miss Emily Davis, and Miss Clough, who were the means of opening College life to women in Oxford and Cambridge.

The Leigh Smiths, the Martineaus, the Wedgewoods and the Darwins have all helped the College. Erasmus Darwin was both Visitor and Chairman of Council for many years, and Major Leonard Darwin is now the Honorary Treasurer. The Rev. Mark Pattison was chairman 1869—1879, and the position is now filled by the Right Hon. Arthur Dyke Acland. Recent visitors have been Miss Anna Swanwick, Sir Richard Jebb, and the Right Hon. R. B. Haldane.

The College is incorporated under the Act empowering it to be registered with limited liability, on condition that no portion of profit be transferred to members of association. It is governed by a body of members who elect the Council of Management, of whom at least one-third must be women.   In accordance with a resolution passed by the Council, and in order to obtain their cordial co-operation, the Principal and two members of the staff are invited to attend the meetings.   The Council works through various committees and elects half the members of a Board of Education, while the staff elects the other half.   This Board discusses educational questions and makes recommendations to the Council.   The staff consists of the Principal, the professors who are recognised teachers of the University, and other lecturers and assistants both men and women, numbering altogether twenty-eight, all of whom are appointed by the Council of Management.

The College holds a unique position as the first and still the only College for women which receives a Parliamentary grant.   As early as 1889, when the first Parliamentary grants to the University Colleges were made, Bedford College claimed to be included amongst them ; and again in 1891, application for recognition by Parliament was made, with the result that the College was inspected on behalf of the Lords Commissioners of Her Majesty's Treasury ; but it was not until 1894, at the time of the quinquennial redistribution of the Parliamentary grant to University Colleges, that Bedford College first received a grant of £700 a year.   This grant enabled the Council to reduce the fees, and when in 1896 it was increased to £1200, the money was almost entirely devoted to increasing the payments of the staff, although the students also received advantages.   This year the grant has been raised to £2000, with an additional grant of £700 for Library and Laboratory equipment.

The London County Council also make a yearly grant of £800.

With these grants, and by the timely help of generous friends, Bedford College has so far been able to meet the demand made upon it for the rapid developments of the higher education of women, but as this demand becomes daily more urgent, the College is now compelled to ask for larger and more lasting assistance. The impetus given to higher education by the reconstitution of the University of London, and by the Order in Council for the Registration of Teachers, has caused a growth of numbers which taxes unduly in every direction the capacity of the premises. Libraries, dining, common and cloak rooms are now all inconveniently overcrowded, the gymnasium is not large enough, and there is not space for physical recreations, which have all to be carried on at a distance from the College on grounds specially hired for the purpose. Further, the College possesses no large assembly hall or museum, and the lecture rooms have become insufficient in number, and more especially in size.

The position is complicated by the fact that the lease of an important part of the premises expires in March, 1909, and there seems no prospect of obtaining any extension of this term. The leases of the rest of the College expire in 1928 and cannot be renewed. Moreover, the ground landlord has informed the College that he declines to sell the freehold, and therefore no scheme of building or extension on the present site is possible.

A VIEW IN THE CHEMICAL LABORATORY, BEDFORD COLLEGE FOR WOMEN.

It is clear that larger premises must be found almost at once, in order that the work of the College may not be seriously hampered or curtailed, as must happen in three or four years time if adequate support is not forthcoming. As regards the conditions which may obtain in 1928, it must be stated that the depreciation in the capital value of the leases has only been provided for to a very limited extent by the accumulations of a sinking fund; and that, consequently, there will be practically no funds available at that date with which to re-establish the College in other quarters.

The task of ascertaining particulars about all available freehold sites in any parts of London, which would be fairly central and easily accessible from all sides, was undertaken by a small committee. The College now stands on over one-third of an acre, and it is estimated that one-and-a-half acres might be adequate for the new building. Freeholds of this size are very rarely available in London and are often only secured, after many years of waiting, by purchasing houses as leases fall in. Besides the length of time, this is generally a very costly way of securing sites. The Council, therefore, think it very fortunate that the committee have heard that a plot of land in a suitable position consisting of nearly one acre is now to be let. They have ascertained that the ground landlord would be willing to sell this to Bedford College, and also that there is every prospect that some of the adjoining land could be secured in the near future, so that ultimately the site might consist of about two acres. The plot of ground now to let is central, and it will

R

be easily accessible from all parts of London and the suburbs. Moreover, it is not far from other institutions connected with the University of London, so that together they would form a convenient group of academic centres ; the arrangements made by the University for the working of the Inter-Collegiate classes would also be facilitated if the College were placed in such a position. The Senate of the University approves of the proximity of several institutions performing rather different kinds of University work, and urges that this is more important than placing isolated colleges in various centres of the population.

The new premises, it is hoped, would supply buildings sufficient for five hundred students, one hundred of whom should be in residence with an adequate resident staff. They would contain the following: Assembly hall, lecture theatre, library and reading room, general museum, dining hall and gymnasium, all of considerable size ; twenty lecture rooms of various sizes, twelve laboratories and research rooms, rooms and library for the Training Department, and two studios, one for drawing from the life ; ample dressing and bathroom accommodation for day students, common and writing rooms, Council and Committee rooms, several offices and waiting rooms, and one hundred study bedrooms. Together with rooms for resident staff, kitchens, servants' hall, and bedrooms.

For land and building the Council are now appealing to the public for £150,000, but they also appeal for an additional sum for endowment. The College is practically without endowment, and is dependent on the fees of

Students, the Treasury grant, and the London County Council grant.

Moreover, the fact that the fees charges are generally equal to, if not greater than, those charged by other University Colleges points to the difficulty which is felt in raising them. It should, however, be mentioned that the total cost of the education per student at Bedford College is less than it is at several other important Colleges.

It is universally recognised that the cost of maintaining higher teaching for either men or women cannot now be covered by the fees which students are able to pay, so that Bedford College is no exception in this respect. If a sum of £100,000 for endowment were obtained, it would not only remove grave financial difficulties but would make progress possible. Moreover, the interest on this fund would only supply a sum which divided amongst 500 students would not amount to as much as one-fifth of the average fee paid by each.

No ancient endowments of Colleges for women exist, and in appealing for funds to men as well as to women, it should be remembered that in the past many Colleges for men have been endowed by women. Colleges for women require even larger endowments than Colleges for men, because parents do not so readily make provision for the higher education of daughters as of sons. Nevertheless there is an increasing need that women should be equipped for professional and bread-earning careers. The good of society also demands the admission of women generally to a larger share in the benefit of a liberal and enlightening education.

It is evident that the amount of the annual Parliamentary grants to University Colleges (£15,000, in 1895; £25,000, in 1897; £27,000, in 1902; and £54,000, in 1905) cannot afford nearly sufficient aid for Colleges without endowment. In France and Germany the amount contributed by the State is far larger in proportion to the expense of education.

For some years the new Education Authority of London will have as much as it can do financially to provide for the elementary and technical education, not to mention the needs of secondary schools, and it is therefore hopeless to expect that it will for many years, if ever, be able adequately to assist University Colleges by providing new sites and buildings or even by assisting the enlargements of premises already occupied.

The special claim put forward on behalf of the Bedford College for Women for public assistance is, that it is a University College for women in which the interests and needs of women are a paramount consideration, and where women can receive an academic education with professors lecturing to classes of women alone, and with laboratories and studios equipped and maintained exclusively for them. The Council feel that the largely and steadily increasing number of students justifies them in the conviction that such a College is needed, and the authorities of the University of London are also convinced that the maintenance and development of at least one University College for women in London is a necessity. Further, Bedford College shares in the Inter-Collegiate scheme arranged by the University of London.

These inter-collegiate courses for higher and post-graduate work for both men and women are held either at the University itself or at one or the other of the "Schools" of the University, and several have already been held at Bedford College in a lecture room set apart for the purpose. Such courses will always be necessary, but it would be a national calamity if a College for women thus connected with the University of London were not properly housed, equipped, and endowed in the Metropolis. With sufficiently large premises Bedford College might well look forward to becoming a centre for some of the best work of women.

The past students of Bedford College are not a rich body, and can only as a rule contribute small sums from professional earnings, to the Building and Endowment Fund, but they have already generously contributed £3,000. The Honorary Secretary of the building and Endowment Scheme is Miss Henrietta Busk, 1, Gordon Square, W.C., an old student of the College, and a present member of the Council. Lady Tate has also promised £10,000 for a library to be erected in memory of her husband, the late Sir Henry Tate, a former benefactor of the College, and the College is now looking for further benefactors, who shall contribute generously, as American millionaires do, to the needs of what is really a national institution.

As an integral part of the University of London this College in its appeal has the cordial support of the Senate. Principal Sir Arthur Rücker eloquently summed up its position in his Report, read at the Univer-

sity of London, on Commemoration Day last May:—
"The very existence of Bedford College, which was
a pioneer in women's education, and which is crowded
with students and is doing admirable work is threatened
by the approaching termination of the lease of the
buildings in which it is at present housed. An appeal
for funds by the Council has been approved by the Senate,
and it is a matter of the utmost urgency that a large
sum should be raised as soon as possible. Otherwise the
Metropolis may witness the disgraceful spectacle of the
ruin of a flourishing College which has for half a century
been one of the principal centres of women's education.'

Summer Gatherings.[*]

BY

ALEX. HILL, M.A., M.D.,
Master of Downing College, Cambridge.

On the occasion which proved to be the last on which the late Sir John Seeley, the Historian, dined in public, I had the privilege of sitting next to him, in Caius College Hall. Our talk fell to the contrast between oriental and occidental ideals, and in illustration of the keenness of the Japanese for education, he told me the following story. "After the self-renunciation of the Daimios and their voluntary abdication of their privileges in 1869, their retainers, the Samurai, found themselves in great poverty; until it was discovered that anyone could make a living in Japan by lecturing on John Stuart Mill and Herbert Spencer." The fundamental laws of economics, of government, of natural science! The Japanese were determined to begin at the beginning! They meant to understand, and therefore, instead of guessing, they consulted the men who had studied most, thought most, and were best qualified to express opinions.

The light in the Western sky is the glow of a sun which rose many centuries ago in the East. Its full

---

[*] Report of an Address delivered to the North London Students' Union.

splendour has been reflected back to the lands which were first tinged by its pale morning rays. It is but five and thirty years since Japan began to catch this glow reflected from the West. Do I need to ask whether, as a nation, she is less bright now than her European rivals?

Speaking of the discoveries which are so often attributed to a happy accident, Pasteur said, "In the field of natural science, chance favours only those whose minds are prepared." The revelations of the West illuminated a people whose whole mental habit was singularly well disposed to receive them and to give them play. How in a phrase can one describe the preparedness of the Japanese mind? The element in their character which made them so singularly ready to accept what is good and to reject what is unworthy in the civilization of England, Germany, France, was the genuineness of their ideals. "Wherefore spend ye money for that which is not bread, and your labour for that which satisfieth not?" Oh! for a number of reasons, great prophet, but chiefly because we have always before our eyes a mirage of something which is better than bread—a wonderful product of the confectioner's art. We grant that it is not so good to eat as bread, but it looks much prettier. Besides, if we must confess the truth, it is the stuff our neighbours always have for tea. We should die of shame if it were thought that we did not know what's what, or, knowing, could not afford to put it on the table.

We have heard a good deal lately about the simple life. The attention which the articles and letters in the *Daily Graphic* have attracted will end no doubt, as every movement in England ends, in what is intended as a beginning. Several Guilds or Leagues will be established. "The League of Simple Livers." "The League of Abnegationists." "The League of Simpletons." The last named league will have the largest following. It will comprise all those, and they are legion, who have not read the terms of the short lease on which their earthly tabernacle is let to them. Modern life is not, ought not to be, and cannot be simple. The street into which our windows give an outlook is a very busy one; there is much to be seen, much to be known. We observe from our windows many whose lives we can lighten or brighten. I have the greatest sympathy with those who mean by the simple life, the honest life, the life free from shams, snobbery, false issues of every kind, but many of those who have written upon the simple life confuse simplicity with emptiness. We need, during the short time before our lease of it runs out, to live as full a life as possible, to get as much into it as the days will hold. But, as much of what? This is the kernel of the controversy. Shall we give more thought to the outside decoration of our dwelling place or to its inside fittings? We have others to think of as well as ourselves. We must consult their tastes. We must try to please their eyes. We live in a street, not on a desert island. Yet we have a private room into which our soul retires at times. Its furnishing, our mental furnishing, should be our first care. The Japanese are not crying out for a simple life. On the contrary, they say "give us everything in your life that is worth the having. Give us everything, but give it good.   Philosophy—let us have Herbert Spencer; Economics—J. S. Mill; ships—send them to us from Barrow; guns—we are a little doubtful of your articles, we prefer those made by Krupp at Essen.   It is useless to offer us rubbish.   Always before accepting a thing we stop to ask is it a good thing of its kind.   Is it of a kind which is better than our own.   Take the case of amusements for example.   We understand that you have some of a rather tawdry sort, they are very expensive, and they make one very tired.   Some of them are cruel, they involve the suffering of animals.   Just at this season, you know, the cherry blossoms are at their best.   We shall stop all work, at the full moon, and spend the day playing and laughing in the orchards, among the flowers.   It is a pretty custom and singularly refreshing both to body and soul.   Later on we may come to you to teach us how to amuse ourselves.   At present we are content to do as our fathers and mothers have done for generations."

Miss Hughes tells us that one of the most admired of Japanese poems runs thus :—

" Morning glory By well bucket taken Beg of neighbour water."

Almost every Japanese cottage has its well, with a bucket suspended by a rope from a swinging beam, and one of the many daily tasks of the peasant woman is to draw the water.   A woman going to her well found one morning that a quickly growing convolvulus had twined its delicate stems round the rope of the well.   To destroy this thing of beauty would be a crime.   The peasant woman passed on to borrow water of her neighbour.

What is amiss with the conditions under which we

live? Why are so many people whining for a simple life? It is not that they want less. It is that they are troubled with misgivings that what they seem to want, even think they want, they really do not want at all.

A great London physician gave this singularly pregnant advice to one of my friends. His patient was a barrister, tall, nervous, over-eager, over-worked. With the patience begotten of routine, Sir William Broadbent tapped a chest which he knew to be sound, and listened to a heart which was beating with the regularity of a church clock. He poked and prodded and did everything that was needed to convince his patient that the visit to the doctor had done him good. But he gave him neither directions nor prescription. Just as my friend was leaving the consulting room he asked plaintively, "But, Doctor, you have not told me what I may eat." "Eat? Eat what you like, but be sure that you do like it." Wonderful prescription! It. transformed my friend. Instead of bolting a couple of sandwiches in his chambers, or worse still, deferring lunch until he had time to snatch a bun and swallow a cup of tea, he lunched at his club. He thought about what he was eating. He rejected many things which before he had eaten without thinking, and had suffered for afterwards.

Where is the physician who will give us equally sound advice with regard to the choice of our mental food? A daily meal at a railway bookstall is apt to agree with the mind as little as a sandwich or sausage-roll from the refreshment bar adjusts itself to our carnal wants. The University Extension movement is the thinker's club. It supplies him with mental food which does not merely put off appetite but nourishes the mind.

The attempt to make University life really a part of common life ; to enable the citizen to live at the same time in two worlds, the world of commerce and the academic world, naturally takes two forms. The University lecturer comes to his pupils during that part of the year when they are tied to their commercial work. But during the short interval of freedom from daily drudgery, what is more natural than that they should live the more attractive life, that they should spend their holidays at their University home and benefit from the ministrations of Alma Mater?

There are few who having once attended a Summer Gathering at Oxford or Cambridge do not make a great effort to go again.

The University Extension movement offers these two complementary opportunities of culture, the lecture *in partibus*, the sojourn in the very heart of academic life.

In America the form of Extension which we know best, the local lecture, has not made much progress. The reason is not difficult to find. "It is hardly to be expected," one of the Chicago lecturers remarked to me, "that a man who has to spend four nights a week in the train will manage to keep up the enthusiasm of his class." Extension is an excellent thing, but it may be overdone. When the tie which unites a local centre to its University is extended beyond about 500 miles, it is apt to lose its elasticity. It hangs slack like over-stretched India-rubber instead of exercising a steady concentric pull.

But if, owing to the vast distances which separate towns in the United States—a bigness which is the glory of our Yankee cousins—the local lecture system does not flourish, the same cannot be alleged of its complement, the Summer Gathering. Some twenty summer gatherings, or Chatauquas, as they term them, are held each year in the United States, attended by more than 20,000 people. These are the foci at which the American lights his lamp, they are the emporia from which he obtains his supply of oil.

For fifteen years I have been Chairman of a society which is frankly an imitation of the Chatauqua Literary and Scientific Circle. I am not going to talk to you about our scheme of reading, for I have always held that an, Extension lecture, which gives to the student the benefit of inspiration drawn from contact with a living teacher is better than any scheme of reading without lectures, however well it may be planned and carried out. But the Summer Assemblies of the National Home Reading Union are identical with those which are held at Oxford and Cambridge, although on a smaller scale. I have attended all of them save one, and can honestly say that each has added to the furniture of that mind-room in which my soul dwells, and each addition, whether ornament or article of use is a thing which I enjoy with a very full sense of possession ; because I realize it with a vividness which does not apply to all the acquisitions which my mind has made since first I began to learn.

Last year we met at York. I had heard, when at school, of the Roman occupation of Britain. Julius Cæsar was to my boy's imagination a very live man. I have seen Roman temples, baths and other buildings in various parts of Europe. But during our week in York we listened to lectures on the Roman occupation of Britain from Mr. Haverfield of Christ Church, Oxford, the greatest living authority on the subject. After one of his lectures we visited Aldborough with him, and wandered about the little Roman town, repeopling it with imperial legionaries, bartering with the British country folk, supervising the making of roads, perfecting the walls and towers, which protected us against a not too friendly population, and in every way taking an active part in the development of the Roman Colony.

Some years ago the Home Reading Union chose the Lake District for its Summer Assembly. There we occupied ourselves with geology amongst other subjects. On the summit of Helvellyn Dr. Marr lectured to us upon the work of ice in carving the features of the landscape. From this lofty lecture room we could *see* the great ice-plough scooping out the basin of Lake Windermere, scarring the sides of the mountains, planing down the hills that tried to block its passage, dropping huge moraines from its melting flanks. We heard the groaning of the rocks as they were crushed in the grip of its deliberate but irresistible might. The drama of nature was re-enacted before our eyes. We were a part of what we saw.

I do not wish to raise regrets in your minds that the University of Oxford was not founded on the shores of Windermere. There are many who think that it would have been a more desirable site than the Valley of the Thames. Even we at Cambridge feel at times that just a little greater diversity in the landscape which surrounds us would add to the picturesqueness of the scenery— might perhaps afford a keener stimulus to mind and body. What I want to point out is the advantage of gaining knowledge at first hand. The impression to which reading gives rise is but the ghost of that clear image which direct experience focusses on the mind. Think how much Oxford has to teach at first hand! Its buildings are much as their founders left them centuries ago. Even the life—the ceremonies, customs, titles are not altogether modern. There is still left for you who go to Oxford from this up-to-date London a trace—just a trace—of mediævalism. Enough for you to taste if not enough to satisfy your thirst; and you will find it of full colour and sound body. A very, very, ancient vintage, but it has not lost its quality through long keeping. Oxford offers for your study two object lessons, each illustrated with a profusion of material—the life of the past in hall and cloister—the activities of the present in laboratory and museum.

At the coming Summer Gathering the programme will be divided into sections. The first two deal with the history and the literature of the Renaissance, the third with the methods of science. Could a greater contrast be conceived? The Renaissance meant the discovery by scholars of the fourteenth or fifteenth centuries that Greeks and Romans knew so much more than they did, and thought so shrewdly about what they knew, that it was superfluous or futile for them to try to find out things for themselves. It was a shorter road to knowledge to study the work of the masters who had written seventeen or eighteen centuries before. Aristotle and Plato knew so much that they seemed to know all that was to be known. The scholars of the Renaissance relied upon authority as the ultimate test of truth. The scientific method is the antithesis to this. *Observe, infer.* There are no facts, or rather none available for scientific purposes. which have not been observed; no theory is true which fails when confronted with facts. Yet this antithesis is not new. The chief place in the Oxford programme will be given to Shakspere and his surroundings. We all know now that Bacon lived in Shakspere's days. Some people turn it the other way about, "Shakspere was an actor and stage manager who brought out plays in Bacon's days— a vagabond who in early life poached deer at Hampton Lucy, in later years he served the public with poached plays—on Bacon."

Francis Bacon, the genius of the Renaissance, was the founder of the Scientific Method. What the scientific method is as a mental process and in its general features will be taught at Oxford by the Waynflete Professor of Moral and Metaphysical Philosophy, and the Waynflete Professor of Physiology. In its special application it will be illustrated by a galaxy of scientific lecturers. Students who attend the Oxford Summer Gathering will have the opportunity of learning from the best of teachers the meaning of the Renaissance. They may soak themselves in its spirit—the spirit of reverence for authority. They will find themselves surrounded by the works of the Renaissance, they will loiter in the haunts of its most famous makers. And as a contrast, the greatest contrast, surely, that can be found, they will see and handle the rocks, the animals and plants, the apparatus which constitute the only authority which science recognizes—the authority not of names and doctrine, but of facts. What exercise could be more fruitful of right thinking. This was the philosophy of Descartes, it was the philosophy of Huxley, who so greatly admired the "French Bacon," as he has often been termed—the philosophy which does not attempt to reach the meaning of things, but concerns itself with the methods by which we attain knowledge enabling us by checking our habits of thought to make sure that we are thinking as effectively as our brains are able to do.

Happy are the lads who spend three years in one of our ancient Universities. But happier still perhaps are those who go to it for training and inspiration at an age when they are able to appreciate the value of its influence. Whether it be a simplification or a complication of life I know not, but it helps us to increase our realization of life. Give us the good of life! Let us spend in attaining it the full measure of our physical strength; the

c

measure of our *energy* is the measure of our potential success in living. Failure is due either to want of force or to waste of force. Life's balance sheet cannot be falsified. How many of us can say that our accounts show no outlay against which we cannot set off an asset which ranks as worth the having.

The treasures brought back from a Summer Gathering have a value which you are unlikely at any after time to call in question.

Workpeople and the Universities.

BY

ALBERT MANSBRIDGE.

THE following thoughts, connected as far as the vast area of the subject will allow, dealing chiefly with the Extension work of the Universities, and entirely with matters of liberal education, are written down in consciousness of a state of affairs which has made it difficult for any educational effort, other than that of the Elementary Schools, to reach the great majority of working people, who are often occupied in ways which tend to render them unconscious of any need for education or of any claim which it may have upon them.

It is recognised throughout that the University in its true sense is a gathering place of men of learning with their disciples; a place where able men are actuated by intense desire to seek truth and to express it; where men are careful to develop enthusiasm and anxious to fan into flame the smoking flax; where men are responsive to the noble impulses of mankind and in touch with intellectual movements; where men add, as master craftsmen, to historic walls and traditional robes choice products of mental and spiritual activity.

There, as elsewhere, higher education depends for its influence upon the intensive force which it exerts. That Universities, University Colleges, and University Extension Centres should be in direct contact with a large number of people is not so important as that their students should be taught, trained, and encouraged to the utmost. Further, as an almost necessary corollary, the University fails if it allows its teaching to fall below an accepted standard—fails in proportion to the fall. Indeed no conception of the University's functions justifies its doing the work of a Public School, a Technical Institute, or a popular lecture Agency. If such institutions are capable of satisfying the educational need of the country, Universities, at the present time, are merely luxuries; this is a conclusion obviously absurd, but not without meaning at the outset of any consideration having for its subject the relations which Universities may legitimately bear to workpeople.

Many opportunities have been provided for working men and University professors to confer upon the extension of University teaching. One such opportunity was taken full advantage of by Vice-Chancellor Dale, of Liverpool University, when he said that "the possession of money, or the want of it, should no longer stand in the way of getting a sound, solid, and complete University Education." There is no essential difference, as far as the University is concerned, between the student from the artisan's home and the student from the public school. A weaver fresh from his loom gained a Brackenbury Scholarship at Balliol, and after a first class in the final schools was elected to a Fellowship at Pembroke College.

It would, indeed, appear that working men, in common with men of other grades, bring their own peculiar richness of thought and experience to a University. "The nations of the earth bring their glory and honour into it." To put it another way—if a University would keep its teaching free from fallacy its collective mind must be composed of elements drawn from all worthy sections of the National life, from labour, from commerce, from church, from pure scholarship. The University is the better for intimate contact with life at all points. Any conception of a University as the parent of a high culture postulates broad and free contact with life. Otherwise its culture will become mere pedantry, its opinions valueless because divorced from practical issues, no "Flame of freedom in the soul," no "Light of knowledge in the eye."

It is thus evident that a University does well if it devises means whereby it may appeal to those not yet under its influence. If it be admitted that the teaching of a University should only slightly overlap the teaching of minor institutions, the need for a University to take all possible steps to direct the course of education to itself is emphasised. Universities have taken many such steps. Representation upon educational institutions near to them may well have a counterpart in representation upon bodies which desire to extend University teaching amongst workpeople as indeed amongst leisured people.

The "experts in supply" induce a maximum result when operating together with the "experts in demand." Precedent for this is not lacking. Official University representatives have frequently addressed working-class congresses upon education, and the majority of the Universities are officially represented upon the council of the newly-formed "Association to Promote the Higher Education of Working Men."

Speaking at Exeter in August, 1904, Canon Parry gave expression to the intense desire of the Cambridge Syndicate to benefit workpeople, "never absent from our thoughts," he said, and, without doubt, the Extension work of Cambridge and of the other Universities has achieved its desire to such an extent as to be an earnest of the years to come. It must be encouraging to modern working-class educationists to reflect that it was an appeal by members of the Nottingham Trades Council which induced the Universities to make such a departure from tradition as the beginning of Extension work.

It has often been said that University Extension has achieved its desire to such an extent only as makes it an earnest of a better future. Indeed, it is commonly observed that Extension students are not so often workpeople as ladies of the leisured and teaching classes. This latter observation has induced the judgment that University Extension in relation to workpeople, if not dead, is, at least, a failure. Much depends, of course, upon what life and success mean. If they mean establishing a state of affairs where the mass of workpeople crowd the Extension course and change *ipso facto* into serious students, then death and failure will ever be the portion of University Extension; but if they mean stimulating an increasing number of students, and endowing those who teach the workers and their children with larger and more liberal ideas of life, then University Extension is successfully alive in its relationship with workpeople.

An ideal which depends for its realisation upon the direct contact of all, or of even most, workpeople with the Universities, may be put aside at once as impracticable, even so, the University must be ready to meet any reasonable demand that groups of workpeople may make upon it.

In order to appraise the influence of University Extension upon workpeople, it is necessary to examine working-class educational movements. Of these, the most prominent is the Co-operative, and it is not too much to say that the history of Co-operative Education is, to a large extent, the history of the influence of the Universities upon it.

The educational watchwords of Co-operation were supplied by Professor Stuart at Gloucester in 1879. "First you must educate your members in your own principles and in those of economic science, and in the history of endeavours like your own, and in the second place you must educate them generally."

Arnold Toynbee dealt with the same subject at the Oxford Congress in 1882. The newly issued official text book of the Union marks that Congress "as the starting point of a new and vigorous growth of educational work. If Co-operators are to arrive at a correct solution of the social problems, which are every day becoming more grave, if workmen are to rightly exercise the unparalleled power of which they have become possessed, then they must receive a social and political education such as no other institutions have offered, an education which I believe Co-operative Societies by their origin and aims are bound to provide."

An examination of the names of men who have pressed forward Co-operative Education in the light of these ideals, reveals very many who are known to have had intimate connection with University Extension work, and who have been inspired as the result of that connection to undertake teaching work in the Co-operative movement. Further, it is matter of experience that those Co-operative students who are enabled by the Co-operative Union to attend the Summer Meetings, go back to their societies quickened in zeal and educated to a larger view of life. In a Co-operative publication of July 1905, it is recorded that a Summer Meeting scholarship offered by the Stratford Society "was won by a working painter, who entered with enthusiasm into the life he discovered for the first time at the University. He has ever since kept in touch with the movement for increasing the opportunities for culture enjoyed by the workers."

This is one instance of many, and will add strength to a plea for the establishment of these scholarships by working-class organisations. By no other means can artisans be enabled to attend Summer Meetings in appreciable numbers. The authorities allow fifty per cent. reduction in the price of tickets, but not only have fares and lodging expenses to be met, but wages lost and employment sometimes imperilled. A foreign point of view is expressed in the remarks of a German professor, who referring to the Exeter meeting in the current *University Extension*, says that "a larger attendance by this class of men (workmen) could not fail to lower the standard." The comments of lecturers and examiners, who know that these men are often the best students, sometimes doing work worthy of the Final Schools, incline us to believe that the standard would be more than maintained. Moreover, the standard is the immediate concern of the University, and must not be lowered. The Oxford Delegacy has so far recognised the importance of working-class teachers as to license those who reach a prescribed high standard. During last year, seven were so licensed. It will be seen at once that it is not essential for the success of University Extension that it should be in direct contact with the vast body of working men, provided that it inspires and trains teachers who can make contact with others.

Another aspect of the question presses for notice. It is common knowledge that those elementary teachers who have placed themselves under the influence of University Extension are the farthest removed from the rut in which many elementary school teachers are to be found. Their minds are freshened and invigorated, they are often inspired by delight in knowledge, and actuated by lofty conceptions of Education. Such teachers are continually in contact with working-class children, and it is reasonable to assume, that to influence them is, in view of their unique and important office, more highly to be valued than to crowd the Extension lecture rooms with grown men. Anything that can save elementary school teachers, and even secondary school teachers, from a temptation to acquire certificate after certificate in studies widely removed from one another, so that their chances of appointment by undiscerning authorities may be improved, is deserving of encouragement, even at financial loss.

It is not easy to trace the influence of University Extension upon trade unionists and members of other working-class organisations as such, because no sustained educational work has so far been accomplished by them, although instances of excellent work are numerous. They have been chiefly concerned with opportunist education, the dealing with topical matters, the insistence upon their own point of view, and they have taken extreme interest in educational politics. The old order of things is passing away and in spite of a tendency towards isolation, a reflex of working-class political strategy, it is to trade unions and trades councils, as well as to Co-operative bodies, that the attention of those who wish to promote the extension of University teaching amongst working men must be directed. The generous support afforded by Trades Unions and Councils to Ruskin College, with its staff of University men, is a matter for present encouragement.

Having established these facts and having defined, in some way, the reasonable attitude of the Universities toward workpeople, it may be well to consider the attitude of the working-classes in general towards the Universities. Any assumption that working people are expectant would be idle. Where indifference does not exist, there is often a sustained note of opposition frequently breaking through the conventionalities of speech. That such an attitude is unreasonable need hardly be said, and there is happily little doubt but that, when things are represented in their true light to those who sound such a note, reasonableness will triumph. It must be remembered that working people have, to a great extent, been left to themselves in spite of the success which has been attained by the University Extension Authorities.

There seems something in the nature of a paradox in what has been said, but it is quite evident that, with rare exceptions, the University Extension Authorities have contented themselves with the provision of lectures acceptable to the cultured man, not necessarily and not always acceptable to the working man. This state of affairs is passing away gradually, but it may be questioned whether the Universities are at present able to send out in sufficient numbers lecturers who, whilst maintaining their own high standard of subject and expression, can interest the average working man. Again, it has sometimes happened that brilliant lecturers, surrounded by experiments and illustrations, have attracted phenomenal audiences and, there being no "apostolic succession" in these matters, a subsequent lecturer of excellent parts, without the experiments, the illustrations, and, it may even be said, the humorous way of presenting things, has found his audience dwindle away. The efforts of University Extension under such conditions are, for the immediate future, sterilised in the district. The intelligent working man's appreciation of University Extension efforts is greatly influenced by this alternate success and failure.

A point of opposition arises in this way. Working men are concerned chiefly with economic difficulties, and a feeling of contempt frequently expressed, is engendered in them by contact with University men who desire to teach them economics, but who have no appreciation of the difficulties of unemployment and the competitive life— a contempt which they would have for a doctor who failed to diagnose his case correctly. The medical schools deal with disease at first hand, it is a more difficult thing to deal with bad economic conditions at first hand, but the workman expects evidence of it or discards at once the economics of the University professor.

Another point of opposition to the Universities is created by the accentuation of what may be termed the socialistic attitude, controlled by the Social Democratic Federation, by the Independent Labour Party, and not so directly, but more potently, by the Labour Representation Committee. It is a socialism with a method of interpretation peculiar to itself, and it considers that the normal teaching of the Universities, as evidenced by its literary output, and the theories advanced by its professors, depends upon interpretation of an antagonistic nature. Therefore they say, "Let us avoid the Universities, let us develop our own culture, our own education in economics. We believe in the study of the humanities, but we think we can do better for ourselves."

The narrowness of this view, which is an obstructive force to be reckoned with, frequently prevents them from seeing that a policy of isolation in education is an absurdity.

There is in all movements what may be roughly termed a collective mind. It will frequently and fortunately happen that heresy in the meeting-room will be common sense by the fireside.

No observer of the working classes will attempt to hide from himself the fact that the average desire for education on the part of socialistic working men is keener than that of working men in general, and it is fortunately a matter of certainty also that the number of individual working men, in spite of the isolation policy, who are directing their energies towards the development of University teaching amongst their fellows is increasing. It is hoped that the increase will be garnered by the Association to Promote the Higher Education of Working Men, which hopes by the joint action of educationists and workpeople to adopt existing and to devise fresh means by which working people of all degrees can be raised educationally, plane by plane, until they are able to take advantage of the facilities afforded by the Universities. This body, at the outset of its work, is confronted by the demand made to define in some way what is meant by the extension of University teaching, and it may be said at once, that, whilst the Association desires to promote courses of University Extension lectures and to infuse a greater element of its working men members into University Extension centres, it will have failed unless intensive class teaching up to University standard is developed. In other words, its success will lie in its being able to promote small classes and reading circles (the hope for large ones being futile) in which education is intensified. Such classes as these can be arranged independently of the University Extension course, and will, as a matter of regrettable necessity, often be. In favourable centres the number of classes may be so extended as to have the value of a University College, if not the fabric of one. The Association will discard any attempt to estimate its influence by numbers, and it hopes that the more popular aspect of its work will be carried on in such a manner as to enable it to maintain the classes, which must always be carried on at financial loss. No idea that working people are clamorously asking for University education confuses the issue in its mind.

In spite of all that has been said about the permeation of the working classes by University teaching, only a small number have been directly influenced, a result surely which will be expected if account be taken of the very long and exacting hours of labour and the economic conditions under which many workpeople live, as well as of the fact that the class has not shown itself backward in adopting the vices of leisured people with less time to accomplish them. At the same time, any working man who wishes to put himself in contact with education, can do so.

The state of affairs is not greatly different from that which existed when, one hundred years since, John Wood, quoting the 38th chapter of Ecclesiasticus, wrote in his little book upon the Edinburgh Sessional School, "'He who reflects that the wisdom of a learned man cometh by opportunity of leisure, and he that hath little business shall become wise,' will not readily expect from a mechanic the wisdom of a philosopher." Still, in these days, there are working-class philosophers and it is these who are sought for in the public councils. There is little doubt but that, though under the best conditions a large number of workpeople cannot be expected to desire University Extension, more will desire it if each man is educated to the utmost of his capacity and opportunity.

In conclusion, the outlook is full of promise. Those who read the signs of the times aright are convinced that the days are passing gradually from the springtime of education to a more fruitful season, and that working men are daily seeing more and more the necessity for education, and the importance of obtaining it in the places of high culture, the seats of the mighty in learning, which must ever exercise the functions of "Universities," so long as education means to them "training for duty to the Commonwealth, its last outcome intellectual force controlled by character, individual energies co-operating for the public good, and fine scholarship given to public service."

Memorial Notices.

"Quique sui memores alios fecere merendo."

SIR WILLIAM MUIR, K.C.S.I., D.C.L., L.L.D..

Formerly Principal and Vice-Chancellor of the University of Edinburgh.

THE University of Edinburgh has lost a faithful friend and a distinguished *alumnus* by the death of its late Principal, Sir William Muir, which occurred somewhat suddenly at his residence in Edinburgh on the 11th of July.   William Muir was born in Glasgow on the 27th of April, 1819, and was educated at Kilmarnock Academy, and at the Universities of Edinburgh and Glasgow.   In 1837, after two years at the East India Company's College at Haileybury, he entered the Bengal Civil Service.   For thirty nine years, William Muir devoted himself to administrative work in India.   His remarkable industry, high integrity and far-seeing statesmanship have won for him a high place among the administrators of Northern India.   During the crisis of the Mutiny, William Muir was in charge of the Intelligence Department at Agra.   In 1867, he was made

Knight Commander of the Star of India in recognition
of his valuable services, and in the following year he
became Lieutenant Governor of the North West Provinces. Under his *régime*, great advances were made in
the departments of Education and Public Health. A
keen interest in higher education was always characteristic
of William Muir, and the Muir College and the Allahabad
University are worthy monuments to his memory.
"Under his auspices," said Lord Lytton, at a farewell
banquet given in Muir's honour in 1876, "we find colleges
established, schools increased, scholarships founded, the
study of vernacular literature extended and its tone
purified, and the humblest village home, even the Zenana
itself, brought within the humanizing influence of whole-
some instruction."

In 1876 he retired from his active duties in India,
though for nine more years he served as a member of
the Council of India. In 1885 he was elected to fill
the difficult office of Principal and Vice-Chancellor of the
University of Edinburgh, and for eighteen years—critical
years in the history of the University—he guided its
course with intelligence, dignity, and tact. During his
Principalship important changes in the constitution of the
University were introduced by the Act of 1889, while
the whole scheme of studies was re-organised by the
Universities Commission. Perhaps the most important
and far-reaching development in the life of the University
during this period was the awakening of the students to
the possibilities of self-government and corporate action.
The kindly interest shown by Sir William Muir in the

D

beginnings of the movement, and his ready encouragement and support of the schemes for a Students' Representative Council, a Students' Union, Playing Fields, and Residential Halls won for him the regard and veneration of every student and the affectionate title of the "Students' Principal."

The universal feelings of respectful affection entertained towards him found expression at his retirement in the public presentation of an address in the M'Ewan Hall. He resigned the office of Principal in January, 1903, and so brought to a conclusion sixty-six eventful years of public service to his country and to his *Alma Mater*.

The University Court on receiving his resignation ordered the following minute to be entered upon the records of the University :—"The University Court, having accepted the resignation of Sir William Muir, K.C.S.I., as Principal, to take effect on the appointment of a successor, desire to record their sense of his faithful services to the University, and their deep regret at parting with him in his official capacity. Appointed in 1885. after forty-eight years spent in almost every grade of the civil service in India, he brought to the administration of perhaps the most cosmopolitan University in the Empire a ripe experience of many races and civilisations, and a knowledge of affairs gained in both prosperous and critical times. With constant assiduity, he devoted that knowledge and experience to the duties of his office, and in every effort, both for the improvement of the University and for the good of its students individually, he exhibited a splendid and unfailing generosity. The respect and affection which he gained from every member of the University during these eighteen years was no more than his fitting reward ; and the members of this Court, in adding their tribute to the universal consensus of academic opinion, would express the earnest hope that every blessing may attend him during the remainder of his eventful life, and would assure him that their respectful affection will follow him to its close."

As an author, he has gained a high position in literature, his "Life of Muhammed" and the " Annals of the Early Caliphate " are regarded as standard works. In recognition of his services to literature and education Sir William received the Honorary Degree of LL.D. from the Universities of Cambridge, Edinburgh, and Glasgow; of D.C.L. from the University of Oxford; and of Ph,D. from the University of Bologna.

Captain MONTAGUE BURROWS, R.N.,

Fellow of All Souls' College and Chichele Professor of Modern History in the University of Oxford.

THE death of Professor Burrows removes from Oxford the oldest Professor in the University. Professor Burrows was born at Hadley, Herts, in October, 1819, and was educated at the Royal Naval College at Portsmouth. He entered the navy in 1835, and as a midshipman he fought in several actions against the Malay Pirates, and was present at the capture of St. Jean d'Acre. In 1843 he became a lieutenant, and after taking part in the suppression of the African slave trade he was promoted to the rank of commander. In 1853 he left the navy and matriculated at Magdalen Hall (now Hertford College), obtaining a first class in classics in 1856, and in law and history in 1857. Professor Burrows was elected Chichele Professor of Modern History in 1862, and until his retirement in 1900 served the University actively and loyally in many directions. He was the author of a number of publications, among which may be mentioned the life of "Admiral Lord Hawke" and the "History of the Cinque Ports." Professor Burrows was a keen politician and took a very active part as one of the leaders of the Conservative party in Oxford. In 1870, he was elected a Fellow of All Souls' College, and his interesting volume "Worthies of All Souls'" is of considerable value as a history of the College. He was an Officer de l'Instruction Publique of France and an honorary M.A. of Cambridge.

Dr. Nicholas Murray Butler.

PRESIDENT OF THE COLUMBIA UNIVERSITY OF NEW YORK.

The visit to this country of Dr. Murray Butler, President of Columbia University, New York, has been in every sense welcome. It has enabled English educationists to show their appreciation of the valuable help and advice he has so generously given to English visitors to the United States. It has provided them with an opportunity to do honour to a man of great academic and adminis- trative distinction, and at the same time to hold out the hand of fellowship to American Universities with which English Universities are so closely connected.

Dr. Butler's career is full of interest. Born in 1862, he was educated at the institution of which he was afterwards to become President. After taking a brilliant degree, he continued his education at the Universities of Berlin and Paris, returning to New York in 1881 as Lecturer in Philosophy at Columbia College. In 1885, at the early age of 23, he served as President of the National Education Association, and in 1886 he founded the well- known Teachers College in New York. In 1902, he was elected President of Columbia University. His published works include "Education in the United States" (two volumes) and "The Meaning of Education," the former containing the admirable series of mono- graphs on American Education prepared for the Paris Exhibition of 1900. At the present time, he is Editor of the *Educational Review*— the leading American educational magazine—the Great Educators' Series and the Teachers' Professional Library. He has also had wide experience of educational administration as a member of various public bodies. In short, it is no exaggeration to say, as Sir Arthur Rücker said in proposing his health at the dinner in his honour on July 5th, that he is regarded as one of the foremost educationists, not only in his own country, but in the world; and it is fitting that the Universities of Oxford and Manchester should have conferred on him the Honorary Degree of LL.D.

During his stay in this country, Dr. Butler has been entertained by Sir Arthur Rücker, by Mr. Alfred Mosely—it is worth mentioning that the success of the Mosely Commission to the United States was largely due to Dr. Butler's organising ability—and by Mr. Cornwall, Chairman of the London County Council. He addressed the National Union of Teachers on the morning of July 22nd, and was afterwards entertained at luncheon. Reference has already been made to the dinner at the Hotel Great Central on July 5th, organised by representatives of the Board of Education and the University of London. The chair was taken by Lord Londonderry, President of the Board of Education, and the guests, to the number of over a hundred, included many of the leading authorities in English education. Dr. Butler's reply to the toast of his health was a great oration which will long remain in the memory of those who were privileged to hear it. It was not, he said, literature for literature's sake, it was not nature for nature's sake, it was not art for art's sake, we were concerned with in educating our people. We looked up to literature and science and art for the sake of humanity and a higher, purer, and truer civilisation. What possible interest would it be to us to strain indefinitely the range of human understanding or the grasp of knowledge if we could bring nothing into the common treasury for the good of mankind? The human standard was the controlling standard, and mankind was the beginning, the middle, and the end of all our work. The most difficult problem in our higher education was to decide how far we should train men to think for themselves, and how far we were to bring our influence to bear on training them to think like other people. He was opposed to a too early and too close specialisation—what was the use of preparing students for life if when they reached it they were unable to live? Our youths to-day were asking, as they asked hundreds of years ago, " Who are the men who know most? Let us sit at their feet and gain from them not knowledge alone, but inspiration as well, the magnetic force of example and of personal contact." A true University could not exist without genuine scholars. It was true that all students could not become great masters of research, but it should be made plain that scholarship of every kind must lead to service—only in this way could we put before the young men of to-day the real goal of a University education.

It is easier to give a *resumé* of Dr. Butler's brilliant speech than to describe its virile and lucid delivery. Dr. Butler is not one of those scholars whose object in life is personal " culture,"—who are content to " burn with a hard gem-like flame." He does not belong to the class of professors who, in Newman's words, are " abstractions and phantoms, marrowless in their bones and without speculation in their eyes." It will be men of the type represented by Dr. Butler who will help our Universities to take their proper place in the public esteem, and will secure their full recognition as institutions contributing in a real sense to national well-being and progress.

An Imperial College of Applied Science.

In view of the widespread interest that has been aroused by the Preliminary Report recently presented by the Departmental Committee on the Royal College of Science and on what has been miscalled the "Charlottenburg" scheme, and of the far-reaching importance of its proposals, we publish below the text of the Report, which was signed by all the members of the Committee:—

To THE MOST HONOURABLE THE MARQUESS OF LONDONDERRY, K.G., PRESIDENT OF THE BOARD OF EDUCATION.

We, the Departmental Committee appointed by your Lordship in April last to inquire into the present and future working of the Royal College of Science (including the Royal School of Mines), and into questions connected therewith, have the honour to submit a Preliminary Report.

I. In conducting the inquiry referred to us, we have held 17 meetings, at which we have examined 21 witnesses.

The evidence which we have received has been largely concerned with the history of the Royal College of Science (including the Royal School of Mines), with the character of the instruction now given therein, and with the possibility of attracting students more advanced in their education than the majority of those who now seek admission. On this branch of our inquiry we should be prepared to submit recommendations which we think will conduce to increase the great usefulness of these institutions, even though conducted in the main upon their present lines; but we have thought it desirable to defer making such recommendations at the present time for reasons which we will now proceed to state.

II. It will be remembered that the terms of reference to the Committee were as follows:—

"To inquire into the present working of the Royal College of Science, including the School of Mines: to consider in what manner the staff, together with the buildings and appliances now in occupation or in course of construction, may be utilised to the fullest extent for the promotion of higher scientific studies in connection with the work of existing or projected Institutions for instruction of the same character in the Metropolis or elsewhere: and to report on any changes which may be desirable in order to carry out such recommendations as they may make."

We recognise the admirable work accomplished by the Royal College of Science not only in training teachers, but in its general method of Science teaching and in the promotion of research. Notwithstanding the marked increase in the number of institutions where teachers of Science can be trained, the demand has so increased that the need for teachers of Science who have been well trained in scientific method is no less now than when the College was established as a Normal School of Science. At the same time it is agreed that there is an urgent national necessity for increased facilities for advanced instruction and research in Science, especially in its application for industry. In view of this fact, and in view of certain munificent offers of aid towards the provision of such facilities in London, we have felt that it was necessary, in order to discharge the reference to us, to survey the resources available for, and the potentialities of, the principal existing and projected institutions of the character contemplated in our terms of reference. We have now proceeded far enough in this survey to satisfy ourselves that the moment is *primâ facie* opportune for a comprehensive scheme. The accomplishment, however, of such a scheme as we have in mind can only be brought about by the realisation of the offers of aid which are referred to above, and by the co-operation of certain influential bodies possessing an interest in such institutions as are dealt with in our proposals.

It has, therefore, become necessary for us to approach these bodies and the persons who have made these munificent offers. But before we proceed any further in this direction, we feel that our position would be strengthened if we could be assured that our proposals will meet with the approval of the Government, and we have accordingly decided, in view of the stage at which we have arrived, to present this preliminary report, in which we outline the scheme we think desirable, and specify the conditions which in our opinion would make it possible.

III. The conditions which, if fulfilled, would, in our opinion, ensure the success of the scheme are:—

(1) The gift of a large capital sum (say not less than £100,000) for buildings and initial equipment.

(2) The gift of a considerable additional site (say not less than four acres) at South Kensington.

(3) The willingness of the Board of Education to allow their

College at South Kensington to be brought into a scheme of common government and administration.

(4) The similar willingness of the City and Guilds of London Institute in respect of their College at South Kensington.

(5) The continuance of the Government contribution including the necessary provision for the maintenance of the new laboratories and other buildings of the Royal College of Science, now approaching completion.

(6) The continuance of the support given by the Corporation and Livery Companies of the City of London to the Central Technical College.

(7) The provision (in the proposed College of Applied Science at South Kensington) of instruction in certain departments of Engineering either by new foundation or by transfer and enlargement of part of the work of some existing College or Colleges (e.g., University College or King's College).

(8) The co-operation of the University of London.

(9) The assurance of a sufficient maintenance fund.

NOTE.—For such a maintenance fund we look to the following sources in addition to those mentioned above under headings 5 and 6.

(a) Any grant from the Vote for University Colleges to which the Institution may be able to establish its claim.

(b) An annual Grant from the London County Council.

(c) The Bessemer Memorial Fund (so far as not applied to capital expenditure).

(d) Fees of Students.

(e) Endowment of special forms of instruction given by persons or bodies interested.

(f) Any portion of funds given for capital purposes which may remain available for income after the necessary capital expenditure.

IV. Given the fulfilment of the above condition, we should be prepared to recommend such a scheme as is indicated in outline in the following paragraphs:—

(1) In considering the problem laid before us by the Government, we are impressed by the fact that the most urgent need in scientific education is the establishment of a centre in which the specialisation of the various branches of study and the equipment for the most advanced training and research should be such as ultimately to make it the chief Technical School of the Empire.

So large a scheme cannot be carried out in a day, but we believe that the present is a favourable opportunity for making a beginning, and in the suggestions which follow we have kept the above end steadily in view. The existence of the Royal College of Science with the Royal School of Mines and of the Central Technical College in close proximity points to South Kensington as the best position for such a centre as we contemplate; and we have made careful inquiry as to the extent of the accommodation which is at present concentrated in that neighbourhood. It is as follows:—

Accommodation for about 200 Students in the permanent part of the existing buildings of the Royal College of Science and the Royal School of Mines.

Accommodation for from 300–350 Students including accommodation for work for about 100 Physics and Chemistry Laboratories in the Royal College of Science, now approaching completion.

Accommodation for about 300 Students in the existing buildings of the Central Technical College.

With the exception of the new laboratories of the Royal College of Science, these buildings are fully occupied by students, but the accommodation for Mining and Metallurgy is quite inadequate, and is to a great extent merely temporary. Further, the accommodation for Engineering, whether in the Royal School of Mines or in the Central Technical College is insufficient to meet the wants of many qualified students who are annually refused admission for want of space, and in no branch of Applied Science is sufficient provision made for advanced or specialised work.

There is no doubt that if arrangements could be made between the Government on the one hand and the City and Guilds of London on the other, the resources of the above-mentioned Institutions could be used with far greater effect and economy.

(2) The buildings and equipment, even if such arrangement were made, though in many respects excellent and extensive, are quite inadequate for existing requirements and still more for the purpose in view. The provision to be made for the future should include not only a fully developed School of Mining and Metallurgy and departments for the principal branches of Engineering, but also for other special subjects.

We do not attempt in this Preliminary Report to draw up a detailed scheme, but the following principal subjects should be within the purview of the Institution:—

As Preparatory Subjects—Mathematics, Physics, Chemistry and Geology: Under the general heading of Civil Engineering—Works of Construction, Mechanical Engineering, Electrical Engineering, Mining Engineering, Marine Engineering and Naval Architecture: Some branches of Chemical Technology, and certainly Metallurgy.

As illustrations of the kind of higher or more specialised application of these subjects, some of which we suggest should be dealt with, we need only mention the applications of Engineering to Railway, Dock, and Hydraulic work; the development of Electricity in the direction of Electric Traction, Lighting and Telegraphyﬁ and Electro-Chemistry. It would be impossible to provide for the whole of the above subjects at once. Some of the more specialised subjects, such as the advanced Metallurgy of Iron and Steel, and certain branches of Manufacturing Chemistry would probably be better dealt with in institutions which are, or may be, established in the provinces. Even, however, if the scheme be restricted by the exclusion of such subjects, its realisation would require at least the whole of the site still available at South Kensington, and great advantage would be obtained by grouping the first extensions immediately round the nucleus provided by the Royal College of Science and Central Technical College.

We believe, however, that if the various London institutions concerned were willing to co-operate fully in the matter, and proper arrangements were made for co-ordination of the considerable resources already existing, the necessary special departments might be established early.

It is quite compatible with an effective realisation of the scheme that separate departments might be conducted in detached colleges.

In view of the terms of reference, we have given special consideration to the provision required for higher education in Mining and Metallurgy, and we are satisfied that the maintenance of a fully equipped Central School of Mines is desirable. While facilities for advanced instruction in Coal Mining and in the Mining and Metallurgy of Iron are now available in some of the larger centres of those industries, it is important that there should be a central school affording a full course of instruction in the Mining and Metallurgy of metals produced in India and the Colonies, but not found, or not found in large quantity, within the United Kingdom. As London is the financial centre of many great engineering, mining, and metallurgical industries in the Colonies, it is in the opinion of several witnesses the best site for a more highly developed School of Mines which shall provide for the needs of the Empire. It has been proved to us that the number of Englishmen who rise to important posts in connection with the mining industries of India, Australia, and South Africa is less than is desirable.

We have, for the present, deferred consideration of the Biological Department of the Royal College of Science.

(3) We consider that the advantages of the Higher Technical Courses, which we contemplate at South Kensington, should only be

available for students who can pass a satisfactory test for admission thereto. The preliminary Science and such rudiments of Engineering as may be prescribed for candidates before entering on these Higher Courses might be obtained either in the laboratories of the Royal College of Science and Central Technical College, or elsewhere in London or the provinces. Admission to these Higher Courses should be restricted to duly qualified students who, it is hoped, would be attracted from all parts of the Empire.

(4) We think it is important that the interests both of Pure and Applied Science should be adequately represented on the body which administers the new institution. It is of the first importance that there should be no divorce between teaching and research in Technology on the one hand and in Pure Science on the other, and we therefore regard it as an advantage that ample provision has already been made by the Government for the teaching of certain Sciences on a site which we hope may be connected even more closely than at present with the highest and most specialised branches of Technology. With regard to both subjects, we believe that it may be necessary hereafter to limit the instruction to the higher branches of both Pure and Applied Science.

(5) We do not contemplate that either the educational or financial administration of the Central College should be vested entirely in His Majesty's Government. Indeed, in the present case there is a special consideration which makes such an arrangement practically impossible. Our scheme, if carried into effect, will entail the hearty union and co-operation of several independent bodies in a common enterprise, and it would be an advantage to be able to accord to each co-operating institution an adequate share in the general control.

These considerations point to the creation of a Council representing all the large interests concerned, including, of course, His Majesty's Government, who must always remain by far the chief supporters of the Institution. We do not now enter into the details of an arrangement of the constitution of the Council, as such details will largely depend on the success of negotiations which must await the decision of His Majesty's Government on the outlines of our proposals as now submitted.

Should the above proposals be accepted it will follow that the State contribution to the Institution will take the form of an annual grant in aid, the Governing body retaining the power to carry over any balance remaining unexpended at the end of a year.

V. We feel that we should not be justified in inquiring whether the Board of Education would be willing to give their support to the foregoing scheme, depending as it does on the fulfilment of all or most of the conditions previously mentioned, unless we had taken steps to ascertain what prospect there is of their being fulfilled. We have good reason to believe that private munificence is prepared to provide a capital sum in excess of the minimum which we consider necessary to a successful issue, and that the Commissioners of the 1851 Exhibition are prepared, with their accustomed liberality where the advancement of higher education is concerned, to make available for a scheme, such as we have sketched, the additional site which will be required. We also confidently look for the co-operation of the University of London. Further, although Public Bodies or Local Authorities which contribute largely to the funds of the proposed Institution may fairly ask for the reservation of some accommodation there for Scholarship holders sent to it by themselves, yet it would appear that a considerably increased income would be available for the support of such an Institution from the fees of fee-paying students. With this nucleus of additional resources thus provisionally secured, we feel justified in approaching the Board of Education. We accordingly desire to ask whether the Board are in a position to inform us (1) that, if it is found possible to establish a scheme such as we have sketched in outline, they will be willing to allow the Royal College of Science (including the Royal School of Mines) to be brought into it under a common government and administration; and (2) that the existing Government contribution to the support of these Institutions will be continued under the new conditions on the scale already made necessary by the provision of the new Laboratories of the Royal College of Science.

With such an assurance, and with such new resources as we have mentioned above, we feel that we could approach, with good prospect of success, other bodies whose co-operation we believe to be desirable, if not necessary, for the complete success of our proposals.

In conclusion, we desire to observe that absence of detail where it might have been looked for in certain portions of our proposals is not to be taken as meaning that we have not considered in some detail the ends which we wish to see attained. Our proposals at the present stage indicate only in outline what we have in view: how near an approach can be made to its attainment must depend on the resources which prove to be available, and cannot, therefore, from the nature of the case, be estimated with precision at the present time. Without, however, attempting now to exhaust the subject, we have submitted proposals framed in such a way as to suggest the establishment of an Institution which will be pre-eminent in its combination of advanced teaching in certain branches of Applied Science, with instruction in Pure Science also developed to a very high standard.

Foreign University News.

THE UNITED STATES OF AMERICA.
(From Special Correspondents.)

Johns Hopkins.

The Economic Seminary has continued its investigations into the history, activities and influence of labour organisations in the United States during the current academic year. Its membership has been narrowly limited to advanced students preparing for a scientific career in economic study, and its primary design has been the development of sound method in economic research. The regular fortnightly evening sessions have been supplemented by briefer morning sessions in alternate weeks. The material resources necessary for the inquiry have been supplied by the continued generosity of the citizen of Baltimore, whose original gift made its inception possible. Appreciable progress has also been made by individual members of the Seminary in the study of specific aspects of the several questions assigned for investigation. During the summer field work was carried on in various carefully-selected localities, and the data thus collected have since been supplemented and corrected by documentary study and personal interview. Certain preliminary studies were completed and published in suitable form, and two senior members of the Seminary submitted monographic studies of the particular subjects on which they have been engaged, in part fulfilment of the requirements for the doctor of philosophy degree. These will appear in the twenty-third series of the *Johns Hopkins Studies in Historical and Political Science.* Early in the next academic year a co-operative volume of "Essays in American Trade Unionism" will also be issued by the Seminary, embodying the preliminary results of the various investigations now in progress and ultimately designed for monographic publication.

The King of Württemberg has presented to the University a bronze bust of the poet Schiller, a replica of a colossal bust, by Dannecker, in Stuttgart. On April 29th, at noon, an assembly of the Trustees, Faculty, Students, and invited guests was held in McCoy Hall, when the bust was formally presented, on behalf of the King of Württemberg, by Major-General Albert von Pfister, of Stuttgart. President Remsen responded, accepting the gift. The

Degree of Doctor of Laws, *honoris causa*, was then conferred upon General von Pfister.

The Johns Hopkins University will begin its thirtieth year of instruction on October 3rd, 1905. The academic year extends from the 1st of October to the 15th of June. The charge for tuition is $150 per annum in the graduate and undergraduate departments, and $200 in the medical department.

The following University appointments have been announced:—

William Osler, M.D., LL.D., Regius Professor of Medicine in the University of Oxford, to be Honorary Professor Medicine.

James W. Bright, Ph.D., Caroline Donovan Professor of English Literature.

C. Carroll Marden, Ph.D., to be Professor of Spanish.

John M. Vincent, Ph.D., to be Professor of European History.

Westel W. Willoughby, Ph.D., to be Professor of Political Science.

James C. Ballagh, Ph.D., to be Associate Professor of American History.

Florence R. Sabin, M.D., to be Associate Professor of Anatomy.

Harvard.

The Commencement exercises at Harvard were attended on June 28th, by President Roosevelt, who was present in connection with the re-union of the members of his former class at the University. Among the distinguished recipients of Honorary Degrees was Sir Edward Elgar, who received the Degree of Doctor of Music.

Mr. Rockefeller's Gift to Education.

It is announced that Mr. J. D. Rockefeller has presented $10,000,000 to the General Educational Board, a body incorporated by Act of Congress for the purpose of promoting education in the United States. The donation is payable on October 1st. In a letter to the Educational Board announcing this gift it is stated that the principal is to be held in perpetuity, and the income is to be used for the benefit of such institutions as the Board may select for periods, in amounts, for purposes, or on conditions to be determined by the Board, which may also employ the income in such other ways as it may deem best adapted to promote a comprehensive system of education in the United States. The income is to be used without distinction of locality and its use is to be confined to higher education. It is designed especially for Colleges as distinguished from the great Universities, although there is no prohibition of grants to Universities. Both gifts are alike available for denominational as well as non-sectarian institutions, although the fund cannot be employed for giving specifically theological instruction. No attempt is to be made to resuscitate moribund schools or institutions so situated as not to give promise that donations made to them will be permanently useful.

Columbia.

At the 151st Commencement exercises of Columbia University in New York City 1,181 Degrees and Diplomas were conferred. Among the recipients of Honorary Degrees were the following:—William Dean Howells, the author; Edwin Anderson Alderman, President of the University of Virginia; William Tufts Brigham, Director of the Bishop Museum of Ethnology at Honolulu; Jacob McGavock Dickinson, of Counsel for the United States before the Alaskan Boundary Tribunal; and the Rev. William Thomas Manning, Assistant Rector of Trinity Church, New York City.

In accordance with the terms of the will of Frederick A. P. Barnard, tenth President of Columbia University, a gold medal is established known as the Barnard Medal for Meritorious Service to Science. This medal is awarded at Commencement at the close of every quinquennial period to such person, if any, whether a citizen of the United States or of any other country, as shall, within the five years next preceding have made such discovery in physical or astronomical science or such novel application of science to purposes beneficial to the human race as, in the judgment of the National Academy of Sciences of the United States, shall be deemed most worthy of such honour. The Barnard Medal was first awarded at the Commencement of 1895 to Lord Rayleigh and to Professor (now Sir) William Ramsay. At the Commencement of 1900 the Barnard Medal was awarded to Professor Wilhelm Conrad von Röntgen. On the nomination of the National Academy of Sciences the award for 1905 is made to Henri Becquerel, member of the Institute of France, for important discoveries in the field of radio-activity, and for his original discovery of the so-called dark rays from uranium, which discovery has been the basis of subsequent research into the laws of radio-activity and of our present knowledge of the same.

Yale.

The Yale Alumni Weekly says:—"It is a somewhat singular fact that the changes of a twelvemonth in a body of several hundred Yale instructors have brought only one appointment by the Corporation of a full professor. He is Charles M. Bakewell, who comes from an associate professorship in the University of California to take a professorship in the Yale Department of Philosophy. Professor Bakewell is a graduate of the University of California; took his Doctor's Degree in Philosophy at Harvard in 1894; for two years following studied abroad; and served as an instructor in Philosophy

E

at Harvard and associate professor in the same branch at Bryn Mawr before going to California. While gaining during the year only Professor Bakewell in the upper rank of her teaching force, Yale has lost two. Dean Sanders has resigned from the Divinity School, and Professor George Trumbull Ladd has gone on the retired list. Special mention should also be made of the transfer of Professor Sneath to be Director and head of the new Summer School. To the list of older Yale teachers who pass from the catalogue should be added Mark Bailey, M.A., who has resigned after a full half-century of service as instructor in Elocution. The changes in Yale's administrative branch have been few, but important. Last December Mr. McClung succeeded Mr. Tyler as Treasurer of the University. After forty years of devoted and successful service as University Librarian, Mr. Van Name has retired, and Professor John C. Schwab will bring to the place his wide knowledge of books and an executive ability which will be of signal value in the ordering of the new library."

Michigan.

Statistics giving the actual number of students enrolled in the University, as they appear in the new number of the University Calendar, show that the attendance for the present year has broken all records. The total includes the students enrolled for the second semester. The following table shows the figures by departments, for this year as well as last year:—

	1904–5	1903–4
Graduate School	94	103
Literary Department	1,323	1,319
Engineering	993	823
Medicine	376	418
Law (net)	877	865
Pharmacy	69	65
Homœopathic	67	69
Dental	132	94
	3,931	3,756
Deducted as counted twice	99	97
Total, exclusive of Summer Session ...	3,932	3,659
Summer Session	304	298
	4,136	3,957

Correspondence from the Universities of Göttingen and Paris, announced for publication in the present issue, is unavoidably postponed.

The Universities.

ABERDEEN.

University News and Notes.

A successful series of Gifford Lectures has recently been given in the University by Dr. Adam, of the University of Cambridge, on the subject of "The Religious Teachers of Greece."

The portrait-medallion in marble of the late Principal, Sir William D. Geddes, has recently been completed, and will be unveiled at the opening of the coming Winter Session. The medallion—which is the work of Mr. Macgillivray, R.S.A.—will be placed in the Geddes Transept of the Library at King's College.

The memorial to the late Professor John Fyfe, from a design by Mr. Douglas Strachan, will shortly be placed in a window of the King's College Library.

It is proposed to place in the Geological Museum a memorial tablet in bronze of the late Professor James Nicol.

At a recent meeting of the Court of the University Principal Lang, who presided, intimated two gifts to the University. Mrs. Beaton, widow of the Rev. Patrick Beaton, of Paris, has given the sum of £200 to found, in connection with the class of Zoology, a prize in memory of her father, the late Professor Macgillivray. The Rev. Dr. Alexander Miller, of Buckie, has added the sum of £100 to the funds of the Caithness prize in History, which he founded in 1898, making the capital of the fund £450. The Court resolved to convey to both donors an expression of the Court's hearty appreciation of the gifts.

The Ordinance by Edinburgh University relative to the inclusion of Geography among the subjects qualifying for graduation in Arts has been approved by the University Court, though some exception was taken to the Ordinance with respect to the institution of Degrees in Veterinary Medicine and Surgery, on the grounds that it is not consistent in one particular with one of the existing Ordinances.

In view of the proposed taxation of land values, the Finance

Committee of the Court has been instructed to take whatever action it may consider expedient in the interests of the University.

Mr. Walter H. Moberley, of Merton College, Oxford, has been appointed Lecturer in Political Science, in room of Mr. Lord, now of Cape Town. Miss Mary E. Thomson was appointed Senior Assistant in Humanity, and Miss J. Forbes, Junior Assistant; W. H. Moberley, Lecturer on Moral Philosophy; and R. Haig Spittal, Junior Assistant in Anatomy.

BIRMINGHAM.

University News and Notes.

Dr. C. E. Purslow has been appointed Ingleby Lecturer for the coming year.

Sir Archibald Geikie, LL.D., F.R.S., has accepted an invitation to deliver the Huxley Lecture in 1906.

In memory of the late Mr. Charles Harding, the Dean of the Faculty of Arts and Mrs. Fiedler have given a donation of £100 to be applied towards artistic decoration of the new Arts Theatre in the University.

Members of the Court of Governors of the University and of the City Council paid an official visit of inspection to the new University buildings at Bournbrook, on Friday, June 30th, but the unpropitious weather caused a somewhat small attendance. There were present the Vice-Chancellor (Alderman C. G. Beale, Lord Mayor) and the Lady Mayoress, the Pro-Vice-Chancellor and Treasurer (Alderman F. C. Clayton), the Principal (Sir Oliver Lodge), Vice-Principal Heath, and a number of representative Governors, City Councillors, Professors, Lecturers and Officers of the University. The visitors were conducted over the buildings by Professors Burstall, Turner and Redmayne. Great interest was manifested in the experimental coal mine that has been constructed in connection with the Mining Department. Considerable progress has been made of late in the erection of the buildings, and it is hoped that the University will very shortly be able to enter into its spacious new home.

Degree Day.

The ceremony for the conferment of Degrees was held on July 8th in the Midland Institute. The Vice-Chancellor (Alderman Beale) conducted the proceedings. In the course of a short address the Principal, Sir Oliver Lodge, made some interesting statements with regard to the recent progress in the work of the University. The past year had seen the opening of a new and highly-equipped dental hospital, and the inauguration of a scheme whereby the University granted a diploma to practice in dentistry. This year would also see the presentation of the first graduates in commerce which had ever been presented in any University in the world. The School of Social Studies was a new development of very considerable interest, which owed its origin very largely to the energy and enthusiasm of Mr. Kirkcaldy. The Chair of Engineering, so long held by Professor Burstall, was now split up into three in recognition of the great development and importance of the subject. In addition to the Chair of Mechanical Engineering there would be Chairs of Civil and Electrical Engineering. In conclusion, Sir Oliver Lodge mentioned two great losses which the University had sustained during the year through the departure of Professor Windle to Ireland and of Professor Macneile Dixon to Scotland. The Vice-Chancellor then conferred a number of Degrees in Arts, Science and Medicine. Upon the presentation of the Dean of the Faculty of Commerce (Professor Ashley) the Degree of Bachelor of Commerce was conferred upon Wilfred Bland, Cyril Barrows Edge, Thomas Henry Sanders and Basil Lewis Thomas. The official Degree of Master of Arts was conferred upon John Churton Collins, Professor of English Language and Literature; and the official Degree of Doctor of Medicine upon Arthur Robinson, Professor of Anatomy.

In the afternoon of Degree Day the Pro-Vice-Chancellor (Alderman F. C. Clayton) entertained the Principal and the University Staff, the members of the Council, the Council of Governors, the graduates and undergraduates, and a large party of friends at the Botanical Gardens, Edgbaston.

University Appointments.

Professor Stephen M. Dixon, M.A., Assoc.M.Inst.C.E., has been elected to fill the recently-established Chair of Civil Engineering. Professor Dixon was born in 1866, and graduated in 1887 at Trinity College, Dublin. In 1892 he became Professor of Civil Engineering in the University of New Brunswick till 1901, when he succeeded Dr. MacGregor at the Dalhousie University in Nova Scotia, where he has done valuable work in organising the School of Engineering.

Miss Rose Sidgwick has been appointed to the newly-created Assistant Lectureship in History, and Mr. M. O. B. Caspari has been appointed Lecturer in Greek Language, Literature and Archæology.

Professor Robert Saundby, M.D., has been appointed a Delegate to represent the Medical Faculty of the University at the International Congress in Medicine, to be held in Lisbon in 1906.

Dr. Stanley Barnes has been appointed Examiner for the Russell Memorial Prize for the current year.

Mr. A. W. Butler has been appointed an additional Assistant in the Day Training College for Men.

Mr. J. H. Sinclair, M.Sc. (Vict.), has been appointed Second Draughtsman in the Engineering Department.

CAMBRIDGE.

University News and Notes.

The King has been pleased to approve the appointment of the Rev. F. H. Chase, D.D., President of Queen's College, Cambridge, to be Bishop of Ely, in succession to the Right Rev. Lord Alwyne Compton, D.D., who has resigned.

At a Congregation held on June 20th the Degree of LL.D. *honoris causa* was conferred on Lord Cromer. At the same Congregation the B.A. Degree was conferred on the successful candidates who had graduated in the First Class in the different Triposes. The Senior Wranglers of the year were not forthcoming, as they are only in their second year of residence and not yet qualified for a degree. The Senior Wrangler of 1904 was presented for his Degree first among the candidates. At a Congregation held in the afternoon the Second and Third Class Honours men were admitted to their Degrees.

The Vice-Chancellor has published the list of donations to the University Benefaction Fund received or promised since November 15th, 1904. Among the donors are Lord Rayleigh, £5,000; Lord Iveagh, a further donation of £1,000; Mr. C. J. Heywood, £100; Mr. J. Lumb, £100; Messrs. J. Shires and Son, £60; the British Association (a contribution from the surplus resulting from the Cambridge meeting), £50; Mrs. W. Foster, £50; Mr. J. Tennant, £50; Mr. G. Weston, £25; Sir W. Broadbent, Mr. B. Broadbent, and Mr. R. Hirst, £20 each. A sum of over £6,000 has also been promised for the University Library. The total amount contributed to the Fund is £81,877. 16s. 5d.

The Surveyors' Institution has offered to provide Scholarships in the University, with the object of affording facilities for the higher education of surveyors in branches of scientific knowledge connected with their profession. It is proposed that the Scholarships shall be called the "Surveyors' Institution Scholarships." They are to be three in number, one to be awarded annually. Each Scholarship is to be of the annual value of £80 tenable for three years.

The University has been offered two nominations for the coming examination for student interpreters in the Far East. Full particulars may be obtained from the Secretary to the Appointments Board, University Office, St. Andrews Street.

The Quater Centenary Celebrations at Christ's College.

The four hundredth anniversary of the foundation of Christ's College, Cambridge, by Lady Margaret Beaufort, mother of Henry VII., was celebrated at Cambridge on July 5th. Upwards of 300 old members of Christ's were present at the ceremonial. The company assembled in the College Hall at five o'clock, and passed in procession into the Chapel, led by the Choir of Westminster Abbey singing Milton's paraphrase of the 136th Psalm. Milton, the most famous of all the *alumni* of Christ's College, was further recognised in the selection of the anthem. The sermon was preached by the Dean of Westminster, who is an Honorary Fellow of the College. In the evening a dinner was held, at which many distinguished guests were present, including the Bishop of Norwich, the Bishop of Toronto, Mr. J. Winfield Bonser, Professor E. W. Brown, of Haverfield, U.S.A., Mr. Justice Buckley, Archdeacon Cheetham, Professor F. Darwin, Professor Percy Gardner, Professor Gollancz, Professor J. Graham Kerr, Professor Morrison, of Birmingham, Professor R. G. Moulton, of Chicago, Professor J. S. Reid, and Professor W. W. Skeat. Among the few past students who were unable to attend were Professor Toker, of Manchester, Professor Vines, from Oxford, Professor H. Marshall Ward, Professor J. W. Hales, and Dr. Bridge. The Westminster Choir sang during dinner the songs in "Comus" set by Lawes for the masque in 1634. The Master proposed the memory of the foundress, and gave the thanks of the College for the organisation of the commemoration service by the Dean of Westminster and for the gift of the bust of Lady Margaret. "Prosperity to the College" was proposed by Archdeacon Cheetham.

University Appointments, etc.

Dr. Baker, of St. John's College, has been re-appointed University Lecturer in Mathematics for five years.

M. A. Beljaene, Professeur à la Sorbonne, has been appointed Clark Lecturer at Trinity College for the ensuing year.

Mr. P. W. Wood, B.A., has been elected to a Junior Fellowship at Emmanuel College.

The tenure of the Fellowship held by Mr. H. M. Chadwick, M.A., Clare College, has been prolonged on account of his researches in Anglo-Saxon language and literature.

At Corpus Christi College the following have been elected Honorary Fellows—: The Ven. W. Emery, B.D., Archdeacon and Canon of Ely, formerly Fellow of the College; the Right Rev. George Evans Moule, D.D., Bishop of Mid-China; and the Right Rev. John Reginald Harmer, D.D., Bishop-elect of Rochester, formerly Fellow of the College.

DUBLIN.

University News and Notes.

A meeting of the Senate of the University was held on July 6th for the conferment of Degrees. The University Caput consisted of the Rev. T. T. Gray, Pro-Vice Chancellor, Dr. Traill, Provost, and Mr. G. L. Cathcart, Senior Master, non-Regent. A number of Honorary Degrees were conferred upon those whose names were announced in the July number of this *Review*. Among the recipients of Ordinary Degrees Miss Eva Jellett may be specially noticed as being the first woman to have graduated from Trinity College since the Degrees of the University were made open to women. Ninety-three women—ten of whom came from Oxford, the remainder from Cambridge—received the B.A. Degree of the University.

An Invitation to the British Association.

At a public meeting held recently at the Mansion House, under the presidency of the Lord Mayor, it was unanimously decided to invite the British Association for the Advancement of Science to hold its annual meeting in Dublin in 1907. A Committee was appointed to make the necessary arrangements for the proposed visit, and an appeal for subscriptions to a guarantee fund in aid of local expenses was authorised. The following were appointed to convey to the British Association the invitation of the Lord Mayor and citizens of Dublin:—The Lord Mayor, the Provost of Trinity College, the Rev. Dr. Delaney, Lord Rosse, Professor John Joly, and Professor Hartley. Three previous visits to Dublin are recorded in the history of the British Association—in 1835, in 1857 and in 1878. On each of these occasions the meetings have been held in Trinity College.

DURHAM.

University News and Notes.

The Easter or Summer Term of 1905 is now a thing of the past, and with it the enjoyments of aquatic sport and river scenery which make Durham so attractive in this all too short term. But it is not only the cessation of these pleasures in Durham which the end of the Easter Term brings, for it also comes as a welcome relief to those fortunate (or unfortunate) ones who are endeavouring to emerge successfully from the struggles of the Final Schools in June. And this year witnessed an exceptionally large number competing for the B.A. Degree, whilst the Theological, Science and Letters finals were well up to the average.

The death of the highly-respected and esteemed Professor of Divinity and Ecclesiastical History, the Rev. Dr. Adam Storey Farrar, cast a gloom over the last few weeks of the term. Dr. Farrar had occupied the Professorial Chair at Durham for the last 41 years, and it is a difficult matter to imagine the University without his picturesque and beloved figure. He was interred in the Cathedral burial ground, and his funeral was attended by a very large number of graduates and undergraduates in academical dress, as well as by University officials and a large concourse of city people and old students. The Professorship left vacant by his decease has been filled by the appointment of the Rev. R. J. Knowling, D.D., Professor of New Testament Exegesis in King's College, London. Dr. Knowling is not unfamiliar to Durham, where he has several times examined for the L.Th. He is also well known in the theological world by his contributions to the Expositors' Greek Testament, Smith and Wall's Dictionary of Christian Biography, and to other recent theological questions.

In consequence of the death of Dr. Farrar, the end of the Easter Term was of a much quieter character than usual, as the annual "June Week" festivities were abandoned. A special number of the *Durham University Journal* was the only additional feature to mark the close of the academical year. The annual University Choral Society's Concert was postponed till next term, and the June Week Ladies' Night Debate was abandoned.

The annual Boat Race with Edinburgh University was rowed on Friday, June 23rd, over the usual course (1 mile 300 yards), and after a good race the Edinburgh men again proved victorious.

The election for the office of President of the Union for the Michaelmas Term took place by ballot at the end of the term, and after a sharp contest, T. C. Walters (Hatfield Hall) was returned.

The new Hall of St. Chad's has completed the first year of its existence, and has enjoyed a very good list of successes in First Year Arts and Theology. The students at present in residence in their temporary quarters number 23, but greater accommodation will be afforded in course of time. The Chairman of the Council of St. Chad's Hall has recently received £2,000 from a generous donor, for the purpose of founding an Exhibition at St. Chad's.

The girding together of the walls of the Norman Gallery at

University College is practically completed, and the rooms in that part of the College will soon be available again for students.

Last year witnessed the publication of the history of Durham University in the College History Series. The task was undertaken and most successfully accomplished by the Rev. J. T. Fowler, D.C.L., Vice-Principal of Hatfield Hall, who is a well-known antiquarian authority.

It is interesting to note that the book famous among 'Varsity men, "Verdant Green," which attempts to portray in a humorous character the experiences of an undergraduate, was the work of a former Durham student, writing under the *nom-de-plume* of Cuthbert Bede (the two great Durham saints). It depicted (?) the life of a student in University College, Durham, in its earlier days; but, for various reasons, the author was induced to apply its contents to Oxford. Some of the original pen-and-ink sketches, copies of which were reproduced in *Punch* at the time, are framed and hung in the Union Reading Room at Durham.

This term has also seen the composition and publication of "The Durham University Song." The words are by W. D. Lowe, M.A. (Univ.), and the music by J. H. Batten, Mus.B. (Hatfield). It is dedicated (by permission) to the Very Rev. G. W. Kitchin, D.D., Dean of Durham, and Warden of the University.

Dr. F. B. Jevons, Principal of Hatfield Hall, is to lecture at Girton College, Cambridge, in August, on the "Evolution and Philosophy of Religion."

The Right Rev. Arthur Gascoigne Douglas, Bishop of Aberdeen and Orkney, whose death occurred on Wednesday, July 19th, was M.A. and L.Th. of Durham, and Hon. D.D. He was also formerly Cansor and Chaplain of Hatfield Hall.

Convocation.

Convocation was "holden" on Tuesday afternoon, June 27th, and proved, as usual, an attractive feature. The grand old Hall at University College (The Castle) was filled with a brilliant gathering, and the crowd of undergraduates at the back of the Hall was as demonstrative as ever. Besides the ordinary Degrees the following Honorary Degrees were conferred:—

D.C.L. (1) The Very Rev. J. H. Bernard, D.D. (Dean of St. Patrick's, Dublin, and Professor of Divinity, Trinity College, Dublin).

(2) Professor Maccalister, M.A., D.Sc., F.R.S., etc. (Professor of Anatomy, Cambridge).

D.Litt. (1) Mr. Andrew Lang.
  (2) Prof. W. Churton Collins, M.A. (Professor of English Literature at Birmingham University).
M.A. (by Vote of Convocation). Sir Frederick Bridge, D.Mus. (Oxford and Durham), organist at Westminster Abbey, Professor of Music in the University of London, and Conductor of the Royal Choral Society.

Amongst those who received "ad eundem" Degrees was the Rev. Dawson Walker (Corpus Christi, Oxford), Censor of the Unattached Students at Durham, and Theological Lecturer, who was admitted to the D.D. The usual Degree list comprised:—D.C.L. (1), D.Sc. (3), B.D. (3), M.A., "ad eundem" (2), M.A. (24), M.Sc. (2), B.A. (37), B.Sc. (24), B.Litt. (26), L.Th. (13), A.Sc. (3), Diploma Theory and Practice of Teaching (2).

EDINBURGH.

University News and Notes.

With simple and impressive ceremony the funeral of Sir William Muir was conducted in the Dean Cemetery and Parish Church at Edinburgh on the 15th of July. In deference to the wishes of the family, the funeral was of a private nature, and the only bodies formally represented were the University Court, the Senatus, the Students' Representative Council, and the University Union.

A service in memory of Sir William Muir was held in the M'Ewan Hall on Sunday, the 16th of July, under the auspices of the Students' Representative Council. The service was conducted by the Rev. Professor W. P. Paterson, D.D., and was attended by Principal Sir William Turner, Lord Dundas, Professors Chiene, Lodge, Darroch, Wyllie, M'Gregor, and Cossar Ewart, by the Executive Committee of the Students' Representative Council, the officials of the Union and a large number of students and friends. The memorial address was delivered by the Rev. John Kelman, M.A.

At a meeting of the University Court, held on July 17th, the resignation was accepted of Professor Alexander Russell Simpson, who has occupied the Chair of Midwifery in the University since 1870. Professor Simpson will carry with him into his well-deserved retirement the best wishes of many generations of students. His loss will be keenly felt by all sections of the University.

Many distinguished foreign professors are visiting Edinburgh in August to take part in the work of the Vacation Courses in Modern Languages which are to be held at the University. The Edinburgh

Town Council has given its patronage to the scheme, and has voted a sum of £100 to the guarantee fund. The Carnegie Trustees have decided to recognise these courses as being of University standing, and to pay, under the ordinary regulations, the class fees of Scottish students attending them.

It is proposed to divide the course of instruction in military subjects into sections, of from eight to twelve lectures each, and to allow a single section to be taken by officers of His Majesty's Forces and others at a fee of half-a-guinea, with an entrance fee for the non-matriculated students of five shillings for the course, or for any section of it.

The University Court has resolved to institute, after consultation with the Senatus, a Lectureship in Gynæcology and to communicate the fact to the Curators of Patronage when making intimation to them of the vacancy created in the Chair of Midwifery by the retirement of Professor Simpson.

In order to provide the means for an extension of tutorial instruction, and thereby to secure increased efficiency of teaching in the Departments of the Faculty of Arts, it has been decided to raise the class fees in that Faculty from £3. 3s. to £4. 4s., as from 1st October, 1906.

The Special Graduation Ceremony.

A special Graduation ceremony was held at the University on July 22nd, when the French Ambassador and a number of distinguished members of the medical profession taking part in the fourth centenary celebration of the Royal College of Surgeons of Edinburgh were admitted to the Hon. Degree of LL.D. Sir William Turner, Vice-Chancellor, presided over a large gathering, and in the course of a brief speech alluded to the old associations connecting the University with the Royal College of Surgeons. It had been impossible for the Senatus to confer Hon. Degrees on all the visitors to the College festival, and so they had to make a selection. They had chosen those who had come from various European countries and from America. They also desired to welcome another visitor to the festival of the College, the Ambassador of France. It was felt that, as the tutor of their founder, King James VI., George Buchanan, had held honourable office as a teacher in the Colleges of France, it would be most appropriate that they, the academic descendants of their founder, should on that occasion honour M. Cambon by giving him the highest qualification it was in their power to bestow, namely, the Hon. Degree of Doctor of Laws. Sir Ludovic Grant, Dean of the Faculty of Laws, presented the recipients to the Vice-Chancellor in the following order:—His Excellency M. Paul Cambon; Professor

Irving Howard Cameron, University of Toronto; Dr. Just Lucas Championière, Paris; Professor Frances Durante, Rome; Professor Anton Freiherr Von Eiselsberg, Vienna; Professor William Stewart Halsted, Johns Hopkins University; Professor William Williams Keen, Philadelphia; Professor Kail Gustav Lennander, Upsala; Professor Sylvester Saxtorph, Copenhagen; and Professor J. Shepherd, Montreal. Precedent notwithstanding, speeches in reply were allowed, and the French Ambassador acknowledged the honour which the University had conferred on the European visitors, and Dr. Keen responded for the Transatlantic visitors.

University Appointments, etc.

Professor Copeland has been granted leave of absence, owing to ill-health, for the next academical year. Dr. J. Halm will act as substitute for the Professor during his absence.

Profesors Chrystal, Darroch, Pringle Pattison, and Bayley Balfour, and Dr. Lowe have been appointed to represent the University on the Committee for the Training of Teachers in connection with the University of Edinburgh, in terms of the minute of the Scottish Education Department of 30th January last.

The University's representatives on the Joint Board of Examiners for the year are as follows:—Mr. F. S. Boas, M.A. (English); Profesor Hardie (Classics); Professor Chrystal (Mathematics and Dynamics); Dr. Alex. Cran (Modern Languages).

On the recommendation of the Senatus, Mr. J. H. Maclagan Wedderburn has been appointed a Lecturer on Mathematical Honours Subjects, his course of instruction to qualify as a half-course for Honours in Arts.

The following University Lecturers have been appointed for the next academical year:—Dr. J. Halm (Astronomy); Dr. L. Dobbin (Agricultural Chemistry); Dr. H. J. Stiles (Applied Anatomy); Dr. T. D. Luke (Practical Application of Anæsthetics). Mr. John Harvey, LL.B., advocate, has been appointed to the Lectureship in Procedure and Evidence, and Dr. George Mackay to the Lectureship in Diseases of the Eye.

GLASGOW.

University News and Notes.

The Summer Graduation Ceremony was held recently. There was a fairly large attendance of graduates and undergraduates and their friends. The Latin prayer was recited by Professor Stewart in the absence of the Principal. At the close of the ceremony Professor

Murdoch Cameron delivered an interesting address, in the course of which he referred to the great progress that had been made during recent years in the study of Medicine in the Glasgow University—a progress which was still going on.

The Brunton prize of £10 awarded to the most distinguished graduate in Medicine has been won by George Allison Allan.

The Calendar of the Glasgow University for the Session 1905–6 has recently been issued. The volume now contains eight hundred pages. Not the least interesting feature is the sketch of the history and organisation of the University. The facilities that are afforded for special study and research are clearly stated. The chapters on the Queen Margaret College and on the Carnegie Trust are of considerable interest. The Calendar also contains the financial statement of the University for the year 1903–4, together with a list of the members of the General Council.

The prize of 20 guineas, offered by Mr. Alexander Littlejohn, of Invercharron, to any member of the shinty clubs of the Scottish Universities for the best essay on the ancient Celtic game of shinty, has been awarded to Neil Archibald Johnston, the Vice-President of Glasgow University Shinty Club.

LEEDS.

University News and Notes.

The first Congregation of the University for the Conferment of Degrees was held at the Town Hall on July 1st. The Vice-Chancellor, Dr. N. Bodington, presided, and was accompanied by the Pro-Chancellor (Mr. A. G. Lupton). A large number of old students of the Yorkshire College were present and received the Degrees of the new University. Fellowships of the value of £100 each were awarded to Joseph Marshall, B.Sc. (Chemistry, 1904), and Osborn Waterhouse, B.A. (English Language and Literature, 1904).

October 1, 1905, has been fixed as the date when the new statute adopted at the last meeting of the Joint Mitriculation Board shall come into force. The new statute has been framed in order to incorporate the new University of Sheffield on the Joint Matriculation Board. The University of Sheffield has been invited to elect a representative on the Court of the Leeds University.

On the recommendation of the Council and Senate the University Court has approved of an ordinance affiliating the Technical College, Huddersfield, with the University from October 1st next.

Mr. A. G. Lupton has been re-elected Pro-Chancellor for the ensuing year.

LIVERPOOL

The Guild of Undergraduates.

Last month saw the close of the first year of centrally organised student endeavour in Liverpool. In retrospect the work of the year is extremely gratifying, and in prospect the promise of future years may be truthfully described as equally hopeful, though the work to be done can never rival in fundamental importance the achievements of last year. Out of a chaos composed of an S.R.C., an Athletic Club and many dissociated and often conflicting departmental Societies, those at the head of affairs at the beginning of last year have evolved an organisation which combines, controls and unifies the efforts of them all. At first there was some opposition, but that very slackness and indifference which the old system had failed to overcome proved to be too prevalent, and the constitution of the Guild went through. Since then it has been altered and amplified. Old wants have been supplied and new exigencies have been met as they arose by new measures, and advances have been made in directions which were hardly thought of at the beginning. All these changes have but developed the initial idea of unifying and directing what corporate energy there was, and by dint of graduated responsibility and decentralisation so to improve and increase it that the "corporate idea" should pervade everything, and so fan into a flame that without which the new type of English University is but little better than a technical school—a corporate life. The material progress, made and in the making, we have mentioned here before—the increased success in athletics, the recognition of the Guild by learned societies in the city, the record Soirée, the "sing-songs" and suppers, the Song-book and the Students' Hand-book, and so on, in all these the influence of the new order can be traced. Many, like the latter examples, are but steps to better things—permanent we hope, but still steps. The highest step of which any of us can think, which some even regard as the ultimate aim, is a Union or Guild Hall, and even that is already almost in sight. The recommendations of the Union Committee of the Council as to the advisability of a Union are already before the Finance Committee of the latter body. The ways of committees are long, tortuous and unsafe, we know but taking all things into consideration, we feel justified in hoping for an early realisation of this scheme of a home worthy of the Guild and of the University.

Degree Day.

This, the second Degree conferring of Liverpool University, was held on July 8th, the actual ceremony taking place in St. George's Hall.

Lord Derby, in his capacity as Chancellor, presided. He opened the proceedings by recapitulating the happenings and developments of the Session, and congratulated the University upon the great progress that had been made during that period. Lord Derby referred to the many generous gifts that had recently been received by the University, such as the gift of £10,500 from the President of the Council to build an extension to the Chemical Laboratories; £10,000 by Mrs. Barrow, in memory of the late Mr. Barrow, to found a Chair in French (which has been filled by our previous able Lecturer, Dr. Bonnier); various annual grants, from £10,000 to £500, from the towns and counties in the neighbourhood; £1,500 to found a Lectureship in memory of Sir W. Mitchell Banks, and a prize in memory of Dr. Ronald Hudson, Lecturer in Mathematics, whose death while mountain-climbing in North Wales cut short what promised to be a career of brilliancy and success; under the will of the late Mr. S. L. Bowes £8,000 for the Department of Modern Languages and Chemistry. In addition, Mr. Edward Whitley has promised £1,000 towards the cost of a building for the Students' Union (a statement that was received with loud applause). The Chancellor went on to speak of the importance of a Students' Union to the life of the University. Such an institution brings people together from all sides, and gives a centre round which associations and friendships may group. The Chancellor then referred to the affiliation to the University of two Training Colleges and one Theological College in the neighbourhood, which had been brought about with a view to uniting the educational forces of the district. He alluded also to the new scheme for evening class graduation, and to the establishment of degrees and courses in Dental Surgery. Candidates for degrees were then presented by the Deans of their respective faculties, and " in virtue of the powers vested in him," the Chancellor conferred the various distinctions in due form. Certificates in various subjects were also given by the Chancellor to a number of students. One Fellowship and four Scholarships of the University were also presented. Sir Joseph Swan then delivered an address in connection with the opening of the School of Electro-technics. Vice-Chancellor Dale having returned thanks to Sir J. Swan, and to Dr. Peace for his services at the organ, the proceedings terminated.

The Electro-technics Laboratories.

Following upon the St. George's Hall ceremony, Sir Joseph Swan, accompanied by Lord Derby and Vice-Chancellor Dale and a numerous company, drove to the new buildings in Brownlow Street, and having been presented with a golden key by the architects,

A VIEW IN THE ELECTRO-TECHNICS LABORATORY, LIVERPOOL UNIVERSITY.

Messrs. Willink and Thicknesse, Sir Joseph formally opened the main door. The visitors made a tour of inspection, and subsequently assembled in the Lecture Theatre, where they united in general congratulations on the opening of the Laboratory.

The new Laboratories are an outcome of the endowment of a Chair of Electro-technics by Mr. David Jardine in 1903, and have been erected at a cost, including equipment, of £13,000. The rooms are excellently adapted to the use for which they are intended, and are conveniently situated, though as yet they are somewhat lacking in furniture and apparatus.

The Degree Day Celebrations.

The local press was good enough to report that the students on Degree Day behaved with their usual resourcefulness and wit in the matter of noise. This may have been so, but to all those who were keenly interested in the effect of the small pamphlet of songs selected from the Liverpool Song-book the afternoon cannot be described as other than disappointing. It proved to the musical few that what might be easy to them was not necessarily so to the mass. And the musical few, those who had taken the trouble to meet and practice the songs, were too small a leaven to waken the general concourse into song. Everything told plainly that new and by no means easy songs set to the best music are not to be picked up like a music-hall catch, and it was seen that for justice to be done to them a considerable amount of organisation and practice by the mass of the students is essential. It is to be hoped that the Song Book Committee—who deserve the highest praise—will not consider their work finished with the publication of their initial *raison d'être*. It was in the evening, at a supper, partaken of by past and present students and many junior members of the staff, after a gymkhana in the Quad., that the full potentialities of the Song-book became apparent. At this supper there were present about two hundred and fifty past and present students. It was one of those functions which are known, we believe, in Liverpool alone, where men and women meet together on the common ground of fellow studentship. There were many speakers and more toasts. The President of the Old Students' Association, one of the founders of the old S.R.C., and other past students spoke. The speech of the President of the Guild was extremely interesting. He reviewed the past year's achievements, and pointed out as amongst the most promising signs of the Guild the complete absence of friction between any of the numerous administrative divisions of that organisation.

The Liverpool Institute of Tropical Research.

What the Liverpool School of Tropical Medicine is to tropical diseases and their causes the Liverpool Institute of Tropical Research bids fair to become to commercial enterprise in the Tropics. Already the Institute is actually at work, though Lord Mountmorres (its Director) and Mr. A. F. Warr have not yet had time to complete the constitution, which will be followed immediately by an application for a charter of incorporation. As an initial step the Institute has recently sent a representative to Paris in order to obtain a mass of information not locally accessible. It may be stated here that the Institute will work in many departments in co-operation with other bodies on an international basis, a free exchange of scientific information being thus effected. Its inquiries will be directed to all tropical countries. The draft constitution of the Institute shows that the general direction of affairs will be vested in an Executive Committee composed of men of distinction connected with Liverpool, its University and its trade. The headquarters of the Institute are in the University buildings.

University Appointments.

Dr. C. Bonnier has been appointed to the Barrow Chair of French. Dr. Bonnier has been Lecturer in French for over five years at the University.

Miss Iles will succeed Miss Graveson as Lecturer in Education. Miss Iles obtained a First Class (Division I.) and Second Class (Division II.) Moral Sciences Tripos, Newnham, in 1901, and subsequently the Cambridge Certificate in Education.

Dr. T. L. Pinches has been appointed to the recently created Lectureship in Assyriology.

The Harrison Chair of Engineering, vacant by the resignation of Professor Hele-Shaw, has been filled by the appointment of Mr. W. H. Watkinson, now Professor in the Glasgow and West of Scotland Technical College. Having served his apprenticeship, Mr. Watkinson entered the University of Glasgow, where he became one of Lord Kelvin's laboratory assistants. In 1888 he was appointed to take charge of the Engineering Department of the Central Science School, Sheffield. In 1893 he returned to Glasgow to take up the position he is now vacating.

The City Council and the University.

The Liverpool City Council have granted a sum of £10,000 to the Liverpool University for the year 1905, subject to an inspection and a report being made to the Council on the University's work.

LONDON.

University News and Notes.

Professor Sir John Macdonell, C.B., LL.D., M.A., has been appointed Dean and Dr. W. N. Hibbert, LL.D., Secretary of the Faculty of Laws.

THE STUDY OF SOCIOLOGY.

The Martin White Committee on the Study of Sociology report that four special courses of lectures in Sociology have been arranged for next year, viz., 40 lectures and 20 seminar classes by Dr. E. A. Westermarck, Ph.D., on " The Comparative Study of Institutions "; a short course of 10 lectures introductory to the Study of Institutions, and a course of 20 lectures and seminar classes on Comparative Psychology by Mr. L. T. Hobhouse, M.A.; and a systematic course of 30 lectures and seminar classes on Ethnology by Dr. A. C. Haddon, Sc.D., M.A., F.R.S.

It was suggested that the following subjects should be included in the University scheme of Sociological Studies:—

(1) An outline knowledge of
    (a) The theory of Biological Evolution ;
    (b) Psychology with special reference to Comparative Psychology.

(2) A detailed study of Human Society :
    (a) The detailed descriptive study of representative groups of mankind ;
    (b) The comparative study of the principal social institutions and developments.

(3) Social Philosophy—the analysis of the principles of social union and the history of political ideas.

(4) Theories of Social Evolution.

(5) Special Investigations of contemporary civilised societies.

The Senate of the University has gratefully accepted the generous offer of Mr. Martin White of the sum of £200 for the establishment of two Bursaries and a Studentship in Sociology.

Bedford College for Women.

The Council held a reception on Wednesday, July 19th, to which were invited the foreign teachers attending the holiday course arranged by the University of London. Teachers from Austria (6),

Denmark (14), Finland (3), France (10), Germany (40), Holland (8), Italy (1), Japan (2), Norway (1), Russia (2), Sweden (17), Switzerland (3) were present, and were received by the following members of the College:—Mrs. James Bryce, Mrs. Ayrton and Mrs. Waller. The College libraries and laboratories were thrown open. A musical entertainment was preceded by a short speech of welcome by Miss Henrietta Busk in the name of the Council. About 200 guests were present, and the legations of Japan, Portugal and China were represented. Letters of regret at absence were received from many foreign embassies, legations and diplomatic agencies.

The Council have appointed Miss Anna Lamberg, Final Honours Upsala, to be Resident Librarian.

The Reid Scholarship in Arts of the value of £31. 10s. for the first year and £28. 10s. for the two following years has been awarded to Miss K. M. Curtis, of the North London Collegiate School, and the Arnott Scholarship in Science of the value of £48 for three years has been awarded to Miss E. M. Stokes, of Dame Alice Owen's Girls' School.

The Council offer a Scholarship of £20 for one year for the Course of Secondary Training beginning in October, 1905. The Scholarship will be awarded to the best candidate holding a degree or its equivalent in Arts or Science. Applications should reach the head of the Training Department not later than September 18th.

The Bedford College Hygienic Diploma has been awarded to H. Bideleux, S. M. Houchen, M. Neatby, M. Sheepshanks, and M. A. M. Stacy.

Cheshunt College.

On June 27th the 137th anniversary gatherings of Cheshunt College were held at the College. At a public meeting Dr. Horton suggested that the buildings, from which the College is to be removed to Cambridge, would provide an excellent home for a missionary training College. Mr. James Brown, Chairman of the Trustees, stated that a generous friend had offered to defray the entire expenses of the removal of the College to Cambridge. It was hoped that they would be able to begin their work at Cambridge in the autumn. It was intended to house the students in rented houses until a new College could be built.

Guy's Hospital Medical School.

The annual distribution of prizes took place on July 12th at Guy's Hospital, when the new Gordon Museum of Anatomy and Pathology was open to inspection. The Museum of Guy's Hospital dates from the latter part of the 18th century. The specimens now number upwards of 12,000. The accommodation has for many years been quite inadequate. The urgency of rebuilding the Museum was fully recognised, but the School was unable to raise the necessary sum of money. Mr. Robert Gordon has very generously erected the buildings at his own expense, and the collection now finds a worthy home. The Dean of the School in his annual report said that the financial condition of the medical schools in London revealed by Sir Edward Fry's Committee had made it plain that it was impossible at the present time for medical education to be adequately maintained without financial assistance or endowment, and for this reason they were again obliged to appeal to the liberality of the wealthy.

King's College.

The annual distribution of certificates and prizes took place at the College on July 5th. The Rev. Dr. Headlam, the Principal, in the course of his opening speech, said that the past year had been moderately prosperous. The increased Treasury grant had placed the College in a more secure financial position. Ever since the reconstitution of the London University the aim of the Council had been to raise all the work of the College to the University level, and to put in the forefront the preparation for the University courses. In this direction there was a steady improvement to record. A first step had been made towards the concentration of medical studies in the preliminary subjects, by an arrangement by which the students of Westminster Hospital were to come to King's College. It was the beginning of what, if it were carried out, would be a great reform in medical education. The prizes were presented by Dr. Gow, the Headmaster of Westminster School.

Royal Holloway College.

The summer term ended on Saturday, July 1st. During the first week of the vacation the examination for the Entrance Scholarships took place at the College. Sixty-three candidates competed for the Scholarships. In the Oxford Schools two Holloway students obtained Second Class Honours in German; in English, one Second Class and two Third; in Mathematics, Moderations, one Second and two Third; and Finals, one Second and two Third. One present and one past student of the College were successful in the Classical branch of the London M.A. Examination.

St. Bartholomew's Hospital Medical School.

The annual prize distribution at the Medical School of St. Bartholomew's Hospital took place on July 12th, in the great Hall of the Hospital. Lord Ludlow, the Treasurer, presided over a large gathering. Mr. Harmer, the Warden of the College, in his report on the work of the School during the past year, said that the total number of students who had worked at the Hospital during the past year was 556, and of these 111 were new students. The Committee of medical officers and lecturers had considered the important question of concentration of the preliminary studies at some centre away from the hospital and had decided that, for the present, it was advisable to continue to teach within the walls of the Hospital, all the subjects of the medical curriculum. The Hospital had sustained a great loss by the death of Mr. Luther Holden, who had served on the active surgical staff for 21 years and who had bequeathed to the Hospital the sum of £3,000 for the endowment of a Scholarship in Surgery. Many distinctions had been gained by St. Bartholomew's men during the year, and in the examinations the School had maintained its high reputation.

The South-Eastern Agricultural College.

The annual distribution of prizes and diplomas took place at the College on July 21st. Mr. M. J. R. Dunstan (the Principal of the College) presided, and the awards were distributed by Lord Ashcombe (Chairman of the Governors of the College). The Principal reported that the students now numbered 89, and that the work during the past year was in every way satisfactory. In the course of an address, Lord Ashcombe referred to the great losses which the College had suffered in the deaths of Mr. Halsey (the late Chairman of the Governors) and Lord Stanhope, both of whom had been connected with the College since its establishment in 1893.

University College.

THE WORK OF THE SESSION.

At the Assembly of the Faculties of Arts and Laws and of Science held at the College on July 5th, the Dean of the Faculty of Science (Professor J. D. Cormack) presented a report on the work of the Session 1904–5, from which the following statements have been taken:—

The Session which is brought to a close by this Assembly may be regarded as very successful. It has been a session of hard work, for staff and students, marked by an increase in the number of students, by an increase in the number of subjects taught, and by the great volume of work which has been turned out.

The number of students in the Faculties of Arts, Laws and of Science is 1,054, as against 947 last Session. In the same Faculties, 323 students (Arts 103, Laws 4, Engineering 38, Science 175, and Economics 3) have been registered as internal students of the University, as compared with 271 at this time last year.

The Commissioners appointed under the Bill to carry into effect the Incorporation of the College in the University, will begin their meetings after the Long Vacation, and it ought to be possible to complete the actual Incorporation by September, 1906. Of the sum of £200,000 required for this purpose, all but £17,000 has been obtained, which, it is to be sincerely hoped, will soon be forthcoming.

The foundations of the new buildings for the Boys' School at Hampstead have been laid, and it is expected that the School will be able to begin work there in September, 1907. The school wing will then be available for College purposes, and every department of the College is eagerly awaiting such increase of space as it may acquire. Not only will the removal of the School provide additional space within the school wing, but it may be found possible subsequently to build a new Department of Chemistry in a portion of the School playground. We hope, however, that a large portion of the School playground will be retained as an open space for the purpose of recreation and exercise.

Many important University improvements are in progress, and among these may be mentioned the scheme for the concentration of preliminary and intermediate medical studies, and the scheme for the re-organisation of the technical teaching in the University.

The work of the Oriental Departments has been facilitated by the possession of the valuable Oriental library of the late Prof. Arthur Strong, which has been given to the College by Mrs. Strong. This gift has been made the more complete by the presentation of the bust of the late Prof. Arthur Strong, whose loss we all deplore.

In the Department of Applied Mathematics the most important event of the Session has been the generous grant by the Worshipful Company of Drapers of £400 yearly for five years to continue the Biometric and Research Work of the Department. This grant will put on a more permanent footing the work already instituted by the same Company two years ago. Six memoirs have been specially published as a Drapers' Research Series, and a number of others are in preparation. The work for these has been rendered possible almost entirely by the financial aid provided by this gift.

The Chadwick Observatory has been completed, but has not been fully in use during the Session, chiefly because the clocks have not yet been installed; and in this connection it is fitting to acknowledge our continued indebtedness to the Chadwick Trustees. Through the generosity of Lord Rosse, Mr. Ludwig Mond, Sir E. Durning Lawrence, Mr. C. R. Kyrke, Miss E. Cave, and other friends the Department has been able to purchase the transit circle, clocks and micrometers, etc., of the late Mr. Crossley. The Council has given permission for the erection of a Transit House on the South Lawn, and it is hoped that this additional astronomical equipment will be available for next Session's work. Further contributions towards the full astronomical equipment of the College are still required.

In accordance with the intention to which reference was made in last year's report, the Botanical Department during the last Long Vacation repeated the experiment of a summer expedition for a detailed survey and study of selected vegetation. On this occasion the visit was to Erquy, on the coast of Brittany. The problems presented by the salt-marsh vegetation proved very attractive, and another visit to the same spot is being organised.

The course of "French Literature in the Middle Ages" was attended by 90 students, and the course on "Old Provençal Palæography and Anglo-Norman Literature" constituted a new and successful feature of the French Department.

The accommodation in the Physics Department, which has recently been so inadequate, is now being increased. The Lecture Theatre is being enlarged, and additions are being made to the Carey Foster Laboratory.

The scheme for architectural students by which they pass through regular day course before entering an architect's offices has now been in existence for two years; 10 students attended the Course this Session. The new evening classes in Architecture which was begun this Session had a class list of 40, mainly advanced students.

The record of the various students' societies shows continued activity. The Union Society has had a very busy year. On its initiative a Students' Representative Council for London University has been formed. Mr. Scott and Mr. Willcox, the President and Secretary respectively of the College Union, are President and Secretary of the new Council. On the invitation of the Union Society, the British Universities' Students Congress has held its annual meeting here. The Musical Society has been specially active, and a Choral Branch which has been formed has had a most successful session. The Engineering Society carried out a very extensive programme which included an unusually large number of papers read by students, and a number of lectures by prominent engineers. An Architectural Society has been founded, at which many papers have been read during the Session.

The College Conversazione was favoured with beautiful weather and there was a large attendance. Great credit and thanks are due to Mr. E. C. C. Baly and Dr. Goodbody for the admirable manner in which it was organised. We were favoured also with delightful weather for the Athletic Sports, which were held for the first time on the College grounds at Acton. The experiment was a great success. It is to be hoped that the grounds will become the property of the Union Society and that many College functions will take place there.

The Foundation Oration was delivered by Professor Sir A. B. W. Kennedy, F.R.S., Emeritus Professor of Engineering. The oration dealt with "The Academic Side of Technical Training : its review of engineering education from the early days, and the interesting suggestions made in regard to future developments are very welcome at this time when the subject is so prominent.

College News and Notes.

The "University College, London (Transfer) Bill" received the Royal Assent on July 11th. The Act provides for the appointment of five Commissioners charged with the duty of making statutes to carry into effect the transfer of the College to the University. Of these Commissioners, two—Lord Justice Cozens-Hardy and Sir Edward Busk—were nominated by the University, and two—Sir John Rotton and Professor J. Rose Bradford—by the College. The remaining Commissioner is to be appointed by His Majesty in Council, and will act as Chairman. Sir Edward Fry, late Lord Justice of Appeal, has consented to allow his name to be submitted to His Majesty in Council for this post, and it is expected that the Order in Council announcing his appointment will shortly be published.

An interesting exhibition of the year's results achieved by Professor Flinders Petrie and his coadjutors in the field of Egyptian archæology has been on view during the past month at University College.

The students of the Engineering School at the College have presented an inscribed bowl and stand to Professor Vernon Harcourt on the occasion of his retirement from the Chair of Engineering, a position which he has occupied for upwards of twenty years.

MANCHESTER.

University News and Notes.

On the occasion of the recent visit of the King and Queen to Manchester an address of welcome was presented to their Majesties on behalf of the University by the Chancellor (Earl Spencer), Vice-Chancellor (Dr. Alfred Hopkinson, K.C.) and the Chairman of the Council (Sir Frank Forbes Adam). The King, in his reply, said:—

> "I am well assured that your University, which bears the name of my late dearly-beloved mother, will, in its new phase of activity, as in the past, realise the anticipations of its public-spirited founders and directors, and that it will ever continue to take a foremost place in the extension and development of all branches of study and research, and to promote the advancement of knowledge and the spread of culture in this great industrial centre.

> "I have no doubt that those who study here will be trained to render distinguished service to the State and to the community, and that they will, by their achievements in science, art, or commerce, contribute to the greatness and welfare of my Empire, and to the fame of their Alma Mater."

The Secretary of State for Foreign Affairs has asked the University Authorities to nominate two candidates for an examination for Student Interpreterships in the Far East. The principal subjects of the examination are Commercial Law and Modern Languages. Student Interpreters are appointed to supply the Consular service in China, Japan and Siam with persons versed in the languages of those countries and otherwise competent to discharge Consular duties.

The Faculty of Technology.

The Manchester City Council and the Manchester Education Committee have approved the scheme prepared by a Joint Sub-Committee of the Education Committee and the University of Manchester for the institution of a Faculty of Technology. For some time past negotiations have been on foot for the establishment of such a Faculty, and recently a Committee representing the Manchester University and the Municipal School of Technology had formulated a scheme that recognised equally the claims of both institutions.

Students of the School of Technology will now be enabled to obtain a Degree at the University. The scheme has received the sanction of the Senate of the University, and it is hoped that the arrangements will be completed in time for the commencement of the coming Session.

·The University and Military Studies.

The Authorities of the University have been informed that the Army Council has decided to offer, in the year 1906, to the University of Manchester, if a satisfactory course of instruction is provided in military subjects, one commission in the Royal Artillery, one in the Indian Army, and at least five commissions in the Cavalry, Foot Guards, Infantry, or Army Service Corps. The question of providing instruction in military subjects of a character suitable for those who aim at obtaining commissions in the Army, has for some time been under the consideration of the University, but no active step could be taken until it was known what commissions were likely to be awarded on the recommendation of the University to those who pass the examination required and comply with the conditions laid down in the regulations of the War Office. These regulations provide that candidates must (a) have resided for three years at an approved University; (b) have qualified for a Degree in the approved subject or group of subjects; and (c) shall produce a certificate of good conduct. The University of Manchester is one of the Universities approved under these regulations.

Now that commissions have been definitely assigned to the University it is proposed by the Council to establish at once a scheme for providing instruction in Military History and Strategy, Military Tactics and Military Topography. It is important that the best possible training should be provided for officers in the Army and that this should effectively be done in a University. A course in the Engineering Department would be specially valuable to those who contemplate entering the Artillery. It is expected that the lectures on military subjects would be attended by Volunteer officers and those who contemplate holding commissions in the Auxiliary Forces as well as those preparing for the Regular Army.

Degree Day.

The University Degree Day was held on July 8th. The Whitworth Hall was crowded with graduates, students and friends. Earl Spencer, the Chancellor, presided. The occasion was rendered one of especial interest by the presence of Dr. Nicolas Murray Butler, the President of the Columbia University of New York. The Chancellor, in the course of a brief speech, cordially welcomed the distinguished visitor to Manchester. In presenting Dr. Butler for the Honorary Degree of LL.D., Professor Michael E. Sadler spoke of him as a leader in educational thought and policy, who by his writings and eloquent speeches had impressed on the minds of his countrymen the deepened conviction that efficient schools, Colleges and Universities accessible to all, differentiated in intellectual aim, but united by a common sense of national duty, were more than ever vital to the welfare of a free and progressive State. Dr. Butler, expressing his appreciation of the honour that had been conferred upon him, said the urban University of the type to which the Manchester University belonged was a new creation. He conceived it to be the function of an urban University to show the urban community, and those who were dependent upon it, how their interests, their health, their growth, their education, and their prosperity might best be increased and furthered by the application of scientific truth and methods to the needs of the moment. The Ordinary Degrees were afterwards conferred upon a large number of graduates.

In the afternoon of Degree Day nearly two thousand guests attended the University Garden Party at the University Athletic Grounds at Fallowfield. Among those present were the Chancellor, Earl Spencer, the Vice-Chancellor and Mrs. Hopkinson, Mr. C. P. Scott, M.P., Dr. Murray Butler (New York), Mr. Donner, and nearly all the members of the University Teaching Staff.

University Appointments.

Mr. J. H. Hopkinson, M.A., has been appointed Lecturer in Classical Archæology. Mr. Hopkinson is a late Craven Travelling Fellow of Oxford University, and has conducted investigations at the British School in Athens, in Crete and in Rhodes and other islands in the Aegean.

The following appointments have been made:—Mr. Jethro Bithell, M.A., Assistant Lecturer in German; Mr. Gilbert J. Fowler, D.Sc., Lecturer in Bacteriological Chemistry in the Department of Public Health; Mr. E. C. Edgar, B.Sc., Assistant Lecturer and Demonstrator in Chemistry.

OXFORD.

University News and Notes.

In Convocation on July 10th the Degree of Doctor of Letters *honoris causa* was conferred upon Nicholas Murray Butler, President of Columbia University, New York. Dr. Butler was introduced by Dr. Farnell, Tutor and Dean of Exeter College, who said that Dr. Butler, having realised that the welfare of States was intimately connected with a wise system of education, had devoted his life to developing and improving the methods of teaching. Dr. Rhys, who presided in the absence of the Vice-Chancellor, conferred the Degree, and welcomed Dr. Butler as " Vir eruditissime, rationisque institutoriæ indagator felicissime." Dr. Butler was afterwards entertained by Dr. Rhys at luncheon in the hall of Jesus College. There were present the Provost of Queen's, Canon Driver, the Presidents of Corpus and Trinity, the Provost of Worcester, Professors Osler, Odling, Poulton, Margoliouth, Dr. Murray, Professor Fine, of Princetown, and others.

The medical graduates of the University have presented an address to the Vice-Chancellor in Convocation, stating the steps that have been taken by the medical profession for the advancement of pathological study in the University. The appeal for support, which had been limited strictly to members of the profession, had resulted in a contribution of over £500, which was destined for the ultimate endowment of the Chair of Pathology. It was to be hoped that the University and the Colleges between them would ultimately place the professorship on a permanent footing. The generous member of the University who had already provided £1,000 had made the further liberal promise to cover the contributions of others of the Faculty by an equal amount. The Vice-Chancellor, Dr. Merry, expressed the satisfaction felt by the University at this unusual demonstration, and his pleasure in receiving the address. He was glad that the importance of the Chair should be thus emphasised. Through the liberality of New College and the Rhodes Trustees satisfactory provision for the study of pathology at the University had been made.

At Christ Church two Scholarships of the value of £50, tenable for one year, are being offered to selected candidates for the India Civil Service who have distinguished themselves in the Entrance Examination for that Service, and who are not, and have not, been members of any College at the Universities of Oxford, Cambridge or Dublin. Personal character will be taken into account in awarding the Scholarships. Successful candidates for the India Civil Service who wish to offer themselves for election to these Scholarships are required to send their names to the Dean before the end of the Government Examination, together with three testimonials as to character, and three references. The election will follow, without further examination, after the publication of the list of selected candidates.

A sum of £600 has been placed at the disposal of the University for the provision during the ensuing three years of a Lectureship in Military History. A lecturer will be appointed for three years dating from October 15th, 1905, at a stipend of £200 a year. He will be chosen by a Board consisting of the Vice-Chancellor, the Regius Professor of Modern History, a person nominated by the Secretary of State for War, a person nominated by the Warden and Fellows of All Saints' College, and two persons nominated by the Delegacy of Military Instruction. The Lectures will not be confined to any special period of history, but will in all cases bear upon the condition of modern warfare. The thanks of the University have been accorded to the donor for his munificent gift.

The Rev. Henry Thornhill Morgan, M.A., Trinity College, has undertaken to continue the unfinished carving in the corridors of the University Museum at his own expense. This generous offer has been gratefully accepted by the University.

In a Convocation held on June 29th the Degree of D.Litt., *honoris causa*, was conferred upon Dom Germain Morin, O.S.B., of Maredsons; and the Degree of M.A., *honoris causa*, upon Commander James John Walker, R.N.

The examiners for the Green Moral Philosophy Prize, 1905, have awarded the prize to Robert Mowbray, M.A., Brasenose College. The subject was " Optimism and Pessimism," which was to be considered from a philosophical standpoint.

The University Sermon which is annually delivered on St. John the Baptist's Day at Magdalen College was preached in the open air from the pulpit in St. John's quadrangle by the Rev. Arthur Ogle.

The Honorary Degree of D.D. has been conferred upon the Rev. Cecil Hook, M.A., Christ Church, nominated Suffragan Bishop of Kingston-on-Thames.

The Commemoration Sermon was preached on June 25th by the Rev. Canon H. Scott-Holland to a crowded congregation, which included many heads of houses and distinguished visitors.

The Encænia.

The Encænia was held on June 28th. There was a large attendance in the Sheldonian Theatre when the Chancellor, accompanied by the customary procession of heads of houses, doctors, proctors, and partakers in Lord Crewe's benefaction, entered the hall. Honorary Degrees were conferred upon the following:—

Honorary Degree of D.C.L.—Major-General Sir Francis Wingate, K.C.B., K.C.M.G., D.S.O., Governor-General of the Egyptian Army; William Holman Hunt; Charles Stewart Loch, Balliol College.

Honorary Degree of D.Sc.—George Howard Darwin, M.A. (Camb.), F.R.S., Plumian Professor of Astronomy and Experimental Philosophy in the University of Cambridge.

Honorary Degree of D.Litt.—Paul Sabatier; Basil Lanneau Gildersleeve, Professor of Greek in the Johns Hopkins University, Baltimore, U.S.A.; Barclay V. Head, Keeper of the Coin Department of the British Museum.

Sir Thomas Raleigh, Reader in English Law, in the absence of Dr. Goudy, Regius Professor of Civil Law, presented the recipients of the D.C.L. Degree.

The Creweian Oration was delivered by the Professor of Poetry, Mr. A. C. Bradley, Balliol College. He alluded to various benefactions to the University, including those of Mr. Rhodes, Mr. Beit, Mr. Wernher, and to the aid given to the Bodleian by Magdalen and Trinity Colleges, and sympathetic mention was made of the late head of Corpus Christi College, and of the late Vicar of St. Mary's.

The prize competitions were recited in the following order:—The Chancellor's prize for Latin verse, "Artes Magicae," Wilfrid A. Greene, scholar of Christ Church; the Chancellor's prize for an English essay, "The Condition and Prospects of Imaginative Literature at the Present Day," Alexander Maxwell, B.A., Christ Church; the Gaisford prize for Greek verse, "Spenser, Shepherd's Calendar, Aegloga Sexta, 'Lo, Colin, here . . . by you trace,'" Frederick A. B. Newman, scholar of University College; the Stanhope historical essay, "The Fronde," George S. Gordon, Oriel; Sir Roger Newdigate's prize for English verse, "Garibaldi," Arthur R. Reade, scholar of Exeter.

University Appointments.

Mr. A. S. Owen, New College, has been appointed to a Tutorship at Keble College.

Ernest J. Trevelyan, M.A., B.C.L., Reader in Indian Law, John A. Simon, M.A., and Leopold S. M. S. Amery, M.A., have been elected to Fellowships at All Souls.

The Rev. Robert H. Charles, M.A., Exeter College, has been elected Grinfield Lecturer on the Septuagint.

Mr. Ritchie, M.A., B.Sc., Fellow of New College and Reader in Pathology, has been constituted, by Convocation, Professor of Pathology, so long as he holds the Readership.

Mr. Henry Julian Cunningham, M.A., Balliol College, Lecturer in Ancient History at Worcester College, has been elected to an official Fellowship at Worcester College.

Mr. Edward Hilliard, M.A., of Balliol and Magdalen Colleges, has been elected Fellow and joint Senior Bursar of Balliol College.

Mr. Abel H. J. Greenidge, M.A., D.Litt., Tutor and formerly Fellow of Hertford College, and Mr. J. U. Powell, M.A., Tutor of St. John's College, have been elected Fellows of St. John's College.

Mansfield College.

The 19th annual meeting of the Trustees and subscribers of Mansfield College, Oxford, was held recently, under the Presidency of Professor A. W. Dale, Vice-Chancellor of Liverpool University. The following were elected as members of the Council:—Sir T. Raleigh, Dr. McClure, Dr. Massie, the Rev. Sylvester Horne, Messrs. A. Dale, A. A. Haworth, Owen Ridley, and A. J. Sheppeard. The Treasurer's statement showed that there was an accumulated deficiency of over £660. But it was stated that news had been received of a handsome legacy left to them by a gentleman who had already shown a great interest in the College, a legacy that would enable them to clear off their liabilities, to do some necessary work in connection with the College buildings, and then leave a substantial sum. The annual report refers to the death of Dr. Alexander Mackennal, for many years Chairman of the College. During the past year the number of names on the books had been 40, 28 Theological and 12 Arts Students.

The sum of £5,000 has been bequeathed to Mansfield College by the late Mr. T. H. Lucking.

The Rev. Dr. Fairbairn, Principal of Mansfield College, will visit the United States at the close of this year to deliver a course of special lectures as " Deems Lecturer " at the University of New York.

SHEFFIELD.

THE INAUGURATION OF THE UNIVERSITY.

University Buildings.

The visit of the King and Queen to Sheffield to open the new University buildings took place on July 12th. The buildings, which have been in course of construction since 1903, are on the collegiate model, surrounding three sides of a quadrangle, the fourth side being left vacant in order to leave room for future extension if required. One side of the quadrangle, which faces Western Bank, a large thoroughfare, contains the necessary offices, common rooms, refectories and the handsome Firth Hall, measuring 100 feet by 40 feet, with an open oak roof; this hall commemorates Mark Firth, who by founding Firth College prepared the way for the present University. Two other sides of the quadrangle overlook Weston Park, one of the chief parks of the city. This park will be of special advantage to the University, as it contains the Public Museums and Picture Galleries of the city, as well as a small Observatory which will in future be taken over and managed by the University. Each of the two sides of the quadrangle that overlook the park consists of four floors (three only on the park side, owing to the slope of the ground), the various lecture-rooms and laboratories of all departments—except those belonging to the Faculty of Applied Science, which are housed in a separate building in St. George's Square, five minutes' walk away from the main buildings—are provided for in these two blocks of buildings. One of these, the north block, is almost wholly given up to the needs of the Medical Faculty, the upper floor being devoted to Pathology, the next below to Physiology, the upper ground floor to Anatomy and to general lecture rooms, while the lowest floor contains a large medical library, to be used by the medical men of the city, as well as other rooms devoted to various purposes. The upper floor of the west block is divided between Chemistry and Biology (including Zoology and Botany), the three lower floors are

G

nearly equally divided between the various Physical laboratories and lecture rooms, as well as the lecture rooms required for the Arts departments, which include Mathematics, Classics, History, English, French, German, Economics and Law. Special provisions are made for research in all departments in which laboratories are required. The Library has not yet been erected, but a special donation for this purpose was announced on July 12th, and this will be taken in hand as soon as circumstances permit.

The University Movement in Sheffield.

The history of the creation of the University of Sheffield may be summarised as follows:—Three separate institutions—the Firth College, the Sheffield Medical School and the Sheffield Technical School—were in 1897 welded into one College, the University College of Sheffield; the interest of the city in the College was quickened in 1902 by the movement started in that year to erect new buildings; and the break-up of the old Victoria University in 1903, occurring at the time when the movement for the erection of the new buildings was in progress, stimulated the larger movement for the foundation of the University. An account of these two movements and of the three institutions out of which the University has grown was presented to each of the three thousand visitors who witnessed the ceremony on the 12th of July.

The Inaugural Ceremony.

The proceedings at the University opened with a procession of visitors and delegates from Oxford, Cambridge, London, Durham, Manchester, Birmingham, Liverpool and Leeds Universities, the University Colleges of Bristol and Nottingham, the British Academy, the Royal Colleges of Physicians and of Surgeons, the Institutes of Civil and Metallurgical Engineers, His Majesty's Treasury and other bodies, who occupied places in front of the pavilion which had been prepared for the opening ceremony. After this procession followed a procession of the Council and Senate of the University, who took their places on the pavilion to await the King and Queen. On the arrival of their Majesties, after presentations of some of the members of the Council and Senate to the King and Queen, a bound copy of the programme of proceedings was handed to the King by the Chancellor, the Duke of Norfolk, and another to the Queen by the Pro-Chancellor, Alderman Franklin. The Royal procession then entered the quadrangle, and took their places on the pavilion. A bouquet was presented to the Queen by the little granddaughter of the late Sir Henry Stephenson, who was for long the principal supporter in Sheffield of the University movement, and may be considered as the second founder of the College. After a prayer by the Archbishop of York, the Vice-Chancellor, Dr. Hicks, F.R.S., who has presided over the College since 1883, read an address from the University, and presented an illuminated copy of it to the King, who at once expressed his hearty thanks, and has sent the following reply:—

"I view with lively satisfaction the establishment of this and other Universities in large industrial centres, and it gives me great pleasure to open the handsome and spacious buildings provided for the University of Sheffield. I have never ceased to watch with great interest the great development of the wide movement for the encouragement of a sound and liberal education among all classes of my people, and I am well assured that the expectations of those patriotic and enlightened men by whose efforts were established the institutions from which the University of Sheffield derives its origin will be justified by the achievements of those who are educated within its walls."

The Chancellor then explained the development of the movement in Sheffield, and the present position of the University, mentioning the names of Sir Henry Stephenson, Sir Frederick Mappin, Dr. H. C. Sorby, F.R.S., and the founder, Mark Firth, as having taken the lead in the movement. In the course of his speech he announced a new gift from Mr. Edgar Allen of £10,000 to be devoted to the building of a library. The Chancellor then asked the King to declare the buildings open. A jewelled key was presented by Mr. H. K. Stephenson, the Treasurer and Chairman of the Buildings Committee, and the King, stepping forward, declared the buildings open as follows:—

> "I have great pleasure in declaring these beautiful buildings open, and in expressing my fervent hope and desire for the long-continued prosperity of the University of Sheffield."

Amidst an outburst of cheering from the students and other guests, the King stepped back to the side of the Queen, a fanfare of trumpets sounded, and the Sheffield Festival Chorus, which occupied a position facing the royal pavilion, closed the picturesque ceremony by singing the anthem "O gladsome light," from Sullivan's "Golden Legend." The Royal procession then retired to view the Firth Hall, and to take part in a military ceremony held in Weston Park. A garden party followed, the King and Queen leaving for a progress through the manufacturing part of Sheffield, the guns signifying their departure by a royal salute.

Besides the ceremony at the University the Royal party attended ceremonies at the Town Hall, and the military ceremony referred to, visited Messrs. Vickers' Steel Works, and unveiled a monument to soldiers of the York and Lancaster Regiment. The whole town was magnificently decorated for the Royal visit, and the day kept as a public holiday. About 800 guests were entertained at luncheon by the University; in the evening there was a military tattoo, a small party was entertained by the Lord Mayor at dinner in the Town Hall, and some of the representatives of Universities and Colleges were entertained at dinner by the Senate and staff of the University.

University News and Notes.

The first meeting of the Court of Governors of the University was held on June 26th, the Pro-Chancellor (Mr. George Franklin) presiding, in the absence of the Chancellor, the Duke of Norfolk. The following were elected to fill the fifteen vacancies on the University Council:—Mr. W. B. Esam, Dr. Sorby, Mr. E. W. Firth, the Bishop of Sheffield, Dr. W. Dyson, Mr. A. J. Hobson, Mr. J. F. Moss, Mr. T. Andrews, F.R.S., Mr. J. Newton Coombe, Mr. A. Wightman, Mr. R. J. Pye-Smith, Mr. S. Snell, Mr. A. Harland, Mr. Frank Mappin, and Dr. John Young.

It was intimated that Dr. Hicks, Principal of the University College, who is named in the charter as the first Vice-Chancellor of the University, has resigned that position. The Pro-Chancellor expressed the warmest appreciation of the great and self-sacrificing services of Dr. Hicks as Principal of the University College, and said that the University would be able to retain him as Professor of Physics. Dr. Hicks feels that his time and thought should be entirely free to be devoted to science. The new Vice-Chancellor is to be appointed immediately.

The heads and principals of the following Schools and Colleges have been invited by the Court to become members of the Court of Governors of Sheffield University:—King Edward VII. School at Sheffield, the Central Secondary School, the Sheffield High School for Girls, the Rotherham Grammar School, King Edward School at East Retford, the Chesterfield Grammar School, St. Cuthbert's College, Worksop, and the Sheffield Training College for Teachers.

ST. ANDREWS.

The Quater Centenary of George Buchanan.

The University Court held its annual meeting for making appointments for the ensuing academical year on Saturday, July. 22nd. It was reported to the Court that the invitation to co-operate in the celebration of the Quater Centenary of George Buchanan in April next had been responded to by the other three Scottish Universities and by nearly all the learned societies to whom invitations were addressed. Friday, April 6th, has been definitely fixed for the celebration, and the functions associated with it will probably begin

on the preceding day and extend into Saturday, the 7th.   The
Universities of Paris and Bordeaux, with both of which Buchanan
was connected, have been invited to co-operate in the ceremonies,
and the Council of the former University has nominated delegates.
The students of these French Universities have been invited to
compete for prizes presented by J. Peddie Steele, Esq., M.D., LL.D.,
of Florence, for translation of certain poems selected by him from
Buchanan's works.   Dr. Steele has offered several prizes to the
St. Andrews students for translations of another group of selected
poems, and of the "Baptists," one of Buchanan's most celebrated
tragedies.   Neatly got-up booklets, containing the text of this group
of selections, and the group prescribed for the translations of the
French students, have been issued by the University.   In addition
Dr. Steele has announced a prize of one hundred guineas for the
best essay on "Sixteenth Century Humanism as illustrated by the
Life and Work of Buchanan."   This prize is open to *alumni* of all
the four Scottish Universities.   The Court has agreed to make a
subscription to the expenses of the celebration, and to invite subscriptions from other bodies interested.   In view of the special
association of Buchanan with the College of St. Leonard, of which
he was Principal, the issue by the University Court of a volume on
the "College of St. Leonard" is opportune.   The book contains a
reprint of the foundation and other documents of the ancient College,
which are prefaced by a historical introduction by Professor Herkless,
the occupant of the Chair of Ecclesiastical History, and Mr. R. K.
Hannay, Lecturer in Ancient History in the University, contributes
valuable notes.

The Installation of the Rector.

The opening of the Winter Session in October will have special
interest from the circumstance that Mr. Andrew Carnegie, LL.D.,
who was last year re-elected Rector of the University, will be formally
installed in office on the 17th October, and deliver an address to
his constituents.   In connection with the installation ceremony a
number of Honorary Degrees will be conferred, according to custom.
The Senatus has selected for recognition several distinguished citizens
of the United States, with whom will be associated one or two eminent
Scotsmen.   The list of honorary graduates has not yet been
announced.   In the course of his visit to St. Andrews Dr. Carnegie
will probably take an opportunity of inspecting the fully-equipped
Gymnasium, the Recreation Park and Pavilions which he gifted to
the students and which have been completed during the past year.
The Park, which lies at the west end of St. Andrews, and forms
part of the lands with which Prior Hepburn endowed the College of

St. Leonard, is a recreation ground of exceptional character as regards situation and convenience, and there are two roomy Pavilions, one for the use of men and the other for women students. The latter adjoins University Hall, the residential Hall for women students.

University News and Notes.

The additional buildings for teaching accommodation at the United College are approaching completion. The Chemical Laboratories and Lecture Theatre have already been partly occupied. The fittings are of a most elaborate description, and great pains have been taken to secure the most highly-perfected apparatus and equipment. The Physics Laboratory and Lecture Theatre and the class-rooms for subjects in the Faculty of Arts will also be fitted in a thoroughly convenient style.

Principal Donaldson has been re-appointed a Trustee of the Carnegie Trust for the Universities of Scotland for a further term of four years.

The Very Rev. Principal Stewart, St. Mary's College, has been re-appointed for a further period of five years a Governor of the Trust for Education in the Highlands and Islands of Scotland.

Mr. Edward E. Morrison, M.A., Bonnytown, Stravithie, St. Andrews, who has been elected an Assessor of the General Council, in room of the Rev. Robert Scott, retired, took his seat at the meeting of the University Court on the 22nd ult.

Intimation was made at the same meeting that the Right Hon. Lord Balfour of Burleigh, K.T., LL.D., the Chancellor of the University, had re-appointed Sheriff Kincaid Mackenzie, K.C., LL.D., as his Assessor for a second term of four years.

The Vice-Chancellor, at a meeting of the Senatus held on July 19th, conferred the Degrees of M.B. and Ch.B. on four candidates, three of whom were women students. These latter have the distinction of being the first women medical graduates of the University.

The following appointments have been made:—Examiner in History, the Rev. John Morrison, M.A., D.D., Edinburgh; examiner in Political Economy, the Rev. Archibald Main, M.A., St. Madoes; examiners for Preliminary Examinations and representatives on Joint Board of Examiners: English, the Rev. Professor Lawson, M.A., D.D.; Classics, Professor Burnet, M.A.; Mathematics and Dynamics, Mr. Alexander Leighton, M.A., B.Sc., Dundee; Modern Languages, Mr. J. Esser, St. Andrews.

The Commissioners for the Exhibition of 1851 have appointed Mr. John Johnston, B.Sc., Dundee, to a Science Scholarship on the Court's recommendation.

WALES.

University News and Notes.

On the occasion of the visit of the Chancellor, H.R.H. the Prince of Wales, to Cardiff on June 28th, an important Graduation Ceremony took place in the Park Hall. The Deputy Chancellor, Sir Isambard Owen, welcomed H.R.H. the Chancellor in a brief speech, and the Prince, in responding, cordially thanked the members of the University for their reception. The Vice-Chancellor then presented the following for Honorary Degrees of the University:—Mr. John Gwenogfryn Evans, Professor Henry Jones, Sir John Williams, M.D., Lord Tredegar and Mr. Joseph Chamberlain. The Latin orator referred to the Chancellor of the University of Birmingham in the following terms:—"Universitatis illius Mediterraneae Cancellarium ac pæne dixerim conditorem illustrissimum, oratorem instigandi suadendique sollertissimum qui insigni publicarum rerum usu et peritia non modo per Britannias omnes innotuit sed totum fere orbem terrarum conquassavit, virum indomitum vehementem indefessum." The ceremony was fully attended by University graduates and their friends from all parts of the country. Though the students seemed to be somewhat awed by the presence of the Chancellor, they gave a characteristically hearty welcome to the recipients of the Honorary Degrees.

University College of Wales.

On July 23rd the Hon. Ailwyn Fellowes, President of the Board of Agriculture, presided over an agricultural conference which was held at Aberystwyth in connection with the Agricultural Department of the College. The meeting was attended by several hundred delegates, representing a number of Welsh County Councils and other bodies. The object of the Conference was to discuss the extension and development of the Agricultural Department of the College and the establishment of a more definite connection between the extension work and that done inside the College.

Mr. Fellowes delivered a short address, in which he congratulated the Conference upon the increased interest taken in agriculture in the Principality. The Board of Agriculture had been able to give £800 a year to Aberystwith College and £200 a year towards the College farm which was to be opened that day. The Agricultural Department of Aberystwith College had the warmest sympathy of the Board of Agriculture, and he hoped that in the future the Board would be able to do still more for agricultural education and for their agricultural colleges.

The Conference passed resolutions in favour of an extension of the work, and invited the County Councils to join the Committee appointed to deal with the matter. After lunching with the Mayor and Corporation, the President and a hundred guests proceeded to the recently-acquired College and Counties' Training Farm, which is situate about four miles outside the town and has an area of 200 acres. The objects of the farm are (1) to provide practical training for students in the Department at the College, and for others who may wish to become pupils on the farm; and (2) to enable the staff of the Agricultural Department to carry out experiments and demonstrations and to be of use and interest to the farmers of Wales generally. The farm has been equipped with the most modern implements and appliances. Mr. Fellowes formally declared the farm open.

University College of North Wales.

The twenty-first anniversary of the formation of the College was celebrated with much ceremony on Saturday, July 1st. The College was formally opened on the 18th of October, 1884, and has made steady progress in every direction during the twenty-one years of its existence. The present staff of the College numbers thirty-three, and the number of students has increased from 58 when the College opened to 329 at the beginning of the current session. Of these 242 are drawn from the six counties of North Wales.

A movement has been started for providing the College with new buildings at the cost of £175,000. A valuable site upwards of ten acres in extent has been given by the Corporation of Bangor, and on July 1st the deed of gift was formally presented to Lord Kenyon, the President of the College, by the Mayor (Councillor W. Bayne). A large and representative meeting was held in the Penrhyn Hall, presided over by Lord Kenyon, when speeches were made by Mr. Lloyd-George, M.P., Sir Isambard Owen, Principal Reichel, and Professor Henry Jones.

A special service for students of the College was held in the Cathedral on Friday, June 30th, when an eloquent sermon was delivered by the Rev. A. J. Mason, D.D., Master of Pembroke College, Cambridge.

University College of South Wales.

The visit of H.R.H. the Prince of Wales to Cardiff on June 28th for the purpose of laying the foundation stone of the new buildings of the University College of South Wales and Monmouthshire marks an important development in the history of higher education in Wales. The strenuous efforts that have been made to provide a worthy home for the College have at last been crowned with success, and the College has entered with fitting ceremony upon a new era. In a fine open space in Cathays Park—the gift of the municipality— in company with the new Town Hall and the new Law Courts, the College buildings are to be erected. The foundation stone was "well and truly laid" by H.R.H. the Chancellor of the University, in the presence of a large gathering of spectators, numbering nearly three thousand. In the course of a brief speech the Prince expressed the great pleasure he felt at taking part in the important ceremony that day, and congratulated the people of Cardiff upon the success that had attended their large-minded generosity and enterprise.

Mr. William Phillips, M.A., has been appointed to succeed Mr. Raymont as Professor of Education and head of the Men's Day Training Department. Mr. Phillips, who is an old student of the College, has been acting for some time as Assistant Lecturer in this Department. Mr. Phillips will enter upon his new duties with the best wishes of all who know him and of all the friends of the College.

UNIVERSITY COLLEGES.

Queen's College, Belfast.

The Summer Session has now come to a close. The class examinations have been held and the professors have a temporary release from duty.

The statistics of the College for the academic year have now been made up. They show that the attendance of students was the largest that the College has had for twelve or thirteen years. Taking all classes into account, a gross total of 501 students were enrolled. The increase was not confined to any one department, but characterised all the Faculties of Arts, Medicine, Law and Engineering, the largest advance being in Medicine.

" The Regulations " of the College for the academic year 1905–6 have now been published, and are to be obtained of the Bursar. They contain full information as to all lectures, examinations, scholarships, studentships, and prizes in the coming session. The pecuniary value of the scholarships, etc., announced for the coming session amounts to over £2,400 per annum.

The applications of candidates for the vacant English Chair were in upon the 21st July. The appointment is expected to be made by the Crown in the near future.

Mr. Thomas Carnwath, B.A., M.B., has been elected to one of the Research Scholarships given by His Majesty's Commissioners of the Exhibition of 1851. The pecuniary value of the scholarship is £150 per annum.

Mr. W. H. Davey, M.A., has passed the final examination for admission to the Irish Bar, taking first place.

Professor Symington, F.R.S., who is President of the Anatomical Society of Great Britain and Ireland, is to preside over the English section of the International Federation Congress of Anatomy at Geneva in August.

University College, Bristol.

Mr. J. H. Priestley, B.Sc., has been appointed Lecturer in Botany in the Faculty of Arts and Science. Mr. Priestley is a former student of the College, and since January last has acted as temporary Lecturer in the Department in the place of the late Mr. George Brebner.

Mr. C. E. Greenall, B.Sc., of Liverpool, has been appointed Assistant Master in the Bristol Day Training College for Men, which opens in September.

H.M. Commissioners for the Exhibition of 1851 have awarded Science Research Scholarships to Mr. Alfred G. C. Gwyer, B.Sc., and Mr. T. F. Sibly, B.Sc. Mr. Gwyer has been engaged during the last session in research on the chemistry and metallurgy of aluminium alloids, and Mr. Sibly has been studying some problems in the geology of the Mendips.

The Council are recommended to award a number of Scholarships tenable at the College during the Session 1905–6, of which may be mentioned:—" Hugh Conway " Scholarship (value £40 per annum, tenable for two years), Elizabeth K. Rendall; Chemical Scholarship (value £25), Francis L. Usher ; Engineering Scholarship (value £25), Herbert E. L. Martin. The Council are also recommended to award the following Diplomas in Engineering:—Senior Diploma: First Class, Basil F. Beverley and Richard N. Hanscombe; Ordinary, Reginald A. Rose. Junior Diploma: First Class, John McMurtrie.

Hartley University College, Southampton.

A summer course of lectures and demonstrations on "Nature Study" has been arranged by Dr. Carvers, Professor of Zoology. It is hoped that next year it may be possible to organise a more extensive scheme of vacation study for teachers and others, including a course on English for foreign students.

The College buildings are about to be considerably extended. Two shops adjoining the College have been acquired, and the site on which they stood will be utilised as occasion demands. It is a matter for great regret that it is not possible to abandon altogether the present highly inconvenient buildings. They are too small; they are situated in the wrong part of the town, hemmed in by shops and slums, and difficult of access from the residential suburbs. But money is not forthcoming; no great scheme of removal and rebuilding can be entertained. Even this makeshift purchase of contiguous property can be effected only by selling out stock—a deadly expedient. We look with envy upon our neighbour, Reading, and upon the rising palaces of education in the wealthy and enthusiastic North.

Owing to the increase in the number of students in the College the Council has decided to appoint two additional assistant lecturers, one in English and one in Mathematics. The applications for these posts are at present coming in.

An attempt is being made to arrange for a conference between the College, the Education Committee of the Borough, and the chief employers of labour in Southampton, with a view to increase the practical value of the technological and commercial work of the evening classes of the College, and to bring these classes into line with the continuation classes held in the Council Schools.

Dr. Michael E. Sadler, in a masterly report on the Secondary Education of Hampshire, deals with the Hartley University College as part of the educational system of the county. He says: "My inquiry into the educational needs of the district has led me to the conclusion that in the case of the Hartley University College it would be wise to concentrate effort on three things—first, on the training of teachers; secondly, on instruction in engineering; and, thirdly, on the creation of a School of Forestry." In so far as the College supplies more than a merely local need its activities would not be limited, it is to be hoped, to the provision of these three important but mundane "things."

Notes and Comments.

Treasury Grants to Universities and Colleges.

It is announced that the main feature in the final report of the Committee on the Allocation of the Grant in Aid to University Colleges has been accepted. It is proposed to establish a permanent Advisory and Inspecting Committee to advise as to the distribution of the grants, and on the question of assisting superannuation funds for College teachers. The Treasury will endeavour during the autumn to constitute such a body. It has been decided that one portion of the grant shall be allocated generally on the principles already adopted, and that the remainder shall be reserved for special requirements. In respect of the former sum, amounting to 90 per cent. of the total, it is proposed that the grant made to each institution should be secured to it for five years. This important provision will enable the Colleges to ensure a welcome condition of stability in their financial arrangements. The following grants are recommended for the ensuing year :—

Manchester	£12,000	Nottingham	£5,800
Univ. Coll. (Lond.)	10,000	Sheffield	4,600
Liverpool	10,000	Bedford (Lond.)	4,000
Birmingham	9,000	Bristol	4,000
Leeds	8,000	Reading	3,400
King's (Lond.)	7,800	Southampton	3,400
Newcastle	6,000	Dundee	1,000

These sums, which are for the current year only, amount to £89,000. The remaining £11,000 will be spent in the purchase of books and apparatus, and in the encouragement of post-graduate work.

The Sociological Congress.

In view of the fact that the International Institute of Sociology has accepted an invitation from the Sociological Society and the University of London to hold its next Congress in London in the summer of 1906, steps are already being taken to ensure the success of the meeting. An Executive Committee, with power to add to its members, has been appointed consisting of the members of the Council of the Sociological Society and representatives of London University. It has been decided to form a guarantee fund to meet the expenditure which will be incurred.

The Association to Promote the Higher Education of Working Men.

The annual meeting of the Association to promote the Higher Education of Working Men will be held in Birmingham on October 14th. Sir Oliver Lodge will preside, and the speakers will be the Bishop of Birmingham and Mr. Bell, M.P. The Co-operative Associations in the Birmingham district and the Trades Council have united in making the preliminary arrangements. Great hopes are entertained that the meeting will be the means of stimulating and encouraging educational work in the great Midlands district.

At the summer meeting of University Extension Students, to be held in Oxford from August 4th to 28th, a Conference will be held under the auspices of the Association for the Higher Education of Working Men, in which the Bishop of Hereford and Mr. W. Crooks, M.P., have promised to take part.

The Carnegie Trust for the Scottish Universities.

The following awards for the academic year 1905–6 have been made by the Executive Committee of the Carnegie Trust under their research scheme :—

RESEARCH FELLOWSHIPS.

Chemical and Mathematical.—J. H. Maclagan Wedderburn, M.A. (Edin.).

Physical.—James R. Milne, B.Sc. (Edin.); and Dugald B. M'Quistan, M.A., B.Sc. (Glas.).

Engineering.—Thomas Oliver, B.Sc. (Edin.).

Chemical.—James C. Irvine, D.Sc. (St. And.); William Maitland, B.Sc. (Aber.); and Alfred W. Stewart, B.Sc. (Glas.).

Agricultural.—Sydney F. Ashby, B.Sc. (Edin.).

Biological.—John Cameron, M.D. (Edin.), D.Sc. (St. And.); W. D. Henderson, M.A., B.Sc. (Aber.); F. H. A. Marshall, D.Sc. (Edin.); and Henry J. Watt, M.A. (Aber.).

Physiological.—Andrew Hunter, M.A., B.Sc. (Edin.).

Pathological.—Carl H. Browning, M.B., Ch.B. (Glas.).

Historical.—Duncan Mackenzie, M.A. (Edin.); and Agnes M. Ramsay, M.A. (Aber.).

Physical.—Robert Jack, M.A. (Glas.); and Henry W. Malcolm, M.A., B.Sc. (Aber.).

Engineering.—William C. H. Cleghorne, B.Sc. (Edin.).

Chemical.—David C. Crichton, M.A., B.Sc. (St. And.); Edward S. Eadie, M.A., B.Sc. (Edin.); Thomas D. Mackenzie, B.Sc. (Glas.); William S. Millar, M.A. (Edin.); Agnes M. Moodie, M.A., B.Sc. (St. And.); David M. Paul, B.Sc. (St. And.); Clerk Ranken, B.Sc. (Edin.).

Agricultural.—William Dawson, M.A., B.Sc. (Aber.); David Milne, B.Sc. (Aber.); and Robert D. Watt, M.A., B.Sc. (Glas.).

Biological.—Thomas J. Anderson, B.Sc. (Edin.); Robert N. Rudmose-Brown, B.Sc. (Aber.); William Macrae, M.A., B.Sc. (Edin.); William Nicoll, M.A., B.Sc. (St. And.); Muriel Robertson, M.A. (Glas.).

Pathological.—Robert D. Keith, M.A., M.B., Ch.B. (Aber.); Elizabeth H. B. Macdonald, M.A., M.B., Ch.B. (St. And.); Janie H. M'Ilroy, M.B., Ch.B. (Glas.); Ivy M'Kenzie, M.A., B.Sc., M.B., Ch.B. (Glas.); and William MacKenzie, M.A., B.Sc. (Edin.).

Historical.—Mary Hamilton, M.A. (St. And.).

Economical.—Constance H. M. Archibald, M.A. (Glas.); and Eric A. Horne, M.A. (St. And.).

Linguistic.—Robert L. G. Ritchie, M.A. (Aber.); and George Stevenson, M.A. (Edin.).

Research grants were also awarded to forty applicants. The total estimated outlay for fellowships, scholarships and grants for the year 1905–6, under the above scheme, amounts to close upon £7,000.

The British Association in South Africa.

In all its long history the British Association for the Advancement of Science has only met twice outside the United Kingdom. On both these occasions the meetings were held in Canada, in 1884 at Montreal, and in 1897 at Toronto. The visit to South Africa this year marks an important development in the history of the Association. The meetings will be held at two centres—in Cape Town and Johannesburg. The inaugural meeting is to be held on the 15th of August at Cape Town, when Professor G. H. Darwin will deliver the first half of his Presidential address. The second half will be given in Johannesburg on August 30th. Professor Darwin proposes to consider evolution in the world of matter as distinct from the world of life, and will illustrate his subject by considering theories of the intimate constitution of matter and theories of cosmogony. Among the lectures that have been arranged the following may be mentioned:—Professor Poulton (Oxford), on "W. J. Burchell's Discoveries in South Africa;" Professor J. O. Arnold (Sheffield), on "Steel as an Igneous Rock;" Mr. A. E. Shipley (Camb.), "Fly-Borne Diseases, Malaria, Sleeping Sickness, etc.;" Professor Porter (Montreal), "The Bearing of Engineering on Mining;" and Professor Ayrton (London), on "Distribution of Power." The work of the sections promises to be of very considerable interest and importance. A most attractive itinerary has been arranged, including visits to Durban, Pietermaritzburg (near where a Kaffir dance will be witnessed), Johannesburg, Pretoria, Mafeking, Bloemfontein, Kimberley, Bulawayo, the Matopos (where the grave of Mr. Cecil Rhodes will be visited), and thence to the Victoria Falls of the Zambesi River. The visitors will then return to Cape Town, and will leave for England on September 20th. It is expected that upwards of 400 members and guests will attend the meetings of the Association this year. High praise is due to the Central Organising Committee at Cape Town for the arrangements that have been made, ensuring a most successful meeting.

———

In the September number of this " Review" there will be published an account of the recent meetings of the British Universities Students' Congress, together with a photograph of the members.

Review

Vol. I.   No. 8.

PRINCIPAL CONTENTS.

LONDON, SWAN SONNENSCHEIN & HODDER.

NEW YORK : ... ...

...COTT & ... PRICES, PENCE 6 d.

AUSTRALIA : ... ... & CO. MELBOURNE, ETC.

From a drawing   *by Henry Lamb.*

Rev. F. H. CHASE, D.D.,
President of Queens' College, Cambridge.

The University Review

NO. 5. VOL. I.   SEPTEMBER, 1905.

The Rise and Progress of the Student Christian Movement.

BY

WALTER W. SETON, M.A. (LONDON),

University College, London.

THE *University Review* owes its origin to a wide-felt desire for an interchange of thought and news between British Universities and Colleges. This desire is one of comparatively recent growth, for it is not long since the Colleges of this country were without any unifying link and had little interest in each other's doings, excepting the historic interest and rivalry of the two oldest Universities. One of the most hopeful signs of the academic outlook of to-day is that the traditional narrow exclusiveness of the College spirit is yielding to an ever broadening interest in the factors which contribute to the advancement of Higher Education. The establishment of Students' Representative Councils, the foundation of Union Societies, the holding of Students' Congresses all point unmistakeably to a fresh vitality which has

A

begun to stir British academic circles ; *esprit de corps*, a factor which has influenced German University life for centuries, has never until now led to an Inter-Collegiate spirit in England.

Out of this same quickening in College life, influencing it, reacting upon it, perhaps even in measure producing it, we find the Student Christian Movement of Great Britain and Ireland[1] which by means of its affiliated Christian Unions in every important College is exercising a continually increasing beneficial force, a binding together of students as notable and potentially as influential as that to which reference has been made. The subject of the following pages is to be a review of the rise and present position of the Student Movement in Great Britain in particular, and throughout the University world in general.

Those who have looked into the position of this Student Christian Movement have satisfied themselves, whether they personally approve of its aims and methods or not, that it is a factor which can no longer be neglected. A movement which embraces in its membership throughout the world over 103,000 students and professors, which includes nearly one in two of all the students in the North American Colleges, which employs for its organisation the whole time of over 200 secretaries (all University men, mostly graduates and salaried), and which owns buildings valued at over a quarter of a

---

1. The name of the movement was changed to the above at the Summer Conference, held at Conishead in July, having been previously known as the British College Christian Union.

million sterling—this movement is a force which cannot be left out of the calculations of a student of academic interests.

No more convenient starting point for a review of the rise of the British Student Movement can be found than the going out to China of the "Cambridge Seven" in 1884. It certainly was a startling announcement for Cambridge and for all the Colleges that the champion cricketer, C. T. Studd, and the stroke of the Cambridge eight, Stanley Smith, were going out as missionaries to China. Rarely, if ever, before had the British Colleges been. so deeply stirred, and the influence of these two remarkable men, along with their five companions who formed the "seven," gave the first strong impulse to the promotion of organised Christian effort among students. Already, several years before, the American Colleges had begun to co-ordinate their Christian work, and the Mount Hermon Conference, convened by Moody in 1886, culminated in the foundation of the Student Volunteer Movement for Foreign Missions in America, which enrolled many American University men who intended to take up foreign missions as a life work. In the following year a similar movement. known at first as the Student Foreign Missionary Union, was launched in London as a result of the visit of Mr. Forman, an American student, who came to England with news of the step taken by the American Colleges. The newly-formed Union was at first on a small scale, and was not successful in influencing the British Colleges as a whole, still less in forming a strong bond between them. How-

ever, the visit of Mr. R. P. Wilder[1] from America to
several Universities, and particularly to Cambridge, in
1891, and the Conference which he convened to meet at
Edinburgh in 1892, produced a reconstitution of the
Union under the new name which it has since retained,
the Student Volunteer Missionary Union of Great Britain
and Ireland ; this Union adopted in the following year as
its basis of membership the following Declaration still in
use: "It is my purpose, if God permit, to become a
foreign missionary."

The object of the Union was not only to enrol students
who had already decided to become foreign missionaries,
but also to bring the claims of foreign missions directly
before students of British Colleges and by their means
ultimately before all the Christian Churches; that is, the
British Colleges were to be made the scope of its activities.
It became very soon apparent to the leaders of the Union
that in order to effect this end it was essential to have in
each College an organised nucleus of men who could
receive the Travelling Secretaries of the Union, and help
them to get a hearing in the College.   A survey of the
Colleges of Great Britain in 1893 showed that there
existed in all only twenty Christian Unions, all uncon-
nected and working without co-operation and with little
knowledge of each other's existence or aims.   A Conference representing twenty Colleges was held at Keswick
in 1893, with the result that a new body, the Inter-

---

1. In this connection, it is interesting to note that Mr. Wilder's services
have been secured as Travelling Secretary of the British College Christian
Union for this Session, and he will accordingly again visit most of the British
Colleges.   Mr. Wilder studied at Princeton University, U.S.A., where he
graduated M.A. with Honours in Philosophy.

Collegiate Christian Union, was founded. Within the first year of its existence, the Inter-Collegiate Christian Union affiliated seventeen out of the twenty existing Unions, and when a second Conference was convened at Keswick under its auspices in 1894 forty-seven Colleges were represented; this was the most representative gathering of University men and women which had ever met in this country. In the year 1894-5, one of unusual activity and rapid development, the number of affiliated Unions rose to forty-five, and at the Conference of 1895 the Inter-Collegiate Christian Union changed its name to "The British College Christian Union," existing side by side with the Student Volunteer Missionary Union, owing its origin to a need created by that Union, but still distinct from it. The objects formulated in 1895 may well be quoted here, as they have remained and are still in the main the objects of the movement:—

(*a*) To unite those Christian Unions in British Universities, Colleges, and Medical Schools, &c., the aims of which are in full harmony with "a belief in Jesus Christ, as God the Son and only Saviour of the world."

(*b*) To establish Christian Unions with similar purposes where none exist.

(*c*) To promote Christian life and activity among the students of Great Britain.

The words in inverted commas in the first clause foreshadow the basis which, after much thought and discussion, was finally adopted at the Summer Conference of 1902 as the basis of the movement as a whole, and of the individual membership of the affiliated Unions, viz., "I desire in joining this Union to declare my faith in Jesus Christ as my Saviour, my Lord, and my God." This simple basis is a valuable indication of the nature of the Student Movement in Britain. The basis harmoniously unites men of all Christian creeds by placing in the foreground of the aims of the movement the points of agreement rather than the points of difference. It possesses a breadth which recommends it naturally to the average student. It is untheological, which is another way of saying it is personal. At the same time the basis is distinctly Christian and aggressive; the Student Movement is not ashamed of its aim to establish the supremacy of Jesus Christ in the Colleges of Great Britain.

It is impossible in the short compass of this review to enter into the details of the development of the movement since its establishment in 1895 to its present position in 1905. A comparison of some points in its position to-day with its position in 1895 must suffice. The Union when first founded affiliated seventeen out of twenty existing Unions. This year there are 151 affiliated Unions, 110 of them being in Universities and non-theological Colleges and forty-one in theological Colleges. The membership in these Unions amounts to nearly 4,600.[1] The Student Volunteer Missionary Union united at its institution 142 men and women

---

1. This does not include the membership in the theological Colleges which is not easily ascertainable.

students who had already decided to become foreign missionaries. In 1895 there were about 500 members enrolled. By the present year not less than 2,500 members have joined, and of these 958 have actually sailed for the mission field. The past academic year (July, 1904—July, 1905) has marked the enrolment of 200 Student Volunteers, a number greater than in any previous year since the foundation of the Union. About 1,000 men and women from the British Colleges are in preparation for their life work abroad, either in the Colleges or elsewhere. It is estimated that two-thirds of the members of the Student Voluntary Missionary Union would not have chosen missions as a calling apart from the influence of the Union; a Union which has directly influenced the life work of 1,600 College men and women is clearly a strong force in the country.

Such then is the position of the Student Christian Movement of Great Britain and Ireland, divided as it now is for administrative purposes into its three departments, the General College Department, the Student Volunteer Missionary Union, and the Theological College Department. It is already represented by a local Union in practically every important College, though there still remain a considerable number of institutions of Higher Education, principally Training Colleges, Fine Art, Music, and Law Schools, which have yet to be entered. Each local Christian Union is a more or less carefully organised institution and certainly, with the possible exception of the Union Societies, there are no College societies which engage in such systematic and generally efficient organisation. Something may now be said as to the methods and policy adopted by the average Christian Union. Its departments of activity may be classified as follows:—

1. GENERAL MEETINGS, at which outside speakers, or student leaders, give addresses specially suited for students on every variety of religious topic, evangelistic, evidential, missionary, devotional, or social.

2. BIBLE CIRCLES. Members of the Union, as well as those who are interested in it but not members, are organised into groups of six or eight for Bible Study ; outline studies, written by student leaders for students, are usually employed. Each member of a circle is expected to engage in daily study on the subject selected and to contribute to the weekly meeting for discussion. A strong Union will sometimes have over a hundred members enrolled in a dozen circles.

3. MISSIONARY BANDS. Groups similar to Bible Circles are formed for the study of missionary problems, each member preparing a definite contribution of missionary information for the meeting of the band.

4. SOCIAL STUDY BANDS are organised similar to the Bible Circles and Missionary Bands in order to interest students in Social Problems and to engage them in practical social work. Many Christian Unions support independent social settlements, while others assist in work carried on by outside agencies.

5. DAILY OR WEEKLY PRAYER MEETINGS are held in the majority of the affiliated Colleges.

All, or at least some, of the above methods of Christian Union work will be found in each affiliated Union.

The work of the central Executive, which is vested
with the direction of the Student Movement, is to support,
extend, and improve all these local activities and to plan
more efficient means for influencing students and
organising work amongst them. These aims it achieves
by the following means :—(1) A General Secretary, the
Rev. Tissington Tatlow, of Trinity College, Dublin, who
gives his whole time to the work of the Union. (2) Five
Travelling Secretaries, generally graduates, two for Men's
Colleges, two for Women's Colleges, and one for
London Colleges, who in the course of the year visit
every Christian Union in the country, and give such
assistance as the Local Committee consider desirable.
(3) A Summer Conference, held in July 1904, at which
large delegations from most affiliated Unions are present;
the last Conference included[1] 418 representatives from
thirty-three Men's Christian Unions, fifty-two Women's
Unions, and twenty-four Theological Colleges. (4) The
publication of a monthly magazine devoted to student
interests, called the *Student Movement.*

Before passing, however, from the subject of the
local Christain Union and its methods, it is necessary to
ask and to answer a deeper question. Can the existence
in a College of a Christian Union be justified? It is a
fact of common knowledge that the Christian Union
exists, but there are many in our Colleges who while
completely sympathetic with its basis, fail to see that the
Christian Union has any part to play in College life.

---

1. The exact statistics of the Conference held this year are not yet available;
the total number of delegates, however, was considerably over 600.

Why, some ask, cannot the Churches do this work for students? Why should it be done within the College itself? Three answers can be given.

In the first place, the function of a College is to educate a man completely. If the College is a lecture shop which does nothing to develop the social and athletic side of student life, it is failing in one of its important functions. A certain kind of social and even athletic development *could* be obtained apart from the College, but as a matter of practice it is found desirable by universal consent that the College should undertake something more than intellectual training. Students, like most other people, have a religious side to their natures which it is the duty of the College to develop. In most cases the College—and this applies particularly to many new Universities and institutions of Higher Education—cannot do this officially on account of a non-religious foundation. The Christian Union does the work then in a far more efficient manner than the College could ever do it officially. The social and athletic side of College life must be left to the students themselves, with of course official encouragement; so too the religious side.

In the second place, if the College cannot well carry on the religious side in the training of its students, neither can the Churches. The average student is far more deeply influenced by a College organisation such as a Christian Union, and even more by personal contact with Christian men in his College than by the Churches. It is not that he is out of sympathy with the Churches, but the Christian Union is a College institution run on lines to which a student is accustomed; it works where the men live, and so it not only gives a colour to their daily lives but gets its own colour therefrom.

In the third place, Christian Union work is necessary because the College days are days of transition for every man. It is the time when he is restating his views on everything of importance: when he leaves school all has to go into the melting pot, and out of that melting pot will emerge sooner or later a new and personal view of life, a new method of thought, a new theology or rather a personal Christianity or the reverse. While this melting process is going on, the home influence counts for much, but the College influence counts for more and specifically the influence of College friends counts for most of all. The Christian Union meets a student at the outset of his College life, and by its environments helps him to restate and to make personal the faith of his childhood. Moreover it helps a man coming from home to keep on the straight amid the tremendous temptations of city life. It is difficult to estimate how many students are thus safeguarded during their College career by the Christian Unions. Without doubt many in the Colleges are being influenced by the Christian Unions, who for one reason or another have not become members. Some broader aspects of the importance of Christian work for students will be mentioned later on.

From this brief account of the policy and objects of the Student Movement it is necessary to return to an event in its history which has influenced profoundly the course of its development, and which leads to wider issues. Reference has already been made to the existence of a similar movement in the American Colleges, to which the British Movement owes its origin.

In 1895, when the American Student Movement was already strong, and when the British Movement had just been founded, there were but three other organised Inter-Collegiate Student Movements in the world, one in Germany, another in Scandinavia, and a third in the mission lands. In that year a conference, attended by representatives of the five movements, met in Wadstena Castle in Sweden, and it was at this conference that the World's Student Christian Federation was founded. It was directed by a Committee consisting of two representatives from each movement, while the office of General Secretary was accepted by Mr. John R. Mott, of Cornell University, a position he still holds. Immediately after the foundation of the World's Student Christian Federation Mr. Mott started on his first tour round the Universities of the world, which was destined to leave important results in the development of the scope of the Federation. After brief visits to many Universities on the way from Scandinavia to India Mr. Mott made a stay of several weeks in India, where he assisted in the formation of a Christian Movement in the Indian Colleges. This movement, along with a similar one in Ceylon, was shortly after admitted to the Federation. From India Mr. Mott proceeded to Australia where he found five Christian Unions in existence, four of them very weak. When he left after three and a half months there were twenty-five thriving

Associations linked together in a national organisation, which under the name of the Australasian Student Christian Movement was affiliated to the Federation. Movements were started also in China and Japan which were visited by Mr. Mott in his tour. In 1896 the Students' Christian Association of South Africa was founded, and united to the Federation. Rapid as was the development of the British Student Movement, the rise of the World's Student Christian Federation has been even more remarkable. At the present time the Federation embraces Christian Student Movements in the following countries or groups of countries : America and Canada ; Australia ; Great Britain ; China, Korea and Hongkong ; Belgium, France, Holland and Switzer- land ; Germany ; India and Ceylon ; Japan ; Scandinavia ; South Africa ; and lands without national organisations. A movement not yet united to the Federation has been started in Italy and another is commencing in Hungary ; in Russia also several Christian Unions exist. Let us compare the position of affairs in 1895 in order to see the extent of the development. (The figures which are given are taken from the Decennial Review of the Federation presented by Mr. Mott to the International Conference held at Zeist in May of this year.) In 1895 the Federation included 599 Student Christian Associations with a membership of 11,725. All these Associations then unaffiliated have since joined the Federation, which how- ever now includes 1,825 Associations with a membership of over 103,000. The efficiency of the older Associa- tions has been greatly increased, so that Mr. Mott estimates that where there was one really efficient Union ten years ago there are five now. In 1895 there were about 11,000 students engaged in voluntary Bible Study in connection with the national movements. In 1904 there were at least 58,000 students enrolled in the Bible Circles of the Federation. One sixth of the total membership of the Australian Colleges has been organised into regular Bible Circles. Similar statistics might be given as to the increased number engaged in Missionary and Social Study but after all, figures are not of any great value. We have, in fact, to deal with a movement which in the short space of ten years has spread over the whole University world, which has already become one of the determining features of academic life and which will probably find in a few years its most important function in the influence which it exercises on the world which lies around and outside the College walls. Nothing is more indicative of the future of the Student Movement than the watchword adopted by the Volunteer Unions of America, Great Britain, and other members of the Federation: "The evangelisation of the world in this generation." A magazine such as the *University Review* is not the place for the discussion of the merits or demerits of this watchword. Suffice it to say that this watchword shows the world-wide horizon of the movement. The charge which is most frequently and, I fear, most justly brought against academic life all the world over by the man—not necessarily a Philistine—who lives outside of it, is that it is unpractical, theoretical, doctrinaire, that it bounds its own horizon; and often, it cannot be denied, that College men seem to live exclusively for their own College ideals, and are shut off from the faintest glimpse of practical life. If I were asked to define what I consider the most valuable contribution which this Student Christian Movement has to make and is successfully making to academic life, I should say that it is a practical outlook on life. The Christian Union aims at teaching men to see life steadily and see it whole. In a properly-constituted Christian Union a man is confronted by the needs of the world, social, moral, and spiritual. He gets a world-wide view of the evangelisation problem instead of a parochial view; he is encouraged in the study of men and their needs in Asia and in Whitechapel. An appeal is made to his sense of honour and to his feelings of heroism to lay out his life for the meeting of those needs. He cannot avoid it without a measure of intellectual dishonesty. College life is primarily intended as a preparation for life generally, but it is this spirit of "apartness" which only too often makes a man worse equipped rather than better equipped for life. The Christian Union prepares men for life in many ways. As has been already suggested it gives them some knowledge of the practical problems of life before they are actually launched upon it. It directs the choice of their life work, so that they can no longer follow vaguely their own ill-defined tastes or those of their parents, but are led to consider how their lives will have the largest sphere of influence. Like other College Societies, it develops the latent powers of leadership, but, unlike most of them, it aims at developing each individual member to his fullest capacity for usefulness. The strategic importance of the work done by the Student Movement lies in the fact that the Colleges produce the leaders of thought and of action in every department of life; that as a class students are more susceptible to religious influence than any other class; that College life, while it is on the one hand an unsettling time, is also in its later stages a settling time, when men learn to make up their minds; that the trained mind—the normal product of a College—is able to do more either for or against the interests of Christianity and morality than an untrained mind. Important as is then the influence of the Student Movement in countries such as Britain or America, its importance in Oriental countries such as India, or Japan, or China, is even greater. It may be said that civilisation has successfully undermined the hold of Hinduism and other native religions on the minds of the educated young men of India. Apart from religious considerations the danger involved in a rapid change of this sort is very great, and the interests of civilisation as a whole are saved by the development of Christian student effort among the rising educated classes of India. So too in China: the greatest danger to civilisation in China lies in the million *literati* who constitute Chinese public opinion. The westernisation of Chinese thought apart from those modifications of western civilisation which are due to Christianity constitutes a real peril. Already, however, the Student Movement has secured a foothold in Chinese Colleges as well as among the *literati* scattered all over the Empire. A Chinese delegate speaking at a recent Federation conference truly observed that students in all countries acted upon the mass of the people like a wind sweeping over a field of reeds. The reeds bend and sway before the wind. It is not an exaggeration to say that from this point of view alone the future of the nations is in the hands of the Student Movement.

Again one of the most important potentialities of the Student Movement is its international meaning. By means of it those who are to be the leaders of thought in all countries are during their student days being linked together in a world-wide movement; it is an axiom that international differences are laid aside and have no place in the intercourse of educated men. Science has a *lingua franca* of its own. But in spite of this there is no organisation apart from the Student Movement which binds together the students of all lands in one common enterprise and with one common aim. How many differences and even quarrels between nations are based on misunderstandings which might be removed by a closer knowledge? In the Federation of Christian Students, each movement learns to know the good qualities of the others; what is equally important, friendships are cemented between the leaders of different nations, apart from and higher than the friendships and enmities of the nations. For example the leaders of the British movement do not confine their interests and their friendships to the leaders in the Japanese Universities, but they extend their sympathies also to the men who are fighting an uphill battle in the Universities of Russia. The Federation shows to all the world that there is an essential unity of Christian men of all lands which is higher than any political unity. As Mr. Mott says: " Probably no single factor in one generation has really done more to promote international fellowship and kindly feeling. Is there not good grounds for belief that the Federation is fusing the nations together by stronger bonds than arbitration treaties or military alliances?" And yet diversity in unity is characteristic of the Federation; the national movements do not lose their own distinctive features, and are not levelled up or down to any one particular feature. As on the smaller scale a London Christian Union may differ in many respects from the Oxford or the Cambridge Inter-Collegiate Union, so the English movement differs completely from the German or the French movement while working for the same ends and using to a great extent the same means. Particularly in Oriental countries does the Federation pursue its policy of getting native leaders to undertake the work required in the Colleges of their own countries and refusing to do the work for them.

And yet once more emphasis may well be laid on the service which the World's Student Christian Federation is rendering in the promotion of Christian unity. Many of the religious leaders of the coming generation are now in the Christian Unions of the Colleges : and in those Christian Unions men of every denomination are learning to give less prominence to religious differences, and to unite heartily on those points on which they agree. Men who during their College career have joined hands over the essential and have striven together for a common ideal are not likely to forget their College experiences when they are in later life leaders of two different denominations; they will have learned to know not the weak points so much as the strong points of each other's system. I have never come across a single instance of a Christian Union Member being led to alter his denomination through Christian Union work; I have heard of two joint Secretaries of a Christian Union working in close harmony for more than six months without discovering that they both belonged to the same small denomination. The Christian Union is demonstrating to the Churches the possibility and the desirability of a harmonious co-operation in Christian service. And if this unity is instructive in Christian countries, how much more so is it in non-Christian countries? Much is said about the denominational differences which are transplanted by foreign missionaries to non-Christian lands. The Student Movement is a powerful apologetic to the educated classes of China or India, who are quite able to see that here they have a solid body of University men and women to whom the one end of enthroning Christ in the life of the Colleges is more than a self-interested denominationalism.

Reference has already been made to the service which the Student Movement has rendered to the cause of foreign missions as a whole. The greatest element in that service is not merely the number of volunteers who have been enrolled in the enterprise, great as that is.

The fact is that the present awakening of missionary interest is due more to the influence of the Student Movement than to any other single force. To quote Mr. Mott once more : "The cosmopolitan sweep and and tremendous momentum of the movement has appealed to the imagination and heart of the Christian world as separate national societies never could have done." The watchword of the British and the American Movements, "The evangelisation of the world in this generation," has been accepted in principle by several of the largest missionary societies, and has distinctly influenced the policy of others which have not so far committed themselves to the watchword. The large influx of graduates into the ranks of the candidates of the missionary societies has served to raise the standard of quality, and the average candidate sent abroad to-day is a better equipped man or woman than the one sent out ten years ago.

Again, the Student Movement is an apologetic for Christianity generally. It is the most complete refutation of the idea that Christianity is losing its hold on the educated classes. Its rapidly increasing membership proves that in the British Universities at least adherence to the Christain faith is not synonymous with being a fool ; for it must be remembered that the movement which received one of its first impulses from men like Studd and Smith has ever since continued to enrol some of the best men which our Colleges can produce. Many instances could be quoted of the offices of President of the Union and President of the Christain Union being held, sometimes for three years in succession, by the same man. In many Christian Unions men are especially chosen as Committee members who are on the Committee of some other Society or Societies, or officers thereof; in not a few cases too, the Committee members are scholars of the College at the same time.

Sufficient has now been said to show that the Christian Union is a College institution which cannot be neglected; that for anyone not sympathetic with its aims it is still useful as a College society; in conclusion it remains to consider how the Christian Union can be made to occupy a still more important place in College life.

In the first place more time must be given to the organisation of its Bible circles and its general meetings. More definite efforts must be made to interest the large number of men in the Colleges who are either opposed to Christian work or indifferent to it. More attention must be paid to the presentation by means of thoughtful addresses of the main positions of Christian Evidences, while definitely including a sane evangelistic motive; students must be helped not to avoid or to stifle intellectual doubts but to solve them. And probably one of the most effective methods of developing the sphere of influence of the Christian Union externally as well as strengthening it internally will be found in the Social Study which seems to be coming to the front at last in practically every Union. Great Britain, Holland, and America are leading in Social Study. In one year Harvard enlisted 475 students not merely in Social Study, but in practical Social work. There is little doubt that when the

Christian Unions engage in social work they will rally hundreds of students in the British Colleges who stand aloof from Christian work, but are fully alive to the necessity of doing something for the alleviation of social wrongs. Needless to say, the Christian Unions will undertake social work for its own sake and not as a sort of cat's paw for extending their sphere of influence; still the extension will come surely enough as an inevitable and welcome accompaniment.

In many of the larger Universities and Colleges the organisation of the various departments of Christian work is becoming a larger task than can be done adequately by undergraduates still engaged in their College work. For the central work many Colleges already need a salaried graduate who can afford to give a year or two to this work before entering his profession. Scores of such graduates are now at work in the American Universities. Such a graduate would undertake the administrative and organising work: the detail of the Christian Union work must remain in the hands of the rank and file of the members.

Finally, the British Christian Unions cannot go on much longer without permanent accommodation. Like the Union Societies they will require rooms and buildings of their own. Many Christian Unions have already rooms inside or outside the College; few have special buildings like many of the American Christian Unions. Before long it will be necessary for the Christian public to come forward with the required funds to equip and endow adequately Christian Union buildings, and to support a graduate staff entrusted with the development of the work of the Union in each College of importance. Obviously students have not the financial resources necessary for this; besides the public has to build the Colleges and equip them (though it often grumbles very much about doing so), and the Christian public will some day have to help to build Christian Union buildings. And then it will be possible to make the Christian Union a still more powerful institution in College life in Great Britain.

The Present Position of Trinity College, Dublin.

BY

JOHN BUTLER BURKE, M.A.

———

"A Land of grievances" where to be "agin the government" is the fashion as well as the rule, such indeed it has been for centuries, the unhappy lot of Ireland to be designated. The story of English rule—or misrule—is long and tedious, and need not be alluded to here but merely with the remark that little good comes of reviving the memory of past wrongs, and the worst policy for a nation is that of dwelling upon the unsatisfactory events which it has encountered, and the iniquities it has had to endure.

Not so much to the spirit of nationality, of a youthful and naturally independent-minded race, is the bewilderment of that unhappy land of saints due, but to the demon of religious strife that tears that race apart and prevents the development of its real character.

The two bogies "Home Rule" and the "Catholic University" have been held up alternately, though with equal ineffectiveness, by the Nationalist party, for their own gratification and the admiration of their constituents at least, and certainly for the disappointment of both.

"Devolution" does not concern him yet, but a Catholic University, which "the man in the street" understands by the Irish University question, is a red flag to him, and has the same chance of being carried as an act of separation between the sister isles.

The settlement of the Irish University question is, however, an entirely different thing, and there are still hopes of inequalities being removed if the matter is put forward in the proper way. But no solution of the education question in Ireland will ever be of any practical use unless the Bishops at Maynooth can give a guarantee that they are satisfied with the plans proposed, and that they will interfere with them no more.

They whose knowledge of University education is second hand find it difficult to understand what that education really means, and what the features are which those who have gone through it value most. The late Cardinal Newman had a clear idea of it. "A University," he held, "is not a seminary nor a monastery, but a place wherein to train men of the world for the world."

But be this as it may, it cannot with fairness be denied, and in fact it is generally admitted, that a grievance in matters of Irish education does exist.

In considering this difficult question, the present position of Trinity College, Dublin, is worthy of special examination. Not the least of the difficulties with which this ancient seat of learning has to contend are the conscientious scruples which have become rooted in the minds of the people, who believe that such institutions as Trinity College have an *atmosphere* which is at once dangerous to faith and morals, and that the students who frequent them run a risk of losing their immortal souls.

Can credulity be ever so debased, that one of the greatest seats of European culture should thus have such insult poured upon it! The obnoxious element in the atmosphere of the place is due to the fact that the majority of the students are Protestants, and that the professors, many of them at least, are men who by their works and exemplary pursuits—for professors should be exemplars—help to give the atmosphere of the place they adorn the tone of that higher culture which is so characteristic of the greater European seats of learning. In their teaching and their writings they try—some of them at least—to impart the true spirit of investigation, and to imply that there is such a thing as truth, and that openness of mind and freedom from bias are the primary and essential qualities in attaining it; that the best interests of the individual as well as of the Race, in the conduct of life as in the pursuit of knowledge, are intermingled with the highest regard for Truth; that "freedom is at once the cause and the consequence of intellectual progress,"[1] and "the life of the higher learning;"[2] that freedom is the Gospel of modern times throughout the civilised world, and it ought, therefore, to be so in Ireland. And this is the objectionable element in Trinity College!

---

1. Huxley, "Science and Education," p. 23.
2. Final Report, Royal Commission, p. 255.

At Oxford and Cambridge there are Chaplains who minister to the spiritual needs of undergraduates, and with very marked success. Opposition, no doubt, gives opinion strength, and these youths, from what I have seen of them—and I have seen a great deal—are more zealous in their religious pursuits than any I have met from the Catholic College in Dublin.

No doubt Trinity College has a Protestant Chapel and a Divinity School. Till recently it has been presided over by a really eminent Protestant Divine, the late illustrious Dr. Salmon, but it is not Protestant in any offensive sense. It is a seat of culture, of learning, and of speculative thought, where freedom reigns supreme. Similar opportunities to those existing at Oxford and Cambridge have been offered to Catholics at Trinity College, Dublin, but have been rejected by their spiritual guides.

Lord Edmund Fitzmaurice said in the debate on the second reading of Mr. Gladstone's University Bill that "if you stare long enough at a star you may persuade yourself you saw a comet." In Ireland the statement that the numbers who receive University education is very much less than in other parts of the kingdom is not borne out by facts. Thus, even in 1873, when Mr. Gladstone introduced his famous Bill, the proportion of University students in

> England was 1 in 4020
> Ireland   „ 1 in 2200
> Scotland „ 1 in 860

whilst the numbers in Ireland have been greatly increased since then.

But as we must take things as they are, it seems to be a great pity that there is not more harmony between Trinity College and the sister College in Dublin, University College. Everybody knows that by paying the usual fee it is possible to keep the terms in Dublin University by examination, instead of by attendance at lectures. Thus students of University College can at present, if they so wish, graduate at the University without attending a single lecture at Trinity College. Just as they can at the Royal University.

All that is required, therefore, is that University College should be properly endowed. In that case, its students instead of taking the Examinations of the Royal University could take those of the University of Dublin, whilst a compromise as to keeping terms by attending lectures at the University College instead of at Trinity would no doubt after a little time be brought about. The objection that the fees which Trinity men pay entitles them to the benefit of attending lectures, whilst those paid by the University College men would not, certainly ought to admit of being surmounted in some way, as for instance by compensating Trinity College for the loss it would sustain if it reduced its fees to those members of the sister College who do not attend the lectures at Trinity. Tutorial fees might in a similar way be reduced and tutors of the other College be recognised. These alterations, however slight in themselves, may mean a great financial loss to Trinity College and could only be effected by some reasonable compromise, so that those at a loss would be compensated.

Moreover, residence and lectures at University College could not be recognised by the University of Dublin, unless that College was raised to the proper level. This would mean an endowment, a portion of which should be raised by the public. The Dublin Corporation and the County Council could do much in raising funds by adding a small tax on the rates, so could the Corporations and County Councils in other parts of the country. It was thus that Birmingham and the other new Universities were so successful in obtaining the necessary funds. A half-penny in the pound throughout Ireland should do much, in addition to a State grant. After ten years or so the number of Dublin graduates from University College would be considerable, and there should be no grounds for complaints of inequality, whilst the alterations would be very much to the advantage of both.

No one could, or would oppose the graduation in the University of Dublin of University College men and other Catholics who do not care to reside or to attend lectures at Trinity.

The difficulty is chiefly about the governing body. Would these new members from University College be regarded as members of Trinity College or merely as graduates of the University of Dublin? It would be very humiliating to University College to have to submit to the latter course, unless it was understood that the College would ultimately become a part of the University by incorporation, and have directly, as well as indirectly, a voice in the management of its affairs. This, however, is the real difficulty in the matter, and it is one about which considerable difference of opinion exists. But it is to be hoped that if a sufficient number of Catholics from University College graduate in the University of Dublin from their own College, that in the course of time they should be able to make their influence felt in the University, and to bring about that affiliation which they want. By graduating as "non-colls,"—as they would be called at Cambridge—they should be able to establish an understanding between the two institutions.

If Catholics will not seek wisdom and learning within the walls of Trinity College, let them at least work in consort with her great inspiring efforts and aspirations. Let them do their best to make the work of Trinity and the work of University College one, in the cause not alone of religious toleration, but of that which we value equally of knowledge and of self-respect.

Dublin, as is well known, has been all through, the great pioneer of progress, although a critic once exclaimed, " The Test Acts have been abolished, but the test remains ! " This is not true of Trinity College, Dublin, however much it may apply to any other institution.

As regards religious toleration, the College was open to Catholics in the eighteenth century, and for more than half a century before the Test Acts by which Nonconformists were admitted to the degrees of the English Universities, Trinity College, Dublin, had thrown open its degrees to the world.   Lord Acton would have graduated in Dublin at the time when he was refused admission to three Colleges at Cambridge.   Likewise in the Higher Education of Women, Trinity College, Dublin, has taken the leading place, and earned for itself the name of the "progressive University."   The admission to degrees, of women who have resided and gone through the required course at Oxford or Cambridge, was the only logical step once the Dublin degrees had been thrown open to women generally.   The many sordid aspersions which have been cast upon this course of action are merely the unworthy criticisms of the vulgar herd, and both Oxford and Cambridge have officially approved of it. It might have been wiser, even if it had not been so logical, to have withheld the conferring of degrees to women who matriculated at Oxford or Cambridge previous to the date of the Grace by Dublin University.

In other matters, as Professor Macneil Dixon has remarked,[1] "it may come as a surprise to some, that in the more strictly academic region the University of Dublin has more than once or twice been first to read the signs of the times.   Her's were the first degrees ever instituted or conferred in Surgery, and her's the first degrees as well as the first University School of Engineering in the British Isles.   Lectureships in Modern Languages, but recently admitted to most English Universities, were founded in Dublin as early as the eighteenth century, and English Literature, lately given

---

1. "Trinity College, Dublin"—College Histories Series.

reluctant place among the studies of Oxford and Cambridge, has for generations formed an important part of the Dublin undergraduate course." It may be remarked here that at the present day there is no Chair of English Literature at Cambridge. The Clark Lectureship at Trinity can scarcely be considered a worthy substitute.

Again, the Classics and the Logics and Ethics *Moderatorships* preceded the Classical and the Mental and Moral Science Triposes, whilst the reconstruction of the Science Honour Schools and the Natural Sciences Tripos followed the establishment of *Moderatorships* in these subjects in Dublin. Trinity College, Dublin, therefore has a right to claim, that amongst the old Universities she has many times taken the first step in great reforms. But Dublin has been under the influence of hostile criticism for three centuries, far more so than other Universities, and it is to that criticism, perhaps more than anything else, that her progress is chiefly due. Through the greater part of her history she has passed through stresses and storms that have never troubled the sweet repose of Oxford and Cambridge. Cambridge and Dublin for long years gone by have worked together, for both in Science and in particular Mathematics, they have occupied the foremost place. In Experimental Science, however, Dublin has been severely handicapped in the way of equipment, whilst the Cambridge Laboratories are all that can be desired. Funds are being raised on behalf of Trinity College for this purpose, and the munificent gift of Lord Iveagh of £34,000 last year, on the condition that

£100,000 is forthcoming in three years, should do much to place her at least on a right footing in these matters.

But Trinity College has kept apace of Scientific and Literary Research so far as its environment has permitted. Its work in the past, before laboratories were necessary, was a brilliant record, and all it requires now to keep up that position are ample funds. The many Trinity College, Dublin men who are so actively engaged in literary research, both inside its walls and without them, indicate the intellectual energy which prevails within its immediate sphere of influence. Its work is naturally not confined to this. In National and Civic life it has played and continues to play a prominent, if not a foremost, part. It supplies the Bar with Judges: it has given England in recent times a Chief Justice of imperishable fame, and at the present time a Solicitor General of unsurpassed abilities, and it has given to the See of York one of its greatest occupants. The present leader of the Nationalist party, Mr. John Redmond, is a Trinity College man, and although the College is a stronghold of Unionism many of the most prominent members of the Nationalist party are graduates of the great Irish University, "which numbers amongst her sons so many shining lights in literature, in history, in politics, and in law."[1]

It is a libel, therefore, to assert that the College has not entered, and that it does not enter into the National life of Ireland, for Ireland owes far more to Trinity College, Dublin, than to any other Institution.

---

1. John Morley's "Edmund Burke."

The greatness of a College is to be measured by the greatness of her sons. Trinity College is the *Alma Mater* of such men as Bishop Berkeley, the founder of Modern Idealism, and Edmund Burke, perhaps the most philosophic statesman in the history of England, whose shade ennobles whatever it reached, who according to Macaulay "in the power of expression was second only to Cicero, but in amplitude of comprehension and richness of imagination was superior to all orators, ancient or modern," The College of Rowan Hamilton, the inventor of Quaternions, who, as the late Professor Tait remarked, has in his works made some of the greatest contributions which Science has received since the giant strides made by Newton and Lagrange. Of Lecky, one of the greatest historians. The College of George Francis Fitzgerald, by common consent one of the most learned physicists of his generation, who occupied the same high place in the estimation of his pupils and contemporaries in the world of science that Lord Acton did amongst historians. He was the spirit who moved and animated all around him, and like a Socrates inspired and aroused the true spirit of enquiry in his pupils and all who came within his sphere of influence. It is to such men as these that the greatness of a College is due. It is such men that act as exemplars and exert a permanent and elevating influence upon the tone, the ideals, and the atmosphere of a College.

What more need be said then, but that as Trinity College has for three centuries performed her work with credit, so let her continue that work unmolested. With her elder sisters she is an ally in waging war against the Philistines. If we cannot say of her, that Dublin has the charms of Oxford "whispering from her towers the sweet enchantment of the Middle Ages;" nor, as of Cambridge, of having sent out the greatest number of great men; we can at least claim for her that "dry intellectual temper" for which she has ever been renowned. Home of "orators and statesmen" and of intellectual gymnasts, the so-called "silent sister" has discharged her duties not in vain, whilst the debt the the world owes her cannot easily be estimated, nor can it ever be repaid.

Expenditure on Education: the Need for an Inquiry.

BY

W. M. J. WILLIAMS.

THE protest of East Ham against the burden of the Education Acts, the rate in that district having reached 2s. 9d. in the pound, has drawn attention to a grievance which is not confined to that, or even to a few districts. East Ham was one of the districts regarded as necessitous to which a special education grant had long been made; but that arrangement comes to an end gradually, being superseded by the Special Aid Grant under clause ten of the Act of 1902. So far as England and Wales were concerned, that Act would, so it was calculated, substitute a grant of £1,300,000 more than the small population grants of the Acts of 1870 and 1897, which together came to about £860,000 a year. But, of course, the Act of 1902 imposed on Local Authorities the maintenance of the schools hitherto called voluntary, and this charge was imposed on necessitous districts in common with others, with the result of an added local expense. Hence such a result as that which has led East Ham to record its protest; a protest which is shared by several other districts of a like nature, and suffering in a similar way.

This incident has only served to accentuate a grievance felt more widely still in regard to the cost of education. It is impossible to peruse county papers without finding complaints of the cost of education; the dissatisfaction is general, and not confined to necessitous places, though some of the grumbling comes, it is well known, from those who grudge every penny spent on education. Neglecting such an objection as this, there remains a wide-spread dissatisfaction regarding the cost of education, and all the more so that the Government has failed to deal with local taxation generally. When Parliament does review local taxation, the education rate will undoubtedly be reconsidered, and especially in relation to the government grants; many being of opinion that some portion at least of the rate should be transfered to the national taxes.

As there is no immediate prospect of a thorough reconsideration of local taxation, and the case is pressing, it is necessary to consider what might be done, and done early. This leads to the suggestion that Parliament should review the method on which grants in aid of educational objects are made. The following summary of the condition and position of such grants will be of interest in this connection.

These Government grants to educational objects are brought together for the most part in Part IV. of the Civil Service Estimates, and are of such a character and magnitude as to deserve serious attention. A short account of the progress of these grants will be suggestive. Let it be understood that they relate to the United Kingdom. In 1887-8 the total was £5,574,178; in 1894-5 £9,647,180; in 1904-5 £15,795.538; and for 1905-6 the estimates are £16,328,947. So in eighteen years these appropriations have nearly trebled; they have risen from £5,500,000 to £16,500,000 annually. In the meantime, the population has grown only about fifteen per cent. The total includes grants to institutions such as museums and galleries, but a very large proportion goes directly to formal educational work. Omitting museums and galleries, but including Colleges, out of the total grant of £16,328,947 for 1905-6 England and Wales take £12,849,848 ; Scotland £1,817,290; and Ireland £1,397,981, or a total of £16,064,819 for direct educational work. The appropriation of such a large sum is clearly worthy of the close attention of the House of Commons and the country.

Without entering upon controversial questions, it may be said that the Education Act, 1902, did nothing to clear up, or even to consider as a whole, the financial aspect of the Education Code. But after an experience of thirty-five years of the Education Acts, it should surely be possible to improve the system of grants. An examination of the basis of these grants will convince anyone that such an improvement is desirable, and the amount to which they have grown calls for an attempt to secure it. The code at present provides parliamentary grants in England and Wales, first on average attendance, and graduated from 15s. to 25s. per head according to the age of the children. Then there is the Fee Grant, a clumsy substitute for the payments of former days; there is the Special Grant Aid of the Act of 1902; grants per head for special subjects; and others again for deaf and dumb and defective and epileptic children. A reference to the estimates adds to this list a considerable number of avenues of grants and expenditure. Administration and Inspection are items of expenditure from the education vote which will raise questions about central and local duties. Other grants refer to pensions for teachers, to the training of teachers, including the very unsatisfactory question of training colleges, and grants to secondary, evening, and technical schools, with all that is suggested by these last. The grant of £197,000 to University Colleges, and to the Intermediate Schools in Wales, is also a subject requiring attention. These Colleges and Schools are now a vital part of our educational machinery, and a part which may be expected to expand still more. Similar questions might be stated respecting the method of aiding education in Scotland and Ireland. Though the volume of aid is much smaller, the questions raised might be stated in like manner, and the objectionable features of the grants arise from similar causes—the gradual development of a national system of Education.

That being the case it may be urged that the House of Commons should pay special attention to the Education Grants. The Select Committee of 1903 on National Expenditure reported that the state of the finances and public expenditure was such that the House would do well to alter its procedure, and in especial to appoint a

Committee on Estimates, which would examine and report upon the Estimates before the House was called to pronounce on the various votes submitted for adoption. Few who know how perfunctorily, how ineffectually, the House of Commons does its peculiar work of guarding and appropriating the people's treasure, would deny the need of such a change. That change is more needed daily, and especially since the adoption of the limited number of sittings devoted to the Estimates—a system which on one occasion permitted £66,000,000 to be voted, without examination and without discussion. What is said of the Estimates in gross can be said also of any section, and the result is that, at once, extravagance is encouraged on the one hand, and, on the other, objects which should receive closer attention and more encouragement are neglected. The fact that national expenditure has grown immensely of recent years should make for a reconsideration of all the chief heads, for it is probable that the achievement of most desirable objects will be postponed by the unwillingness, nay, the inability of the taxpayer to add to the total of the revenue. In short, it would be wise to examine and report on such an important branch as the National expenditure on education—whether the allocation of grants to various institutions might be improved.

Happily, a disposition to make such an enquiry is evinced by the authorities already; but to enable the reader to judge how the present large appropriation is divided, the following summary of the Education Estimates is given:—

EDUCATION, SCIENCE, AND ART.—TABLE A.

	1905-6.	1904-5.
United Kingdom and England:	£	£
Board of Education ...	12,652,548 ...	12,235,758
British Museum	170,501 ...	170,171
National Gallery	19,014 ...	17,065
National Portrait Gallery ...	5,619 ...	5,682
Wallace Collection ...	6,593 ...	6,539
Scientific Investigation, &c..	53,900 ...	46,407
Universities and Colleges, Great Britain, and Intermediate Education, Wales	197,300 ...	151,200
Scotland:		
Public Education	1,817,290 ...	1,753,724
National Gallery	5,405 ...	6,550
Ireland:		
Public Education	1,391,721 ...	1,393,625
Endowed School Commissioners	910 ...	935
National Gallery	3,096 ...	3,082
Queen's Colleges	5,050 ...	4,800
Total ...	£16,328,947	£15,795,538

Even this large total, an eighth of the public national expenditure, is not inclusive of all the appropriations to educational purposes. There are large items in the estimate for the Board of Agriculture for agricultural and dairy education, not to mention the cost of maintaining the Royal Botanic Gardens at Kew. The Scottish Universities too, which appear in the sums given above for Universities and Colleges for £42,000 only, receive no less than £30,000 more under the Local Taxation Account Act of 1892. All such items should be brought together in order to enable the House of Commons to review the appropriations made for various educational purposes.

Let attention be concentrated on that portion of the appropriation for 1905-6 under the head of *United Kingdom and England.* This amounts to no less than £13,105,475. How is this subdivided? For the purposes of this paper attention may be confined to three items, viz., Board of Education, Scientific Investigation, and Universities and Colleges, &c. The appropriations for the maintenance of the British Museum and the National Galleries of various names and characters may be omitted, though worthy of inclusion in any thorough inquiry into the subject.

Of the grants to scientific investigation amounting to £53,900 this year, the Royal Society (£15,500) and the Meteorological Office (£15,300) together appropriate £30,800. Both have received special departmental attention, and the latter's organisation and working has been the subject of inquiry this year. Still, the House of Commons, and still more the public, has but a hazy idea of the purposes to which these appropriations are made.

Coming to the huge sum of £12,652,548 which is required for 1905-6 under the head of *Board of Education,* the following table will be found instructive :—

TABLE B.

	1905-6. £	1906-7. £
A—Administration	169,322 ...	165,487
B—Inspection and Examination	259,919 ...	259,349
C—Grants to Public Elementary Schools, &c. ...	10,951,104 ...	10,688,400
D—Grants to Training of Teachers and Pupil Teachers, &c.	479,843 ...	385,795
E—Grants to Secondary Schools	242,500 ...	216,500
F—Expenditure on other added Schools and Classes ...	410,740 ...	381,145
G—Royal College of Science, London	22,723 ...	21,659
H—Royal College of Art ...	12,443 ...	12,196
I—Museums and Circulation	59,972 ...	61,041
K—Works and Furniture, South Kensington ...	28,861 ...	29,746
L—Geological Museum ...	3,755 ..	3,862
M—Geological Survey of the United Kingdom ...	17,833 ...	17,075
N—Committee on Solar Physics	1,801 ...	1,771
Gross Total ...	£12,660,816	£12,244,026

Such a table is real pemmican. Examination, however, yields some reflections not altogether comforting. The comparison between the two years reminds one of the steady growth of expenditure on education, but that growth would stand out much more prominently were we to take say the last twenty years. It is open to the most enthusiastic educationalists among us to say that when expenditure has leaped up thus by millions the time has come to take a full survey of that expenditure as a whole. Such a survey has not yet been ordered ; but in view of the probability of further developments of educational effort, the very interests of progress call for such an inquiry.

When we come closer and examine the various items, or rather subheads, of this large estimate, the necessity for inquiry becomes more clear. An inquiry, let it be said again, into the disposition of the large sum placed in the hands of the Board of Education, and not into our education policy, or any of the larger questions pertaining to it. The nation is, as a whole, in favour of a vigorous education department, and is prepared to pay for it, to pay a larger sum than at present, if necessary ; but it must be shown that the money is applied well and wisely, and that cannot be said now, deliberately, because the question as a whole has not been considered, at any rate by the House of Commons which is responsible for voting the money. Each subhead under Table A starts some important questions of administration. Administration, Inspection and Examination may be taken together, as they involve the working arrangement of the central office. Whitehall and South Kensington face one another here. True, since 1899, the Board of Education has appeared instead of the Department, and some attempt to co-ordinate their work has been made; but in taking up the Education Estimates as a whole, the organisation of the Board of Education would be reconsidered, not only as regards the South Kensington Branch, but also in relation to the growing establishments of the various local education authorities. Some very interesting evidence might be expected in this connection. Subheads C, D, E, and F are concerned with that work of which the public and Parliament think when education is referred to. It will doubtless be impossible to shut out from any inquiry into these various grants for education the question of the burden borne by the central and the local authorities respectively. Admittedly, when the Acts of 1902 and 1903 were passed, the financial provision made was only a patch on an old boot. The Royal Commission on Local Taxation has reported in favour of transferring a portion of the local burden to the central funds; but the question is not free from difficulty, both financial and other. And, certainly, were an inquiry made into our education grants this aspect of the matter would deserve further consideration.

The subdivisions of the items in this Estimate open up quite a chapter of details, all of which call for close attention. A mere enumeration of them will suggest that policy is in a tangle, and that a re-survey might result in straightening it out somewhat. Here are some of these subdivisions of grants: Pensions and gratuities to teachers; annual grants for public elementary schools, involving £5,681,964; grants in lieu of fees, reaching now £2,702,500; grants for education of blind, deaf, defective, and epileptic children, nearly £40,000;

aid-grants to local authorities under the Act of 1902, already £2,432,000; grants for the training of teachers, £309,843; building grants for Training Colleges, £10,000 in 1905-6 (a very doubtful item); grants for the education and training of pupil teachers, £160,000; grants for secondary schools and day classes in science and art, £242,500; grants for evening schools, £390,000; for scholarships, royal and local exhibitions and prizes in science and art classes, both in local schools and national Colleges, £18,780; and other smaller sums.

This enumeration of the subdivisions of these grants does more than suggest the wide field they cover. The field is undoubtedly large; let any reflect who has seen something of the London local department, or the work of our large county boroughs, and the endless ramifications of the work done by our county local authorities. But the enumeration does something more pertinent: it reminds us of the building up, gradually and conflictingly, of our public work in education, to call it a system might challenge contradiction; it points in particular to the essentially patchy nature of the grants by which the State's contribution to education is made. Is it possible to improve this method of granting State assistance? Popular opinion affirms that improvement is possible, and demands a change. Inspection of the various grants confirms the popular impression, though possibly for very different reasons. The inter-relation of the capitation, the fee, and the aid grants is ripe for attention. And does not the case of those districts which have long been found poor in proportion to population require a repair of the wrong done to them by the present unsatisfactory nature of the aid grant? Perhaps it may be found that it will be possible to reduce the confusion of grants, and to give relief to certain localities, by making the local contribution always and everywhere a certain poundage according to the proportion of population and assessment of property. That the intricate and confusing nature of these large grants is felt, and inevitably so, should be realised by the authorities, especially by those at the centre.

A review of this question could not be closed without a narrow inquiry into the position of the grants for training teachers. Especially urgent is the question of the Training Colleges. Not only is the sum involved considerable—some half a million—not only is the supply of teachers defective, and this is a matter crucial to the well-being of our national life, but it is also the most obscure of all our educational arrangements, the Training Colleges being yet, contrary to all sound policy, founded for the most part for denominational rather than for educational ends. Then it is clear that if the Act of 1902 left the finance of elementary education in a tangle, that of secondary education is a wilderness. To find the State making a grant of £242,000 for secondary schools, and £390,000 for evening schools of a nondescript educational character, is pitiable, at the same time leaving all the rest to the option of local authorities. It is to be hoped that these facts are enough to point to the unsatisfactory condition of such grants as a whole.

Of the other subdivisions of Table B it is unnecessary

to say anything here save of the Royal Colleges of Science and of Art. The other divisions are concerned with educational museums and similar work, and would no doubt come under the reference of a committee of inquiry. And of the Royal Colleges it is enough to say that the question is already under the eye of the Government through the report of the Committee on Technological Instruction. The suggested Committee on Education Estimates, however, could not avoid considering what the State might and would do in relation to this pressing question. It is clear that, however large private benefactions for this object may be, the call upon the State will be urgent, and will be permanent. The fact that the provision now made is inadequate in every respect would make this an important branch of the inquiry into Education Estimates.

The estimate for *Universities and Colleges in Great Britain, and for Intermediate Education in Wales* appears this year as follows:—

TABLE C.

	1905-6. £	1904-5. £
A. University of London	8,000	8,000
B. University of Manchester	2,000	2,000
C. University of Birmingham	2,000	2,000
D. University of Wales	4,000	4,000
E. University of Liverpool	2,000	2,000
F. University of Leeds	2,000	2,000
G. Scottish Universities	42,000	42,000
H. University Colleges, Gt. Britain	100,000	54,000

I. University Colleges, Wales   ...   12,000 ... 12,000
J. Intermediate Education, Wales:
  Examination and Inspection   1,200 ...   1,200
K. Do.: In aid of Schools ...   ...   22,100 ... 22,000

   Grand Total   ...   £197,300 £151,200

This estimate again opens up a great vista before the mind. ' The Universities here supported are by no means the only ones which might be considered by such a Committee of the House as should deal with this matter. The Scottish Universities receive not only the £42,000 recorded above, but as has been already said, they get £30,000 additionally from the Local Taxation Account. The Scottish people have been wise and persistent in getting money, and wise also in appropriating it to educational ends. As to the other items for Universities it should be observed that the grants now made are for those corporations as distinguished from Colleges of the same name and place. That is so both in England and in Wales. The remaining items call for some attention. The Colleges of Great Britain are now promised £100,000, an advance on the sum granted the previous year of £46,000. These have just been the subject of a departmental inquiry by a Committee consisting of Mr. Haldane, M.P.. Sir F. Mowatt, Mr. C. A. Cripps, M.P. and Dr. Woods, of Trinity College, Oxford, with Mr. H. Higgs as secretary. Their report gives an account of these grants to the modern University Colleges, beginning with £15,000 divided between eleven Colleges in 1889-90, which grant became £27,000 in 1903-4 to

D

fourteen Colleges, and £54,000 in the following year. In this financial year, 1905-6. the grant is £100,000.[1] The grants for intermediate education in Wales are now a special feature of these estimates; why they should remain special, and why England should not be organised in some such way are questions which occur instantly. In the £22,100 for Intermediate Schools, some ninety-six Schools in Wales and Monmouth participate. It is a very modest grant, but though small it is admitted officially and known to common observation as a potent stimulus in the remarkable educational development of the Principality, of which the foundation of the new University Buildings at Cardiff, recently laid by the Prince of Wales, is only one of the visible signs.

This compressed account of the grants for education may be deemed enough to support a demand for a parliamentary inquiry into the present disposition of these grants. It has been suggested that since 1870 we have gained a vast experience; and that hitherto our appropriations of money have been necessarily experimental; it has been pointed out that the Act of 1902 did not contain powers to aid any examination of the system of grants to education. That Act, and the whole of the code from 1876 downwards, have been concerned chiefly with elementary education; it is now more than time that secondary education should be dealt with formally and seriously. The co-ordination of all kinds of education, of which we have heard so much, will involve

---

1 For particulars as to allocation of this grant see No. IV. *University Review*, page 461.

a reconsideration of the State's support of education. This paper will have failed in its purpose if it does not make it clear that the present allocation of millions of public funds, not to speak of local rates, is confused and known to be wasteful, and that it will not bear the strain of the future demands which will be made upon the State. To safeguard the taxpayer by assuring him that good use is made of his substance, and to encourage him to continue his support ungrudgingly until our boys and girls, our young men and maidens, even our mature researchers, are as well equipped for life as those of any other nation, these are the reasons why such an inquiry is advocated. Such an inquiry should be conducted by the authority of Parliament, by Parliament directly, and not by a Departmental Committee, so that the votes may be recast and consolidated. The report which would ensue, it may be hoped, would do much to clear up dark portions of this question, to further both economy and efficiency, and would issue in a new Education Act which might bring weal to us all.

The Teaching of History in Elementary Schools.

BY

AN ELEMENTARY SCHOOL TEACHER.

OF all the subjects included in the curriculum of the modern English Elementary School, the subject of History is the one least understood by the Teachers, and the one most badly taught by them.

This arises from several causes, chief among which may be mentioned, first, the dislike most Elementary Teachers have for History; second, the bad training these Teachers have received in the subject; and third, the failure of the Board of Education to insist on an uniform course of study in Historical subjects for the Teachers, and an uniform course of instruction in History for the children in the schools under its control.

To take the causes in the order they appear above. It is a remarkable and a saddening experience to find how great is the dislike, in some cases the utter aversion, the majority of Elementary Teachers have for History, either as a subject of study or instruction.

On all hands they will confess to this, and take no shame to themselves while doing so; rather do they think they are voicing the sentiments of all sensible men. They conceive a contempt for the subject, and, as a result the weekly lesson in History suffers not only in its delivery, but also in its place in the school time table,—a fact which again affects its delivery.

In school time tables the History lesson is found in various places, according to the tastes of the Master of the School, or the demands made by other subjects upon the time devoted to secular instruction. Rarely, if ever, will it be found occupying a prominent place. It is a stop-gap subject, pushed in when all the other subjects have been provided for. The amount of good resulting from a lesson in History, delivered in the last half-hour of Friday afternoon, is better imagined than calculated.

The delivery of these weekly lessons in History needs improvement. The Teacher who grades his sums in Arithmetic, and proceeds from the known to the unknown in Science, and who would be horrified at the idea of teaching the Geography of a Continent before his listeners were conversant with Geographical terms, deems it a fit method of teaching History, if he dismember the story of Britain, seize upon one of the parts, and bestow on it a cold formal description, full of irrelevant details. If the period be lacking battles, so much the worse for its chances of accurate and sympathetic delineation.

It is obvious, of course, that the Assistant Teacher,

who does the major part of the actual teaching, cannot be blamed for this method.   He works according to a syllabus or scheme, drawn up by the Head Teacher.   Some of the History schemes in use in Elementary Schools are marvels of misdirected energy, and a slavish adherence to them (which is the part the Assistant is expected to perform), only results in a further waste of energy.

Another thing for which the Assistant is not responsible, but the evil of which affects him closely, is that the scheme of instruction in History, in use in one School, is unlike that in use in most other Elementary Schools. Examples abound, where, not even in Schools in the same town, and under the same Educational Committee, are the schemes uniform.

The Assistant may be exonerated from blame in the drawing up of these schemes, but there remains the blame undoubtedly his for faulty teaching,

The greatest defects noticeable in the teaching of History are, (1) too much "telling," (2) too many useless dates, (3) a narrow view of the subject, and (4) an utter absence of local colour.

It may not be out of place to offer here a few suggestions to indicate where these faults may be remedied. In the first place it is true that it is in the nature of the subject to require a certain amount of "telling"; but it is in calculating the quantity of it that the Elementary Teacher most signally fails. It is possible to teach the subject, with profit and pleasure to Teacher and children, by pursuing a method, in which the children are made to put themselves, their town, their district, hundreds of years back before the History lesson proper is approached. History should be made a personal matter, and the amount of "telling" necessary will decrease appreciably, the facts, when told, will be understood more fully, the significance or insignificance of personages in the story will be more accurately gauged.

Dates, which should be used sparingly, are often given in abundance, with no indication of their relative value. As the History taught in Elementary Schools can be, after all, only Elementary History, only those dates which possess an intrinsic value should be used. It is a physical impossibility for children to remember the mass of dates some teachers present to them; and if they were capable of performing the task they would have performed an achievement of doubtful value. Twenty dates, or thirty at the most, are quite sufficient for a child to know at the end of the normal Elementary School career. A selection should be made, not at haphazard, but of those dates which might be styled "landmarks of History."

Teachers, again, in Elementary Schools are very weak in the perspective of History. To them History means the History of England. It is, of course, the only History most of them know. They give the children a digest of their own insular knowledge, and in this way unfortunately foster the worst traits of the ordinary English—ignorance of, and contempt for, any other race but their own. This is done in spite of the many opportunities the teaching of English History holds out to the Teacher to widen the children's horizon. There have been events, of course, which have had no counterpart outside these islands; but on the other hand, many of our great Historical questions have had an European, and some a world-wide interest.

With regard to the absence of local colour, here again the Teacher fails to make the most of his opportunities. Our country is rich in historic remains, and every town and district boasts the possession of something which can be made the subject of an "object lesson in History."

The fatal result of this neglect of local colour is that the children fall into the habit of dissociating themselves from, or rather of never associating themselves with, the personages or events of the History lesson.

It is a fact to be regretted, but the truth of which cannot be controverted, that the children in an ordinary Elementary School, to whom the Norman Conquest has been taught, will be quite unable to say what became of the Normans of whom they have just learnt. They might even show by their looks that they considered the question an unfair one.

Very different indeed would have been their attitude if they had been taught to look upon William and Harold, and the other men who fought at Hastings, as their own relations. It needs no proof to show that in any class in any English School will be found descendants of the men who forced John to sign the Charter, or of the men who followed Drake round the world, of the men who charged with Cromwell, or of those who suffered with Charles.

The children are not taught the value of their birthright, that they possess a share in England's victories and defeats. England has been made what it is, and has attained the position it now occupies, by men and women to whom the children are related—the Conqueror's blood is still in the island, Cromwell's spirit is with us to-day, in the Teachers who teach and the children who listen, but the listeners do not know it, and the average Teacher fails to grasp the bare Educational utility of the fact. He rarely does more than scratch, and that very perfunctorily, the surface of our national history.

But for all these faults exhibited by the Teacher, the sins of omission and commission, the Teacher himself is not entirely responsible. He treats his little listeners as he was treated, and both Teacher and taught experience the effects of the intellectual cramp which overtakes people whose lives are spent in a narrow groove. They are like dwellers in a valley, who think that because they cannot see over the local hill there is nothing on the other side.

Supposing, for the sake of argument, that the teaching of History our Teachers receive in the days of their apprenticeship is a negligible quantity, and that what they receive in the Training College is to be their stock in trade; one would reasonably expect that this would be thorough and comprehensive.

Unfortunately it is not so. It differs only in being more extensive. The evil methods of the apprentices pursue the successful Scholarship candidate into the Training College, and he suffers from a re-hashing of old methods, old catchwords, old results. Perhaps the Education Department knew this when it decreed that the student, whose memory enabled him to answer the Scholarship History questions with credit, should be excused from studying the subject while in residence. Knowing what agonies the candidate has suffered in the past in the guise of instruction in History, and what lies in store for him, the experts at Whitehall say, in effect, "Do well, and have done with it."

Manifestly the Department has avoided its duty, in thus allowing so important a subject to be shelved, and has shirked the performance of an unpleasant task in not enforcing the teaching of *real* History to the students, to whom will be committed the training of generations of British citizens. The students, themselves, never having experienced the delights of *Historical* teaching, are indifferent, and those who fail to secure the desired exemption, are quite content to plod on in the same dull groove, preferably unaided.

An incident which happened in a Training College in the west of England, some few years ago, will illustrate this. When the students who had just entered the College for the normal two years of training had assembled for their first History lecture, the Master asked them if they desired him to deliver lectures in the subject, or to give them private lessons. He had very good reasons, (which need not appear here), for offering them the choice he had indicated. The Lecturer was known by the students to be a man of sound scholarship, a good teacher, and a master of English ; yet, strange to relate, his offer to deliver lectures, which would doubtless have repaid publication was rejected without a dissentient vote.

Among those students were some with a genuine love for the subject; but it is to be feared that the majority looked upon History in the same light as the Head Master of a certain Elementary School, who gave it as his opinion, that "it's a pity these people you read of in history books did not die sooner."

It has been said that History makes a man wise, and that History repeats itself; more Historical Teaching of a better quality is needed both in our Training Colleges and in our Elementary Schools, if the rising generation is to derive any wisdom or guidance from this branch of study.

J. TURNER.

Memorial Notices.

"Quique sui memores alios fecere merendo."

CHRISTOPHER HEATH, F.R.C.S.

Emeritus Professor of Clinical Surgery in University College, London.

Many generations of London medical students will have heard, with deep regret, of the sudden death on the 8th of August of Mr. Christopher Heath, Emeritus Professor of Clinical Surgery in University College, London, and Consulting Surgeon to University College Hospital.

Born in London in 1835, Mr. Heath was educated at King's College School, and received his medical training at King's College and King's College Hospital. At the time of the Crimean War, Mr. Heath, at the age of twenty, joined the Baltic Fleet and was awarded a medal for his services. In the following year, 1855, he was appointed Demonstrator in Anatomy, at Westminister Hospital, and six years later he became Lecturer in that subject. It was in 1866 that he first became connected with University College Hospital by accepting the positions of Assistant Surgeon and Teacher in Operative Surgery. In 1871 he became Surgeon to the Hospital, and on the

THE LATE MR. CHRISTOPHER HEATH,
Emeritus Professor of Clinical Surgery in University College, London.

retirement of Sir John Erichsen, in 1875, he was appointed Holme Professor of Clinical Surgery in University College, a position he filled with eminent ability and success until his retirement in 1900. Mr. Heath was the author of a number of notable text books on surgery, chief among which may be mentioned his " Practical Anatomy," " Minor Surgery," and " Students' Guide to Surgical Diagnosis." He was a prominent member of the Royal College of Surgeons, and in 1895 became President of that body. Mr. Heath had acted as an Examiner in Surgery for the Universities of Cambridge, Durham, and London.

On the occasion of his visit to the United States of America, in 1897, for the purpose of delivering the Lane Medical Lectures at the Cooper Medical College, in San Francisco, the McGill University of Montreal conferred upon him the Honorary Degree of LL.D.

By his death the surgical world has lost a practical and impressive teacher, a brilliant operator, and a clear and expressive writer. It will be difficult to fill the position left vacant by his death.

AUGUSTUS SAMUEL WILKINS, M.A. (LONDON).

Professor of Classical Literature in the University of Manchester.

By the death of Dr. A. S. Wilkins, the University of Manchester has lost a devoted friend and one of its most distinguished professors. A long illness, borne with characteristic fortitude, terminated fatally at Llandrillo-yn-Rhos, North Wales, on the 26th of July. Professor Wilkins was born in 1843, and was educated at Bishop Stortford School, and afterwards at University College, London, and St. John's College, Cambridge, where he gained five University Prizes, and came out fifth in the first class of the Classical Tripos, and served a term as President of the Union. As a staunch Nonconformist however, Dr. Wilkins was prevented from obtaining a Fellowship of his College—the natural reward of his brilliant University career. It is good to know that he was one of the last to suffer in this way. In 1869, at the age of 26, he was appointed Professor of Latin in the Owens College, which at that time was situated in Quay Street, Manchester. Here his abilities as a teacher and scholar were soon recognised, and from the first he became one of the most valued members of the College staff. Professor Wilkins devoted himself with energy to serve the growing educational needs of Manchester, and in all the great developments of the Owens College he took an active part. Among his many valued contributions to literature may be specially mentioned his admirable edition of Cicero's "De Oratore." Honorary degrees were conferred upon him by the Universities of St. Andrews, Cambridge, and Dublin, and he was also elected an Honorary Fellow of University College, London.

To all who have been his pupils, the death of Dr. Wilkins will be accompanied by a keen sense of personal loss. A colleague has said of him " He had the widest sympathy with every good cause. Whether it was that

THE LATE DR. A. S. WILKINS,
Professor of Classical Literature in the University of Manchester.

which he believed to be right politically or in the religious world or in the academic world—all alike had his sympathy. He will live in the memory of many of his old students as one who directed their thoughts with regard to literary matters, improved their literary tastes, and gave them a keener insight into what accurate scholarship ought to be. Everyone who has worked with him will feel that they never could have had a more truly loyal colleague or a better friend."

British University Students' Congress, 1905.

The first British University Students' Congress was held in London, from June 28th to July 1st, under the auspices of the newly-formed London University Students' Representative Council. The Congress was attended by representative students from every University in the United Kingdom, with the exception only of the Universities of Oxford and Cambridge, these, unfortunately, having no organisations representative of the general body of their under-graduates. The Union Societies of both Universities, however, had been asked to send representatives to the Congress, but neither felt able to accept the invitation in view of their non-representative character. It was the cause of great regret to the London University S.R.C., and to the Congress, that the undergraduates of Oxford and Cambridge were not represented on this occasion.

Five representatives had been invited from each University, but owing to the great distance from London of many of the Universities it had not been possible for all to send the full number of delegates. Excluding the Chairman and Secretary of the Congress, who were *ex-officio* members, there were sixty-three delegates representing in all, fifteen Universities.

The Congress opened on Wednesday, June 28th. The delegates were received in the General Library at University College, London, by Sir Arthur W. Rücker, F.R.S. (Principal of the University of London), the Right Hon. Lord Reay, G.C.S.I. (President of University College, London), and Dr. T. Gregory Foster, M.A. (Principal of University College, London). Lady Rücker and Mrs. Gregory Foster kindly assisted in the reception.

The meetings of the Congress were held in the Botanical Theatre at University College. Mr. W. L. Scott (President of the London University Students' Representative Council and of the Union Society of University College) occupied the chair.

During the four meetings of the Congress the following matters were brought forward for discussion:—

From a Photo

by Gunn & Co., Richmond.

MEMBERS OF THE BRITISH UNIVERSITY STUDENTS' CONGRESS, 1905.

Mr. J. I. Macpherson (Edinburgh) moved, and Mr. H. J. Norman (Edinburgh) seconded, a resolution:

"That any system of education which fails to provide for physical as well as mental development is necessarily incomplete."

Mr. Napier (Glasgow) proposed the addition of the words:

"And that representations be made to the University authorities urging them to organise along practical lines adequate means of physical exercise for students."

The resolution thus amended was carried.

Mr. A. R. Skemp (Manchester) moved:

"That in the opinion of this Congress, University employment registers fulfil a function of very great importance both to members of the University and to the community generally, and that this Congress strongly approves the establishment and development of such registers."

This was seconded by Mr. A. C. Ward (Leeds), and carried unanimously. It was decided to send a copy of the resolution to the registrars of all the Universities and Colleges of the United Kingdom.

Miss M. A. Kelly (Bedford College, London) moved a resolution approving the system of State support for Universities, and expressing an opinion that the adoption in this country of such a system would aid the cause of education. Mr. G. T. Reid (London School of Economics) seconded the resolution, which was carried by a small majority.

The following resolution was proposed by Miss B. Butler (Westfield College, London), and seconded by Mr. R. J. McAlpine (Liverpool), and carried unanimously:

"That wherever practicable the work done by a student at one University should entitle him to an equivalent standing at any other University."

An interesting discussion was held on a resolution, proposed by Mr. H. P. Pickerill (Birmingham), and seconded by Mr. W. C. Moston (Birmingham):

"That this Congress approves, and will take steps to establish, the annual holding of Inter-University Sports and Athletics."

The debate gave rise to a scheme for the formation of an Inter-University Athletic Union, whose duties would be to get together athletic teams composed of the best players from all the Universities of the Kingdom. The resolution was agreed to, and a Sub-committee was appointed to arrange an Inter-University Athletic Meeting to be held next year.

E

Mr. J. Forbes Watson (Edinburgh) moved, and Mr. H. V. Rabagliati (Edinburgh) seconded a resolution, which was carried:

"That in view of the work done by, and the present position of, the International Committee of the University of Edinburgh, and considering the increasing importance of study in foreign Universities, this Congress do appoint a representative committee to examine into the possibility of extending the application of that committee's organisation to the other Universities of the United Kingdom."

The committee asked for in this resolution was forthwith elected, and was composed of the Secretaries of the students' representative organisations of the various Universities.

In addition to the foregoing resolutions the following reports of Committees appointed at the English and Welsh Inter-Universities' Students' Congress, held last year in Manchester, were considered and adopted:—

1. The Report of the Residential Halls Committee was presented by the Secretary, Mr. A. C. Ward (Leeds). The report showed that a considerable amount of work had been done in collecting information as to the residential system of fourteen British Universities and Colleges, eleven American Universities and four Australian Universities.

2. The Report of the Inter-University Magazine Committee was considered at some length, and finally adopted.

3. The Report of the Committee appointed to consider the voting and other clauses in the constitution and laws of the Congress, was dealt with in sections. Clauses incorporating the Scottish and Irish Universities and Colleges in the constitution were adopted. It was decided that voting at meetings of the Congress should be on the basis that each delegate is entitled to one vote. It was agreed that in future each University should be allowed to send not more than three representatives.

The Report of the British Students' Song Book Committee, presented by the Secretary, Mr. C. G. Dehn (late of Manchester), stated that negotiations had been entered into with the Scottish Students' Song Book Company with a view to co-operation.

The following Sub-Committees have been appointed by the Congress, and will report on the results of their work to the next year's Congress:—

1. *The Inter-University Magazine Committee.* This Committee will act as a means of communication between the directors of the Magazine Company and the annual Congress.

2. *Residential Halls Committee.* This Committee will consider the various schemes outlined in the report of last year's Committee

on this subject, and will endeavour to formulate a definite scheme with a view to recommending its adoption to the authorities of the Universities.

3. *Employment Registers Committee.* An inquiry will be made into existing forms of employment registers, and the Committee will endeavour to formulate a scheme for Inter-University connection between the various registers.

4. *Inter-University Athletics Committee.* This Committee will arrange for Inter-University Sports to be held next year, provided that at least ten Universities are willing to render both athletic and financial assistance. If these Sports can be arranged, the Guild of Undergraduates of the University of Birmingham has very kindly invited the Universities to meet at Birmingham.

5. *British Students' Song Book Committee* will endeavour to complete some scheme for the production of a British Students' Song Book, in co-operation, if possible, with the Scottish Students' Song Book Company.

6. *Inter-University Volunteers Committee.* This Committee will consider the best means to increase the numbers of the various University Volunteer Corps, and will discuss the possibility of the formation of an Inter-University Volunteer Battalion.

7. *A Committee for the Encouragement of Physical Training* Will endeavour to devise some scheme whereby greater facilities may be given to University students for physical training, with a view to such scheme being placed before the authorities of the Universities, if approved of by the Congress.

8. *A Committee for the Consideration of the Constitution and Laws of the Congress.* To consider the constitution and laws as they stand at present, and to suggest any alterations and additions that may be necessary.

During their visit to London the delegates were entertained at various social functions, nearly all of which had been arranged in honour of the Congress. The entertainments included a Garden Party at the Royal Holloway College, Conversaziones at the University of London, University College, and King's College, a River Party on the Thames at Maidenhead, a Smoking Concert at the Holborn Restaurant, and an entertainment for women delegates in the Botanical Gardens.

In the limited space of a magazine article it is only possible to give a very brief account of a Congress whose meetings extended over four days. A full account of the proceedings, however, will be published in the official report, which, it is hoped, will be ready early in October.

B. B. W.

The Higher Education of Working Men.

The objects of the Association are to promote the Higher Education of Working Men primarily by the Extension of University Teaching, also (a) by the assistance of all working class efforts of a specfically educational character, (b) by the development of an efficient School Continuation System.

Under the auspices of the Association to Promote the Higher Education of Working Men an important Conference was held in the Examination Schools, at Oxford, on August 12th. The meeting was attended by over two hundred representatives of trade unions, co-operative societies, education authorities, and branches of the Association. The Dean of Christ Church, who presided over the Conference, in the course of his opening speech, said it seemed to him, if this Association were to continue in the path of success which it had taken already and the Universities were to be brought into contact with it, that they would be spreading through the nation an ideal of what learning ought to be, and in one particular respect an ideal of what method ought to be. A cordial welcome to Oxford was extended to the Conference by Mr. J. A. R. Marriott, the Secretary to the University Extension Delegacy.

The chief business of the meeting was the discussion of the following important resolution, which was proposed by the Bishop of Hereford:—

"That this Conference, representative of co-operative societies, trade unions, and educational organisations, having regard to the educational wastage consequent upon young people of both sexes either neglecting or being prevented by conditions of employment from utilising the facilities afforded by education authorities for instruction in the evening, urges the Board of Education to ascertain from the local education authorities how far and under what conditions employers and employed, in their respective areas, would welcome legislation having for its ultimate object compulsory attendance at evening schools."

In the course of his speech the Bishop said that the present truncated system of popular education involved an enormous amount of waste; he felt that the avoidance of this waste and the beginning of a wiser public action with regard to the well-being of the nation, was to be found in the continuous education of the people. He was sure that the mass of the people were not nearly so well educated as they ought to be and had a claim to be. Every local education authority should be given the power to make education continuous up to the age of seventeen.

Councillor Emes, of Bristol, in seconding the resolution, said that in the present eagerness for educational reform there seemed to be a danger of overloading the curriculum without obtaining a corresponding educational benefit. Continuation schools, in his opinion, were absolutely necessary, and attendance thereat should be made compulsory.

The Earl of Crewe hoped that the Government might be induced to institute a local option in the matter, so that districts which really had higher education at heart might be able to set such an example as would shame the more backward districts into following them.

Special attention was paid by the meeting to the speech of Professor Michael E. Sadler. In supporting the resolution, Professor Sadler said that it was his duty last year to ascertain where England stood comparatively in regard to the attendance at evening continuation schools, and to his surprise, he found that only one country in Europe—Switzerland—could show a better attendance at continuation schools than England and Wales, although our system was entirely voluntary. He would like to see the Board of Education include a list of the great firms which already had required attendance at evening schools as a condition of apprenticeship. He believed they would never get compulsory continuation schools until they laid upon employers of labour the statutory duty of securing a technical and civic education for their young workpeople. He would like to see joint committees of employers and trade unions and educational students, so that when compulsory schools were being established they might have some more definite idea of what they meant to teach. The ideal in education should be that the man who learned was learning, not in order simply to get more money or advance from class to class, but to make himself of more service to his country.

The resolution was carried, there being but two dissentients.

Mr. W. Crooks, M.P., moved the second resolution:—

> "That this Conference, having regard to the immediate necessity for strengthening the instruction, already available in the evenings, for men and women engaged during the day, urges that the evening lectures, given under the direction of the University Extension authorities, and the reading circles organised by the National Home Reading Union, be co-ordinated with each other and with the evening classes now being offered by the local education authorities."

In the course of a characteristic speech, Mr. Crooks spoke of the poorer section of the working classes which looks upon education as a positive disadvantage and upon educationists with suspicion. He asked that there should be more opportunities of acquiring knowledge, and he felt that these could be obtained through evening continuation schools.

After an interesting discussion, in which the Secretaries of the Rochdale and the Reading branches of the Association spoke of the success which had attended the work of the Association in their districts, the resolution was put to the vote, and unanimously carried.

It may be said that the Conference was, from all points of view, a complete success. It was a serious contribution to the difficult problem of working class education. The Conference was the first held by the Association for the discussion of definite educational objects, and its success is felt to be all the more encouraging.

Foreign University News.

AUSTRIA—HUNGARY

(From a Private Correspondent.)

AUSTRIA.

Vienna.

At last the strenuous efforts of the Italian members of the Austrian Parliament have been rewarded with success, for the Government has promised to grant permission for the establishment of an Italian College, so earnestly desired by the Italian population throughout Austria. The Minister of Public Instruction, Herr Von Hartl, has declared that the Government is not averse as a matter of principle to the establishment of new Colleges, but it would prefer to see the extension of existing Universities not only on financial grounds, but also because of the serious difficulties that have to be faced in providing capable teaching staffs for the new institutions. In the present case, however, the Government has no intention of objecting to the establishment of an University in which the Italian language is exclusively used, for it recognises the right to higher education possessed by the Italian-speaking population of Austria. The Italian members of Parliament are anxious to see Trieste as the seat of the University, contending that its large number of educational institutions, libraries and hospitals, its prosperous inland and maritime trade, and its large Italian population render its choice especially suitable. It is said, however, that the Slavonian population of the district does not welcome the proposal.

The Federation of Private Professors *(Privatdozenten)* of the Austrian Universities has instituted a prize of 300 crowns for an essay on the " Private and Public Position of University Professors " (having reference more especially to the Colleges of Germany and Austria). The author is allowed the fullest latitude in dealing with the subject. In making the award particular stress will be laid on the most complete treatment of the question, and on the comparisons made with the position of professors in educational institutions in other countries.

Following the annual custom, two special vacation courses in all the different branches of Medicine are being held in the months of August and September in the Faculty of Medicine of the University of Vienna.

Prof. Hermann Nothnagel.

Widespread regret has been caused by the recent death of the world famous Dr. Hermann Nothnagel, Professor of Pathology and Clinical Medicine in the University of Vienna. He was born in 1841 in Braudenburg, Germany, and studied under favourable conditions in Berlin and Königsberg at a time when the science of medicine was making rapid strides in the branch of Pathological Anatomy and Psychology—an advance which was very largely due to the combined efforts of Virchow, Johannes Müller, and Rokitausky. Nothnagel having acted for a while as Profesor at Jena, was called to Vienna in 1882. It was here that he acquired the reputation of being one of the best of clinical teachers, introducing to many generations of medical students the well-tried methods of his teacher Traube. He was an excellent speaker, both on the public platform and in the lecture room. Many of his vigorous sayings will be long remembered, such as, for example, his aphorism " Only a good man can be a good doctor." He was an enthusiastic disciplinarian, and was possessed by a keen sense of duty. He was an outspoken opponent to the study of medicine by women, and would never allow a woman student to enter his lecture room. Professor Nothnagel's contributions to medical literature are of the greatest value, and not a few may be considered classics. He held the position of Imperial Counsel, and was a member of the Austrian Upper House. He was correspondent of the Academy of Sciences, and held many other high distinctions.

Salzburg.

A new district has been formally constituted here for University training. Dr. Povinelli has been appointed Chairman, and Dr. von Hattingberg, Deputy-Chairman.

The University courses will start at the beginning of September, and will include 19 courses of lectures and two scientific excursions.

Great regret has been caused by the recent death of Herr Dr. Richard Schuster.

Prague.

In the German University the number of students has been on the increase during the past few years. One hundred and thirty-three candidates have recently graduated in the following faculties: Divinity, 3 ; Law, 81 ; Medicine, 39 ; Philosophy, 10.

THE LATE DR. HERMANN NOTHNAGEL,
Professor of Pathology in the University of Vienna.

HUNGARY.

Agram.

The great resentment caused by the order prohibiting the use of the University tricolour has recently manifested itself again. The order has been in force since 1895, and the students of the University are organising a vigorous campaign in favour of its immediate withdrawal.

The recently appointed Professor Greksa has been prevented by the demonstrations of the Croatian students from giving his introductory lecture.

FRANCE

Paris.

The following information as to the conditions of residence of foreign students in Paris has been received from the Secretary of the Bureau des Renseignements of the University of Paris.

In pursuance of the decree of 1888 a foreigner wishing to reside in France is required, within a fortnight after his arrival, to declare to the authorities:—

1. His surname and Christian name.
2. His nationality.
3. His place and date of birth.
4. Last place of residence.
5. His standing or means of livelihood.
6. If married, the name, age, and nationality of his wife, as well as of his children under age.

If he settles in Paris or the immediate neighbourhood, he must make his declaration at the Prefect's; if in the provinces, at the Mayor's. Vouchers and papers are necessary. If he changes his abode, he must declare the fact to the Prefect or Mayor, as the case may be.

The student coming from abroad with a view to attending the University lectures will find all difficulties removed by one or other of the following institutions and associations:—

INQUIRY OFFICE OF THE UNIVERSITY OF PARIS.

A special service has been started at the Sorbonne by the City of Paris and the University, particularly with a view to assisting foreigners. It centralises and publishes all information relative to the best means of study to be found at Paris: lectures, classes, laboratories, museums, libraries, etc. This information has been collected and classified, and states the conditions of admission, dates and hours of classes, etc.

The office, directed by Dr. Blondel, is situated at the junction of the galleries of Science and Sorbon (entrance in the Rue des Ecoles).

It is open to visitors from 10 to 12 and 2 to 5 every week-day all the year round (except on general holidays).

Interpreters are attached to this office.

All correspondence should be addressed to Monsieur le Directeur du bureau des Renseignements de la Sorbonne, Paris.

INQUIRY OFFICE (41, rue Gay-Lussac).

This office has been opened at the Musée Pédagogique. One of its objects is to bring into closer connection teaching institutions in France and abroad.

Foreign Universities are supplied with information concerning organisation of studies, despatch of French students abroad, etc. The office is in constant communication with the teaching staffs in French Universities and with the members of the committees formed to promote the interest of foreign students in France. All correspondence should be addressed to the Director of the Musée Pédagogique (inquiry office), rue Gay-Lussac, 41, Paris.

COMMITTEE OF PATRONAGE FOR FOREIGN STUDENTS.

This Committee aims at giving assistance to foreign students, by furnishing them with all useful information whether bearing on their studies or their accommodation. A subsidy voted annually by the French Parliament enables the Committee to grant a foreign student recommended by his Government a scholarship of 200—350 francs, to be employed solely in the payment of University fees.

The Committee has prevailed upon the French steamship lines to grant a reduction of 30 per cent. to students coming to attend classes in France. The same reduction is allowed on the return voyage.

Every day (except Friday) between 5 and 6 p.m., in the committee rooms at the Sorbonne, a Secretary can be consulted by students wishing to obtain precise information as to the scholastic advantages offered by different institutions.

FRANCO-SCOTTISH ASSOCIATION.

This is divided into two sections—one French and the other Scottish. Frenchmen and Scotsmen and everyone who would take interest in the work of the Society can be admitted.

The object of this institution is to bring into closer connection the Universities of France and of Scotland, in encouraging mutually the sojourn of their students, to facilitate the historical studies of the relations between France and Scotland, and to institute alternate meetings in those countries.

GENERAL ASSOCIATION OF PARISIAN STUDENTS (43, rue des Ecoles).

Founded in 1884, its object is (1) to facilitate the conditions of the material life of the student; (2) to assure him intellectual and moral support. It gives him material help by offering him a comfortable place where he may obtain books, read the papers, and talk with friends. He obtains reductions in the prices of books, magazines, theatres, and even in the principal necessities of life. It helps him more directly in procuring for him lessons if he wishes. It offers him intellectual and moral support by its organisation in different sections (sections of law, medicine, letters, sciences, chemistry, etc.).

In this way the new member finds himself at once in relation with comrades of his Faculty or School. Every section has its library. The Association is open from 8 a.m. to 12 p.m.

The Association is independent of any political or religious party. Every student regularly inscribed in any Faculty or School of Paris is admitted to the Association. The subscription is 18 francs.

UNIVERSITY HALL (95, boulevard Saint-Michel).

University Hall is a hostel for French and foreign students, teachers, and professors which affords not only board and lodging but also surroundings favourable to the pursuit of studies, and means of introduction to the intellectual life of Paris. The residents are at liberty to invite their friends and to make arrangements for common profit and entertainment. No one is admitted without having been first proposed and seconded by two residents. A large library forms the common hall. Mealtimes are fixed by the residents. References may be obtained from well-known literary men in France and abroad. Lessons in French may be obtained in University Hall by the residents.

INTERNATIONAL GUILD (6, rue de la Sorbonne).

The International Guild gives students of all nationalities hints and advice on the conduct of their studies and the accommodation to be found in Paris. The foreign section familiarises newly-arrived students with the French language and literature which enables them to attend, from the first, the lectures and lessons of the Sorbonne and the Ecole des Hautes Etudes. To this end the Guild has opened for the benefit of foreigners classes devoted to the study of French pronunciation, comparative grammar, literature and history.

THE UNITED STATES OF AMERICA.

(The following information has been taken by kind permission from "The Michigan Alumnus" and "The Yale Alumni Weekly.")

Yale.

CONFERMENT OF YALE DEGREES.

Professor Williston Walker was the advocate of the candidates for the Yale Honorary Degrees at the Commencement exercises, June 28th. The candidates were, as usual, seated on the platform, and having been presented by Professor Walker, and having received the Degree with a few appropriate words from the President, were hooded by Professor John C. Schwab and Professor Samuel S. Sanford. The occasion was notable not only on account of the presence of many distinguished Americans, but because of the presence of Sir Edward Elgar, who received the honorary degree of Doctor of Music. At this ceremony Yale conferred fourteen honorary degrees, as follows:—

MASTERS OF ARTS.

Henry Waters Taft, a graduate of the University in 1880, a lawyer of the New York bar, and member of the New York Board of Education and a trustee of the College of the City of New York.

Alfred Ernest Stearns, teacher and administrator, Principal of Phillip's Academy, an American preparatory school of high importance and distinguished history.

Samuel Waldron Lambert, a graduate of Yale, recently appointed Dean of the Medical Faculty of Columbia University.

Huber Gray Buehler, the head of the Hotchkiss School at Lakeville, a great preparatory school closely linked to Yale University.

James Wallace Pinchot, principal founder of the Forest School of Yale University.

DOCTORS OF DIVINITY.

Frederic William Keator, a graduate of Yale, recently oppointed Protestant Episcopal Bishop of Olympia.

John Franklin Genung, a graduate of the University of Leipzig and now Professor of English Literature in Amherst College.

DOCTORS OF SCIENCE.

Theodore William Richards, Professor of Chemistry in the University of Harvard.

George Ellery Hale, Director of the Yerkes Observatory and Professor of Astrophysics in the University of Chicago.

DOCTOR OF MUSIC.

In presenting Sir Edward Elgar for the degree of Doctor of Music, Professor Walker said: "A composer of musical creations of the highest merit, honoured for his genius and his achievements as a master of the oratorio . . . . marked in his home-land by ample scholastic recognition and by the appreciation of his Sovereign, and commanding the homage of the musicians of Germany, of France, and of America, he is heartily welcome among us. We felicitate ourselves on his presence with us at this anniversary of this venerable University, and see in it a fresh evidence of the union in sympathy and mutual recognition that is knitting together by bonds of ever-increasing closeness the two great English-speaking nations. We would ask that Yale do her part to express the admiration of America for his talents and his services by conferring upon Sir Edward Elgar the degree of Doctor of Music, already his by the gift of English Universities, and thus do herself the honour of enrolling him among her graduates."

DOCTORS OF LAWS.

Lebaron Bradford Colt, now serving as one of the Presiding Justices of the United States Court of Appeals.

Abraham Jacobi, born in Germany, a student at the Universities Greifswald, Göttingen, and Bonn; a specialist in the diseases of children, and a writer of authority upon medical practice.

Edward Anderson Alderman, recently elected first President of the University of Virginia.

Augustus St. Gaudens, the famous sculptor, trained in the National Academy of Design and in the Ecole des Beaux Arts of Paris.

AN IMPORTANT CHANGE IN THE CORPORATION OF YALE UNIVERSITY.

"The change in the membership of the Corporation of Yale University made on June 28th, 1905, is very significant in several ways.

The first charter required the members to be "ministers of the Gospel inhabiting within this Colony, and above the age of forty years." The charter of 1745, which by common consent is regarded as the law of the University, omits the clerical phrase, and names the Corporation as an "Incorporate Society, and Body Corporate and Politic, and shall hereafter be called and known by the name of the President and Fellows of Yale College in New Haven, and that by the same name they and their successors shall, and may have perpetual succession and shall and may be Persons in the Law capable to plead and be impleaded, et cetera."

It is now regarded that whatever was intended by the first charter as to the continuance of the clerical element, it having been omitted in the charter of 1745, a free course is left open as to the composition of the body. The omission of the clerical element may not have been anticipated, but it was not forbidden. What lay in the minds of the second generation of founders cannot be guessed, but they may have had a clear sense of the wisdom of not laying " a dead man's hand " on an institution founded for all generations.

Hence, two years ago, when a vacancy occurred, it was filled not by a minister from " within this Colony," as the first charter required, but by the choice of Rev. Dr. Jefferson from New York. The departure from the " Colony " of Connecticut not having been challenged, it is reasonably to be expected that the change from the ministry to the layman will be received without opposition, since one is not more inhibited than the other.

In the present election, following the resignation of Rev. Dr. Munger, the vacancy is filled by Mr. Payson Merrill, a member of the Bar of New York. This event is of special significance as a precursor of a series of like events and others of even wider importance. It reveals a change of public sentiment and especially that of the University in regard to the order of the past. There is a growing expectation and demand that the Corporation shall not always continue to be made up largely of Congregational ministers in Connecticut.

The reasons for this are:—

First. That it keeps the University under the control of one of several denominations to which it sustains equally vital relations of interest and support. It is felt that what was wise and necessary two hundred years ago when the Congregational churches were a civic standing order, and were the only possible founders of a college, has entirely passed away on account of radical changes both in Church and State. These changes are so thoroughly understood by the public that it requires corresponding changes in the governing body.

Second. The University at its organisation was virtually a school of theology; it is that no longer, but an institution for general learning. The incongruity of such an institution being under the control of a fixed clerical majority is regarded with impatience by the American mind, yet without antagonism to the clerical element or influence. It is simply impatience with what is outworn and may block a better order."

UNIVERSITY NEWS AND NOTES.

During Commemoration Week the Yale Corporation received from Professor Samuel S. Sanford a unique gift in the shape of a collar and jewel, so-called, to be worn by Presidents of Yale, as a badge of office, on official occasions of the University. President Hadley wore it for the first time on Commencement Day, June 28th. The collar is made of enamel, gold, silver and precious stones. There are twenty links in the collar, of which ten are gold shields surrounded by laurel wreaths of silver gilt. Six of the shields bear emblems of the different subjects of Yale training—such as theology, law, mathematics, literature and the arts. Four of the shields are left vacant for the record of the future. The collar is joined at the bottom by a large and very beautiful sapphire with radiating rays of diamonds, representing Yale's motto of Truth and Light. Depending from this by a small medallion is the jewel, so-called, about three inches wide by four long. Its chief feature is a seal, combining the seals of Yale, the City, the State and the Nation, done in white and blue enamel and surrounded by sapphires. Around the seal, in letters of blue enamel, are the words: "Honos Alit Artes."

The Yale Summer School opened officially on July 6th, but registration continued during several days later. The total registration numbers about 250 students, drawn from a large region that includes 26 States of the Union, Canada and the Philippine Islands. About nine-tenths of the students are women and a very large proportion are teachers. The courses attracting respectively the largest number of students are History, Psychology, English and Teaching.

Returns from all the examinations show that 454 candidates have thus far taken the final entrance examinations for the Academic Department as compared with 433 last year, corresponding figures for preliminary examinations being 373 and 433. In the Scientific School examinations there is a small gain in finals and a loss in the preliminaries.

By the strenuous efforts of the Professors of the Yale Divinity School, the deficit of $30,000, accumulated in the last four years, has been cleared away.

The racing on the Thames River between representative crews of Yale and Harvard resulted in Yale winning the eight-oared race and Harvard winning the four-oared race and the freshman eight-oared race. In the presence of upwards of twelve thousand people, the Yale Baseball Nine won a brilliant victory over the Harvard team by 7 runs to 2.

President Hadley states that Yale has received a gift of one

million dollars from John D. Rockefeller. The only condition of the
gift is that it be added to the permanent revenue producing funds
of the University, while its income is to be used as the President and
Fellows may see fit. Graduates and friends of the University have
also given sums in different amounts to the total of another million
dollars. This announcement of these generous and welcome gifts
has given great delight to Yale *alumni*.

Harvard.

HONORARY DEGREES.

Harvard conferred the following seven Honorary Degrees at her
Commencement exercises in June:—

MASTER OF ARTS.

Frederick Pike Stearns, Chief Engineer of the Metropolitan Water
and Sewerage Board.

DOCTOR OF SCIENCE.

James Homer Wright, Pathologist, Teacher and Investigator.

DOCTORS OF LAWS.

Henry Marion Howe, Professor of Metallurgy in Columbia
University.

Reginald Heber Fitz, a teacher of Pathological Anatomy.

James Burrill Angell, for thirty-three years President of the
University of Michigan.

Edward Douglas White, United States Senator.

William Howard Taft, Teacher of Law, Judge, President of the
Philippine Commission, and Secretary of State for War.

Michigan.

A SOCIOLOGICAL CLUB.

A society for the study of social questions has just been organised
among the advanced students at the University of Michigan under
the name of "The Sociological Club." It is a continuation of the
Chicago Commons Committee, which has hitherto been subordinate
to the Students' Christian Association.

Its chief function will be the maintenance of an annual residence
scholarship at the Chicago Commons for the purpose of sociological
study. The holder of the scholarship this year has been Miss Anne
E. Huber, of Detroit, a member of the senior class, and her report
was on the subject: "The Recreations of Working Girls." Chester
S. Carney has recently been appointed to the scholarship for next
year.

Appointment to this scholarship is made by a Faculty Committee composed of Professors Henry C. Adams, Charles H. Cooley, and Fred M. Taylor. Funds for the maintenance of the scholarship are raised each year by subscription.

In addition to this work, the society holds monthly meetings to discuss sociological topics or to hear the results of special investigations undertaken by its members. The first President of the organisation is George A. Fox.

The Classical Association of the Middle West and South.

An important meeting of classical teachers was held recently in Chicago, and an organisation was effected, to be known as the Classical Association of the Middle West and South. The object of the Association is the advancement of classical studies within the territory indicated, and the promotion of the common interests of the members through its meetings and publications.

Professor Benjamin L. D'Ooge, A.M., of the Michigan State Normal College, was elected secretary-treasurer of the new organisation, and Professor Walter Dennison, A.M., of the University of Michigan, was elected a vice-president.

It was decided to publish a journal of the Association, to be called *The Classical Journal*. Professor Henry A. Sanders, A.M., of the University of Michigan, was appointed a member of the Board of Editors.

A New Electrical Laboratory.

An addition is to be built on the west end of the physical laboratory at the University of Michigan for the accommodation of the electrical laboratory. The new portion will cost $30,000. The lower floor will be used as a laboratory, and the second floor will be furnished as a lecture room, which will seat about 400 students.

The June Graduation Ceremony.

The sixty-first annual Commencement held on June 22nd, 1905, saw the graduation of 775 students from all departments of the University,—eleven less than were graduated the preceding year. The Commencement procession was formed, as always, a little after nine o'clock in the morning. Following the guests of honour, the Faculty, and alumni, the graduates of each department arrayed in cap and gown, with tassels of distinctive colour, came in long procession. The Commencement oration was delivered by Henry S. Pritchett, President of the Massachusetts Institute of Technology. President Pritchett spoke on "Shall the University Become a Business Organisation?"

F

Degrees were granted as follows:—

DEPARTMENT OF LITERATURE, SCIENCE, AND THE ARTS.

Bachelor of Arts	295	
Master of Science (in Forestry)	3	
Master of Arts...	34	
Doctor of Philosophy	7	339

DEPARTMENT OF ENGINEERING.

Bachelor of Science (Marine Engineering)... ...	4	
Bachelor of Science (Chemical Engineering) ...	9	
Bachelor of Science (Electrical Engineering) ...	18	
Bachelor of Science (Mechanical Engineering) ...	24	
Bachelor of Science (Civil Engineering)	32	
Master of Science	2	89

DEPARTMENT OF MEDICINE AND SURGERY.

Doctor of Medicine	61	61

DEPARTMENT OF LAW.

Bachelor of Laws	217	217

SCHOOL OF PHARMACY.

Pharmaceutical Chemist	17	
Bachelor of Science (in Pharmacy)	2	
Master of Science (in Pharmacy)	2	21

HOMŒOPATHIC MEDICAL COLLEGE.

Doctor of Medicine	12	12

COLLEGE OF DENTAL SURGERY.

Doctor of Dental Surgery	35	
Doctor of Dental Science	1	36
Total ...		775

In addition to the degrees regularly conferred the following honorary degrees were granted:—

MASTER OF ARTS.

Clarence M. Burton, Ph.B. '73. Learned investigator of early history of Michigan, and especially of Detroit.

Mary Clare Spencer, State Librarian.

DOCTOR OF LAWS.

Henry F. Pritchett, President of Massachusetts School of Technology.

Dr. Theodore A. McGraw, A.B. '59. Eminent teacher and practitioner of surgery, Detroit.

William Warner, eminent lawyer and United States senator.

DOCTOR OF SCIENCE.

William W. Campbell, B.S., Director of Lick Observatory.

Columbia.

NEWLY APPOINTED PROFESSORS.

Hermon C. Bumpus, Ph.D., Director of the American Museum of Natural History.

Edward Thomas Devine, Ph.D., Schiff Professor of Social Economy.

John Dewey, Ph.D., LL.D., Professor of Philosophy.

George Stewart Fullerton, Ph.D., Professor of Philosophy.

George Hastings, Diplomé of the Ecole des Beaux Arts, Director of Atelier.

Charles F. McKim, Litt.D., Director of Atelier.

The Universities.

CAMBRIDGE.

The President of Queens' College.

The news of the appointment of the President of Queens' College, the Rev. Dr. Chase, to succeed Lord Alwyne Compton as Bishop of Ely, has been received with satisfaction throughout the University. Dr. Chase was born in 1853, and was educated at King's College, London, and afterwards at Christ's College, Cambridge. Here, among other distinctions, he gained a high position in the first part of the Classical Tripos in 1876. In 1881 he was appointed Lecturer in Theology at Pembroke College, and three years later he became the first Tutor of the Cambridge Clergy Training School, which was then being founded. In 1887 he became Principal of this School, a position he held until his appointment as President of Queens' College in 1901, which followed shortly after his election to the Norrisian Chair of Divinity. In 1902 he became Vice-Chancellor of the University.

The Vacation Term for Biblical Study.

The third Vacation Term for Bible study at Cambridge concluded on August 19th. This year the work has been conducted at Girton College. The students numbered about 70. Six courses of four lectures each were given during the term. Among the lecturers were Dr. Chase, Canon Kennett, Dr. Barnes, Dr. Jevons, Professor Nairne, Professor Barrett and Professor Max Kellner, of Cambridge, U.S.A. It is hoped that in future the meetings will be held annually.

The Library Association at Cambridge.

The twenty-eighth annual meeting of the Library Association was opened at Cambridge on Tuesday, August 22nd, under the presidency of Mr. Francis Jenkinson, M.A., Litt.D., the University Librarian. The attendance of members numbered upwards of two hundred and fifty, many of whom were lodged in Trinity and St. John's Colleges. Dr. Alex. Hill, Master of Downing College, extended a cordial welcome to the Association on behalf of the University. In the course of his Presidential address Dr. Jenkinson gave an interesting sketch of the work of Henry Bradshaw, the famous librarian and bibliographer to whom the Cambridge University Library owes so much. In 1860 the collection of 15th century books in the University Library contained about 830 different volumes. Bradshaw, with immense zeal and self-devotion, set to work to enlarge this collection, often himself buying and presenting works which the University could not afford. His purchases were made on a well-considered plan. Every book acquired had its place and helped to illustrate some development or to fix some landmark, or else furnished some problem which he hoped to solve. His greatest achievement was at the sales at Brussels, in 1884, when he bought 145, 15th century books at a cost of £551. The impetus given by Bradshaw lasted for some years after his death, and by the end of the century the collection amounted to 2,200 separate works, or nearly three times as many as there had been forty years before.

Among a number of interesting papers read at the meetings of the Association was one by Mr. H. G. Aldis, Secretary to Cambridge University Library, on the organisation and methods of the University Library. Mr. Aldis pointed out three characteristic features of the Library. Firstly, its great age, which, though it conferred the pride of historical continuity, at the same time involved the legacy of mediæval methods; secondly, the copyright privilege, which means a continuous addition of a large amount of material of very diverse value; and, thirdly, the readers' privilege of free access to the shelves. The University Library now contains upwards of 720,000 volumes and over 80,000 maps. A total of 56,000 items is annually received into the library.

DUBLIN.

The Training of Secondary Teachers.

It has long been a reproach to Dublin that no arrangements existed for the training of secondary teachers. No lectures were provided for candidates for the Diploma in Education until two years ago, when courses of public lectures on subjects connected with education were instituted by Mr. E. P. Culverwell, M.A., P.T.C.D., who has lately been appointed to the Chair of Education, and the very large attendance of teachers and of the public—the audience at one of the Winter Courses being maintained at over 500—showed the growing interest in the subject.

Following this a Committee was appointed in the Spring of 1904 by the Board of Trinity College to consider and report on the question of providing a school for the training of secondary teachers such as already exist in connection with most of the English Universities. The outcome of this was that arrangements were made by the Board last Trinity term for instituting a School for the training of secondary teachers, both men and women.

As the Council of Alexandra College had also resolved on a scheme for the training of women teachers for secondary schools, the two governing bodies took counsel together with a view to avoiding the necessity of providing, at the initiation of the schemes, two entirely separate staffs, while each College will issue its own certificates of attendance. A good deal of the instruction in the two schools will be given in common, the Alexandra College students attending a considerable portion of the theoretical lectures in Trinity College, while the Trinity College students will have the benefit of the services of the Mistress of Method appointed by Alexandra College.

The Trinity College School will be under the direction of the Professor of Education in the University of Dublin, assisted by a Master of Method.

Until this School was founded there was no school in Ireland for the training of men teachers for secondary schools.

The Graduation of Women at the University.

The following statistics have been compiled in view of the interest that has been aroused by the action of the University of Dublin in presenting its Degrees to women who have passed the qualifying examinations of other Universities. It may be said that these figures competely contradict the many exaggerated statements that have been made with reference to the number of *ad eundem* Degrees that have been conferred.

The number of B.A. *(ad eundem)* Degrees conferred is as follows:

June, 1904	... ...	6
Dec., ,,	... ...	39
March, 1905	... ...	15
April, ,,	... ...	86
July, ,,	... ...	94
	Total	240

Of these the following have proceeded to the M.A. Degree:—

June, 1904	1
Dec., „	20
March, 1905	13
April, „	67
July, „	50
Total	151

The number of women students now on the register of the Trinity College attending lectures, etc., is as follows:—

Senior Sophister Year	3
Junior „ „	11
Senior Freshman Year	13
Junior „ „	32
Total	59

A Diploma in Economics and Commercial Knowledge.

The Board of Trinity College have instituted a Diploma in Economics and Commercial Knowledge. This Diploma will be granted for proficiency in the various branches of a higher business education, as tested by an examination which will be held every year, beginning in 1906. The course includes obligatory and optional subjects. The former are (1) Economics, descriptive and theoretical; (2) Economic and Commercial History; (3) Commercial Geography; (4) Accountancy and Business Methods; (5) Commercial and Industrial Law. As optional subjects the candidate may select a modern language (French, German or Spanish), any one of a number of economic subjects, and any one of the following branches of economic and business organisation: banking, railways, insurance, agriculture. Candidates must pass in *three* subjects, of which Economics, theoretical and descriptive, must be one. Candidates who satisfy this condition may pass in the remaining subjects at a subsequent examination. The Diploma will not be issued until the candidate has passed in all the obligatory subjects. The examination will be open to anyone who has matriculated in any University or University College; who has passed the Middle or Senior Grade Intermediate Examination; who has the certificate of any recognised Technical School or School of Commerce; or who possesses any other qualification deemed sufficient by the Board. It shall be in the power of the

Examiners, if it is thought advisable, to hold parts of the Examination at night. The fee for members of Trinity College will be one guinea, for other candidates two guineas. The Diploma will be accepted as equivalent for the exercises required for keeping the Hilary and Trinity Terms of the Senior Sophister year, but not for the B.A. Degree Examination. Further information may be obtained from Professor C. F. Bastable, Trinity College, Dublin.

DURHAM.

University News and Notes.

A "Durham Association" is in process of formation in the Diocese of Canterbury for the purpose of drawing together the members of the University living in the South of England. Similar associations exist in other parts of the country. Members of the University wishing to join the above Association are requested to notify their names and addresses to John Highwood, M.A., D.C.L., The Laurels, West End, Staplehurst, Kent.

At the recent British Colleges' Christian Union Annual Conference, held at Conishead, " Durham " was represented by delegates from the Durham Inter-Collegiate Christian Union and from the Christian Union of the College of Medicine.

Athenian Colours (i.e., 'Varsity Colours for cricket) have been awarded for this year to H. J. Hawkins (Hatfield Hall), F. W. Mitchell (Hatfield Hall), G. C. D. Horton (Hatfield Hall), and T. Blaylock (College of Science).

Durham College of Medicine.

A new wing is in the course of erection at the College. This wing will accommodate the Departments of Physiology and Bacteriology, and will also contain a Students' Gymnasium and a set of Students' Union Rooms.

The Calendar for 1905–6 has been published. Amongst early events enumerated in the Almanack we notice the following :—

September 18. Examination for the Degree of Bachelor in Hygiene, for the Diploma in Public Health, and First and Second Examinations for Degrees in Medicine and Surgery begin.

September 22. Examination for M.D. (Practitioners) and M.S. Degrees, and Third and Final Examinations for M.B. Degree begin.

September 26. Examination for Certificate of Proficiency in General Education and University Medical Scholarship begin (at Durham).

September 27. M.D. (Essay) and B.S. Examinations.

September 30. Convocation at Durham and Degrees Conferred.

The Winter Session of the College of Medicine will be opened on Monday, October 2nd.

The annual meeting of the Durham University Medical Graduates' Association was held on June 9th at the Rooms of the Medical Society of London, 11, Chandos Street, Cavendish Square, W. Dr. Hembrough (President) was in the chair, and there were also present Mr. H. T. Herring—the new President—and Dr. Selby Plummer (Vice-Presidents), Sir George Hare Philipson (President of the College of Medicine). The annual dinner took place the same evening at the Imperial Restaurant, Regent Street, at which 84 members and guests were present.

A general meeting of the subscribers to the "Turnbull Memorial Fund" was announced for July 18th in the Anatomy Theatre at the College of Medicine, to decide upon the best way of preserving the memory of the late Dr. Turnbull, for many years Demonstrator of Anatomy at the College.

During the past 12 months 1,474 specimens have been examined in the Bacteriological Department of the University of Durham College of Medicine, showing an increase of 352 over the previous year.

Harold John Hutchens, M.R.C.S., L.R.C.P., D.P.H. (Oxon.), has been appointed Demonstrator of Comparative Pathology and Bacteriology. Dr. Hutchens possesses the coveted distinction of being a member of the Distinguished Service Order.

Dr. Page has most ably continued the course of lectures on Medical Jurisprudence, so unfortunately interrupted by the lamentable death of Dr. Murphy.

Pending the appointment of another lecturer in Dr. Murphy's place, Dr. McDowall will examine in Medical Jurisprudence in the Third Professional Examination in September.

The resignation is announced of Dr. McDowall from the Staff of the Infirmary. Many thanks are due to him for his work in the Psychological Deartment.

Armstrong College of Science.

In the allocation of the Treasury Grant to University Colleges, we notice that the sum of £6,000 has been allotted to Durham University College of Science.

Graduates and undergraduates generally will feel the deepest sympathy with Dr. Bedson, Professor of Chemistry, on the terrible bereavement he has suffered in the loss of his eldest son in a recent motor-cycle accident.

The new buildings of the College, constituting the front wing and the large Examination Hall, will be ready for occupation at the commencement of the coming Session, 1905–6. It is expected that His Majesty the King will formally open the buildings in July, August, or September of next year. In this connection it is interesting to note that Lord Armstrong has accepted the invitation of the Newcastle City Council to be Mayor of the city next year.

The Rev. W. M. Davison, M.A., M.Sc., B.C.L., Assistant Lecturer in Mathematics in the College, has been appointed Vice-Principal of S. Catherine's Training College for Women, Tottenham.

The following appointments have recently been made:—
Demonstrator in Physics—Mr. T. P. Black, M.A., B.Sc., Ph.D.
Demonstrator in Geology—Mr. D. Woolacott, D.Sc.
Demonstrator in Metallurgy and Surveying—Mr. H. Dean, A.R.S.M.
Demonstrator in Mechanical Engineering—Mr. James Hall.
Demonstrator in Electrical Engineering—Mr. W. W. Firth, M.Sc.
Normal Mistress and Lecturer on Education—Miss S. E. S. Richards, M.A.

EDINBURGH.

University News and Notes.

A graduation ceremony took place in the M'Ewan Hall on July 28th. The occasion was possessed of more than ordinary interest by the fact that it marked the retirement of Professor A. R. Simpson from his Chair of Midwifery after 35 years' service. At the commencement of the ceremony the Honorary Degree of Doctor of Laws was conferred upon Dr. J. Horace Round, the historian. After the presentation of a large number of Ordinary Degrees, nearly all of which were medical, an eloquent address was delivered by Professor Simpson, which will long be treasured in the memories of those who were privileged to hear it. At the close of the ceremony an illuminated address from the students and recent graduates was presented to Professor Simpson by the President of the Students' Union, Mr. H. J. Norman. In conclusion, the Vice-Chancellor, Sir William Turner, expressed, on behalf of his colleagues in the professoriate and himself, their respect and esteem for Professor Simpson, who carried with him their united wishes for health and strength in his retirement.

The graduation ceremony was followed by a reception and luncheon in the University Union, which was attended by upwards of two hundred guests. At the luncheon Mr. H. J. Norman (President of the Union) occupied the chair, and among those present were Sir William Turner and Miss Turner, Professor Simpson and Miss Simpson, Professor and Mrs. Chiene, Professor and Mrs. Saintsbury, Sir Ludovic Grant, Dr. Horace Round, Professor .W. W. Keen, of Philadelphia, and Miss Keen, and Mr. Fitzroy Bell.

The first meeting of the newly-constituted Board of Management of the Royal (Dick) Veterinary College, Edinburgh, was held on July 24th. It is proposed to establish a Chair of Comparative Anatomy in the Edinburgh University and a Chair of Physiology in the College. It is intended to have the College incorporated by Parliament in the ensuing Session. The Dick College will continue, as heretofore, to be a teaching institution qualifying for the examinations of the Royal College of Veterinary Surgeons and the Veterinary Degrees of the University. Until the College is incorporated the Town Council of Edinburgh will continue to act as the trustees of the founder, the late Professor Dick, with the Board of Management as advisers.

University Vacation Courses.

The Edinburgh University Vacation Courses for the study of foreign languages have been held during the month of August, and have achieved a considerable success. The aim of the organisers of the scheme on this occasion has been to provide instruction, both theoretical and practical, in the French, German and English languages. Among the lecturers may be mentioned Professor Morillot (Grenoble) and Professor Passy (Paris); Professor Jeanroy and Professor Henri Guy, of the University of Toulouse; Professor Viëtor, of the University of Marburg; and Professor Witkowski, of the University of Leipsic; and Professor Kirkpatrick, of Edinburgh, and Mr. A. A. Jack, late Fellow of Peterhouse, Cambridge. The courses of lectures were attended by upwards of a hundred foreign students and twice that number of English and Scottish teachers and students, as well as by some twenty-five French and German professors and lecturers. The use of lecture rooms, library and reading rooms in the University had been granted by the authorities, and on August 1st the students were welcomed by the Lord Provost of Edinburgh and Principal Sir William Turner. A number of enjoyable social functions were organised in connection with the courses, including soirées, concerts and dramatic recitals and readings. Excursions to places of interest in the neighbourhood of Edinburgh were also greatly enjoyed by the visitors.

LEEDS.

University News and Notes.

The resignation is announced of Professor Edward Ward, who has occupied the Chair of Surgery during the past six years. The Council of the University has accepted the resignation, and has recorded its high appreciation of the services which Professor Ward has rendered to the University. To the vacancy thus created Mr. Harry Littlewood, the present Lecturer in Practical and Operative Surgery in the University, has been appointed.

The Council of the Royal College of Physicians has added the University of Leeds to the list of Universities whose examinations are accepted in lieu of the first and second examinations of the Royal College of Physicians.

LIVERPOOL.

University News and Notes.

While the prospect of the erection of Union buildings on an adequate is now practically secure, it is clear that the building cannot be made ready for occupation until at least two years hence; and for that reason the University authorities are favourably considering the advisability of renting and furnishing a house to serve temporarily. This house, it is proposed, should be opened at the beginning of the coming session. The leaders of student opinion believe that this step, if taken, would have the effect of both showing and stimulating the need for a permanent Union.

The Guild of Undergraduates has been provided with two commodious rooms for purposes of administration during the coming session. The rooms are situated in the building recently vacated by the Zoological Department.

The Liverpool School of Tropical Medicine having offered its services to the Mayor of New Orleans in the work of dealing with the outbreak of yellow fever in that city, received the following telegram in reply:—" Grateful thanks on behalf of this city, and accept co-operation of Liverpool School of Tropical Medicine." Professor Ronald Ross and Professor Rubert Boyce left Liverpool immediately in the Cunard liner *Campania* en route for New Orleans.

Viscount Mountmorres has gone to the United States on behalf of the Institute of Tropical Medicine, and Mr. Montgomery, of the School of Commerce, is visiting Germany on behalf of the School.

The Institute of Tropical Research.

The opening meeting of the Council of the Instute of Tropical Research was held on July 31st, when Sir Alfred Jones was unanimously elected Chairman. The following generous guarantees towards the expenditure of the Institute were announced at the meeting:—Sir Alfred Jones and Mr. W. H. Lever, £1,000 each for four years; Mr. T. Sutton Timmis, £250 a year; and Mr. H. Sutton Timmis, £50 a year. The following were appointed to act as a Professorial Board:—Professor E. C. K. Gonner, Statistics; Professor J. Harvey Gibson, Botany; Professor W. A. Herdman, Zoology; Professor Benjamin Moore, Physiological Chemistry; Professor Ronald Ross, Tropical Hygiene and Sanitation. Lord Mountmorres was appointed Director, and Dr. Eric Drabell, Economic Botanist.

As the aims of the Liverpool Institute of Tropical Research become better known it is seen that they are both ambitious and practical in the extreme. And unless the amount of energy required for their achievement far outstrips the aid of the increasing number who will be benefitted, they are feasible too.

The objects as put forth in the Institute's prospectus are as follows:—

1. Collecting and tabulating all kinds of information regarding Tropical Countries, their products, natural resources, industries, and economic conditions, which can be of service either to commerce or to science.

2. Studying the botany, zoology, geology, ethnology, minerology, meteorology, and physiography of Tropical Countries, more particularly in their relation to the commercial and political development of British Tropical Colonies.

3. Investigating all kinds of scientific problems which arise in connection with the trade of the tropics, and the industries dependent on it.

4. Training experts in the various branches of applied science concerned with the work of the Institute.

5. Supplying information and advice to all interested in the Tropics.

The means adopted to effect these objects are:—

1. The organisation of scientific and exploratory expeditions to Tropical Countries.

2. The establishment of a bureau in Liverpool where the latest scientific and commercial information may be obtained.

3. Research work in the laboratories of the University by a staff of experts under the guidance of University professors.

4. The publication of reports, pamphlets, and monographs, and the delivery of lectures and addresses.

5. Correspondence and exchange with Government Departments and learned societies, both at home and abroad.

It will be seen from this rough outline that the programme of the objects and work of the Institute is a very wide one. Such work is already being carried out in Germany, France and the United States, but has never before been attempted in England, which has for centuries been more closely connected with the Tropics than has any other country. Perhaps the following example of what has already been done will not be out of place. At a Lancashire cotton mill the operatives working at looms which had been refitted with wood which could not be identified, but which was called "African box-wood," suffered from a mysterious illness. Through the instrumentality of the Institute the wood was sent to the University Laboratories, where it was recognised and proved to contain an alkaloid of very deadly properties, well calculated to produce the symptoms exhibited by the operatives. It is not too much to say that the Institute promises to become of vast importance, and the University of Liverpool rejoices that her workers and her laboratories are able by its means to render useful service to those who have done so much to establish her in the position she now holds.

The University Club.

The University Club is looking forward to the opening of its spacious and convenient new premises in the centre of the city, which should be ready for occupation early next term. This Club, though not in any way formally connected with the University, has played an exceedingly important part in its life since 1894. It includes among its membership a large majority of the Council and Staff of the University, as well as a good many members of the City Council, and other prominent citizens, and it has since its formation in 1894 formed an invaluable meeting place for the exchange of opinions between " town and gown." Indeed, the remarkably good relations between city and University which distinguish Liverpool are in no small degree to be attributed to the existence of this Club. In its quiet and charming rooms overlooking the site of the new Cathedral the discussions and dinners took place in which the need for the establishment of an independent University was first promulgated; and the success of the movement may be partly attributed to the part played by the Club first in preparation and then in active agitation. On the more purely social side the Club has been distinguished by the intimate good feeling, the informal and comradely relations, which have been maintained among its members. No more homely or simple Club exists anywhere, and all must hope that the change from its present retired and simple quarters to the much larger and more flaunting rooms in the heart of the city will not have the effect of destroying the peculiar character which the Club has possessed. Such a character is very easily destroyed, and if we lost it many would feel that we had lost one of the most attractive features of University life in this city.

An Interesting Publication.

We should before this have noted the publication of the life of William Rathbone by his daughter, Miss Eleanor Rathbone. Both the subject and the author of this work have been intimately connected with the University, Miss Rathbone formerly as a student and now as a lecturer in the new School of Social Studies; William Rathbone as the first Vice-President and the real founder of the Institution. The book possesses the unusual qualities (in modern biographies) of brevity, vividness, and the most charming modesty; as a record of one of the purest of philanthropic lives, it can be commended to every reader. But to the Liverpool man, and perhaps especially to the Liverpool University man, it is full of pleasure. Space permits us only to allude to one episode. In the year 1881 the early advocates of the foundation of a College in this city were hard at work endeavouring to stimulate interest and to raise funds; but in three years they had only obtained conditional promises to the amount of £3,000, and £100,000 was required. William Rathbone had been full of sympathy and interest, but being a very hard-working member of Parliament he had not been able to give any time to the cause. In 1881 he was persuaded to give up a safe seat and to stand for a very uncertain one, with the result that he was defeated. "At the declaration of the poll, his reception of the figures was characteristic. For a moment his face clouded; then, turning to Mr. W. S. Caine, who stood near him, he said: '*Now* we'll have the College.'" We had the College within the year. For William Rathbone not only collected money, and gave it himself; he inspired on all sides interest and enthusiasm. He turned a dream into a practical proposal, a failing scheme into a triumphant fact. To William Rathbone beyond all others (and there were many others) the actual foundation of University College is to be attributed; and it would indeed be unbecoming if we were to allow the publication of this worthy memorial of a noble life to pass without a word of tribue for the vast debt which the University of Liverpool owes to him.

LONDON.

The Study of Sociology.

The Senate of the University has decided that the Syllabus in Sociology (the Comparative Study of Social Institutions) for the B.A. Honours in Philosophy and B.Sc. (Economics) Honours Degrees for Internal and External Students (Calendar for 1904–05, Vol. II., 236 and 850, and Vol. III., 26 of the Arts Section, and 8 of the Economics Section) shall be as follows:—

1. Sociology in its relations to Biology and Psychology. The principle of evolution applied to Social Phenomena.
2. Forms of Social Organisation.
   (a) The Family—Maternal and Paternal Descent. Power of the Head of the Family. Joint and individual property. Regulation of Marriage. Position of Women.
   (b) Society—The Clan and Tribe. Monarchy, Feudalism, the City State. The Modern State. Federal Government.
3. The Maintenance of Social Order.
   The Blood Feud. Retaliation. Compensation. Primitive Courts and Processes. The Oaths and the Ordeal. Growth of Public Justice, and Rational Procedure. Responsibility. Punishment and Prevention of Crime.
4. The Social Structure. Slavery, Serfdom, Free Labour, and Industrial Co-operation. Caste and Class Distinctions. Civil and Political Equality.
5. Religious and other beliefs in their bearing on social relations. Influence of Magic, Animism, Ancestor-worship, Polytheism, the World Religions, on Social Morality. Antithesis of Temporal and Spiritual Powers.

Syllabuses in Ethnology and Psychology.

The following Syllabuses have been arranged in Ethnology and Psychology for the B.Sc. (Economics) Honours Degree for Internal and External Students (Calendar for 1904–05, Vol. II., 850, and Vol. III., 8 of the Economics Section):—

PSYCHOLOGY.

1. The Psychological Standpoint.
2. Comparative Study of Mental Structure—
   (a) in Animals and Man, (b) in Child and Adult, (c) in Primitive and Advanced Peoples.
3. The Psychological basis of Social Institutions.

(*a*) Ideas of Moral and Political Obligations. (*b*) Nature and development of Moral Faculty. Psychology of Sympathy, Self-love, Moral Sense, Conscience. The idea of Personality. (*c*) Psychology of Responsibility—Analysis of Will, Desire, Impulse, Motive, Intention.

4. Psychological Element in (*a*) Æsthetic, (*b*) Scientific, and (*c*) Development.

ETHNOLOGY.

The physical, mental, cultural, and social characteristics of the main varieties of mankind.

The present geographical distribution of races and peoples, and their former wanderings.

The antiquity of man; the physical characteristics of prehistoric peoples and the evolution of their culture.

A detailed acquaintance with a selected continent, or area, comprising a knowledge of the main social groups in the region selected, their environment (physical and biological), occupation, property, culture, social structure, religion, expansion, and their influence upon one another.

A Chair of Protozoology.

The Senate has received a communication from the Secretary of State for the Colonies, offering the University the sum of £700 a year for five years for the purpose of instituting a Chair of Protozoology. Of this sum, £200 a year is stated to be a contribution from the Rhodes Trustees, and £500 a year to represent a moiety of a grant originally made from the Tropical Diseases Research Fund (established under the auspices of the Colonial Office) to the Royal Society for the promotion of research work, and by the Royal Society surrendered for the purpose of endowing the Chair. Having considered reports upon this offer from the Academic Council, and from the Board of Advanced Medical Studies and the Boards of Studies in Botany and Zoology, the Senate decided to accept the offer, to devote the whole of the £700 a year as salary to the Professor, and to set aside a further sum of £200 a year to defray the cost of assistants and laboratory expenses in connection with the Chair.

University News and Notes.

A Committee consisting of the Chancellor, the Vice-Chancellor and Chairman of Convocation, Sir William Collins, Dr. T. Gregory Foster, Rev. Dr. A. C. Headlam, Mr. H. J. Mackinder, Lord Reay, Sir Owen Roberts, Sir Albert Rollit, and Mr. Sidney Webb, has been appointed to consider and report upon the organisation of Commercial Education in the University.

G

Mr. Edgar Schuster, the Francis Galton Research Fellow in National Eugenics, has presented a report containing a preliminary account of inquiries which have been made into the inheritance of disease, and especially of feeble-mindedness, deaf-mutism, and phthisis. Arrangements have been concluded with Mr. John Murray for the publication of a work on Noteworthy Families in Modern Science, written by Mr. Francis Galton in conjunction with Mr. Schuster. This is to appear as Volume I. of the publications of the Eugenics Record Office, and will contain accounts of the families of some fifty Fellows of the Royal Society.

Miss Ethel Mary Elderton has been appointed Secretary to the Eugenics Record Office.

The Worshipful Company of Goldsmiths have expressed their willingness to bear the expense of building a gallery and erecting additional bookcases in the room which contains the Library of Economic Literature collected by Prof. H. S. Foxwell, M.A., and presented to the University by the Company two years ago.

Mr. Reginald A. Rye has been appointed Assistant Librarian.

Sir John Wolfe-Barry, K.C.B., LL.D., F.R.S., has resigned his membership of the Council for External Students.

The Chancellor has appointed Mr. G. W. Knox, B.Sc., to be his representative on the Court of the University of Sheffield.

Dr. T. Gregory Foster, Ph.D., Principal of University College, and Lady Lockyer have been nominated by the Senate for appointment by Bedford College as representatives of the University on the Council of that College.

Under the will of the late Dr. Nathaniel Rogers the Senate offers a prize of £100, open for competition to all members of the medical profession in the United Kingdom, for an essay on " The Physiology and Pathology of the Pancreas." Candidates are informed that the Examiners will attach importance to the results of original observation. Essays, by preference typewritten or printed, must be sent in not later than May 1st, 1907, addressed to Percy M. Wallace, M.A., Secretary to the Senate.

Bedford College for Women.

The following contributions have been promised to the building scheme of Bedford College for Women :—Mr. and Mrs. G. T. Pilcher, £1,000; Miss Shaen (one of the daughters of Mr. William Shaen, for some years Chairman of the College), £1,000; and the Clothworkers' Company, a donation when the sum collected has reached £50,000.

The Commission appointed under the University College Transfer Act of last Session held its first meeting on August 15th at the

University of London. The Commission has made an order postponing the day on which the transfer of the College to the University is to take effect to September 1st, 1906.

Cheshunt College.

The Board of Education has completed the scheme for the future of the Cheshunt College. Despite its removal to Cambridge the College will still retain its original name. The scheme provides for the sale of the present property at Cheshunt, and for the erection as soon as convenient of suitable buildings at Cambridge. A Board of Governors will be formed, consisting of co-optative and representative members, the present trustees being the first co-optative Governors, the others representing the University of Cambridge, the Countess of Huntingdon's Connexion, the Congregational Union, the London Missionary Society, the teaching staff, the subscribers, and the former students.

A number of houses have already been engaged at Cambridge for the accommodation of students next Session.

King's College.

The Council of King's College have appointed the Rev. F. E. Brightman, M.A., to give a course of lectures on the Ancient Liturgies, in the Lent term of the Session 1905–06.

The Council have elected Professor J. M. Thomson, F.R.S., as Vice-Principal, and the following as Deans of the various Faculties for 1905–06:—Prof. W. C. F. Walters, M.A., Arts; Prof. S. A. F. White, M.A., Science; Prof. W. D. Halliburton, F.R.S., Medical Science; A. Whitfield, M.D., F.R.C.P., Medical; Prof. D. S. Capper, M.A., M.I.C.E., and Prof. H. M. Waynforth (Sub-Dean), Engineering; W.|N. Hibbert, LL.D., Laws; R. W. K. Edwards, M.A., Evening Classes.

The following arrangements have been made for the opening of the next Session:—October 3rd: Admission of new students; distribution of prizes in the Medical Faculty and address by Prof. Clifford Allbutt, M.D. October 4th: Lectures begin; inaugural lecture by Prof. A. Dendy, D.Sc.

WOMEN'S DEPARTMENT.

Miss Soltau, late Office Secretary of the National Union of Women Workers, has been appointed to the joint office of Accountant and Librarian.

The Library has received a grant of £50 from the Treasury Funds, which is being expended on the purchase of books.

A new Zoological Laboratory will be constructed and equipped before the opening of the coming Session, and the Botanical Laboratory will be enlarged.

Royal Holloway College.

The following appointments have been made for next Session:— Prof. Louis Brandin, M.A., Ph.D., as Visiting Lecturer in French Philology; Miss M. E. D. Honey, B.A., as Assistant Lecturer in French; Mr. Thomas Seccombe, M.A., as Visiting Lecturer in Modern History; Miss H. Fraser, B.Sc., as Demonstrator in Botany; Miss F. D. Ghey as Assistant Lecturer in Classics.

The Rev. Canon Beeching, M.A., will give a course of lectures on English Lyrical Poetry.

University College.

Mr. Frederic Mackarness, M.A. (Oxon.), Advocate to the Cape Supreme Cape, has been appointed to the new Chair of Roman-Dutch Law. He will begin his courses in October next. Dr. George A. Buckmaster has been appointed to a Teachership in the Department of Physiology; Dr. Skuckburgh has been re-appointed Lecturer in Ancient History; Mr. F. J. Kean, B.Sc., has been appointed Demonstrator in the Department of Mechanical Engineering, and Mr. B. B. Willcox in the Department of Applied Mathematics.

The Session of the Faculties of Arts, Laws and Science will begin on October 3rd, and the Session of the Faculty of Medicine on October 2nd.

MANCHESTER.

University News and Notes.

Miss Hilda D. Oakeley, M.A., has been appointed Tutor for Women Students and Warden of the Ashburne House Hall of Residence. Miss Oakeley obtained a First Class in Literæ Humaniores at Oxford in 1898. In 1899 she was appointed to a Research Studentship in the School of Economics, and in the same year to the Wardenship of the Royal Victoria College for Women, of the McGill University, Montreal, where she was also a Lecturer in Philosophy.

Mr. Eric M. Wilkins has been appointed to a Leech Fellowship in Medicine; and Mr. Frank Foster to the Vulcan Engineering Fellowship.

The Gilchrist Trustees have elected Miss Violet D. Adams, Gilchrist student. Under the new conditions recently issued by the Trustees the Studentship, which is of the value of £80, tenable for one year, is open to graduates of either sex who have taken Honours in Modern Languages at the Final Degree Examination of the University, and who are proposing to enter the profession of teaching in a secondary school. The purpose of the Studentship is to enable the holder to pursue a special course of study abroad with a view to qualifying for teaching Modern Languages in a secondary school. Miss Adams graduated this summer with First Class Honours in Modern Languages and Literatures in the University.

In memory of the late Mr. W. H. Dayas, who was principal Professor of the Pianoforte at the Manchester Royal College of Music, it has been decided to endow a gold medal—to be known as "the Dayas Memorial Medal"—which will be awarded triennally to the best pianoforte student of the College.

The funeral of the late Professor Wilkins took place at Colwyn Bay on July 27th. The ceremony, which was of a brief and simple character, was attended by a number of friends and colleagues of the late Professor.

The Faculty of Commerce.

The prospectus of the Faculty of Commerce for the Session 1905–06 has recently been issued. The introductory note states that the work in the Faculty comprises, "first, teaching in the subjects which are fundamental in all commercial and administrative education; second, instruction in more special branches of study; and, finally, research and investigation. The object of the training provided is not merely to give useful information, but to develope and discipline the mind, both generally, and with special reference to the problems which must be faced in business and public life. It is no substitute for experience, but it should broaden the outlook, train the faculties to analyse new commercial and economic situations, and impart organised knowledge. Alike to the man of business and to those who are engaged in administration, systematic economic study is to-day of the highest importance, as a consequence, on the one hand, of the complexity and international character of modern commerce, and, on the other hand, of the widening scope of public interests and duties. This fact has for some time been freely recognised, especially in the United States, Germany, France and Belgium, where the Universities, or institutions of University standing, have vigorously taken up studies in Commerce and Administration."

OXFORD.

University News and Notes.

The vacation is the cause of a "plentiful lack" of news of a strictly academic nature. In the meantime the Oxford Summer Meeting has taken possession of the buildings and the machinery of the University. From the Examination Schools, which are now the centre of the meeting, the last proclamations of the University went forth at the beginning of August. These were the Honours lists in the two largest of the final schools. The first to appear was that in Literæ Humaniores, which was headed by Balliol with seven names in the First Class. This, we believe, constitutes a "record" for the College. In the Modern History School there were only twelve names in the First Class altogether, and these included four women students. Balliol, with two Firsts, could again claim a nominal superiority, as no other College obtained more than one. The Second Class contained the names of 55 students, of which eight belonged to New College, six to Balliol and four each to University and Exeter.

The United University Club is closed for re-building, and its very pressing need for alteration is a testimony to the many generations of University men which it has served. The Club dates from the time when George the Fourth was King. It possesses a good, but incomplete, collection of the famous Oxford Almanacks for which Turner painted the well-known pictures of the Oxford Colleges which are now in the Ashmolean collection. Perhaps the best known of these is the view of Magdalen Tower and Bridge, a scene which has since been the motif of so many artists.

In a Convocation held on August 10th, presided over by the Vice-Chancellor (Dr. Merry, Rector of Lincoln College), the Degree of D.D., *honoris causa*, was conferred upon the Right Rev. Walter Farrar, B.D., Keble College, Lord Bishop of Antigua.

The Committee for the Supervision of Instruction in Geography have appointed Mr. N. F. Mackenzie, M.Inst.C.E., Senior Instructor in Surveying at Cooper's Hill College, to be Instructor in Surveying for the next academic year.

The next term begins on October 12th.

The University Extension Summer Meeting.

The twelfth summer meeting of the University Extension Movement began at Oxford on August 4th. Over one thousand tickets were issued for the first part of the course, which continued till August 15th. The second part was held from August 17th till the 28th. The foreign students numbered 256, consisting mainly of Germans (87), Americans (49) and Scandinavians (26). For the first time Russia and Spain sent a few students. It is interesting to observe that quite a number of these foreign visitors are sent by their Governments to study and report on the work and organisation of the Extension Movement. The students were welcomed by the Vice-Chancellor (Dr. Merry, the Rector of Lincoln College) in the Examination Schools. The opening address was delivered by Professor James Stuart, LL.D., Fellow of Trinity College, Cambridge, and formerly Professor of Mechanics. He sketched the history of the University Extension Movement from its inception, and explained the ideals which had inspired its founders. It arose, he said, in the belief that the nation wanted higher education and that the Universities were best fitted to supply this want. The more illiterate the pupils the more necessary was it to provide teachers of first-rate attainments and ability. The founders of the movement put teaching before examination, and desired that the latter should be rather an instrument of teaching than a means of controlling teaching. They hoped from the beginning that the University extension lectures and classes would become a means of assisting the educational training of teachers of elementary schools, and in many districts they established classes specially for pupil teachers, which were greatly appreciated. The Education Committees that had been created throughout England by the Education Act of 1902 seemed to him to be the very bodies which were aimed at by the founders of the University Extension Movement. Professor Stuart strongly advised the University Extension authorities of to-day to put themselves into communication with those bodies, and to be prepared if if necessary to adapt the system to their requirements. A new obligation had been put upon the Universities to aid the nation in the future development of that class of higher education which the Universities were so well qualified to supply.

The subjects for study during the meeting formed a continuation of the work done at the last summer gathering in 1903, and throughout, both in selection and in treatment, the aim has been to explain methods, suggest problems and inspire interest rather than to give the finished and classified results of inquiry.

The students were given ample opportunities of sight-seeing in Oxford and the neighbourhood. Garden Parties were held at Balliol and Wadham. A debate was held in the Union, when the Rev. W. Hudson Shaw moved a resolution in favour of admitting women to the Parliamentary franchise. The motion was carried by 532 votes against 104.

A number of the men students were given rooms in Balliol, and the women students were distributed between Somerville, Lady Margaret's and St. Hugh's.

The meeting was in every way an unqualified success, and the work of the organisers is quite beyond praise.

SHEFFIELD.

The New Vice-Chancellor.

Sir Charles Eliot, K.C.M.G., C.B., has been appointed Vice-Chancellor of the University of Sheffield. Considerable interest has been aroused by the appointment of this brilliant scholar and experienced publicist. Born in 1864, Sir Charles Eliot was educated at Cheltenham College, and afterwards at Balliol College, Oxford, where he graduated as M.A. in 1885, having gained many academic distinctions during his University career. In the diplomatic service he has had a wide experience of men and affairs in many countries. He has served as Secretary to the Embassies at St. Petersburg, Constantinople, and Washington, as *Chargé d'Affaires* in Morocco and Servia, as British High Commissioner of Samoa, and as His Majesty's Commissioner in East Africa, a position he resigned in 1904. It is certain that Sir Charles Eliot possesses all those qualities that are necessary for such a position as that of Vice-Chancellor of the new University of Sheffield, and it is felt that he may with confidence be relied upon to guide its course aright. The University is to be congratulated upon the wise choice it has made.

UNIVERSITY COLLEGES.

University College, Bristol.

The Council of the College, at a special meeting held on Wednesday, July 19th, appointed Mr. George H. Leonard, M.A., (Camb.), to the Chair of Modern History, and Mr. Richard P. Cowl, M.A. (Dublin), to the Chair of English Literature and Language. Hitherto these Chairs have been held as a joint one by Prof. Rowley, who now resigns after 29 years' service. Mr. Leonard has held the post of Lecturer in History at the College since 1901. Probably few men in England have so intimate an acquaintance with local history in Bristol and many other centres, or a fuller knowledge of the historical aspect of social and economic questions. Mr. Cowl is Lecturer in English Language and Literature, and special Lecturer in Middle English Language and Literature, in the University of Birmingham. Educated at Trinity College, Dublin, he there obtained first place in first class honours in Modern Literature (thrice), second place in first class honours in Literature (twice), the gold medal and senior moderatorship in Modern Literature, the classical scholarship, first class honours and moderatorship in Classics, prizes in International and Roman Law and Political Economy, and the gold medal of the Philosophical Society. Mr. Cowl is also author and editor of several works, and comes with very high credentials from Dr. Edward Dowden, Dr. Churton Collins, and Dr. W. Macneile Dixon, Professors of English Literature in the Universities of Dublin, Birmingham, and Glasgow respectively.